EATING
clean

The 21-Day Plan to Detox, Fight Inflammation,
and Reset Your Body

amie valpone *creator of thehealthyapple.com*

FOREWORD BY MARK HYMAN, MD

PHOTOGRAPHY BY LAUREN VOLO

Houghton Mifflin Harcourt
Boston New York 2016

Copyright © 2016 by Amie Valpone
Interior photography © 2016 by Lauren Volo
Food styling by Marina Velasquez
Prop styling by April Valencia
Book design by Tara Long

For information about permission to reproduce selections from this book,
write to trade.permissions@hmhco.com or to
Houghton Mifflin Harcourt Publishing Company,
3 Park Avenue, 19th floor, New York, New York 10016.
www.hmhco.com

Library of Congress Cataloging-in-Publication Data
Valpone, Amie.
Eating clean : The 21-Day Plan to Detox, Fight Inflammation, and Reset
Your Body / Amie Valpone ; foreword by Dr. Mark Hyman M.D. ; photog-
raphy by Lauren Volo.
pages cm
Includes index.
ISBN 978-0-544-54646-2 (trade paper) ISBN 978-0-544-54647-9 (ebook)
1. Detoxification (Health) I. Title.
RA784.5.V35 2016
613.2dc23
2015020865

Printed in China
C&C 10 9 8 7 6 5 4 3 2 1

To my parents, who nurtured me through my tears and smiles when I was ill,
and whose unconditional love I will carry in my heart forever.
To my body, for taking me on this incredible journey,
and hanging in there while I figured out what was best for us.
To my sister, who inspires me and is truly my best friend.
And to all of you, for having the courage to embrace this new lifestyle:
I believe in you.
Believe in yourself, challenge your doctor, eat clean, live clean,
and accept nothing less than your best life ahead.

contents

foreword

Mounting evidence points to a unique and unappreciated trigger for obesity and chronic illness: Exposure to small traces of environmental chemicals in the environment. Consider this: The average newborn has 287 chemicals in its umbilical cord blood. We are born toxic, and it only becomes worse from there. Sadly, the consequences are wreaking havoc on our health and our waistlines.

Toxicity manifests in ways of which we're not always aware. In one study, rats given toxic chemicals gained weight and increased their fat storage without increased caloric intake or decreased exercise. In six months, these rats were 20 percent heavier and had 36 percent more body fat than rats not exposed to those chemicals.

If you struggle with weight loss, you are probably toxic, which means you can gain weight without eating any more calories or doing any less exercise. Toxins increase your appetite and scramble brain signals that control hunger, slowing down your metabolism and contributing to weight gain and diabetes.

I call this epidemic diabesity, the continuum of health problems ranging from mild insulin resistance and being overweight to obesity and diabetes. Diabesity is the single biggest global health epidemic of our time, contributing to heart disease, dementia, cancer, and premature death.

Numerous factors contribute to diabesity, including a sugary, processed diet, lack of exercise, poor sleep, and chronic stress. But environmental factors are an often-overlooked culprit that wrecks insurmountable havoc.

It comes down to this: If you're toxic, it makes you sick and fat. We can no longer ignore the toxic burden that bombards us.

Many patients arrive in my clinic very toxic. They feel awful, carry extra weight (usually around their midsection), and struggle with numerous problems including low sex drive and constant fatigue. These patients are understandably frustrated. They've visited numerous doctors who prescribe medications or otherwise have attempted ineffective treatments. This Western-medicine perspective doesn't help my patients and in some cases only makes their situation worse.

As a Functional Medicine practitioner, I take a different approach to toxicity and all its ramifications. Functional Medicine is a personalized medicine that focuses on the underlying causes of disease. In a word, it is the medicine of WHY, not WHAT.

In other words, instead of asking what disease you have and what drug should be used to treat it, we must ask WHY the disease has occurred. What constitutes the underlying causes that lead to illness and how do we look under the hood to find out what's going on? With my patients, I often discover dietary and lifestyle changes—including a detoxification program—radically transform their health.

This improvement doesn't occur overnight. It oftentimes requires trial and error, along with some detective work. But in the end, these patients feel better, look better, and reverse their risk for diabesity and other chronic diseases.

If you struggle with toxicity and all its miseries, I'd love to work with you at my practice, but I realize not everyone can do that. That's why I'd like to "prescribe" Amie Valpone's *Eating Clean*, which is the next best thing to a Functional Medicine doctor visit.

Amie approaches detoxification and optimal health from a genuine place. She has struggled with toxicity and many of its health-robbing ramifications. Along the way, she's developed a roadmap she shares in this groundbreaking book that can also help you heal your health, your weight, and your life.

I've witnessed this transformation, and I'm confident the tools in this book can also help you. Within these pages you'll find an effective, easy-to-implement game plan that reduces food sensitivities, processed foods, added sugar, and other junky ingredients so you reclaim your weight and your health. More than anything, *Eating Clean* becomes about self-empowerment. But let's talk food. Delicious, nourishing, easy-to-prepare recipes form the heart of this beautifully illustrated book. Along with appetizers, entrees, and sides certain to satisfy your most finicky eater, you'll find refreshing beverages and even decadent desserts that nourish and detoxify your body while helping you become lean, vibrant, and healthy.

These recipes taste fabulous. Choosing a favorite isn't easy, but right now I love Amie's grab-and-go snacks like Abundant Mango Cardamom Walnut Bars. As an extremely busy practitioner, I can appreciate having healthy snacks to keep hunger and cravings at bay.

Far more than just a cookbook, Amie outlines a comprehensive, effective plan that can dramatically improve how you feel, think, and live. "In this book, I'm going to show you how to transition from feeling tired, achy, and miserable to feeling better than you ever have," Amie writes. "I did it, and you can, too!"

Detoxifying, becoming lean, and reducing your disease risk, one delicious bite at a time.

—*Mark Hyman, MD, nine-time*
#1 New York Times *best-selling author*

how to
DETOX YOUR DIET
AND YOUR LIFE

even good girls can
get deathly ill

I was in my mid-20s, and I was practically bedridden. My legs were swollen, my muscles hurt, my belly was a balloon, and despite what had once been a healthy appetite, I weighed only 98 pounds. My gut was a mess, my immune system was trashed, and my once exuberant energy was non-existent.

My life had come to a complete halt. I was so sick, I had to quit my job and spend all of my time and money going from doctor to doctor and hospital to hospital, trying to figure out what was wrong with me.

I couldn't understand it. I was always such a good girl. Seriously! I never smoked or did drugs. Aside from a little drinking in college, I was a saint as far as my health was concerned. I avoided processed and fast foods. I ate lean proteins and greens. I exercised. I wore Neutrogena sunscreen to keep my skin "healthy," used Off! to avoid bug-borne illnesses, and drank my daily allotment of unfiltered tap water.

My childhood had been completely normal, too. I wasn't raised downwind of a power plant. I grew up in a cute beach town in New Jersey, eating chicken and spinach most nights for dinner. My mom washed our clothes with Tide and cleaned the floors with bleach, and my dad used pesticides on the lawn like everyone else on the block, but we had no family history of chronic disease or allergies. I was lactose intolerant, but that was about it.

I thought I was doing all the right things. So why had this happened to me?

A LIFE-CHANGING DIAGNOSIS

I was a 25-year-old marketing professional in Manhattan, with a few big corporate notches on my belt. I'd worked at Ralph Lauren and *Vogue* magazine, and was settling into my new job at the NBA when I noticed something odd: my legs were swelling up.

I'm not talking about a little premenstrual water weight. I'm talking 40 pounds of water in my legs. I'd wake up in the morning and be fine, but as the day wore on, the water would collect to the point where I could barely bend my knees or even take my pants off.

Freaked out, I finally went to the emergency room. They took my vitals. Turns out my white blood cell count was 1.1 (normal is 4.0). As you can imagine, this diagnosis was very concerning, but because I seemed completely fine for the most part, they let me go home to wait for the rest of the test results.

I was eating lunch at my desk the next day when the doctor called and said I needed to leave work immediately. He gave me an address downtown. I showed up and found myself at a Manhattan cancer hospital. I called the doctor and told him he must have sent me to the wrong place.

"No," he said, "that's where you're going. You have leukemia."

Huh?

UM, WAIT, MAYBE NOT

I was shocked, to say the least. I thought I ate well and lived well, and what? I had cancer? It couldn't be.

Without so much as a how-do-you-do, the medical staff had me bend over so they could administer a bone marrow biopsy. It was one of the most painful procedures I've ever experienced (imagine taking a corkscrew to the tailbone). The whole time, I kept telling myself, "Amie, you know your body best. You

know this isn't right. Just hang in there and we'll get through this."

Turns out it was a false scare. Upon further testing, they determined that I did not have leukemia. Something *was* wrong with my bone marrow, though. It was gel-like, which is normally a sign of malnutrition. Basically, my body wasn't absorbing anything I was eating—healthy or not. Moreover, my cells couldn't hold on to fluid, which is why it was running through me and collecting in my legs.

I was relieved I didn't have leukemia. The problem was, I was still sick, and no one knew why.

WESTERN MEDICINE MAKES ME A LAB RAT

Because I was so thin, the professionals at the Mayo Clinic and the New York hospitals assumed I was anorexic, or bulimic, or both. Of course, I wasn't! I was eating what most people consider a healthy American diet, and I'd always had a very hearty appetite. The nutritionist told me to drink more milk (dairy), eat more whole wheat bread (gluten), and get more conventional red meat in my diet (linked with inflammation), and that it didn't matter if it was all organic or not.

Really?

Meanwhile, my white blood cell count remained chronically low. Over the course of the next two years, I had 24 vials of blood drawn every other week, to monitor my blood levels. I felt like I was living at the hospital.

I was also sent to a host of physicians. Liver doctors. Kidney doctors. Vascular surgeons. Rheumatologists. Hematologists. I saw every GI (gastrointestinal) doc up and down the eastern seaboard. They didn't have answers; they had guesses. And all of them turned out to be wrong.

I was told I had hypothyroidism, so they put me on Synthroid, a thyroid-regulating drug. No change. In the meantime, my immune system had been severely damaged, and as a result, I had no good bacteria in my gut—only way too much "bad" bacteria. My belly swelled to the size of a pregnant woman's. People honestly thought I was pregnant and asked when my due date was!

The doctors put me on the strongest antibiotics available to help combat the bacterial overgrowth. This further taxed my immune system, because it wiped out everything. When I asked if I should be taking probiotics to help rebalance and support my good gut flora, they said no.

These were teams of doctors at the best hospitals in the country—who was I to question them?

I STARTED TO FIGURE IT OUT— BUT MY DOCTORS LAUGHED

Feeling more sick and tired than I had ever felt, I did what any girl would do: I Googled. I started reading about my symptoms. The more I researched, the more I learned. Eventually, I was able to surmise that I had—in addition to my other maladies— developed leaky gut syndrome, a condition in which the intestinal walls become so compromised they let bacteria and pieces of undigested food leak out into the rest of the body. This, in turn, causes a host of autoimmune issues, inflammation, and more. I had also developed chronic candida, a yeast overgrowth in my gut.

I received no help from my slew of doctors. Leaky gut and candida? They literally laughed at me. I might as well have told them I had fairies living in my large intestine.

Meanwhile, I developed myositis (inflammation in my leg muscles), which gave me cramps that hurt so badly I could barely walk. The rheumatologist put me on steroids. Sure, they took the pain away, but what I didn't realize at the time was that there was a price to pay: they affected my cortisol (stress hormone) levels and increased my symptoms of adrenal fatigue and candida.

THE CRAZY HYPOCHONDRIAC

Eventually, I became so sick that life as I knew it stopped. I couldn't work and had to go on disability. My social life went out the window. Even worse, my friends, coworkers, and the other people in my life who I thought supported me started to think I was crazy. Surely if a doctor couldn't pinpoint what was wrong, there must not be anything amiss, right? As far as anyone could tell, it was all in my head.

But I knew better. I wasn't faking it. By the time I checked myself into a hospital in Philadelphia, I had developed what's called *C. diff* colitis, a deadly condition in which a form of bacteria called *C. difficile* proliferates in the colon.

It's particularly dangerous when your immunity is weakened, as mine was. Without any other bacteria to compete with, *C. diff* essentially takes over and destroys anything in its path. The Centers for Disease Control and Prevention (CDC) notes that the condition is linked to 14,000 American deaths each year.

I was given 24 hours to live.

INSURANCE COVERAGE DENIED, TIME TO GO

What does one do when given that kind of grim prognosis? Eat one last amazing meal? Say her goodbyes? Pray or meditate?

All I could do was lie in bed and moan. The morphine barely relieved what felt like being repeatedly stabbed in the belly. My parents looked on in shock—they couldn't believe this was all that remained of their once bubbly, full-of-life daughter.

I was in the hospital for five days. Amazingly, after intense treatment, my chronic stomach pain and other symptoms eased. The *C. difficile* was cured. Tests showed the bacteria were no longer destroying my intestines. There was hope!

Yet my legs were still swollen, I was still suffering from chronic fatigue, and I was only 95 pounds.

That might not seem surprising after such an ordeal, but as the days went by, I couldn't gain weight. The bacteria were gone, but my blood work still looked terrible. Lab tests showed that everything from my platelets, hemoglobin, white blood cells, liver, and kidneys were still incredibly inflamed.

My team of doctors kept trying (and guessing), but after multiple CT scans, MRIs, X-rays, and more and more blood work, they still didn't have any answers. They told me: "We've run every test imaginable, Ms. Valpone. We can't find anything else wrong with you. There's nothing we can do."

With no official diagnosis, my insurance had no reason to continue covering hospital care. I was told I had to go home.

I got into the car with my mother. It was the lowest point in my life. What was left but a future full of sickness and pain?

FINDING PEOPLE WHO COULD REALLY HELP

I'm sharing my story with you because I have a feeling you may have gone through a similar experience. Maybe you didn't get as sick as I did—or maybe you suffered something even worse—but chances are, you found yourself at the end of your rope, failed by Western (conventional) medicine, with nowhere left to turn.

I was raised like most Americans. I revered doctors and prayed at the altar of conventional medicine. But after years of suffering, I came to realize something: they couldn't help me. I'd been in and out of some of the country's best hospitals, and I was actually worse off than when I started.

After three years of this insanity, I found a woman who changed everything: Susan Blum, MD, MPH, of the Blum Center in Westchester, New York. A Functional Medicine physician, Dr. Blum was different from any other doc I'd seen.

She talked to me for an hour, as opposed to ten minutes. She didn't just take my vitals and hand me a prescription; she asked me questions about what I ate and when. She asked me about my lifestyle, my stress levels, my sleep habits, and my work. She was even interested in what kind of pipes I had in my house. Unlike Western medicine doctors, who follow a disease model (seeking the problem in one area of the body), this Functional Medicine doctor wanted the whole picture.

Dr. Blum's testing revealed I had numerous parasites, chronic fatigue, significant bacterial overgrowth, and countless pathogens that traditional testing hadn't identified. In addition, I had heavy metal accumulation that was off the charts and chronic candida.

Her diagnosis surprised me. All this time, I hadn't been suffering from a disease, per se; rather, my body was overrun with toxins, made worse by the conventional medical approach, which kept dumping in more and more prescription drugs.

I started working with Jeffrey Morrison, MD, a detox expert in Manhattan, who put me through a full-scale detoxification, including IV chelation, which removed metals from my body over the course of several treatments that spanned two years. Even my mercury fillings had to be removed by a specialist, as any mercury I might have inhaled during the procedure could have caused brain and liver failure.

Richard Horowitz, MD, another functional medicine physician, determined I also had Lyme disease, even though I had tested negative for it for over a decade. (Turns out they were false negatives from Western medicine labs.) He determined that because I didn't have a bull's-eye rash, I possibly got the Lyme disease from a tick when I was a child.

Two months after that diagnosis, Alan Warshowsky, MD, found my ovaries were covered with big, black cysts. I was diagnosed with polycystic ovarian syndrome (PCOS), a condition that had been overlooked at every hospital and doctor's office, even after numerous ultrasounds.

All the medications I'd been taking did nothing for any of these conditions. In fact, they most likely made them worse.

Bottom line: I didn't need more meds. I needed exactly the opposite—a complete and total detox.

FINALLY, THE RIGHT DIAGNOSIS

It was time for another blood test. I'd had hundreds of them up to that point, but Integrative and Functional physicians go beyond what your general practitioner (Western medicine doctor) tests for, and they conduct a more detailed analysis to get an accurate picture of what's going on in your body via comprehensive urine, saliva, and blood tests. This includes testing for a gene with such a ridiculously long name; it's abbreviated as MTHFR. (It stands for "methylenetetrahydrofolate reductase," in case you're curious.)

In layman's terms, if you have a genetic mutation to the MTHFR gene (and 35 percent of people do), you aren't able to detoxify as efficiently or effectively as someone without this enzyme. Because of this, toxins accumulate, which can interfere with bodily functions and ultimately lead to serious conditions including irritable bowel syndrome, arthritis, and cancer. There are two different genetic mutations assessed for the C667T mutation and the A1298C mutation. Currently, more research has shown the C667T to be more medically relevant to detoxification and methylation. Methylation is a biochemical process that our body needs to function; it helps keep inflammation in check, repairs your DNA, and helps recycle molecules needed for detox. You can maximize your methylation by eating foods rich in folate (leafy greens, fruit, whole grains, and beans to get adequate levels of B6 and B12 vitamins), keeping the bacteria in your gut healthy, avoiding processed and canned foods, avoiding caffeine and alcohol, and minimizing your consumption of animal protein, sugar, and saturated fat. More

information on methylation can be found on my website, TheHealthyApple.com. I cannot stress enough how important methylation is for detoxification, disease prevention, and wellness. (See Integrative and Functional Medicine Testing on page 379 for more information about MTHFR.)

Having the MTHFR mutation also makes you more susceptible to toxins in your environment, particularly any heavy metals, pesticides, herbicides, antibiotics, and growth hormones in your food. As a result, these substances, which bind to fat receptors, have more of a toxic effect on you than someone without the MTHFR mutation. This also means chemicals in tap water, conventional food, household cleaning solutions, and beauty products can pose a greater threat. Toxic exposures, medications, decreased stomach acid, smoking, poor diet, malabsorption, and genetics can all affect your methylation process.

I most certainly was suffering toxic effects on a grand scale—mainly from heavy metals such as mercury, lead, and cadmium. My levels were off the charts, and it was contributing to my hypothyroidism, leaky gut, candida, polycystic ovarian syndrome, Lyme disease, and severely suppressed immune system. On top of that, my methylation was a mess, so I wasn't detoxing any of these toxins out of my body.

THE BIG LIFESTYLE DETOX

Meanwhile, I did my own homework, and soon took measures to detox my lifestyle, from my food and water to my cleaning products and skin care. Most important, my diet changed dramatically.

While Western docs had been telling me to eat conventional dairy for calcium and assuring me that gluten was fine based on nearly a dozen colonoscopies and endoscopies—despite the fact that glutinous grains made me feel bloated, lethargic, and sick—my Integrative doctors found quite the opposite. In fact, gluten and dairy—in addition to soy, refined sugar, corn, eggplant, eggs, peanuts, processed foods, and more—were big contributors to my problems. (And, you guessed it, you won't find any of these ingredients in this book!)

A few months after my detoxification began, I did an elimination diet (which I've outlined for you on page 23). Through the 21-Day Elimination Diet, I was able to identify what foods were causing inflammation in my body.

I removed all processed, packaged foods from my diet as well. I avoided literally anything in a package because of preservatives, colors, and dyes. Even seemingly harmless things like emulsifiers and food-grade fillers are hard for the body to detoxify.

Also off limits were any canned foods, because heavy metals in the can lining seep into the food. I ruled out conventionally (meaning "nonorganic") farmed crops because of the high levels of toxic pesticides. For me, organic wasn't a luxury anymore; it was my only option.

For a long time, I got by on protein and vegetables. For two years, I ate—no joke—vegetables and medical protein powders pureed in a food processor like baby food because my leaky gut was so bad and I reacted to everything I put in my mouth.

Yum!

EVERYONE DOESN'T NEED TO GET THIS EXTREME—BUT FOOD CAN HEAL YOUR LIFE

Mine is probably the most extreme tale you've ever heard, but I have to be honest: these adjustments changed my body and my life for the better.

People asked me how I did it. I tell them I *had* to. There was no choice. But it wasn't a burden. In fact, I was fascinated by it. Who knew there was so much that could put you at risk, or that could have such an effect on you? I was so intrigued that I went back to school to earn a degree in Integrative Nutrition and to learn more about how food can heal the body.

I made it my life.

In the end, my illness was a blessing in disguise.

THIS HAPPENED TO ME FOR A REASON—I WAS MEANT TO HELP YOU!

To this day, I am gluten-, dairy-, egg-, refined sugar–, corn-, peanut-, and soy-free. I can't eat out of a box or a can—but then again, I feel better without it. I have been able to add back into my diet things like nuts and seeds, asparagus, lemon, black pepper, and avocado, which caused bellyaches and pains for many years. My menstrual cycle is back on track after eight years without a period. (While most women bemoan their monthly, let me tell you, when mine returned, I wanted to throw a parade.) My legs are no longer swollen, and my color and vigor are restored.

All because I changed my diet, detoxed my lifestyle, and took charge of my health. Myself.

It turns out that thousands of people are living just like I did, suffering as a result of toxins, autoimmune disease, and unexplained symptoms. I'm guessing you may be one of them, or you know someone who is. Unfortunately, few people have access to information that explains how they can get off the medical hamster wheel and truly help themselves.

When I started to feel better, it occurred to me that I could help. I'm not a doctor and I'm not a scientist, but I've experienced firsthand the effects of toxicity and the resulting helplessness and hopelessness. No one told me what toxins were, why I should care, or how to reduce my exposure to them. No one told me the items we see on shelves are not as safe as we think.

Truth is, you could eat and drink and be exposed to the same things I was and not experience what I did. For you, it could be something else in your food or environment that is causing your symptoms. But no matter what your own personal struggle looks like, I'm telling you, you can feel unbelievably better when you start making changes today.

WHAT THIS BOOK CAN DO FOR YOU

In this book, I'm going to show you how to transition from feeling tired, achy, and miserable to feeling better than you ever have. I did it, and you can, too!

It all starts with food. Food is my obsession. I love to cook real, whole, organic foods, and I do it every day. Though I've lived in New York City for over a decade, where there are twelve restaurants on every block, I've never ordered takeout. Not once.

In fact, I love cooking so much that I have made a career out of food. I'm the founder of TheHealthyApple.com, a popular detox and recipe blog that gets upward of 100,000 hits a month. I'm a personal chef, recipe developer, and contributor to major publications such as Food Network, Fox News, *Prevention*, *Glamour*, *SELF*, *Reader's Digest*, *Clean Eating*, *Vegetarian Times*, *Fitness*, and *SHAPE*. I taught myself food styling and photography, and now spend my days writing, creating recipes,

and working with healthy brands that line the shelves at Whole Foods Market.

I'm going to tell you about detoxing, too, and show you how the everyday foods and products you may be using right now might be destroying your health. I'll show you how to clean out and detox your diet, your body, and your life—and get back to being the person you used to be. (Or even better!) Best of all, I can promise you that every step and every recipe in this book is not only doable but also 100 percent enjoyable. Once you get into the clean-living lifestyle, you're never going to want to go back!

I've been on this path for over a decade, and I'm right by your side. This book was written for you. Because without you supporting the new recipes I post every Monday on my website, following me in my travels on Facebook, @TheHealthyApple, or just checking in on Instagram to see what yummy foods I've discovered, I wouldn't be the person I am.

So get comfy, make a cup of my Dandelion Liver Detox Tea (page 299), and keep on reading to learn how to better your life forever and begin your own path to health.

amie's eating clean manifesto

Before we dive into the nitty-gritty of detox, let me share with you a general overview of what I believe about food, diet, and eating clean for your best health. This will give you a quick introduction to where I'm coming from, as it forms the basis for all my recommendations in this book.

1. There is no one ideal diet.

I believe you can benefit from a cleaner, greener diet. But that doesn't mean you need to eat exactly what I eat. While there are some precepts for clean, toxin-free eating, which I will explain in the following chapters, there are many ways to eat healthy.

I'm not into labels. This isn't about being a vegan, vegetarian, or flexitarian. If you want to come up with a name for what this is, knock yourself out, but the most important thing is to eat foods that make your body feel good.

2. If a food makes you feel lousy, it's not for you.

I don't care what's trending or hot or highly recommended by the buzziest superstar or best-selling author. You are the expert on what you can eat. Your friend, trainer, or mom may swear up and down that unpasteurized dairy is the golden key to health or that millet is king, but if it makes you feel ill, pass it up.

Same goes for animal protein: some people swear you shouldn't eat it, but there's no need to feel guilty if you feel your best after eating a grass-fed burger. The right foods for you should make you feel satisfied and energized, not sick and sleepy. There is no preordained, across-the-board "right," just what's right *for you.*

3. DETOX IS NOT THE SAME THING AS A JUICE CLEANSE. NOT EVEN CLOSE.

This is a common mistake. Take spinach, a powerhouse green and juicing favorite. It's also one of the most contaminated vegetables when it comes to pesticides. It's on the Environmental Working Group's (EWG) Dirty Dozen list for that reason. (Check out page 48 for information on the EWG's Dirty Dozen.)

Apples are another example of a healthy food often used in juice cleanses that can be full of toxins. (Conventional apples rank number one on the EWG's Dirty Dozen.) Putting them in a blender together with other fruits and veggies and drinking the resulting mixture through a straw doesn't make them healthier. You'll just be delivering the toxins to your body in super-easy-to-digest form.

The best way to detox, in my book, is to go organic and remove the toxic exposures that make you sick and bloated. (More on that on page 14.)

4. DETOX IS A WAY OF LIFE.

You can't detox over a single weekend; there is no shortcut. If you care about your health, detox needs to be an ongoing process that becomes a way of life. Instead of approaching it in fits and bursts, it's better to develop a deep understanding of the harmful environment we live in, and then bring that awareness to everyday life, gradually eliminating toxins from the body.

Every. Single. Day.

5. THERE'S MORE TO HEALTH CARE THAN WESTERN MEDICINE.

Western medicine (also known as conventional or allopathic medicine) has its place, no question. It saves lives every day. But where it excels in emergencies, it falls short on day-to-day lifestyle guidance.

Why? Your physician does not go home with you. (If he does, can I have his number, please?) No one knows what you experience but you. Most doctors are highly skilled in one area, but don't have the time or expertise to know what lifestyle changes you need.

I highly recommend you do your homework on different kinds of Integrative and Functional Medicine doctors. Check out my website, TheHealthyApple.com, for more information on Integrative and Functional Medicine. These are MDs who treat the body as a whole, looking not just at the physical self, but the mental and emotional self, too. I didn't stop searching until I found an Integrative Medicine team that could help me get my life back, and they did. So even if you are struggling, don't give up! There are options beyond Western medicine.

One more crucial thing to keep in mind: You're the expert on your body. Explore what methods and practices make you feel best, and share these notes with your doctor at each visit. You might just pass along something useful to someone else, and it will go a long way in enabling your doctor to combine his wisdom with yours. You and your doctor are a team. It's time to start playing your part.

6. FEED YOUR BODY, NOT JUST YOUR BELLY.

Hunger and appetite together drive you to do one very important thing: eat. When you feel that pang of hunger, you know what you need to do. But eating is about more than just quieting your appetite. You do not subsist on calories alone; you need a spectrum of nutrients and vitamins to feed your body on a cellular level.

Foods have so much more to them than calories, and yet many people think caloric intake is the bottom line. Au contraire, my friend! The number of calories a food has is merely information, and as with any other kind of information, less isn't necessarily better, just as more isn't necessarily bad.

A 100-calorie snack pack is in no way equal to 100 calories of avocado. Counting calories is the last thing you should worry about when you're trying to eat clean. A handful of nuts may be calorically dense, but there's a lot of goodness packed in there that you can't get somewhere else.

Choose foods based on how they nourish every cell in your body, rather than by how many calories you believe they will glue to your waistline. When you're eating clean, believe it or not, those calories don't add up to love handles and saddlebags.

7. Processed foods can't hold a candle to one-ingredient foods.

Food in its whole form is the healthiest version. That's my rule of thumb, and it should be yours. The majority of what you eat should have one ingredient. What's in cabbage? Cabbage. What's in an orange? An orange. If most of your meals come from a box, then it's worth rethinking your diet.

Because we live in the 21st century, I get that there is a fair amount of packaged convenience foods you probably won't cut completely out of your life. If the only way to know what you're eating is to read about it on the side of the package, though, you are, as I always say, eating sawdust.

The more a food is processed, the less of its original nutrition remains. Sure, some foods need to be heated to make them palatable and to ease digestion, but I'd rather you do more of the processing yourself, be it heating, blending, or chopping, and leave less of it to manufacturers.

8. Pay now or pay later—organic is cheaper than medical bills. (Trust me.)

The point of eating organic is not to reap more nutrients. The reason you should choose organic is to avoid toxins like pesticides, growth hormones, antibiotics, and herbicides found in conventional foods, which can make you sick.

Every time we pick up a fork, we choose whether we put chemicals in our bodies or not. Your food makes the biggest difference; you can live a healthy life (like I did), but if you continue to eat conventional foods and expose yourself to hidden chemicals, you'll probably end up sick from toxicity masking itself as a disease, unexplained symptoms, or illness at some point.

No one educated me on toxins. Western medicine doctors didn't know, my family didn't know, I didn't know, no one knew. It wasn't until after I started working with Integrative and Functional Medicine doctors that I realized biting into a juicy conventional cucumber that had been sprayed with toxic pesticides and herbicides was like eating something sporting one of those warning labels you find on chemicals underneath the sink.

Somewhere along the line we've gotten the idea that food shouldn't cost us anything. Not true. The total sum of my medical bills came to just shy of half a million dollars. And no, it wasn't all covered by insurance. Yet we're so enamored with getting a great deal that we're bargaining with our health and our lives.

Good, healthy food is perhaps the greatest investment you can make in yourself and your future. You have one body, and it has to last. So before you give in to the urge to save a few bucks by opting for conventional strawberries or factory-farmed eggs, think about what you're worth. If your health doesn't seem worth it to you (and that's a whole other discussion), consider that you're paying not only for the quality of the food itself, but for the many hands that helped cultivate it in a way that's least harmful to the earth and to your family. A healthy world makes for a healthier population.

9. Eating clean needs no defense.

Too many people would sooner eat a thing that makes them sick than hurt someone's feelings or risk coming across as "high maintenance." This is madness. There's no reason you need to feel bad or embarrassed about the foods you can't eat! You should never feel ashamed for being the best friend to the only body you have been given.

You can be mindful of your needs without being unkind or offensive to others. What you cannot do is sacrifice your health over food, no matter what social toll it takes. There are lots of ways to address this, whether it's calling a restaurant ahead or bringing your own homemade treats to a friend's home for dinner. (See pages 59–67 for tips on traveling, eating out, and entertaining.)

If you loathe making your diet the center of the discussion, have a quick, simple answer. When you pass on the bread or ask about gluten in a dish, and you get the inevitable, "Do you have celiac disease?"—and you don't—just say, "I just find I feel a lot better without gluten." End of story.

10. YOUR DIET SHOULD CHANGE WITH THE SEASONS.

Through the magic of the modern food economy (and I say that slightly tongue-in-cheek), there are plenty of foods you can get year-round. But that doesn't mean you should be eating them. In fact, the healthiest diets shift throughout the year.

There's a reason you want bright, juicy berries in the summer and crave the heartiness of butternut squash in the fall. This is when these foods are at their peak, and when you should be eating them.

It makes me laugh when people say eating clean is boring. Hardly! Part of the fun of eating is the pure anticipation. I can barely wait until August when tomatoes are at their ripe, perfumed best. I love the fall season for its rich, caramelized root vegetables like parsnips and carrots. Eating these foods when they're naturally in season is also the best way to get the highest level of nutrients out of them—smart all the way around! (Check out TheHealthyApple.com, my website, for a complete list of what's in season, when.)

11. A HEALTHY DIET GIVES YOU MORE OPTIONS, NOT FEWER.

It's easy to think that when you identify foods you can't stomach, your world gets smaller. Quite the opposite. Most people think inside the box, or bag, as it were, and never venture outside of their same old sawdust snacks.

Eating clean is not restricted eating; it's an adventure beyond the box. It's getting outside of your old habits, and all the problems they bring with them. When you decide to see food in a new way, more doors open than close, and once you walk through them, you'll never want to go back again.

why detox?

After years of struggling with mysterious symptoms and illnesses, visiting doctor after doctor, taking test after test, and spending hundreds of thousands of dollars on my health, it all boiled down to one simple answer for me: toxicity.

Our bodies were built to deal with natural pollution created by digestion, respiration, and metabolism, but they're not designed to handle the enormous amount of artificial pollutants we're exposed to in today's chemical-filled world. The only way to deal with this toxic overload is to assist the body's natural self-cleansing mechanisms with detoxing.

How toxic are you? The following quiz will give you some idea. Answer the questions with a simple yes or no.

HOW TOXIC ARE YOU?

- Do you experience brain fog?

- Do you have frequent headaches?

- Are you irritable?

- Do you need coffee to wake up in the morning?

- Do you need wine or other alcohol to wind down at night?

- Is your skin dull or lackluster?

- Do you suffer from eczema, psoriasis, or acne?

- Do you have insomnia?

- Are you often bloated or puffy?
- Do you have congestion, allergies, or sinus issues?
- Are you frequently fatigued?
- Do you have an autoimmune disease?
- Do you struggle with constipation, gas, or diarrhea?
- Do you have acid reflux?
- Do you have difficulty losing or gaining weight?
- Do you have joint pain?

Now add up your yes answers. The more you have, the greater the potential toxic burden you may be carrying.

Although it is impossible to eliminate all the toxins in our environment, we can reduce some of them and work toward balancing out the remainder. The goal is to minimize external pollution and maximize our internal cleansing functions, which means reforming our diet, reorganizing our daily priorities, and refining our lifestyle.

WHAT IS A TOXIN?

A toxin is basically anything the body identifies as a poison. Most come from three main sources:

1. External toxins come from outside our bodies and include things like car exhaust, industrial pollutants, and heavy metals.

2. Internal toxins are those we put inside our bodies, like pesticides and herbicides from nonorganic produce; antibiotics and growth hormones in nonorganic animal products; food additives and preservatives; and chemicals in skin care and cleaning products. Alcohol, caffeine, gluten, soy, dairy, processed foods, refined oils, refined sugar, and pharmaceutical drugs can also wreak havoc on our bodies and raise toxicity.

3. Self-created toxins are naturally produced by the body as a by-product of normal metabolism. These include waste products formed during digestion and other normal metabolic processes.

Over the past several decades, our exposure to toxins has increased through pollution, water contamination, pharmaceutical drugs, widespread use of pesticides, and increased use of chemicals in our food and personal care products. As we age, these contaminants accumulate in our fat tissues and organs, increasing our overall toxic residue. This build-up may result in health complications and illness, with accompanying symptoms like those mentioned in the quiz.

You can reduce your toxic exposure by changing your diet, your home environment, personal care products, supplements, water source, and even the quality of the air you breathe. Such changes will help put you on the path toward optimal health and well-being.

WHY ISN'T THE BODY TAKING CARE OF THIS?

In addition to being exposed to more chemicals than any previous generation, most of us today are also experiencing chronic stress, overstimulation of the senses, insufficient rest and relaxation, and excessive dependence on stimulants and intoxicants. These factors keep our autonomic nervous system racing in the fight-or-flight mode, which is the stress mode (aka. the sympathetic mode). This exhausts our adrenal glands, weakens our immune response, and floods our bloodstream with acid-forming residues produced by stress hormones and the metabolic reactions they trigger.

Unable to process and eliminate this growing overload of toxins through our normal detox channels, we are forced to store them instead in our bones, liver, muscles, tissues, bowels, joints, fat, lymph, and any other tissue where they can't directly poison the bloodstream. If these toxic deposits are not dislodged now and then, it's only a matter of time before they damage our tissues and cause cellular malfunctions that can lead to cancer, Alzheimer's, heart disease, heavy metal accumulation, and other devastating and possibly fatal conditions.

Toxins may seem harmless in small amounts, especially when you don't have an overt reaction. But they're sneaky—they can lie dormant for years, accumulating in our bodies and eventually overwhelming the liver to cause inflammation, which then leads to disease. Inflammation can occur anywhere in the body where toxins exist. If it exists in the joints, then you may get arthritis. If toxins are harbored in the colon, you may get colitis.

Our bodies need vitamins, minerals, enzymes, clean food, purified water, and working processes such as proper methylation to remove these toxins. The liver and intestinal tract perform most of the work, but the kidneys, lungs, lymphatic system—and even the skin—each play a large role. These organs all work together to eliminate toxins so they won't hang around in your body's tissues creating health issues, weight gain and, above all, toxicity.

If we continue to overload our systems with toxins, however, and fail to assist the body in its detoxification efforts, our natural drainage system can become clogged, allowing waste to build up in the bloodstream and circulate throughout the body. That's when we start to notice symptoms like unexplained headaches, fatigue, joint pain, and more.

TOXINS ALSO INTERACT WITH DNA

Did you know that toxins can also interact with your DNA, effectively turning on or off certain inborn tendencies toward disease? They have the ability to interact with DNA SNPs, single-nucleotide polymorphisms (mutations), or "snips." These are the most common type of genetic variation, each representing a difference in a single DNA building block.

We could all be born with genetic predispositions to cancer, but only some of us will get it because of the toxins we're exposed to and the lifestyles we live that turn on these DNA snips. That's why some people get sick from mold, and some people don't. The study of epigenetics tells us that our DNA does not run our lives; we have the ability to turn our genetic predispositions to illness on or off based on our toxicity level, detox abilities, and more.

The good news is there are small changes you can make today that will affect your body for the rest of your life. I actually don't advocate doing too much too soon. Take time to make these changes, but don't put these things off until you find yourself sick and tired one day down the road. Start making tiny changes to make you feel amazing, today.

WHAT'S CAUSING YOUR TOXIC OVERLOAD?

If you've been struggling with low energy, accelerated aging, weight loss or gain, chronic illness, and memory problems—or if you're simply feeling foggy and groggy—you might be in toxic overload mode.

Begin by taking these three steps:

1. Identify where your toxins are coming from

2. Gauge how toxic you are

3. Identify what these toxins are doing to you (and your family)

It's important to remember that everyone reacts differently to allergens, drugs, chemicals, and toxins—some of us are more sensitive than others. In addition, when you try to pinpoint exactly what is making you toxic, it can be hard to find a single issue. Most often, it's a combination of several factors.

your typical toxic morning

Not sure where your toxins originate? Here's a brief example of a typical morning full of toxic exposure.

▸ You wake up in a bed that's made with off-gassing foams your body has been absorbing all night, including toluene (emitted from polyurethane), stain-resistant perfluoroctanic acid, fire-retardant chemicals, and antimony. You walk across your synthetic carpet that's filled with chemicals and head to the bathroom.

▸ You brush your teeth with toothpaste made with a warning sign (because of toxins like triclosan and fluoride), using tap water filled with chemicals. You rinse with mouthwash that may contain formaldehyde and ammonia, as well as colors and chemicals leached from the plastic bottle.

▸ You shower. Your water exposes you to chlorine, fluoride, copper, lead, traces of herbicides and pharmaceutical drugs, and other by-products. You reach for shampoo, conditioner, and a bar of soap that may all be filled with parabens, dyes, coloring agents, artificial preservatives, and other lubricants. You dry off with a towel that contains chemicals from laundry detergents and dryer sheets.

▸ You apply your makeup, lotion, hair products, and more, which are filled with chemicals that seep into your skin and scalp. You put on your aluminum deodorant and get dressed in clothes fresh out of the plastic from the dry cleaners, filled with chemical fumes and residues along with exposing yourself to the invisible gases from your carpets, rugs, paint, and furniture.

▸ You drink conventional coffee, which is filled with chemicals, affects the nutrients you need to detox, and gives you a false boost of energy. Do you add a fake sweetener or refined sugar? Bonus toxin points.

▸ You add conventional milk to your cereal, which is filled with antibiotics and hormones. The plastic wrap inside the cereal box contains vinyl chloride; your cereal may contain HFCS (high fructose corn syrup), wheat, and additives. The fresh conventional berries you toss into your cereal are filled with pesticides.

▸ You clean your dishes using a chemical dish detergent and clean the countertop with Windex, which is filled with unnoticeable fumes that you breathe in and absorb through your lungs and skin.

▸ You get into your new car, which smells like a new car always does, because it's emitting gases from fabrics, solvents, plastics, and glues. Yikes—you just started your day, and look at all the toxic exposures! We can't escape every toxin, but we can do our best to diminish the toxic load we bombard our bodies with on a daily basis.

Following are some of the possibilities.

NUTRIENT DEFICIENCIES

To function properly, our bodies require plenty of vitamins, minerals, antioxidants, amino acids, and essential fatty acids, as well as fresh organic fruits, vegetables, healthy fats, and lean proteins. If we aren't feeding our bodies enough micronutrients, we are essentially starving our cells.

The following all contribute to our toxic load: inadequate quality protein; processed foods and refined sugar; refined oils; conventional meat, dairy, eggs, and poultry that are exposed to chemical pesticides and shot up with hormones and antibiotics; and conventionally grown fruits and vegetables sprayed with pesticides and herbicides.

LEAKY GUT SYNDROME

We have nearly five pounds of good bacteria in our gut. These friendly bugs fight off harmful bacteria, parasites, and fungi, and form a healthy barrier on the intestinal wall so harmful germs can't enter the blood and lymph systems. They also help you digest food and fiber and optimize the assimilation of vitamins and minerals in your bloodstream to nourish you.

When we eat an excess of the wrong foods, however, or take too many antibiotics, or become exposed to heavy metals and toxins, we can develop leaky gut syndrome. This is when the gut barrier is breached, causing intestinal permeability. Undigested pieces of food can enter our bloodstream, where the immune system identifies them as invaders and attacks. That is why some people become sensitive to various foods and suffer inflammation as a result of what they're eating. (See page 378 for information on how to get tested for leaky gut syndrome.)

HIDDEN FOOD SENSITIVITIES

Food sensitivities can also play a role in toxicity. Some of you may already be aware of foods that don't agree with you. Food sensitivities are different from food allergies. If you eat shellfish or peanuts and immediately have an anaphylactic reaction such as breaking out in hives, you've got a food allergy.

Food sensitivities, however, are harder to detect because the reactions—headaches, insomnia, fatigue, and foggy brain, for example—may not occur for 24 to 72 hours after you eat the problematic food. (These can be uncovered, however, through my 21-Day Elimination Diet on page 22 and Food Sensitivity Testing on page 377.) I've learned from the Integrative Medicine doctors I've worked with that the gold standard of testing for food sensitivities is the food elimination diet, which will uncover the foods that may be causing inflammation in your body.

In a way, food sensitivities are no different than any other chemical exposure; they create a heightened state of physical reaction to a chemical that interferes with cellular function and can trigger an immune response.

STRESS

Chronic stress disrupts our hormone balance and increases inflammation. If we're faced with immediate danger, like our ancestors were—such as a hungry lion about to attack—stress hormones like cortisol and adrenaline are necessary for survival.

But in today's world, many of us are suffering from chronic stress that has nowhere to go. We're tired, wrung out, worried, and frustrated over a number of things in our lives, causing our stress hormones to flood our bodies on a regular basis. These toxic hormones must be eliminated from the body via our detoxification pathways, or they will lead to weight gain, headaches, fatigue, digestive problems, and other health issues.

LACK OF MOVEMENT

Many of us are living sedentary lifestyles. We sit at work, sit on our commute, and sit to watch television when we get home. Finding time to exercise is becoming more and more difficult for many people. Yet exercise is one of our most potent weapons when it comes to detox. When we move, we increase circulation of both the blood and the lymph, and we encourage the digestive system to do its job—both things that support the body's elimination of waste.

A lack of exercise, on the other hand, contributes to weak intestinal health and poor circulation, which makes elimination more difficult and decreases the amount of lymph pumped through the system. Over time, your body is unable to detox as well as it should.

the difference between conventional and organic

Throughout this book, you'll come across the terms "conventional" and "organic." The difference between the two lies in how the farmers grow the crops and the materials they use to do so. For a food to be labeled USDA certified organic (you'll see the USDA symbol), the food is grown and processed according to federal guidelines that prohibit the use of synthetic fertilizers, pesticides, herbicides, irradiation, sewage sludge, hormones, antibiotics, and genetic engineering. Conventional foods (aka not organic) don't follow these restrictions, which means they're loaded with antibiotics, hormones, herbicides, pesticides, and many other toxic chemicals that, in turn, can lead to toxicity in our bodies.

WHAT IS ORGANIC?
I eat organic—you won't find any conventional food in my kitchen. Eating organic helped me heal from chronic illness because I removed all the toxins I was ingesting on a daily basis and my body didn't have to work so hard to process all those chemicals and antibiotics that were lurking in my food. Be aware, however, that while there are numerous products in the grocery store that are organic, they aren't all necessarily healthy. Skip the organic, processed cookies and candy and focus on whole, one-ingredient organic foods such as gluten-free whole grains (wild rice, millet), lean proteins (beans), healthy fats (nuts, seeds, avocados), and produce (berries, spinach). If a label says that the product is made with organic ingredients, it doesn't mean the entire product is organic, only that some of the ingredients are organic, so read closely and look for the USDA certified organic seal on the package as well as the number "9" on your fresh produce stickers to ensure the food is organic.

WHAT IS EATING CLEAN?
Eating clean is eating whole, organic foods (like all the recipes in this book)—nothing processed from a box or can. (One exception to my "no-cans" rule is for culinary coconut milk; you can use a BPA-free can of culinary coconut milk.) That means no gluten, dairy, soy, refined sugar, artificial sweeteners, nonfat/low-fat or "light" products, fried foods, and refined or hydrogenated oils (including but not limited to canola oil, margarine, grapeseed oil, corn oil, soybean oil, and vegetable oil). See my list on page 24 of the Toxic 13 foods to avoid when you're eating clean.

probiotics and prebiotics

Your gut contains a hundred trillion bacteria, and you always want more good bacteria than bad bacteria in your gut. Probiotics are friendly "good" gut bacteria that protect your gut. Taking a high-quality daily multistrain probiotic supplement will help you add beneficial bacteria (see page 380 for a suggested brand and page 382 for suggested probiotic-rich foods). Talk to your Integrative doctor about what strains are right for you. You may need to continue to take probiotics for a while to maintain a healthy balance of good gut bacteria. It's also important to eat foods that are rich in prebiotics, which feed the good bacteria in your gut. Examples of prebiotic foods are leeks, onions, asparagus, garlic, dandelion greens, and Jerusalem artichokes.

INTENSE EXERCISE

While regular exercise supports detoxification, you do not want to overdo it. If you join a new program that's far too advanced for you, for example, or push yourself too hard in your exercise efforts, the body interprets that exertion as stress, and releases toxins instead of removing them. Overexercising also negatively affects the adrenals, causing you to be even more exhausted. Slow, steady exercise such as walking, yoga, and stretching is the way to go!

YOUR DNA

We each have our own pile of DNA we've inherited from our parents. As I mentioned earlier, it's the interaction between our DNA along with our lifestyle and food choices that can lead to disease. You may not be missing the MTHFR gene to help you detox (see page 7), as I am, but you may have other triggers that are best avoided to help your body detox every day.

LACK OF SLEEP

Sleep is necessary for hormone balance, cellular health, fatigue reduction, brain health, and stress management. Getting seven to nine hours a night is ideal; any less than that interrupts your normal biology and throws your hormones out of whack, which can affect the efficiency of your body's waste management system.

ENVIRONMENTAL ELEMENTS

We're bombarded by toxins in mercury dental fillings, pesticides, pollution, cigarette smoke, cleaning products, tap water, personal care products, plastics, and much more. When we inhale, touch, or ingest these chemicals, they interfere with our normal cell function, which contributes to our toxicity and leads to inflammation. Reducing your exposure to all of these elements will help lower your body burden from toxins, allowing you to detox easier, reduce inflammation, and encourage overall better health.

YOUR TOXIC TRIGGERS

Any food can be considered a toxic trigger if it causes a negative effect in your body. Each of our bodies is different, so it's not about following one diet for everyone. It's about knowing, listening to, and trusting your own body.

There are some common toxic triggers, however, that affect most people. These include gluten, dairy, soy, refined sugar, refined oils, corn, alcohol, eggs, peanuts, processed foods, and caffeine. You will not find any of these ingredients in this book.

Other common triggers are nightshade veggies (which include tomatoes, peppers, eggplants, and white potatoes). In this book, I do not use white potatoes or eggplants for this reason. You will see a few recipes with tomatoes and peppers, though, because I've found they don't bother me and most of my clients, but you can always remove them if you wish!

Remember, these foods may or may not be toxic triggers for you; however, there is a growing number of people who are finding they have sensitivities to many of them. The best method for discovering your toxic triggers is to test them with my 21-Day Elimination Diet (page 22) and Food Sensitivity Testing (page 377), and then reboot your body and replenish with probiotics, prebiotics, and enzymes to aid digestion.

Enzymes and You

Enzymes are catalysts to each chemical reaction in the body. Think of them as the sparks that start the fires. They're very important for our digestion, help us absorb nutrients into our cells, and assist in excreting waste from these cells. The right amount increases the effectiveness of our natural detox processes. For more information on enzymes, check out my website TheHealthyApple.com.

The following are examples of how food enzymes and our human enzymes can be affected.

▸ **DEPLETED SOIL.** Worn-out farmland produces foods that are lower in health-supporting enzymes.

▸ **REFINED FOODS.** These are exposed to heat, which damages enzymes and nutrients; chemical preservatives; and coloring and flavoring agents, which block the effectiveness of enzymes that do get into the body.

▸ **IRRADIATION.** This process is used to keep harmful organisms out of your food, but it can also rob food of vitamins A, E, K, and B, as well as essential amino acids, healthy fats, and enzymes.

▸ **PESTICIDES.** They inhibit the absorption of minerals that come from the soil; enzymes need minerals to work properly.

▸ **ANTIBIOTICS.** Taking antibiotics can alter your gut environment, creating the perfect breeding ground for internal toxicity. Also, eating conventional animal products (which are full of antibiotics) can affect us as well.

▸ **TOXIC EXPOSURE.** Your toxic load affects your enzyme activity. Heavy metals such as aluminum, mercury, and lead wreak havoc with enzyme interactions.

▸ **STRESS.** Digestive enzymes are compromised when you face stress, both emotional and physical, and can affect your digestion and proper absorption of foods.

the 21-day elimination diet

Okay, folks, here's the plan that will lead you into the transformation of your lifetime.

I've gathered my best tips and notes to make your detox a breeze. My goal is to revamp your pantry and give your kitchen, your immune system, and your gut a makeover. Get ready for increased energy levels, decreased inflammation, and more overall well-being than ever before!

Whether you work full time, have a family of six, have been diagnosed with an autoimmune disease or other illness, or just want to clean up your diet, this section is going to blow your mind. I'll show you how to plan ahead and make your new life (free of gluten, refined sugar, dairy, peanuts, soy, corn, caffeine, white flour, and eggs) super-duper easy, and delicious.

If you let me, I can make your transition a smooth one. Before you know it, these whole foods will be on the top of your mind and those old "foodlike substances" will taste like cardboard! The purpose of this book is to help you gain a new perspective that will allow you to begin your detox and clean-eating journey through realistic, lifelong shifts (not a quick-fix diet).

I don't want you to be overwhelmed. It's important to understand that none of us are perfect and you can move along at your own pace—no need to do everything in one day!

When it comes to eating clean, don't deprive yourself of healthy, homemade foods (like the ones in this book). Be flexible. Try to make five nights of dinner at home and use the other two nights to enjoy leftovers. Find your own happy medium that works for you and your family, and please, don't try to be perfect. I'm surely not, but I do my best to keep myself healthy and sane!

The Elimination Diet is 21 days in which you will cut out the most common food triggers (see the list of the Toxic 13, page 24) from your lifestyle. The idea is to stop eating the foods that are negatively affecting your health. With this anti-inflammatory diet, you'll feed the good bacteria in your gut, reduce inflammation, improve your body's ability to fight off pathogens, and lose weight.

After the 21 days are over, you'll add each food back into your lifestyle, one by one. If you have symptoms, then you'll know which foods bother you. I love this program because it's tailored to each individual; you get to figure out what agrees with your body and what doesn't.

This 21-Day Elimination Diet Detox will help you:

- Reduce your exposure to toxins in your food

- Boost your detox pathways

- Balance your blood sugar (with healthy fats and quality proteins)

- Improve your gut function

- Eliminate current toxins in your body

- Nourish your body's cells to support their natural function and capacity to detox

- Eliminate foods that wreak havoc on your body and create unwanted bloat

- Learn what foods fuel your body and be done with feeling tired and foggy

- Improve your digestion and get your bowels functioning

- Reduce inflammation that leads to bloating, headaches, and/or gut imbalance

- Properly absorb your food

- Feel grounded, alert, powerful, and ready to take on the world of eating clean every day of your life

- Jump-start and reboot your metabolism

BEFORE YOU START

Before you get started, ask yourself the following questions:

- What foods do you eat most often?

- What foods would you have trouble giving up if you had to remove them from your diet?

- What foods do you eat to feel better or to get that jolt of quick energy?

- What foods do you reach for when you are sad, mad, or frustrated?

- What foods do you crave?

Think about these questions, and write down your answers in a journal. They will help you understand your food habits and the emotional aspects of your eating, and help you get in touch with how you respond to various foods. It's also good to record these answers so you can look back after you have finished the 21 days, to see what has changed.

WHAT TO EXPECT

During the 21 days, there's no deprivation—only an abundance of fresh ingredients. As you eliminate trigger foods, you might notice that your sugar cravings, chronic symptoms, and imbalances disappear.

I've seen numerous clients find relief from migraines, irritable bowel syndrome, acid reflux, muscle pain, autoimmune diseases, hives, rashes, acne, anxiety, depression, cravings, and much more using this simple program. When you focus on consuming delicious whole, fresh, organic foods like nuts, seeds, fruits and veggies, as well as beans, legumes, extra-virgin olive oil, coconut oil, nut butters, and nut milks, you'll feel anything but hungry.

It's best to realize, though, that eliminating takes time and commitment. At first, you may experience unpleasant symptoms such as headaches, insomnia, irritability, and fatigue. These are common side effects after years of cumulative toxicity. This is a new way of eating and living; your body needs time to get used to it.

Meanwhile, your brain will likely tell you (sometimes in a very loud voice!) that it wants the addictive processed foods you were eating before. Just keep going. You will get there, and believe me, you will finish feeling great.

Step 1: Eliminate the Toxic 13

I could give you a big long list of every food you should stay away from on this diet, but that can get really confusing, so let me give you just a short list—the Toxic 13! If you get rid of the following items and remove them completely from your house—you'll be well on your way to feeling better fast. For the next three weeks, remove all trigger foods from your diet, including the Toxic 13 listed below and those in the "Exclude" column in the chart on page 26. You won't find any of these ingredients in this book.

1. Gluten

2. Dairy (no milk, cheese, yogurt, etc.)

3. Soy

4. Corn (no cornstarch)

5. Caffeine

6. Eggs

7. Refined sugar (and no chemical sugar alternatives)

8. Alcohol

9. Shellfish

10. Peanuts

11. White potatoes (no potato flour or potato starch)

12. White flour (no baked items made with white flour. Yes, this means no gluten-free all-purpose flours such as white rice flour!)

13. Any processed food sold in a package or can (i.e., food mixes, chips, snacks and snack bars, popcorn, pizza, etc.) For my recipes that call for culinary coconut milk, which most often comes in a can, make sure to purchase BPA-free cans.

You might also want to avoid nightshade veggies (see page 21) such as eggplants, if you have found them bothersome in the past.

Now one note of caution—look closely at the foods you're eating now, you may find that almost all of them contain at least one of the ingredients above. (Corn and soy can be particularly sneaky, especially in processed foods.) Try not to get too discouraged. Focus on what you can eat for the next 21 days and let the other foods fall by the wayside.

Step 2: Replace Trigger Foods with Anti-Inflammatory Goodies

Wondering what you should eat for the next 21 days instead of the Toxic 13? See the chart on pages 26–27 to make it easy for you to see your options at a glance. You can eat all the foods in the "Include" column, but you must avoid the foods in the "Exclude" column. For a full list of ingredients that contain hidden forms of gluten, dairy, and soy, go to TheHealthyApple.com/EatingClean.

If you find you need more foods to add to your "Include" list, see my Anti-Inflammatory Pantry List on page 375. I'm also going to give you more tips and tricks for substitutions and replacements in the next chapter. And for those of you who like to plan your meals for the week, see page 371 for my 2-Week

Detox Meal Plan to help you plan healthy meals and snacks without feeling deprived.

Step 3: Substitute

Instead of Refined Sugar

Any type of sugar is converted quickly into glucose by the body and used for fuel, but how healthy that fuel is depends on where the sugar comes from. Natural sugars, such as those found in fruits, are typically accompanied by other nutrients like fiber and antioxidants, making them healthy foods overall.

Refined sugar, found in products such as store-bought cookies, on the other hand, is processed through bleaching, extreme heat, chemicals, and it's stripped of any other nutrients or fibers, resulting in a nutrient-devoid food.

Processed sugar is easily digested and goes right into your bloodstream, which causes your blood glucose levels to shoot sky high. This puts strain on your organs, causing wear, tear, and aging.

High-fructose corn syrup (HFCS) is even worse. Found in everything from soup to cookies to cereals to sodas, it's made from corn syrup that is scientifically altered to contain a higher percentage of fructose than glucose. HFCS makes foods taste sweeter, which means manufacturers can use less to get the same sweet taste, thereby saving money. Unfortunately, through research we're finding that the body doesn't process fructose the same as it does glucose, and that HFCS may be more connected to weight gain and even pancreatic cancer than regular sugar.

Even what many people think of as a "health" food, like low-fat yogurt, is often filled with added sugars that make it unhealthy. In fact, we can consume a lot of sugar without even knowing it. These days, sugar is in our sweets and treats, our yogurt and salsa, but also in our salad dressing, bread, cereal, condiments, soup, and more. Read your labels!

USE: The best alternatives to refined sugar are whole, natural sweeteners such as organic honey and organic pure maple syrup. Pure maple syrup is especially good because it is brimming with essential vitamins, minerals, trace elements, and other nutrients drawn from deep within the earth by maple trees.

Instead of Dairy

Dairy creates mucus in the gut and make us feel generally terrible, especially if we are lactose intolerant. It's also an inflammatory food, and can lead to a number of digestion problems and acne.

USE: I have been lactose intolerant my whole life, so dairy was never in my meal plan or in my lunchbox. Now, I make my own nut and seed "mylks" such as almond, hemp, and cashew. I use the word "mylk" when I'm referring to my homemade dairy-free coconut, nut, and seed drinks on pages 290–292. You can choose to use these mylks for any recipe calling for nut milk or simply purchase unsweetened nut milk from your store if you're short on time. Remove cow, sheep, and goat dairy products, which means avoiding milks, cheeses, yogurts, ice cream, and butter. Try my Dairy-Free Vanilla Bean Coconut Ice Cream (page 334), Dairy-Free Creamy Cashew Cheese (page 308), Moo-Free Cashew Sour Cream (page 309), and Creamy Mock Mayo (page 313) instead, and use extra-virgin olive oil or coconut oil in place of butter for baking.

Instead of Conventional Meat

Conventional meat and eggs are often filled with inflammation-causing ingredients such as growth hormones, antibiotics, and other artificial substances. Sodium nitrites—which have been linked to cancer—are used to preserve cured and processed meats like ham, bacon, and sausage to keep them looking moist and appetizing. Steer clear of these, please!

(*continued on page 29*)

	✓ *include*	✗ *exclude*
Fruits and Vegetables	Organic fresh or frozen (without additives) whole fruits and vegetables. Limit peppers, tomatoes, oranges, grapefruit, strawberries, grapes, and bananas only if problematic.	Corn, eggplant, conventional fruits and vegetables, potatoes, canned fruits, canned vegetables creamed vegetables, edamame
Dairy Substitutes	Almond, hazelnut, walnut, hemp, rice, and other nut and seed milks; coconut milk; culinary coconut milk; coconut oil; coconut butter	Soy milk, tempeh, tofu, and all forms of dairy, including milk, cheese, cottage cheese, cream, yogurt, butter, ice cream, nondairy creamers, ghee, powdered milk, sheep's milk, cow's milk, goat's milk, whey protein
Gluten-Free Grains, Flours, and Starches	Rice (brown, black, wild), millet, amaranth, certified gluten-free oats, teff, tapioca, buckwheat, quinoa, bean pasta, brown rice pasta, quinoa pasta, bean flours (chickpea flour), seed flours, nut flours (almond flour, almond meal), coconut flour	Wheat, couscous, bran, farina, barley, corn, kamut, rye, spelt, triticale, oats, corn pasta, polenta, cornmeal, cornstarch, white flour
Proteins	All beans, split peas, lentils, legumes, nuts, seeds, gluten-free whole grains, a small amount of organic, doctor-approved protein powders from hemp, artichoke, or pea protein	Soy products, protein powders, seitan, eggs
Nuts and Seeds	Raw (unroasted and unsalted) tahini, nut and seed butters, hemp seeds, sesame seeds, pumpkin seeds, sunflower seeds, hazelnuts, pecans, almonds, walnuts, cashews, macadamias, pine nuts, Brazil nuts	Peanuts and peanut butter, pistachios
Oils	Cold-pressed extra-virgin olive, flax, hemp, avocado, and coconut oils	Butter, margarine, shortening, processed oils, canola oil, processed salad dressings, mayonnaise
Drinks	Purified water; organic green, white, or herbal tea (noncaffeinated); seltzer; mineral water; organic freshly squeezed juices	Alcohol, coffee, caffeine, soda, processed fruit juices, tap water

	✓ include	✗ exclude
Sweeteners ✓	Pureed and whole fresh fruit, sulfur-free dried fruits, pure maple syrup, organic honey, cinnamon sticks, fennel seeds, cardamom seeds, fresh and dried fruit peels, unsweetened cocoa powder, carob and carob powder, raw chocolate, raw cacao, unsweetened coconut flakes	✗ Refined sugar, white sugar, brown sugars, high-fructose corn syrup, evaporated cane juice, Splenda, Equal, Sweet'N Low, fruit juice concentrate, agave nectar, brown rice syrup, beet sugar, processed stevia
Other ✓	Sriracha or pure pepper hot sauce, raw unfiltered apple cider vinegar, red and white wine vinegar, organic balsamic vinegar, freshly squeezed citrus juices, spices, dried herbs, Himalayan pink salt, sea salt, black pepper, peppercorns, whole-grain and Dijon mustards, chickpea miso paste, coconut aminos, no-sugar-added whole fruit jam, sea vegetables (seaweed, dulse, kelp, nori, kombu), fresh herbs, vegetable broth, garlic (if tolerated), fermented sauerkraut, kimchi, fresh horseradish, pure vanilla and almond extracts, saffron, pickles	✗ Processed chocolate (with dairy and sugar), processed ketchup, relish, processed barbecue sauce, teriyaki, gum and mints, protein bars, popcorn, chutney, MSG, tamari, traditional soy sauce, gluten-free soy sauce, soy miso paste

hidden names for sugar

agave nectar	corn sweetener	evaporated cane juice	grape sugar	molasses
Barbados sugar	corn syrup	Florida crystals	HFCS (high fructose corn syrup)	panocha
barley malt	corn syrup solids	fructose	icing sugar	raw sugar
beet sugar	crystalline fructose	fruit juice	invert sugar	refiner's syrup
brown sugar	date sugar	fruit juice concentrate	lactose	rice syrup
buttered syrup	dehydrated cane juice	galactose	malt sugar	sorbitol
cane juice	dextran	glucose	malt syrup	sorghum syrup
cane sugar	dextrose	golden sugar	maltodextrin	sucrose syrup
caramel	diastatic malt	golden syrup	maltose	treacle
caster sugar	ethyl maltol	granulated sugar	mannitol	turbinado sugar
confectioners' sugar				yellow sugar

what to do when cravings strike

When you're craving...

▸ Coffee—drink organic dandelion root tea or my detox teas (pages 298–299) with honey and my Healthy Homemade Dairy-Free Nut (and Seed) Mylks (page 290).

▸ The processed breakfast buffet at your 11:00 a.m. meeting—spread ripe avocado on gluten-free whole-grain toast with a sprinkle of sesame seeds (for calcium!) before you head into the meeting.

▸ Afternoon processed chocolate candy bar—eat a handful of raw almonds with fresh organic berries and a dash of unsweetened cocoa powder or my Simply Sweet Maple Roasted Chickpea Croutons (page 144) for crunchy protein-packed options. Healthy fats and protein will help satisfy your cravings.

▸ Store-bought processed cake at a party—make my Joyful Hot Cocoa (page 297) and serve it with my Easy Raw Chocolate Coconut Banana Tart with Amie's Grain-Free Pie Crust (page 344).

▸ Junk food when you're traveling—pack my grain-free crackers (pages 156–162) with avocado and Dairy-Free Raw Macadamia Nut "Ricotta" Cheese (page 309); or my tasty hummus recipes (page 301–303) served with chopped raw veggies.

▸ The vending machine when you're stressed at work—snack on a handful of my roasted nut recipes (page 140–142) and my grain-free crackers (pages 156–162) with my Dairy-Free Creamy Cashew Cheese (page 308).

▸ The bread basket at dinner—order an organic green salad appetizer with avocado, nuts, olive oil, and vinegar, and bring along my Transformed Crunchy Breadsticks (page 143) or my grain-free crackers (pages 156–162) for your own "bread" basket. Dip the breadsticks and crackers into tomato sauce or a mixture of garlic and extra-virgin olive oil.

▸ Sugary cocktails—drink seltzer, herbal tea, one of my three detox teas (pages 298–299), my Caffeine-Free Chai (page 289), or sip on mineral water with fresh lime or lemon.

▸ After-dinner treat—drink my Frozen Hot Chocolate (page 293) to cure your sweet tooth.

▸ Candy on weekend afternoons—sip a cup of my No-Soy Chickpea Miso Soup (page 187); there's a reason this recipe serves one. The salty flavors of chickpea miso can cure any stubborn afternoon sweet tooth.

USE: If you choose to eat animal products, choose organic and cage-free/grass-fed. Although you may feel healthy while eating organic animal products, this cookbook is 100 percent vegetarian, and also contains many vegan recipes, so you won't find any that include meat, poultry, seafood, eggs, or dairy. In this book and on my website, TheHealthyApple.com, I use lentils, beans, nuts, seeds, and whole grains as healthy proteins. Feel free to add your own organic, lean animal protein to my recipes, if desired.

Instead of Caffeine

Caffeine is processed by the liver, using the same detox pathway as some toxins you are trying to remove from your body. It acts as a stimulant and taxes our adrenals. It can also make other foods, like iced teas and sodas, addictive. Getting off caffeine releases you from cravings. And yes, decaf coffee still contains some caffeine, so it's off limits.

USE: If you usually drink caffeine, start your detox with green tea. It contains some caffeine, so you'll want to taper off it after about the first week, but it's a great beverage to use during your transition. After that, go for organic dandelion root tea or burdock tea and other organic, caffeine-free teas. (See pages 298–299 for three tasty detox tea recipes.)

Instead of Eggs

There are no eggs used in this cookbook. Instead of eggs, I use ground flaxseeds or whole chia seeds combined with water to form a gel, which acts as your egg substitute.

USE: If you choose to eat eggs, look for the USDA organic seal on the carton.

Instead of Wheat/Gluten

For many people, wheat/gluten causes headaches, joint pain, weight gain, and digestive issues. Often, people don't realize these symptoms are related to their food. Part of the problem is that the wheat/gluten we consume today is not the same as the wheat we ate a hundred years ago. Today's wheat is a hybrid and genetically modified strain that is made of molecules that haven't ever been seen in wheat before. Plus, it's overprocessed and is more like sawdust than a grain.

USE: Use the recipes in this book to eat naturally gluten-free without relying on processed all-purpose gluten-free flours, breads, and other nutrient-devoid foods that are advertised as "healthy."

Instead of Soy

There is no soy used in this cookbook. See page 42 for examples on how to create creaminess in your recipes without soy.

USE: If you decide to eat soy, look for the USDA organic seal on the package.

Step 4: Monitor Your Progress

Each day during the 21-Day Elimination Diet ask yourself: What did I eat and drink? What are my thoughts? How am I feeling? How did I sleep?

Use the chart on page 30 to track your progression. Go to TheHealthyApple.com/EatingClean, download this chart, and make 21 copies. Fill in one chart for each day. You can keep the charts in a binder or create a file for yourself on the computer—whatever is easiest for you. If you fall off the wagon, you'll have to start over from day one to get accurate results. No cheating!

Step 5: Support Yourself

This plan isn't just about eating. Use the "Additional Notes" column to write anything that comes to mind for you that day, such as how much water you drank, your quality of sleep, your bowel movements, stress level, etc. Moreover, adding other healthy activities into your life can help reduce stress, improve your mood, and support your detox efforts. When you find your cravings getting the best of you, or when you're in a bad mood and just really want that frosted donut, pause and take a deep breath! The next page has a

YOUR DAILY ELIMINATION DIET JOURNAL

day ____

Meal/Snack	What I Ate/Drank	How I Felt Immediately Afterward	How I Felt 1 to 3 Hours After Eating	Coping Techniques I Used Today	Additional Notes for the Day

few ideas for coping techniques that you can use to support yourself during the 21-Day Elimination Diet. You can add them to your "Coping Techniques" column in the chart to remember what worked for you each day. Do one of the following instead:

‣ **REST:** Take a nap. Sometimes when your body is tired and you don't let it rest, it will respond by inducing food cravings. Try taking a nap before you cave in!

‣ **LIGHT EXERCISE (FOR AT LEAST 30 MINUTES):** This is huge, as it gets the blood and lymph pumping, which supports your liver function and encourages detox and good digestion. Try taking a walk or light jog, swimming, biking, or engaging in another enjoyable activity, but don't overdo it. Hard exercise causes a rapid accumulation of lactic acid in your tissues, and the last thing you want to do during detox is produce more waste products. My favorite way to move is by dancing in my apartment to upbeat fun music like Beyoncé!

‣ **MEDITATE:** Stress fills the body with toxins and makes us crave all the wrong things. Meditation is a great stress reliever. Take ten to twenty minutes to meditate or sit in stillness. Feel your feet and your hands and just sit with your body.

‣ **STRETCH:** Do some stretching or light movement—yoga or tai chi are both great options. They help relax a tight body, which reduces stress and helps eliminate lactic acid in the muscles. Both are also linked with an improved immune system and reduced aches and pains.

‣ **TAKE A DETOX BATH:** Baths are not only relaxing, they can also be great ways to detox. Soak your body or feet in hot water with sea salt or Epsom salt and a few drops of organic detoxifying essential oils. (Try Aura Cacia grapefruit seed and peel, sage, and rosemary for additional detoxing action.) The magnesium in the Epsom salts draws out toxic waste

and replenishes the body's supply of this important mineral.

‣ **SKIN BRUSHING:** Dry skin brushing boosts your blood and lymph circulation and exfoliates your skin, clearing your pores of dead tissues. This practice consists of applying a long-handled, natural-bristle brush to your skin with quick, short strokes. Brush your dry skin (before your shower or bath) toward your heart, starting with the soles of your feet and moving up your legs and arms, and then on to your stomach, brushing clockwise to stimulate your digestive tract. This practice takes less than five minutes to do and leaves your skin with a glow!

‣ **TRY REBOUNDING:** Rebounding is simply jumping up and down on a rebounder (small trampoline) to help move the fluid in your lymph system. Our lymph system clears toxins we absorb through our environment, therefore bouncing will help your body eliminate toxins that are locked within your lymph.

‣ **SIT IN AN INFRARED SAUNA:** Unlike ordinary saunas, far infrared saunas (not generic infrared saunas) heat you from the inside out to reach your deepest tissues and organs, which helps mobilize toxins to be carried away via your sweat. Many of my doctors had me sit in a far infrared sauna to "sweat out" heavy metals and candida, and help with my Lyme disease symptoms.

‣ **TAKE A DETOX SHOWER:** You can stimulate the circulation of your lymph and blood at the end of your shower by switching from warm water to a rinse of icy-cold water for a few minutes. Be sure to use a shower filter on your shower head so your skin is not absorbing the toxins from your tap water. You'll feel rejuvenated!

‣ **DRINK WATER:** Get yourself a nice tall glass of cool, purified, filtered water. To increase the detox action, add ½ teaspoon high-quality sea salt (my favorite is from Frontier Organic).

▸ **DRINK TEA:** Make yourself a cup of organic herbal tea. Great options include dandelion root, nettle, cleavers, burdock, and red clover. Try my Warm Cleansing Tea (page 299).

▸ **ENJOY A MUD MASK:** Masks can help pull toxins out through your skin, leaving you with a healthy glow. Dead Sea mud and bentonite clay both have cleansing and detoxifying powers. Algae and kelp can also absorb toxins when applied to the skin with clay or in a seaweed mask. These masks are even more effective when you sweat them out.

▸ **ENJOY MUSIC/ART:** These activities can relieve stress and calm the body. Listen to your favorite music, paint with watercolors, draw, craft, or do something you enjoy to calm and quiet your mind. I listen to happy music daily and paint watercolors on blank index cards for relaxation.

▸ **EAT CLEAN:** I have plenty of clean recipes (there's more than two hundred in this book) for you to choose from (starting on page 111), along with my detox meal plan (page 371).

DON'T GET DISCOURAGED—YOU CAN DO THIS!

If you're reading this book, you've accepted that something in your life needs to change. Acceptance may seem hard—especially if you think it means you have to give up things like a social life, eating out, and "feeling normal." But it's easier than you think!

The key is to adopt a new mind-set. This book will introduce you to a bunch of new (delicious) foods and healthy lifestyle changes that you otherwise would have never thought to try. You are giving your tummy and your health their best fighting chance—like a gift to your future self.

All you have to do is start with one step (like getting the Toxic 13 out of your kitchen from step 1, or filling your pantry with the healthy foods from step 2). Only you know what you can afford, what you're willing to change, and what you can tackle without feeling overwhelmed. Once you take that first step, though, you'll feel empowered to take another. And then another.

Buy yourself a big calendar and hang it on a prominent wall or tape it to your fridge. Take a red marker and for every day you eat clean and take care of yourself (mind, body, and spirit), put a big red X over that day. After a few days you'll see a chain, which will grow longer and longer as you go. Once you have a few months' worth of that red chain, you won't want to break it because you'll be feeling great.

Now that you have a few doable steps to plan into your 21-Day Detox calendar, you're ready to make some shifts in your kitchen! The next section focuses on cleaning out and stocking up. What do you still need to get rid of, and what can you add to your refrigerator, freezer, and pantry to make eating clean tasty, easy, and fun?

8 steps to clean out and stock up

Getting healthy (and staying healthy) may take some serious shifts in your daily habits, but don't worry about revamping your lifestyle overnight. These changes take time. Start when you feel ready and take a deep breath.

My "aha" moment was getting chronically ill, but you don't need to go through something that dramatic. Funny thing is that before I got sick, I cooked my own meals, brought my lunch to work, and never ate fast food. I thought I was eating healthy, but I had no idea how toxic seemingly healthy food could be.

Whether it's the birth of your first child, a scary health diagnosis, or just wanting to clean up your diet, eating clean for a few weeks will convert even the pickiest eater. My father is living proof. With a name like Tony Valpone, you can imagine—this Italian man lived off white bread, white pasta, and way too many processed snacks. Not anymore! He's dropped excess weight, and decreased his inflammation, and he's bouncing off the walls with energy way beyond what a normal person might have at the age of sixty-eight. Sound like a miracle? Nope. He's the real deal.

You can do it, too! The steps, tips, and suggestions in these next two sections are dedicated to making this transition relaxed and fun.

Step 1: Create a Clean Kitchen

First things first—ditch the foods that are making you feel yucky, bloated, puffy, yada yada yada. You've already done some of this, but it's time to check your cupboards again. Move over, gluten. Adios, dairy. Sayonara, refined sugar. Never again, corn. Bye-bye processed foods.

Now that you know why these foods have gotta go (reread Why Detox?, page 14, if you're feeling a little unsure), it's time to say bye to your old pantry staples and hello to a whole new world of fun, flavor, and creativity with whole, organic foods.

STEP 2: CREATE YOUR EATING CLEAN PLAN

Before you set foot in the grocery store, it's key to have a strategy. I don't want you freaking out and running out of the store inhaling a pint of conventional ice cream and crying.

You don't want to risk spending a small fortune on new foods, only to have no idea what to do with them. There's nothing more discouraging! Instead, here's how to get started on your new-and-improved anti-inflammatory detox:

‣ **TAKE INVENTORY.** Go through your fridge and pantry (after you've cleaned them out!) and see what you have that you can keep (see page 375 for my Anti-inflammatory Pantry List).

‣ **CHOOSE YOUR FAVORITES.** Sit down with this book and flag the recipes you want to prepare. Plan your meals at least a couple of days ahead of time, though ideally for the week. Don't forget snacks! My meal plan on page 371 is a great place to start.

‣ **MAKE A LIST.** Write down all the ingredients you need to prepare these meals. Don't worry if your list is quite long the first time you do this; it'll shrink as time goes on. Go to TheHealthyApple.com/EatingClean for a shopping list to my meal plan. The more you cook, the more ingredients you'll collect. Plus, you'll be stocking up on quality ingredients, so you'll only need to use a pinch for flavor.

‣ **GET ON A SCHEDULE.** Every Sunday night, make a plan: pick three gluten-free grains, five veggies, and four healthy fats to use in your meals and snacks for the week. For example: quinoa, wild rice, and millet; zucchini, spinach, carrots, and kale; avocado, almonds, walnuts, and hummus. You can easily create all your meals and snacks for the week from this group of foods you choose. Even if you plan to buy lunch at work, pack my Easiest Guacamole (page 305) or Kalamata Olive and Cashew Tapenade (page 304) for snacks with raw veggies, or toss a sealed mason jar filled with cooked millet (see how to cook millet on the gluten-free grain chart on page 104) into your fridge and add it to your desk-side salad. Fake out that takeout and bring a few of these healthy additions into your cubicle each week. My Freckled Sesame Almond Clusters (page 140) make a fabulous party snack, but also do wonders for a boring salad. Catch my drift?

---

where's the protein?

This cookbook is vegetarian and many recipes are vegan (minus a few recipes that contain honey), meaning there are no animal products (no dairy, eggs, meat, poultry, seafood, etc.). You can enjoy these recipes if you are vegan, vegetarian, or even if you are an organic carnivore, because you can serve my recipes paired with your choice of animal protein, if desired. The protein in my recipes comes from organic beans, legumes, gluten-free whole grains, and raw nuts, and seeds.

Knowing how to buy food is almost as important as figuring out what to buy. Here are my favorite ways to shop smart and simple:

‣ **USE COMMON SENSE.** This is the best way to not only end up with a fridge full of groceries that you'll want to eat, but also to save money. Don't buy quick-to-spoil items in bulk and don't buy foods you know in your heart you'll never eat. If you hate asparagus now, chances are you'll still hate it in a week. See page 39 for rounding up your list of top ten go-to foods.

‣ **STREAMLINE YOUR SHOPPING TRIP.** Organize your shopping list by where you'll find those items at the store, such as produce, grains, spices, frozen foods, etc. It'll save you time and help you to avoid forgetting any items. Do your best to stick to the list and avoid making spur-of-the-moment impulse buys.

‣ **BE FLEXIBLE.** You might have kale on your shopping list, but once you get to the store, you may see they're having a sale on collard greens or they only have Swiss chard. Sometimes you have to let your wallet do the talking. You can always improvise—it might just be better than what you had planned in the first place. Check out the Smart + Simple Substitutions chart on page 44–45 for easy swaps.

‣ **STOCK YOUR FREEZER.** If my local food store is having a sale on a vegetable I love, I'll grab a pound or two, along with my favorite marinating ingredients, combine them when I'm home, and either roast or grill them. Then I transfer the veggies to a sealed container and freeze them for a future meal when I don't have time to devote all night to

---

get out of the grocery store

I don't think there's anything scarier (well, maybe a few things) than shopping for food in an overly lit, overpriced megastore that's loaded with cardboard boxes and advertisements for fake foods. Here are a few ways to make food prep and shopping that much lovelier, cheaper, easier, and more fun!

‣ **HEAD TO THE FARMER'S MARKET.** See what's fresh and in season, taste samples, and ask for tips on how to best prepare those ingredients. There's no better way to know where your food is coming from and how it's grown than to talk to the people who grow it.

‣ **DON'T FEAR ONLINE SHOPPING.** One of the easiest ways to ensure your pantry is stocked with healthy foods is to shop online. I was always skeptical of ordering food from a website for my organic necessities until I found frontiercoop.com, abesmarket.com, amazon.com, thrivemarket.com, and vitacost.com. I can order everything from gluten-free oats and organic mustard to raw unfiltered apple cider vinegar and have them delivered to my door without rummaging through ten health food stores. It has changed my life and has allowed me to use that saved time for taking care of myself.

‣ **PLANT A MINI HERB GARDEN.** Don't have a garden or a green thumb? No problem! Put a pot or two (or three or four) of herbs on your windowsill. That's the Manhattan way!

---

cooking. Trust me—a well-stocked freezer is like finding ten bucks in your coat pocket. Almost anything freezes well except for cooked potatoes, salad greens, celery, cabbage, and cucumbers. Freeze as much as you can in small batches. Organic fruits like berries are great to freeze immediately since they often go bad quickly in the fridge. You can use them in smoothies instead of ice, or defrost and use in desserts. You can also mix them into oatmeal or add them to coconut yogurt. I defrost frozen fruit in the fridge overnight and use the next morning. Frozen veggies like spinach, broccoli, cauliflower, and squash can be easily added to recipes. Freeze your own, or buy organic brands like Earthbound Farm or 365 Everyday Value from Whole Foods Market (both of which also offer organic frozen fruits, too).

▸ **TAKE RISKS.** Try one new whole-food ingredient each week. Not only is it good for your body, it's good for your brain—plus, it will encourage you to get a little creative with your meals. And who knows, you may find a new ingredient you love! My favorite risk? Eating nori (seaweed sheets). They're totally going to knock your socks off. And so is jicama. You'll see. Check out my Nori Crisps (page 37) and Raw Jicama Romaine Wraps with Dilly Lime Drizzle (page 170).

Step 4: Pantry Makeover

Throughout this book you'll notice a few ingredients that I keep coming back to—the foods that I can't live without. Call them superfoods, call them nutrient dense, call them your new best friends. Whatever you want to call them, it's time to get to know them.

There's no need to go out and buy them all at once, but consider adding them into your rotation a few at a time. By having them in your kitchen, you'll be able to easily add flavor and nutrients to almost any dish you're cooking, without chemicals, refined sugars, and any other sneaky ingredients.

▸ **CHICKPEA MISO PASTE:** This deeply flavorful Japanese staple used in soups, sauces, marinades, and salad dressings is made from chickpeas instead of soybeans. Woo-hoo for no soy! This miso changed my life; it's fermented, so it's great for gut health, too. Double bonus! I love using the organic Miso Master brand.

▸ **SEAWEED:** Sea vegetables are loaded with iodine, iron, minerals, vitamin C, antioxidants, and phytonutrients. You buy them dried and can rehydrate them in water in five minutes. Arame and wakame are great in soups and salads or sprinkled over steamed and roasted veggies. I add kombu when cooking beans (for a boost in nutrients and to help break down their starches), but you can also make a seaweed salad by cooking the kombu on the stovetop in water and adding a drizzle of coconut or extra-virgin olive oil before serving. Nori is a great snack, especially when rolled up with some avocado, hummus, and veggies. Check out my Sunrise Nori Wraps with Spicy Tahini Drizzle (page 168). Other sea veggies such as kelp and dulse are sold in granules and look like red pepper flakes. They're naturally salty and add great flavor to a dish. My No-Soy Chickpea Miso Soup (page 187) is a fun way to include dulse!

▸ **TURMERIC:** This spice gets its yellow coloring from a compound called curcuminoid, which is anti-inflammatory and stimulates the natural detoxification process of the liver and gallbladder. I add it to ice water with fresh lemon, as well as to herbal teas and my Warm Cleansing Tea (page 299).

▸ **WHOLE MUSTARD SEEDS:** Instead of using processed mustard from a jar—which is often filled with refined sugar and additives—these seeds add flavor to soups and salads while also stimulating stomach acid production to ensure you digest your food better. They're a great source of selenium, too. Try my tasty (and super-easy) Sweet Home Honey Mustard recipe using mustard seeds (page 315).

nori crisps—an easy snack!

Nori is known for its oceany flavor in sushi and miso soup, but you can use this dried Japanese sea-weed for wrapping veggies in place of tortillas, or brush it with water, sprinkle with sea salt, and toast in the oven at 250°F for 15 minutes. Crumble the toasted crisps over veggies, stir-fries, and salads for a little kick of flavor. Its papery texture makes it fun to serve and it looks great as a garnish, too.

> **FRESH GINGER:** Ginger stimulates the liver to flush out toxins. Fresh ginger is great for teas, salad dress-ings, and marinades, and it's delicious finely grated for a quick, flavorful touch!

> **CACAO:** Cacao beans are found inside the cacao fruit, and cacao is the primary ingredient in all chocolate. It's high in antioxidants, magnesium, and many other nutrients, and tastes bitter and chocolaty without the sugar and additives. You can add cacao nibs or powder to granola, smoothies, cereal, and trail mixes, as well as to desserts. Use it in place of cocoa powder for an extra punch of nutrients in my Joyful Hot Cocoa (page 297). I use the organic Navitas Naturals brand.

> **CINNAMON:** Cinnamon adds a touch of sweetness to your food and drinks. It comes from the inner bark of the cinnamon tree and has great antibacte-rial and antimicrobial properties. It's also filled with fiber, calcium, iron, manganese, and antioxidants. Sprinkle ground cinnamon on desserts, sweet pota-toes, squash, or baked fruit.

> **DAIRY-FREE NUT CHEESES:** These protein-packed "cheeses" add creamy texture and dairylike flavor to any dish and make great spreads for my grain-free crackers (pages 156–162) and raw veggies. You can make your own; I have a ton of options from my Dairy-Free Brazil Nut Parm Cheese to my Dairy-Free Creamy Cashew Cheese and more (see pages

307–310). To give your tummy a happy boost, add 1 teaspoon powdered probiotic to the food proces-sor when making these cheeses.

> **EXTRA-VIRGIN OLIVE OIL:** This crucial staple is made without being treated or altered in any way, so there's not much you have to look for other than an organic version. Make sure your oil comes in a dark glass bottle so that heat, oxygen, and light can't accelerate the oxidation process and destroy its nutritional properties such as antioxidants and vitamin E. I love using olive oil not just for cooking, but also for my beauty needs—as a moisturizer on my lips and eyes, a hydrating cuticle soak, and mixed with sea salt as an exfoliator.

> **GRAIN-FREE CRACKERS:** Having these crackers on hand is helpful for throwing together quick snacks and meals, especially when you're in the mood for a "real deal" cracker instead of sandpaper from a box. You can make grain-free crackers without any fillers, gluten, grains, or additives (that are often in boxed varieties) with the recipes on pages 156–162.

> **GLUTEN-FREE PIZZA CRUSTS:** Just like my crackers, you won't find any white flour or Xanthan gum in these tasty pizza crusts. Plus, who doesn't love pizza? These are super-healthy pizzas that are load-ed with flavor and fiber. Think butternut squash pizza crust and more. Check them out on pages 234, 235, and 236.

buying healthier groceries

Sneaky ingredient obstacles and pitfalls such as misleading labels are everywhere in the grocery store. Here are a few rules of thumb to keep in mind as you shop:

▸ **ALWAYS READ THE INGREDIENT LIST:** To this day, I'm guilty of walking through a health food store and grabbing an "organic" product like Dijon mustard, vegetable broth, or salsa without looking at the ingredient list. When I get home, I realize the "healthy" food is filled with refined sugar, flavorings, and other ingredients. My advice is to look at every label, or contact the brand of the product if you have questions. Most brands have contact pages on their website. Ask questions about ingredients, GMOs, organic certification, sourcing, and more.

▸ **BUY WHOLE FOODS:** Purchase one-ingredient whole foods that don't have an ingredient list (like apples, avocados, etc.), or choose foods with a short list of ingredients that you can pronounce and understand.

▸ **AVOID NUMBERS:** No ingredient on any box or package label you purchase should ever have a number in it. Red no. 40 and yellow no. 6 (along with all the other colors and numbers) weren't grown from the ground or on a farm. Your taste buds may love the chemical flavors on Dorito chips, but your body surely can't identify them.

▸ **WATCH OUT FOR HIDDEN INGREDIENTS:** Be cautious of hidden gluten, dairy, sugar, soy, additives, whey, chemicals, and eggs that are found in cake and pancake mixes, coleslaw dressings, salad dressings, marinades, mustard, chocolate, candy, mayonnaise, icings, hollandaise sauce, and protein powders.

▸ **LOOK FOR THE "9":** Check out the little stickers on your fresh produce. Fruits and veggies starting with the number "9" are organic.

▸ **SHOP ONLINE FOR BULK:** Bulk bins are helpful for buying things like legumes and grains for less money, but make sure you trust your store. A bin can be an easy spot for bacteria and mold to form, and that's not worth the cheaper price point. Mold and bacteria will contribute to gut health and inflammation! Trust me—I know from personal experience. My suggestion is to shop online for bulk; it's much cheaper and safer! Shop Frontier Organics (FrontierCoop.com) online and get bulk bags sent directly to your door.

▸ **AVOID GUM AND CANDY:** They're filled with chemicals and nothing about them is good for you. For years I was addicted to sugar-free gum and Snapple. After cutting them out, I feel so much better. Instead, use fresh lemons, limes, herbal teas, and fresh ginger to create flavor in your meals so you don't crave sweets.

‣ **RIPE AVOCADO:** It's a creamy replacement for dairy that can be used as a dip or spread for a decadent dish. Avocados are also a great addition to smoothies and pureed soups. And a party ain't a party without my Easiest Guacamole (page 305).

‣ **RAW NUTS AND SEEDS:** Nuts and seeds should be a welcome, easy addition to your kitchen prep, as they add healthy fat and protein to any dish. I always have containers of raw nuts, seeds, home-made trail mix, and my Maple Sriracha Roasted Pecans (page 142) on hand for grab 'n' go snacks. Be sure to purchase raw, unroasted, unsalted nuts because if they were roasted by the manufacturer, they most likely contain MSG, added sugar, and refined salts as well as GMO oils. Dry roasted nuts from the store can also have flavors added to them. You can easily toast or roast 2 cups of nuts or seeds at a time yourself and keep them in sealed glass containers for up to a week. See page 108 for how to toast and roast raw nuts and seeds. Raw almonds, pine nuts, hazelnuts, pecans, and walnuts add tasty, crunchy texture to any dish, whether tossed in a salad, stirred into coconut yogurt, or sprinkled on roasted veggies. Sweet macadamias are delicious in baked desserts or atop ice cream, and cashews are a great base for creamy sauces, desserts, and dips. Along with nuts, you can use raw seeds in meals and snacks; try pumpkin, sesame, sunflower, chia, ground flaxseeds, and hemp seeds. Try my nut and seed "mylks" (page 290) and my Butter Me Up Honey-Almond Nut Butter (page 307) in your morning oatmeal. Or toss nuts and seeds into soups and salads for a crunchy topping, create a few roasted nut recipes for a party (pages 140–142), or just enjoy raw nuts and seeds by the handful as a quick protein-packed snack. All nuts and seeds are best stored in the fridge or freezer.

‣ **MAKE YOUR OWN ALMOND FLOUR:** Process 1 cup of whole, raw almonds in a high-speed blender or food processor until they reach a fine flour consistency. Be sure not to blend too long or the oils in the almonds will release and the flour will clump together. If that happens, just break apart those clumps with your hands. Remove any almond pieces and chunks that weren't processed. One cup raw almonds yields about 1 cup almond flour. Store in a sealed container in the refrigerator until ready to use, for up to two weeks.

‣ **MAKE YOUR OWN GLUTEN-FREE OAT FLOUR:** In a high-speed blender, blend gluten-free rolled oats for a few seconds, or until they reach a very fine flour consistency. One cup rolled oats makes about 1 cup oat flour. Store in a sealed container in the refrigerator until ready to use, for up to two weeks.

STEP 5: MAKE YOUR OWN "TOP TEN" AND HANG IT ON YOUR FRIDGE

As you transition to this new way of eating, it's crucial to keep one simple thing in mind: don't forget that at the end of the day, you're nourishing your body—not anyone else's—so eat what makes you feel your best. Just because I call for an item in a recipe doesn't mean you have to eat it. Don't care for tomatoes? Not a fan of Swiss chard? No sweat. There are tons of other options to take their place. I created this "Top Ten" list for myself a few years ago when I needed a reminder every day for ingredients that would help support my detox. Don't be shy about fruits and veggies; try to aim for eating 1 pound of produce each day. They're rich in phytonutrients that can promote detoxification, reduce inflammation, and offer numerous other health benefits. Many herbs and spices are also rich in anti-oxidants and phytonutrients that reduce inflammation, support detoxification, aid digestion, and boost immunity. Supporting your digestive flora (the good bacteria in your gut) with fermented foods, such as chickpea miso, helps fight off infections and keeps your gut (where almost 80 percent of your immune system lives) healthy. We also need to support our

superfood: coconut

▸ Coconut oil is my favorite oil to bake and cook with because it has immune-boosting properties and is antiviral, antimicrobial, and antifungal—great for those of you who have candida, which can cause bloating, bad breath, and acne. It's easily absorbed by the small intestine and doesn't require the full digestive process. It converts to fuel faster than any other fat, making it a great source of energy. It has a high smoking point, so it's great for heating over high heat. It remains solid at room temperature, but turns to liquid when heated. Coconut oil tastes a bit like coconut and can add a coconut-y flavor to your food. Use coconut oil to grease your pans when baking and cooking. Coconut oil can also be used in baking recipes in place of butter or oil. The substitution ratio for butter or oil is 1:1.

▸ Coconut milk is made from combining coconut meat with coconut water. It's a great dairy-free alternative to cow's milk. Choose unsweetened so you're not getting added sugar in your milk. Check out my Easy Homemade Coconut Mylk recipe (page 292) for a simple way to make this milk when you don't have any coconut meat in sight. Do not use this type of coconut milk (which has a thinner consistency and is found in the refrigerated section of the grocery store) in recipes calling for culinary coconut milk (which has a thicker consistency); see below.

▸ Culinary coconut milk is found in BPA-free cans. These cans are sold in full-fat and lite options. The solids separate and rise as coconut cream. To get the coconut cream, spoon the cream from the top of the opened can and reserve the remaining clear milk for another use. Use only unsweetened coconut milk in your cooking, not the sweetened coconut cream meant for cocktails.

▸ Coconut flakes and shredded coconut add a touch of sweetness to smoothies, salads, cereals, and my dairy-free ice creams (pages 334–339)!

▸ Pure coconut water is the clear liquid inside young green coconuts. Coconut water can also be found in tetra (cardboard) packs. It's high in potassium and minerals. Use it in my Coconut Curry Carrot Soup (page 197).

▸ Coconut aminos is a delicious, rich, dark, and salty soy-free sauce that has a slightly sweet aftertaste. It's a wonderful replacement for soy sauce in marinades, sautés, and dressings and as a seasoning for roasted nuts and seeds. I use coconut aminos in many of my recipes for a boost of flavor. When a coconut tree is tapped, it produces a nutrient-dense "sap" from the coconut blossoms. This sap is a great source of vitamin C, B vitamins, minerals, and amino acids, which are vital to our health. I use the Coconut Secret brand; the only ingredients are organic coconut sap and sea salt!

liver to break down toxins and facilitate their elimination, which is why dandelion root tea is on this list! It's important to see cooking and preparing your detoxifying meals as a fun, positive experience as opposed to something you're forced to do.

While you experiment with different ingredients and flavors, keep track of your favorites. That way you'll always know what to keep in stock in your kitchen, what to bring with you when you travel, and what to come back to if you ever start feeling antsy with your new pantry. Plus, it'll make shopping a lot easier if you keep a list of your go-tos on your fridge. (Never rely on memory at the store—you'll only end up with what you don't want and none of what you do.) To inspire you, here's my list (for specific brand recommendations, see pages 381–382).

Amie's "Top Ten" Organic Ingredients

1. Sea salt (or Himalayan pink salt) and freshly ground pepper (okay, that's two, but they're a pair!)

2. Lemons for eating, drinking, and cleaning

3. Fresh herbs (parsley, basil, and cilantro are my favorites to add quick flavor)

4. Cruciferous (detox) veggies like arugula, broccoli, cauliflower, and Brussels sprouts

5. Leafy greens such as Swiss chard, collard greens, kale, and spinach

6. Unsalted raw nuts and seeds

7. Ground or fresh turmeric

8. Dijon mustard (or try my Sweet Home Honey Mustard, page 315)

9. Dandelion root tea for cooking grains and beans (or for drinking with fresh lemon, hot or iced)

10. Chickpea miso paste (soy-free)

STEP 6: GIVE YOUR FRIDGE (AND FREEZER) A MAKEOVER

Getting healthy isn't just about buying healthier foods—you actually have to eat them! Here are a few ideas for making your life easier once you get home from the grocery store.

▸ **BE A MINIMALIST.** If your fridge is overstuffed, it's hard to see what you have. Organize what's left over from your initial pantry clean-sweep, and then take inventory of your fridge every week so you don't forget about certain foods when they're pushed to the back.

▸ **GET A BETTER VIEW.** Put nutritious foods on the middle shelf so they are at your eye level.

▸ **SLICE AND DICE RIGHT AWAY.** Make veggies and fruits more convenient to eat by cleaning and cutting them up as soon as you get home so they're ready to go the next time you raid the fridge.

▸ **DITCH THE PLASTIC.** Remove any plastic wrapping from fruits and veggies and store them in organic cloth bags. Store fresh herbs in open mason jars filled with water to keep them fresh and flavorful.

▸ **SPOIL-PROOF YOUR PRODUCE.** Improperly storing your produce can actually make it spoil more quickly. To get the most mileage out of your dollar, make sure that ethylene-producing items aren't ruining things for the whole lot. (Fruits and veggies that ripen as they age release this gas as a by-product, which causes other items to rot.) Plums, pears, and melons should be stored in unsealed cotton bags in separate bins of the fridge. Avocados, bananas, and tomatoes should be kept on the counter in their own zone—not sharing a bowl with your apples.

▸ **FLAVOR SAVOR.** Want to give your recipes an instant hit of yumminess? This trick works great for pastas, whole-grain dishes, stews, or when you're going to sauté veggies and sauces. Freeze leftover hearty herbs like rosemary and thyme in extra-virgin olive oil; this will protect them from freezer burn and browning. Fill ice cube trays three-quarters full with chopped herbs, cover with oil, and then freeze until solid—about twenty-four hours—then transfer to a sealed container in the freezer for up to one month.

▸ **STREAMLINE YOUR SPICES.** I'm more likely to use my spices when they're accessible. That's why I keep them in a drawer, label-side up, instead of on the counter where things get hidden. When you refill a jar of spices, put a label on the bottom with the date. After six months, ground spices can lose their flavor and need to be replaced.

▸ **COOK A BATCH OF GLUTEN-FREE GRAINS.** Cook a big batch of teff, millet, gluten-free oats, brown rice, or quinoa on Sunday so you can use them to create recipes all week long. These grains are perfect to add to your morning porridge, afternoon salad, or evening fajitas. Check out pages 104–107 for specific

---

create creaminess without dairy, sugar, gluten, and soy

Most people use heavy cream, cow's milk, tofu, or other processed ingredients to make a recipe creamy. Here are a few ways to get that yummy silkiness you're craving without dairy, sugar, gluten, and soy!

▸ Soak nuts or seeds in separate bowls (see chart on page 108). Blend soaked and drained ingredients in a blender individually to create a creamy base you can add to your recipes for a protein-boost, too.

▸ Add steamed and pureed carrots, squash, parsnips, rutabaga, pumpkin, sweet potato, and zucchini to soups for silkiness.

▸ Add a ripe avocado to thicken up soups and add a creamy consistency. You can also remove the dairy-filled cheese from your pesto and use ripe avocado instead. Swap out pine nuts for walnuts and you'll add a dose of omega-3s too!

▸ Add a ripe or frozen banana to a smoothie.

▸ Add full-fat culinary coconut milk to soups and smoothies.

▸ Add a few scoops of cooked risotto or other cooked gluten-free whole grains for richness in a soup or porridge.

▸ Add cooked gluten-free rolled oats to smoothies and desserts for thickness.

cooking instructions for each type of gluten-free grain.

- **FOCUS ON HEALTHY FAST FOOD.** Every weekend, prep a few grab 'n' go staples so you'll have them on hand for snacking or quick meals. These pre-prepped bites should include gluten-free whole grains, lean proteins, fiber from fresh produce, and healthy fats. Easy as that!

- **BEAT THE TAKEOUT URGE.** To re-create that crave-worthy Chinese takeout flavor in a snap, make sure to always have organic shallots, ginger, and garlic in the house—prepped and ready to go. Either buy them prechopped or freeze dried, or chop them yourself and store them in glass containers in the fridge. Add a leafy green like bok choy along with onions and bell peppers to the mix, and toss them in a hot pan for a quick meal.

- **HONOR THE RECEIPT.** Post your grocery receipt on the refrigerator door. This visual reminder will help you eat healthy items before they go bad. Cross off the items you've eaten so you know what you have left waiting for you. What better way to encourage yourself not to let things go to waste?

Step 7: Make Simple Swaps

Making healthy trades—or swapping out unhealthy food items for cleaner ones—can help you get acclimated to your new detoxed lifestyle. Remember, this doesn't have to happen overnight. Instead, upgrade your food in stages so you feel in control, and get inspired by the benefits you see as time goes on.

As for where to start, think about what you want to address first. If you suffer from colds or ear, nose, and throat problems, consider upgrading to almond or other nut and seed milks and removing dairy. If you're battling irritable bowel syndrome (IBS), bloating, or other gut issues, think about first cutting out gluten and yeast-filled foods like breads, pastas, and baked goods. Even if you don't currently

suffer from any ailments, I promise that you'll feel better than you thought possible by simply making small changes.

Step 8: Bottle Your Condiment Habit

With all your store-bought barbecue sauce, ketchup, teriyaki marinades, and taco seasonings in the trash, it's time to explore ways to scratch that itch for some extra flavor in your meals. No one said healthy food had to be boring! Check out Dip It, Spread It, Dress It (page 300) for your very own homemade Creamy Mock Mayo, Sweet Home Honey Mustard, Amie's Easy Home-Style Sun-Dried Tomato Ketchup, and Moo-Free Cashew Sour Cream without the dairy, eggs, gluten, refined sugar, or soy!

- **GO BIG ON THE SPICES, HERBS, AND AROMATICS.** These include allspice, basil, bay leaf, black pepper, caraway, cardamom, cayenne pepper, chicory, chili powder, cilantro, cinnamon, cloves, coriander, crushed red pepper flakes, cumin, dill, fennel, garlic, ginger, Himalayan pink salt, sea salt, horseradish, parsley, leeks, lemongrass, marjoram, mint, mustard seeds, mustard powder, nutmeg, onion, oregano, paprika, rosemary, saffron, sage, sesame seeds, shallots, star anise, sumac, tarragon, thyme, turmeric, and pure vanilla and almond extracts. And that's just the beginning! I also love spice blends like garam masala and za'atar. Check out my Mini Baked Chickpea-Free Falafel with Cannellini Bean Za'atar Sauce (pages 240–242). Buy a bunch of spices and herbs to experiment with different flavors and combinations. Then bottle your favorite creations so they're ready to go as you cook. Try making your own, or use my Dukkah recipe (page 326).

- **GO DIY.** Make your own sauces and condiments at home; there's no need to buy processed, bottled condiments filled with high fructose corn syrup, refined sugar, and unpronounceable ingredients when you can check out Dip It, Spread It, Dress It (page 300) for lots of ideas.

SMART + SIMPLE SUBSTITUTIONS

instead of ›	*use*
Refined white table salt ›	Himalayan pink salt or sea salt
Teriyaki sauce ›	Mixture of apple cider vinegar, cinnamon, ground fennel seeds, cardamom, cumin, and coriander
Sour cream ›	Moo-Free Cashew Sour Cream (page 309)
Tamari or soy sauce ›	Coconut aminos (a soy-free flavoring)
Dairy milk ›	Make your own coconut, almond, or other nut and seed milks (pages 290–292)
Starchy white rice ›	Gluten-free whole grains like quinoa, millet, teff, buckwheat, black rice, and wild rice, or use cauliflower that's been shredded in the food processor to look like rice (find my Spicy Chili Lime Chickpeas with Cauliflower "Rice" recipe on page 255)
Processed, store-bought granola bars ›	Best Friend Bars (page 357)
Pro-inflammatory peanut butter ›	Anti-inflammatory Butter Me Up Honey-Almond Nut Butter (page 307)—great spread on a brown rice cake
Processed crackers ›	Grain-free crackers (pages 156–162) with hummus recipes (pages 301–303)
Bottled juices ›	Make your own Detoxing Greeny-licious Juice (page 289)
Sugary granola ›	Amie's Grain-Free Granola (page 121) or Honey Cinnamon Quinoa Granola (page 118)
Sugary gluten-free cakes and breads ›	Charismatic Cranberry Spice Quinoa Bake (page 126) and Morning Glory Carrot Muffins (page 127)
Store-bought dressings and dips ›	Dip It, Spread It, Dress It (pages 300–329) has a variety of sauces, dips, dressings, and more

SMART + SIMPLE SUBSTITUTIONS

instead of ›	*use*
White pasta	Grain-free veggie "noodle" recipes using squash, carrots, or zucchini (see pages 222, 224, and 271)
Processed tortilla wraps	Nori sheets or my Savory Chickpea Flour Crepes (page 274)
Store-bought dessert pie crust	Amie's Grain-Free Pie Crust (page 344)
Croutons	Make your own Gluten-Free Herbed Croutons (page 190)
Processed, sugar-laden chocolate	Currants, unsweetened cocoa powder, carob, or cacao (powder or nibs)
Soda	Seltzer with freshly squeezed lemon juice and berries
Coffee	Cozy Bellyache Ginger Tea (page 298) or Dandelion Liver Detox Tea (page 299)
Bottled ketchup	Amie's Easy Home-Style Sun-Dried Tomato Ketchup (page 315)
Canned tomatoes	Fresh diced tomatoes, or my Oven-Roasted Cherry Tomatoes with Poppy Seeds (page 283)
Canned tomato sauce	Heirloom Tomato Sauce (page 318) or Sun-Dried Tomato Sauce (page 320)
White-flour, starchy bread crumbs	Grain-Free Protein-Packed Breadcrumbs (page 283)
Store-bought gluten-free white flour pizza crust	Homemade gluten-free pizza crusts (pages 234, 235, and 236)
Thickeners, like cream and flour	Thicken soups with a cup of pureed cannellini beans, culinary coconut milk, or ripe avocados

▸ **BE CREATIVE.** Satisfying a craving for preservative-packed condiments can be as easy as flavoring with ingredients like chickpea miso, sauerkraut, kimchi, pure organic maple syrup, honey, apple cider vinegar, balsamic vinegar, Easy No-Foil Roasted Garlic (page 329), mustard seeds, unsweetened coconut flakes, shredded coconut, cocoa powder, raw cacao, Himalayan pink salt, sea salt, and organic unsweetened dried fruits like dates, mango, cranberries, cherries, and golden raisins (sulfur-free and no added sugar).

▸ **JUST ADD TEXTURE.** Instead of throwing breadcrumbs into a dish, sprinkle foods with finely ground raw nuts or ground flaxseeds. Try my super-easy Grain-Free Protein-Packed Breadcrumbs (page 283) if you're feeling creative!

▸ **GET ZESTY.** Use fresh lemon, lime, grapefruit, and orange zest to add flavor to everything from salads to roasted veggies to desserts. The zest contains pungent oils that are much more flavorful than juice—and it won't turn green veggies a drab color like citrus juice does. Just don't zest the bitter white pith, only the outer skin.

▸ **INFUSE YOUR RICE.** Instead of using oil to flavor rice and quinoa while cooking, add a jasmine or rooibos tea bag to create flavor.

▸ **LEARN THE POWER OF REDUCTION.** Reduce ½ cup of organic vegetable broth or freshly squeezed orange juice in a hot saucepan to make a flavorful glaze that you can drizzle over veggies.

▸ **COOK WITH FRESHLY SQUEEZED JUICE.** If vegetable broth or water doesn't cut it for flavor in your recipes, use organic fresh carrot juice instead. It's great for adding quick, healthy flavor.

▸ **GET ON A FIRST-NAME BASIS WITH HERB CUBES.** Put 1½ cups leftover fresh herbs in a blender or food processor and add ½ cup extra-virgin olive oil, a pinch of sea salt, and black pepper. Puree until smooth, and then spoon the mixture into an ice cube tray, filling each well to the top. Stash in the freezer and toss into soup, hot pasta, or risotto, or defrost at room temperature and drizzle it over beans, grains, or lentils.

▸ **HIGHLIGHT, DON'T DISGUISE.** Instead of trying to cover up the taste of veggies, find new ways to enhance their natural flavor. Once you've embraced their true-to-nature goodness, you won't feel the need to reach for the bottle of processed ketchup. You'll wanna dig into Amie's Easy Home-Style Sun-Dried Tomato Ketchup (page 315) instead.

▸ **SPLURGE ON PREMIUM SALT.** Table salt—that fine-grained refined item you find in a shaker on almost every table in this country—has been stripped of most minerals during the refining process. In many cases, it's also been loaded up with anticaking agents and iodine. Do not use table salt for any of the recipes in this book! My salt measurements are using sea salt or Himalayan pink salt only. Every brand of sea salt is different, so be sure to salt to taste, if needed. Sea salt and Himalayan pink salt are actually good for you because they promote a healthy balance in your body and are filled with minerals. And a little goes a long way! I like using the finer-grained version for seasoning as I cook and a small sprinkle of the larger flakes for finishing dishes; the delicate flavor brings any recipe to the next level. When you're making the recipes in this book, feel free to add more sea salt, to taste because some of our palates prefer more salt than others. For my recipes, I used Frontier and Simply Organic sea salt for premium taste and quality.

Now it's time to look beyond your pantry. Toxins are also likely to be lurking on your seemingly clean fresh produce, in the crystal-clear water from your sink, and in many other places you may not be aware of.

your guide to fresh herbs

Along with bottled spices, consider herbs your new best friends in the kitchen. They're the easiest, fastest, and cheapest (not to mention healthiest) way to add freshness and flavor to your food. Here's what you need to know:

▸ Leafy herbs such as mint, basil, and parsley are best treated like cut flowers. Trim the stems on the diagonal and put the herbs in a glass of fresh water in the fridge. Change the water every day. Store fresh cilantro, oregano, and dill by wrapping them in damp towels and a cotton bag and refrigerating for up to a week.

▸ Add fresh woody herbs such as rosemary and thyme to infuse a dish at the beginning of the cooking process. Try using sturdy rosemary sprigs (stripped of their leaves) as skewers for grilled kebabs.

▸ Add fresh, leafy herbs such as cilantro and parsley at the end of the cooking process; they're brightest when raw.

▸ Fresh tarragon leaves have a strong anise flavor. Try them in hummus or salads.

▸ Don't throw away tender dill stems—add them to stock or soup for a boost of flavor.

▸ Tie whole fresh thyme sprigs in a bundle with parsley to flavor soup (simply remove the bundle before pureeing or serving).

▸ Put a new twist on pesto by replacing the fresh basil and pine nuts with a little fresh mint and raw cashews.

▸ Try fresh marjoram in place of oregano for a sweeter, less earthy flavor in a marinade.

DRIED HERBS

A good rule of thumb for using dried herbs instead of fresh is to use one-third the amount of dried herbs to replace fresh herbs. If your recipe calls for 1 tablespoon chopped basil, for example, use 1 teaspoon dried. Add dried herbs at the beginning of cooking unless you are using cilantro, basil, or parsley, which are more delicate and will lose their flavor. If you don't have fresh or dried handy, just omit the herbs altogether and add a pinch more sea salt and pepper for flavor. For my recipes, I used the Simply Organic and Frontier brands of dried herbs.

I'm going to show you how you can avoid these chemicals and fill your plate with a rainbow of colors to jumpstart your detox system and keep your immune system running smoothly. After experimenting with hundreds of foods over the last ten years, I've found what works for myself, along with many of my readers and clients. Eating this way gives me incredible mental and physical energy. I also see progress daily with people who clean up their lifestyles and start their journey to healthier eating and living with these tips.

WHAT ABOUT FAT?

As you're slowly adjusting your diet, you may wonder about fat. For years, we've been told to avoid it, but recent research has demonstrated that this isn't good advice.

Our cells and hormones need fat to survive, but it needs to be the right kind of fat. Did you know that the types of fats you consume determine how well your cells function? Fat from a bag of chips, for example, causes inflammation in your cells, but fat from walnuts, ground flaxseeds, avocados, and extra-virgin olive oil help your cells function at optimal levels. These foods have anti-inflammatory properties, as well, so they can help put out the inflammatory fires in your body.

Many of my clients have a fear of fat. They've been taught to live in the diet aisle and buy fat-free foods. Those fat-free foods you see in the grocery store are not safe, healthy, or good for you. They're leftover from the 1980s, when everyone was terrified of fat. Manufacturers responded by replacing the fat with refined sugar, sodium, chemical fillers, and artificial sweeteners—all ingredients that contribute to inflammation and weight gain.

Be sure to look at labels on your granola, barbecue sauce, ketchup, teriyaki sauce, nonfat flavored yogurts, cereals, and snacks. Instead of these

---

the dirty dozen and the clean fifteen

On a budget? If you can't buy all of your food organic, it helps to know which fruits and veggies are the cleanest and dirtiest so you can make informed decisions at the store. Since these lists are different year to year, check out the EWG website for the most up-to-date "cleanest" and "dirtiest" lists of produce at EWG.org. Check out WhatsOnMyFood.org for more info on what is on your food!

THE DIRTY DOZEN: HIGH-PESTICIDE FOODS

Each of these foods contains high concentrations of pesticides relative to other produce items. Washing doesn't remove all the pesticides, so always choose organic.

THE CLEAN FIFTEEN: LOW-PESTICIDE FOODS

Tests found low total concentrations of pesticides on these. Because they are the least likely to hold pesticide residues, you can purchase conventional varieties if you need to.

---

options, choose fresh organic fruits and veggies along with gluten-free whole grains, beans, legumes, and healthy anti-inflammatory fats like avocados, raw walnuts, ground flaxseeds, coconut oil, flaxseed oil, and extra-virgin olive oil. These are nutrient-dense foods that will support your body instead of work against it.

LABELS, DECODED

Another important part about detoxing your lifestyle is learning to read labels—and read them carefully. Marketers are smart, and they know we want the foods we purchase to be natural and full of nourishing goodness. At the same time, they care about keeping costs low and profits high, so they may throw in some organic raisins, but then fill the rest of the product with chemical preservatives, artificial sweeteners, and synthetic flavorings.

What do the labels on food packages mean? Sometimes a lot less than you may think. Review this list, and realize that it's best to take most marketing claims with a grain of salt. The most important part of the label is not the shiny, impressive front, but the lonely, boring ingredient list.

▸ **ALL NATURAL OR NATURAL:** Some of the ingredients may be derived from nature, but this term is not regulated. "Natural" and "organic" are not the same thing. Some products are more natural than others, so my best advice when looking at a product that says "natural" on the packaging is to look at the ingredient list and see for yourself how natural the product really is. Some natural foods are highly processed, while others aren't as processed, so you can be the judge here.

▸ **USDA CERTIFIED ORGANIC:** The only food label that is both strictly defined and regulated by the government and requires third-party certification is the USDA organic logo. When you see the green-and-white USDA organic seal, it means the product

has 95 percent organic ingredients and was grown, processed, and handled according to certain guidelines regarding herbicides or conventional pesticides, synthetic fertilizers, growth hormones, antibiotics, irradiation, and genetic engineering. It was also produced with an emphasis on water and soil conservation. This is the only type of food that can carry the USDA certified organic seal. Also, all certified organic products are non-GMO, but not all non-GMO products are certified organic.

▸ **MADE WITH REAL FRUIT:** There's no way to know if the product was made with actual fruit, or only a few splashes of fruit juice. There is no regulation on this claim.

▸ **FREE RANGE AND FREE ROAMING:** These claims are not standardized, but the animals are supposed to be exposed to the outside for some period each day. (However, this could be for only a few minutes.)

▸ **NON-GMO:** A GMO (genetically modified organism) is a living organism whose genetic material has been artificially manipulated in a laboratory through genetic engineering (GE). Genetically modified crops are often used for animal feed, but many have been introduced in our food system. A growing body of evidence connects GMOs with health problems, environmental damage, and violation of farmers' and consumers' rights. If a food isn't identified as Non-GMO Project Verified or organic, look at the label to identify any genetically modified ingredients that you may want to avoid such as canola oil, corn oil, cottonseed oil, high-fructose corn syrup (HFCS), soybean oil, and soy lecithin. The five major food crops sold in the United States that are typically genetically engineered (according to the U.S. Department of Agriculture) are corn, soybeans, cotton, canola, and sugar beets, which means that the majority of the processed food sold today (most of which contain one or more of these ingredients) contain

sugary snack swaps:
lose the sugar, keep the flavor

▸ Instead of soda, try seltzer with fresh lime, strawberries, and lemon.

▸ Instead of sugar in your coffee or tea, use cinnamon, nutmeg, and allspice with my Homemade Almond Mylk (page 290).

▸ Instead of butter on white toast or bagels, try spreading coconut oil on my Savory Chickpea Flour Crepes (page 274) or on gluten-free whole-grain toast with a dash of freshly grated orange zest.

▸ Instead of processed jelly on white toast, try my Chia Seed Berry Jam (page 329) on my grain-free crackers (pages 156–162).

▸ Instead of processed bottled juice, try my Detoxing Greeny-licious Juice (page 289).

▸ Instead of processed pumpkin pie at the holidays, enjoy a few scoops of Homemade Pumpkin Puree (page 123) with a drizzle of Butter Me Up Honey-Almond Nut Butter (page 307) or my Perfect Pumpkin Gelato (page 332).

▸ Instead of barbecue sauce, use Dijon or spicy mustard or my Sweet Home Honey Mustard (page 315).

▸ Instead of agave nectar, use organic honey or organic pure maple syrup.

▸ Instead of a refined sugar chocolate bar, use raw cacao nibs, carob, cacao powder, or unsweetened cocoa powder.

▸ Instead of canned or boxed vegetable broth, which often contains added sugar, make my Cleansing Detox Veggie Broth (page 194).

▸ Instead of Thousand Island or another processed dressing, use apple cider vinegar or fresh lemon juice and extra-virgin olive oil with hemp seeds or chia seeds.

▸ Instead of tonic water, use seltzer or mineral water with fresh lemon slices.

▸ Instead of a fancy Starbucks Frappuccino, make my Caffeine-Free Chai (page 289).

▸ Instead of coffee, try my Dandelion Liver Detox Tea (page 299) with my Homemade Almond Mylk (page 290)

genetically modified ingredients. You can find more information on GMOs and helpful resources on finding non-GMO products from the Non-GMO Project at www.livingnongmo.org.

HOW TO SATISFY YOUR SWEET TOOTH

I already talked a little bit about sugar cravings, but I want to give you some more tools to use against them, now. Sugar can be a very powerful substance. Even after eating clean for a while, you may find yourself craving it now and then.

That's okay. You can have your sweet stuff without destroying your new detox plan. Just don't get your sweet fix from refined, processed white sugar, or from high-fructose corn syrup and other artificial sweeteners. Healthier options below include organic honey and organic pure maple syrup. These require almost no processing, contain no fillers or additives, and have no toxic pesticides or chemicals.

You can't deprive yourself, and sometimes you need a little bite of sweetness to feed your soul. If you have a craving, try these alternatives instead, and remember—sweets are best eaten on occasion and with intention. In other words, when you have a craving for a little sweetness in your life, bring your full awareness to the present moment and enjoy each bite of flavor. No mindless snacking here!

▸ **MEDJOOL DATES:** Dates contain fiber, calcium, and potassium. They are a great alternative sweetener for baking and cooking because they bind ingredients and enhance sweet flavor without any processed ingredients. Medjool dates are plump and soft and tender, but regular dates can be used as a less expensive option. Pit, chop, and then cover them with purified water and soak for at least forty minutes or up to seven hours.

▸ **100 PERCENT PURE MAPLE SYRUP:** This syrup is pure, boiled sap from the maple tree. Make sure

you get pure organic maple syrup and not brands that add sugar.

▸ **SHREDDED COCONUT AND COCONUT FLAKES (UNSWEETENED):** This can be used in cakes, breads, cookies, raw truffles, and many other dishes for flavor and texture. Try toasting your coconut flakes for an extra sweet touch like I do in my breakfast recipes on pages 114 and 115, and soup on page 197. (Instructions for easy toasting can be found on page 114!)

▸ **PUMPKIN PUREE:** Instead of using oil to make brownies and sweet breads, pumpkin puree is healthier and keeps baked goods moist. Make your own homemade pumpkin puree (I show you how on page 123), or if you can't find fresh pumpkins, try Pacific Foods organic pumpkin puree, sold in a cardboard box, not a BPA-laden can. Use pumpkin puree in my Perfect Pumpkin Gelato (page 332) and my Open-Faced Pumpkin Enchiladas with Moo-Free Cashew Sour Cream (page 309).

▸ **ORGANIC UNSWEETENED COCOA (OR RAW CACAO) POWDER:** This is soaring with antioxidants! I use it in my dessert recipes (pages 330–368).

▸ **ORGANIC HONEY:** Unlike the processed honey you find in most food stores, this honey is loaded with nutrients, has a thick, cloudy color, and is full of antimicrobial properties. It's also rich in enzymes, phytonutrients, and antioxidants. Add it sparingly to desserts, tea, and coconut yogurt. In this cookbook, when a recipe calls for honey, I used organic honey if I needed more of a "liquid" honey. Some recipes call for raw organic honey because it works better in those particular recipes.

▸ **HIGH-QUALITY PROTEIN:** If you're having sugar cravings, it could be that something else in your diet is out of balance. Make sure you're eating enough protein; focus on high-quality organic protein, healthy carbohydrates, fiber, and healthy fats at every meal and snack. Protein is key to keeping your blood sugar stable so you feel satiated longer.

‣ **MORE HEALTHY FATS:** Yes, I said more fat. Healthy fats like avocados, extra-virgin olive oil, coconut oil, and raw nuts and seeds will help stabilize your blood sugar and put a stop to those sugar cravings!

‣ **PROBIOTIC-RICH FOODS:** These reduce your sugar cravings by regulating the yeasts in your gut through fermented foods (organic chickpea miso, sauerkraut, kimchi) and drinks (kombucha, etc.).

‣ **UNSWEETENED CAFFEINE-FREE TEA:** These soothing drinks help distract your cravings. Add fresh mint leaves and lemon slices for natural sweetness. Try my tasty tea recipes (pages 298–299).

‣ **FRESH FRUIT:** Keep fresh fruit right where you can see it at all times. Try raspberries, blueberries, apples, and bananas. Pair these fruits with a healthy fat to keep your blood sugar levels steady—enjoy a handful of raspberries with raw almonds or a banana with sunflower seed butter.

reintroduction—bring the good foods back

You don't have to get sick to get healthy. You can transform your health with clean, organic foods because food is medicine, and healing your gut is the start to an amazing life.

Many of the symptoms we experience are caused by toxins, especially those in our food system. I've learned about the connection between the health of our gut and the efficiency of our immune system, the clarity of our skin, the ease of our digestion, and our risk for disease.

When you repair your gut and eliminate the root of inflammation, symptoms disappear. Finally, you realize what it's like living in a healthy state of mind (and body!). If you haven't been diagnosed with a disease or illness and you're just looking to clean up your food and improve your gut health, those tiny booboos that you may not have realized were ailments may suddenly disappear. I'm talking about things like aches and pains, allergies, mood swings, loss of libido, acne, bad breath, body odor, eczema, fatigue, and constipation.

The first step on your journey was to remove toxic foods and other foods that might have been causing inflammation in your body—such as gluten, dairy, soy, eggs, refined sugar, and processed foods. The next step is to slowly reintroduce some of those foods, so you can either a) confirm that they were, indeed, problematic for you, or b) discover that certain foods are okay to add back into your diet.

Try adding back the foods (in their certified organic whole-food form) you want to try to incorporate into your lifestyle, but remember—everything in moderation. And please, no matter what, steer clear of those processed foods! I know your taste buds love them and you may still crave them sometimes, but remember—you were taught to want these foods. Now you can learn (and I can help you) how to not crave them. Trust me. I did it, and so can you. The key is to start slow.

The best thing about all this is that you don't have to suffer any longer or feel sick, tired, or weighed down with the gunk found in processed, packaged foods. This detox and reintroduction program will restore wellness into your lifestyle and revamp your gut so it can help you sustain a healthy life. You'll feel vibrant, healthy, and more "alive."

Just wait and see!

STARTING FRESH

At this point, you've completed the 21-Day Elimination Diet. You've given your body a chance to detox and clean out, and you've got a rare opportunity to start fresh. It's not often that your body is in the condition it is now, so take advantage of it, and proceed carefully!

I think this is the fun part because you get to do some detective work. Now you can find out which foods bother you, and which ones don't. As long as you do this right and don't rush it, you'll have a lot of great information that will guide your eating choices in the future.

BEFORE YOU START: FOOD SENSITIVITY/ INFLAMMATION TESTING

Because there are so many potential ingredients in foods that can cause symptoms, I recommend that if you are still having unwanted symptoms after you do the 21-Day Elimination Diet (and before you start reintroducing foods), you ask your Integrative doctor

about food sensitivity testing (see page 377). It's a simple blood test that will show you your food sensitivities that you may not be able to notice yourself. The blood test will show foods (beyond the Toxic 13) that are causing silent inflammation in your body. My results from these blood tests, for example, showed that I was sensitive to foods such as basil and grapefruit, which meant that those foods were causing inflammation in my body.

Food sensitivities and intolerances are not to be confused with food allergies—I was not allergic to basil or grapefruit. These foods ended up causing inflammation and stress to my digestive system, so I avoided them for six months until my gut healed. Then I was able to slowly add them back into my lifestyle as long as they didn't become troublesome.

If your food sensitivity blood test results reveal foods that are causing inflammation, the typical approach is to avoid those foods for six months, and then slowly start to add them back in (following the 7-Step Reintroduction Process explained on the next page), checking to see if they are still bothersome. You can then get another blood test, if desired, to see if your results have changed, or just pay close attention to how your body feels after eating certain foods. Again, food sensitivity blood tests are optional and can be used if you are still experiencing unwanted symptoms after eliminating the Toxic 13 foods from the 21-Day Elimination Diet on page 24.

Once you've completed your 21-Day Elimination Diet, you're ready to begin reintroducing foods!

TESTING, TESTING, ONE-BY-ONE

This part of the process is simple, but it does take time. There is a tendency to rush it. Please go slow so you can monitor any reactions, and remember that some symptoms may not even seem like food reactions, at first.

You're going to add back into your diet one food at a time. This is called the "reintroduction" phase, because you're taking foods that you used to eat (as long as they're healthy foods and not processed foods!)—foods that you eliminated over the past 21 days—and reintroducing them into your body. The point is to find out once and for all just how you and that specific food are getting along.

The process requires only seven steps. Before you start, make copies of the Food Reintroduction Chart (page 57) for each food you plan to reintroduce, as you'll be using this chart to record the foods you try and any reactions you may have. You don't need to add back all the foods—you may only wish to try to add back one or two, and that's okay. I personally did not add back any of the Toxic 13 into my lifestyle, but it's up to you to choose what foods you want to try to eat again.

7-Step Reintroduction Process

1. **CHOOSE A SINGLE FOOD OR BEVERAGE:** There are thirteen foods listed in my Toxic 13. Start with one food (such as soy) to reintroduce at a time. Let's say you eliminated soy because of the elimination diet, but you really like edamame and you'd like to try it again. So you choose soy. (But choose organic because most conventional soy comes from GMO crops.) If you'd rather not try to add back soy to your lifestyle, then choose another food to reintroduce such as corn.

2. **MAKE SURE YOU ADD BACK THE SPECIFIC FOOD IN ITS WHOLE FORM (EX. ONE-INGREDIENT FOOD):** You have to be really careful with reintroduction, as many foods are made up of a combination of ingredients. Soy milk, for instance, also contains carrageenan and flavorings. If you add soy back in that way, and then you experience a reaction, you can't be sure if it was from the soy, the carrageenan, or the flavorings. So make it as simple as possible and start by adding in one-ingredient whole foods. In this case, try plain steamed organic edamame because the only ingredient

is soy. Just be aware that soy, gluten, dairy, and corn are often hidden in tons of processed foods, so read your labels.

3. **TRY THE FOOD:** Do this very carefully. Start by eating that food at least twice a day for three days. Note how you feel in your journal. Keep everything else the same in your diet. This is crucial to getting good results out of your testing!

4. **IF YOU HAVE A REACTION:** If you have a reaction such as a headache, brain fog, rash, fatigue, stomach upset, or other symptom, write it down in your journal. Write down these feelings after you eat, even if your symptom seems unrelated to what you ate. If you're not sure whether the reaction was caused by the specific food (such as edamame), go ahead and try it again the next day and record any symptoms. If a food causes an immediate allergic reaction, such as throat swelling, seek medical care immediately, unless you are otherwise instructed by your doctor.

5. **IF YOU DON'T HAVE A REACTION:** If you don't have any reactions, note that in your journal as well, and try the food again the next day during the three-day trial period.

6. **AFTER THREE DAYS:** After three days in a row of trying this food, you should have a pretty good idea how your body is getting along with it. On the fourth day, don't eat this food at all and pay attention to how you feel. Note how you feel in the chart on day four without eating the food. Do you feel any different? If you had no reaction throughout the four days, you can safely assume that particular food is okay to add back into your diet—just keep an eye out for any changes in the future. If, on the other hand, you realize the food is bothering you, remove it from your lifestyle for good! (See my pantry makeover tips on page 36.) Then give your body a day or two to recover from any reactions you had. So,

if the edamame (soy) gave you a headache, for instance, wait twenty-four hours after the headache is gone before trying to reintroduce another new food. That headache is a sign that soy is a problem for you and it's time to try adding back another food such as dairy.

7. **START AGAIN:** On the fifth day (or sixth, or seventh, depending on how you feel and any required recovery time), you can start this cycle again. Choose another food you'd like to add back into your diet, and test it out by reintroducing it twice a day for three days (then one day off) in a new chart, and record your symptoms and progress throughout those four days.

For each food that you reintroduce, make sure you are listening to your body to feel the symptoms you experience. In the chart on the opposite page, describe your reaction to the food, which will help you remember what foods caused issues when you ate them.

Food Reintroduction Chart

Download and print out this chart from TheHealthyApple.com/EatingClean and fill it out as you reintroduce each food (gluten, dairy, soy, corn, etc.). Take your time. It's important to isolate and thoroughly test each food separately in order to properly rule it out or in. To make it easy, use the following scoring method to measure your reactions (or lack of reactions):

‣ X=No Reaction

‣ M=Mild Reaction

‣ S=Severe Reaction

Mark an X, M, or S in each of the boxes on the chart based on what you experienced with the food you're testing. You can write in other symptoms in the blank column on the far right.

In the "Other Symptoms" column, pay attention to how you feel and write in words that describe

any symptoms you may experience such as how did you sleep, how many hours did you sleep, how many bowel movments did you have, how were your bowel movements (constipation, diarrhea, etc.), if you were nauseous, gassy, bloated, energized, calm, experienced brain fog, heart palpitations, body odor, post-nasal drip, sinus pressure, or bad breath. Be sure to drink enough water throughout the day so you don't end up dehydrated, which will lead to unpleasant symptoms, as well.

WHAT FOODS TO REINTRODUCE?

If you decide to add foods back into your lifestyle and you're not sure where to start, here are some options for you:

‣ **DAIRY:** Try one whole, organic food containing dairy at a time. Maybe you start with organic milk, then try a little piece of organic cheddar cheese, then a quarter cup of organic yogurt, etc. Note your reactions to each individual food.

‣ **GLUTEN:** Be sure to test each type of gluten-containing grain—such as wheat, barley, and rye—separately, to determine the best results. Certain types of gluten may cause problems in some people and not in others. You may find you have trouble with wheat and not rye, for example.

‣ **SOY:** Find the purest form of soy you can. If you are going to eat it, choose organic edamame instead of processed soy products such as soy milk.

‣ **EGGS:** If you choose to add back eggs, go for organic. Try the egg yolks and the egg whites separately; some people can tolerate the yolks and not the whites!

‣ **NIGHTSHADES:** See page 21 for more info on nightshades. I can tolerate tomatoes and peppers (as can most of my clients, which is why I use these foods in this book), but I cannot tolerate eggplants

	Headache	Other Aches/ Pains	Bloating/ Heartburn/ Diarrhea/ GI (Gastro-intestinal) Symptoms	Brain Fog	Acne Breakouts	Fatigue	Other Symptoms (Sleep qual-ity, bowel movements, etc.)
day 1 (Eat the Food Two Times)							
day 2 (Eat the Food Two Times)							
day 3 (Eat the Food Two Times)							
day 4 (Do Not Eat the Food)							

and white potatoes (which is why these two foods are not in this book). Try each item one at a time to see if you have a reaction.

▸ **UNREFINED SUGAR:** Start slow here! And only use unrefined sugar in the form of organic honey and pure maple syrup. A little bit of sugar goes a long way—especially if you've gone without it for a while. The less sugar you consume, the better you'll feel, so add back only those items that you really miss. Try honey in your herbal tea, for example, or a little on your oatmeal or dessert, if desired.

▸ **ARTIFICIAL SWEETENERS:** It's best to stay away from these—trust me, they're not doing anything good for your body. I even removed processed stevia from my lifestyle! I recommend that you don't add back any artificial sweeteners.

▸ **CORN:** Again, go for the purest form of this food first. Choose fresh, organic corn on the cob and see how you do. If it doesn't bother you, you can try some other corn-based foods, but remember that most conventional corn today comes from GMO crops, so choose organic.

▸ **PEANUTS:** If you decide to add back these legumes (yes, peanuts are legumes, not nuts), choose organic unsalted raw peanuts, but note that peanuts are high in mold, so if you have a history of candida, IBS, other belly issues, or sinus issues, these can be troublesome.

▸ **CAFFEINE:** Start slow, perhaps with a little green tea. Caffeine does have some health benefits, but it can also be very taxing for sensitive systems. If you've gotten to the point where you can do without it, my recommendation would be to keep it out and enjoy herbal teas instead!

▸ **ALCOHOL:** Same as above. Watch for symptoms. You may be surprised to find out that even just a little alcohol can make you tired, irritable, or anxious. It can also interfere with your sleep and your detox pathways. Best bet is to avoid alcohol as much as possible.

WHAT NEXT?

Congratulations! You've finished the 21-Day Elimination Diet; you've cleaned out and restocked your refrigerator, freezer, and pantry; and now, using the 7-Step Reintroduction Process, you're starting to figure out your food sensitivities.

If you are anything like me, you might be surprised at the results. Either way, take some time to celebrate your accomplishments. If you made it to this point, you need to pat yourself on the back. That took a lot of time and effort, and I hope you're already noticing the benefits.

Remember, this is about upgrading your lifestyle one step at a time, so stay patient with yourself. Continue to prioritize your health issues and focus on the ones that are causing you the most pain. If you discovered that dairy is a problem for you, for instance, you can remove dairy and switch to my tasty dairy-free nut cheeses (pages 307–310) and dairy-free nut or coconut "mylks" (pages 290 and 292). There are always nutritious options, so don't get discouraged. Instead, just imagine all the new tasty foods that are coming into your life! Fresh herbs, fruits, veggies, and spices (think garlic, berries, avocado, broccoli, walnuts, flaxseeds, turmeric, beans, and black rice) are loaded with phytonutrients, which help our bodies detoxify from everyday toxins. Try to focus on the positive aspect of adding more of these whole foods at every meal instead of focusing on missing the Toxic 13 foods you're removing.

As you begin to gain control over your diet, you'll notice more energy and other positive changes in your sinuses, skin, bowel movements, and more. Think of this as a time you can connect with yourself and decide how you want the rest of your life to look and feel. It's your choice. Listen to your body, and it will tell you exactly what to do.

Meanwhile, you may be running into some difficulties when you're traveling, eating out, or entertaining friends. While you're still experimenting with reintroducing some foods, let's tackle those issues—and make them nonissues, pronto!

traveling, eating out, and entertaining

Just because your diet may seem limited doesn't mean you have to resign yourself to a life of seclusion and rubbery kale. I am one of the most social people I know—and I live in Manhattan, the city that never sleeps. I thrive on getting out, seeing friends, and meeting new people. The energy of Manhattan makes me feel alive. Plus, I'm constantly jet-setting across the country to meet people like you at conferences and events, as well as working one-on-one with celebrities in exciting locations.

So instead of turning down invitations and opportunities because of the many food-based booby traps out there—gluten dressed up in dips, GMOs hiding in oils, sugar lurking almost everywhere—I've found that by planning ahead, I can always enjoy myself and stay healthy, no matter where I am.

TRAVELING—HOW TO SURVIVE IN THE AIR, ON THE ROAD, AND ON THE RUN

I travel. A lot. Even when I'm not traveling, I'm running around New York City to meetings and often don't have time to sit down for lunch or snacks. While there are more healthy hot spots popping up on each corner—and in airports—every day, many don't have options to nosh on that I can enjoy. So how do I stay healthy when I'm outside of my routine (and my kitchen)?

I plan ahead and bring my own meals and snacks. (You won't catch me eating airport or airplane food!) When I arrive at my destination, I find a Whole Foods Market or health food store where I can buy fresh organic veggies, fruits, raw nuts, seeds, herbs, avocados, and lean proteins.

To help you maintain the good work you've done on your detox plan, try these tips for traveling healthy:

▸ **IF TRAVELING BY PLANE:** I bring my own carry-on just for my meals and snacks. Raw nuts, seeds, my Honey Cinnamon Quinoa Granola (page 118), Abundant Mango Cardamom Walnut Bars (page 147), Maple Sriracha Roasted Pecans (page 142), and ripe avocados (with bamboo utensils for eating) are key items to bring along with you. Yes, you can bring these through security as long as there is no liquid.

▸ **IF TRAVELING BY CAR OR TAKING A ROAD TRIP:** Pack a big cooler with gluten-free whole-grain salads (see Serving Ideas for Cooked Gluten-Free Whole Grains, page 102) mixed with veggies like broccoli, cauliflower, carrots, cherry tomatoes, celery, collard greens, and kale. Throw in a few sandwiches on gluten-free whole-grain bread or pack my grain-free cracker recipes (pages 156–162) with my tasty hummus recipes (pages 301–303). You can also tote along my Butter Me Up Honey-Almond Nut Butter (page 307) and my Chia Seed Berry Jam (page 329) for a super-healthy AB & J sammie.

on-the-go snacks

▸ Freckled Sesame Almond Clusters (page 140)

▸ Lundberg Farms Organic Brown Rice Cakes spread with Butter Me Up Honey-Almond Nut Butter (page 307)

▸ Best Friend Bars (page 357) and No-Bake Fuel Up Bars (page 138)

▸ Organic sulfur-free unsweetened dried fruit with raw nuts or seeds

▸ Roasted Chickpeas: Sweet and Savory (page 144)

▸ Homemade grain-free crackers (pages 156–162) with Butter Me Up Honey-Almond Nut Butter (page 307) or hummus recipes (pages 301–303)

▸ Hempy Cocoa Coconut Truffles (page 351)

▸ Inspiring Raw Layered Oat Squares (page 150)

▸ Morning Glory Carrot Muffins (page 127)

▸ **IF STAYING IN A HOTEL:** I often ship heavier products to my hotel so I don't have to lug them in my suitcase or risk the liquid contents getting confiscated at the airport. My grain-free crackers (pages 156–162), Amie's Grain-Free Granola (page 121), Homemade Almond Mylk (page 290), nut butters, frozen fruits and veggies (they'll defrost in your fridge), Himalayan pink salt or sea salt, fresh limes and lemons, coconut oil, and raw seeds and nuts are all great staples for your home-away-from-home pantry. When you're making a hotel reservation, request an empty fridge (or two) in your room and see if you can request a kitchen to cook simple portable meals.

▸ **IF STAYING WITH FRIENDS OR FAMILY:** E-mail them a list of the foods you can and cannot eat ahead of time. Ask if there's a food store or farmers' market where you can buy fresh food.

What to Pack

Packing a selection of versatile ingredients yields lots of yummy options. Here are my favorites when I'm on the go. If you opt for store-bought, check out pages 381–382 for a list of my favorite brands.

▸ **ON-THE-GO OATMEAL:** Pack dry, gluten-free rolled oats in a small stainless-steel container and add hot water at the airport, rest stop, or coffee shop. You can also toss in my Rosemary Plum Jam (page 328); chia, hemp, and ground flaxseeds; raw nuts; sulfur-free dried organic fruits; unsweetened shredded coconut; nut butters such as almond, cashew, or walnut; or unsweetened cocoa powder.

▸ **THERMOS SMOOTHIE:** Add flavor to your favorite smoothie recipe with freshly squeezed citrus juice or my coconut, nut, and seed "mylks" (page 290). If you have access to a high-speed blender (I've been known to pack mine in my suitcase—more of a must-have than a hairdryer, in my case), you can

purchase organic frozen fruits to make your own smoothies.

▸ **SUPER SALAD:** Toss leafy greens with avocado, sun-dried tomatoes, chickpeas, and raw nuts and seeds. Make your own dressing by packing sea salt, freshly ground black pepper, your favorite spices, fresh lemons or limes, and extra-virgin olive oil. Toss in a few fresh herbs, if desired. Fresh parsley, scallions, and cilantro are always in my travel bag; they give my meals an instant flavor boost. If you don't have time to make your own salad, Earthbound Farm makes handy to-go Powermeal Bowls that are perfect for travel.

▸ **WRAP IN A SNAP:** Slather my Savory Chickpea Flour Crepes (page 274) with spreads, like my Curried Maple Hummus (page 302), Sweet Home Honey Mustard (page 315), Sun-Dried Tomato Sauce (page 320), or The Easiest Guacamole (page 305). You can also spread nut butter onto my crepes with sliced pears, and ground cinnamon for something sweet. My favorite savory combo is my Kalamata Olive and Cashew Tapenade (page 304) with Big-Flavor Marinated Roasted Bell Peppers (page 278), Easy No-Foil Roasted Garlic (page 329), black beans, and spinach wrapped up for lunch! Big leaves from romaine lettuce, collard greens, Swiss chard, and Bibb lettuce can sub in for a gluten-laden tortilla in a pinch. Use these leaves to make lettuce wraps stuffed with your favorite veggies, gluten-free whole grains, healthy fats, and lean proteins.

▸ **MEAL IN A CUP:** Give your cup of coconut or almond yogurt a boost by filling it with my Amie's Grain-Free Granola (page 121), Honey Cinnamon Quinoa Granola (page 118), Energizing Maple Cranberry Amaranth "Granola" (page 122), or Nature's Path Qi'a Superfood Chia, Buckwheat, and Hemp Cereal.

MY FAVORITE HEALTHY TRAVEL TIPS

You know how it goes. You look forward to your trip, but when you arrive, you just don't feel "right." Maybe it's digestive issues, jet lag, brain fog, or other things that make your trip less fun than it could be.

I have a few tips to help with that. Start by asking for an extra fridge in your hotel room so you know you'll have plenty of room for food. Healthy food is key to feeling good. Put frozen organic fruit or veggies in the fridge and they'll defrost for you by the next day. Then you can enjoy them in salads or with guacamole and hummus for a snack.

I always bring a small empty spice jar of ground cinnamon for extra sweetness. It's great to sprinkle on fresh fruit or gluten-free oatmeal, or you can take a teaspoon after a meal to help regulate your blood sugar, too. This helps with my polycystic ovary syndrome (PCOS) and insulin resistance!

Use a bead case (like the ones you used back in the 1980s to make necklaces—remember those?) to help organize your supplements and vitamins while traveling. Use a marker to write the time to take each supplement on the bead case so it's easy for you to remember ("E" for taking on an empty stomach and "X" for taking with food).

To manage jet lag without caffeine and Tylenol, drink purified water (unfortunately, bottled is your best bet at the airport—look for brands in glass bottles, like Pellegrino, instead of plastic).

Sip herbal tea or hot water with lemon. Bring your own organic herbal tea bags so you can rest assured your tea is not contaminated with pesticides and heavy metals, since it's likely the water is. Steer clear of airport, plane, and train (and rest stop) food—it's filled with preservatives and is most likely not organic.

EATING OUT

Eating out may seem challenging with GMO canola oil, refined salt, hidden sugar, dairy, soy, MSG, and gluten used in just about every menu item at many restaurants. No thank you!

RULES OF THUMB

▸ **PREVIEW THE MENU:** Find it online or call before you go. Don't be afraid to ask to speak with the chef. See if they can arrange for substitutions and accommodations ahead of time. (Have a backup plan in case the kitchen doesn't get the memo.) If you need to, ask if you can bring your own food and have them send it out on their plates. You can also bring my grain-free crackers (pages 156–162), roasted nut recipes (pages 140–142), and other snacks (page 139) in place of the glutinous bread basket and butter staring you in the face.

▸ **ASK QUESTIONS:** Ask how the food is prepared and with what ingredients. That way you know the oil they used to fry their French fries isn't being used for your broccoli!

▸ **DOUBLE THE VEGGIES:** Request double the veggies instead of starches like greasy fries and white potatoes. You can ask for veggies to be grilled, roasted, steamed, or sautéed—just make sure they use extra-virgin olive oil or coconut oil (you can even bring your own). Many restaurants use canola oil, which is made from corn and filled with GMOs and pesticides.

▸ **NO SAUCES:** Request that your meal be served without sauces and dressings—where sugars, dairy, soy, MSG, refined salts, and gluten often hide.

▸ **BRING YOUR OWN HIMALAYAN PINK SALT OR SEA SALT:** Store your salt in a tiny travel-friendly container. It does wonders for bringing out the flavors in your food with just a pinch!

▸ **CREATE YOUR OWN MEAL:** Ask the chef to create a meal for you with a lean protein (beans, legumes), gluten-free whole grains (black, brown, or wild rice; quinoa; buckwheat; amaranth; millet; etc.), healthy fat (avocado, olive oil, coconut oil, nuts and seeds), and lots of veggies. Season your meal with fresh lemon juice, extra-virgin olive oil, and your handy jar of salt.

▸ **CUSTOMIZE YOUR APPETIZER:** Ask for a dish of extra-virgin olive oil and minced garlic. Add a pinch of your salt, dip my grain-free crackers (pages 156–162) into the oil mixture, and enjoy. This is a whole lot better than bread and butter that are chock-full of antibiotics, growth hormones, GMOs, pesticides, and gluten.

▸ **AVOID SALAD BARS AND BUFFETS:** Because people are using the same spoons and tongs to reach into different foods, cross-contamination is likely. Plus, most of these foods are probably soaked in butter or canola oil and loaded with refined table salt. Yuck!

▸ **BRING YOUR OWN PICK-ME-UPS:** Pack an avocado, raw nut butter, and raw nuts or seeds with you just in case you need them. My snack recipes (page 139) will be your saving grace. Make these snacks on the weekends for easy grab 'n' go options all week.

▸ **PACK A COOLER:** If you're going to a wedding or other event, pack a cooler and stash it in your car or in the coatroom. I always keep a stash in my car and sneak out for a nibble—I did this at my best friend's wedding and no one had a clue!

ENTERTAINING

Everyone asks me, "How do you have a social life if you can't go out to restaurants?" That's easy. Stay in instead! Play host or hostess to your friends. Throw potlucks, or good old-fashioned dinner parties. Whether it's a small birthday party, a summer BBQ, a casual dinner party, a bridal shower, or a holiday cocktail party, it's always smart to ask your guests ahead of time what they can and cannot eat.

▸ **ASK WHAT THEY LIKE:** Don't just focus on what they can't eat; collect a list of everyone's favorite foods, too. Ask your guests to recommend their favorite recipes or see if they'd be willing to bring something.

▸ **MAKE SIMPLE SWAPS:** Scan the list of foods that your invitees can't eat and see if there are easy substitutions. For instance, use my Creamy Mock Mayo (page 313) in place of processed mayo. There are always options. My website, TheHealthyApple.com, is full of healthy swaps.

Simple Entertaining Menu Ideas

To get you started, here are some simple menu ideas you can use for your next dinner party or casual get-together.

▸ **GLUTEN-FREE WHOLE-GRAIN BUFFETS:** Set out steaming hot bowls of whole grains like millet, wild rice, or quinoa, and let your guests choose their own sauces and toppings to mix in. If you want, make a theme for the flavors—Mexican, Italian, Asian, or Mediterranean. This can be for a weekend "DIY porridge" brunch served with pure maple syrup, walnuts, and cinnamon, or for a dinner party with fresh herbs, pine nuts, my Moo-Free Cashew Sour Cream (page 309), Peppy No-Cheese Parmesan (page 307), and Cumin Cashew Cream Sauce (page 230).

▸ **VEGGIE "SUNDAES":** Using a variety of different methods, like sautéing, grilling, and roasting, cook up a wide assortment of in-season fresh veggies and put them in separate ramekins. Guests can create their own combinations to serve as tacos, fajitas, burritos, salad bowls, or whole-grain dishes.

▸ **DIY RAMEN COUNTER:** Let guests start with a base of my No-Soy Chickpea Miso Soup (page 187) and then choose their own "add-ins." See the same page for my miso soup garnish suggestions.

My golden rule for entertaining: Save time and

fresh 'n' tasty tapas plate

Sometimes the most informal way of eating can be the most satisfying. A tapas plate is an easy way to feed guests—plus, it's stylish and fun! Here are a few suggestions to pair various recipes in this book together for a tapas plate. Each combination serves six to eight as appetizers or small plates. For more festive menu ideas, check out my website, TheHealthyApple.com/EatingClean, for Celebration Menus for Thanksgiving, birthdays, and more.

SPRING TAPAS
- Sweet Pea Crostini with Dairy-Free Creamy Cashew Cheese *175*
- Oil-Free Traditional Hummus *301*
- Grain-Free Golden Herbes de Provence Crackers *161*
- Freckled Sesame Almond Clusters *140*
- Marvelous Mango Salad with Raspberry Ginger Dressing and Toasted Sunflower Seeds *215*

SUMMER TAPAS
- Oil-Free White Bean and Basil Hummus *302*
- Grain-free crackers *156–162*
- Spicy Honeydew Melon and Cucumber Gazpacho *189*
- Grilled Green Beans, Shallots 'n' Scallions with Romesco Sauce *171*
- No-Eggplant Garden Herb Ratatouille *234*

FALL TAPAS
- Humble Pickled Pears and Apples *287*
- Grain-Free Perfect Parsley Sunflower Crackers *156*
- Celebration Delicata Squash *260*
- Dairy-Free Creamy Cashew Cheese *308*
- Cranberry Kale Salad Smothered with Walnuts and Broccoli Pesto *208*

WINTER TAPAS
- Dairy-Free Sunshine Macadamia "Cream" Cheese *310*
- Blanched Sea Salt Almonds *142*
- Grain-Free Lemon Peppered Almond Crackers *162*
- Oven-Roasted Cherry Tomatoes with Poppy Seeds *283*
- Nuts about Butternut Squash and Kale Salad *210*

VEGETARIAN ANTIPASTO PLATTER
- Dukkah *326*
- Mediterranean olives
- Panzanella with Gluten-Free Herbed Croutons, Cherry Tomatoes, and Fresh Herbs *268*
- Easy No-Foil Roasted Garlic *329*
- Quick Balsamic Portobello Mushrooms *273*
- Big-Flavor Marinated Roasted Bell Peppers *278*
- Dairy-Free Sunshine Macadamia "Cream" Cheese *310*
- Grain-free crackers *156–162*

PRE-DINNER TAPAS SPREAD
- Divine Paprika Chickpea Croutons *144*
- Kalamata Olive and Cashew Tapenade *304*
- Sun-Dried Tomato Sunflower Pâté *304*
- Gluten-free crusty whole-grain bread
- Beaming Quinoa Tabbouleh with Coconut Chili Cashews *245*
- Fire-Roasted Peppers and Tomatoes with Herbs *280*
- Grilled Cauliflower Bites with Romesco Sauce *266*

kitchen space on the day of the party and cook what you can ahead of time. Many of my desserts (page 330) and gluten-free whole grains (like the ones in my gluten-free grain chart on pages 104–107), in particular, can be made in advance, frozen, and thawed out the night before your big meal.

SURVIVING THE HOLIDAYS

Classic holiday foods can be a recipe for disaster when you are trying to eat clean or if you have food intolerances and sensitivities—pesticide-stuffed turkeys and hams; gluten-filled stuffing; refined sugar–laden cakes, cookies, and pies; soy-laced canned gravy. But with a little creativity, you can tweak your traditional holiday menu into a clean-eating and anti-inflammatory spread. You'll want to whip up my Epic 'n' Easy Banana Bread (page 362) and my Grain-Free Nutty Apple Pear Crumble (page 358) for every holiday gathering.

Appetizers

‣ Set out my grain-free crackers (pages 156–162) with a variety of toppings: dairy-free nut cheeses (page 307–310), Zesty Orange Marmalade (page 328), Raw Strawberry Ginger Citrus Marmalade (page 327), Oil-Free Traditional Hummus (page 301), and Big-Flavor Marinated Roasted Bell Peppers (page 278).

‣ Quinoa-stuffed mushrooms are a great stand-in for the usual glutinous bread-filled mushrooms. Spoon protein-packed quinoa into button mushroom caps and bake until the mushrooms are tender and juicy. Your guests will never know they're gluten-free! You can also let wild, black, or brown rice have its time in the spotlight in place of the quinoa. Or get a little fancy and swap bell peppers, heirloom tomatoes, or large onions for the mushroom caps, stuff 'em to the brim, and then bake away! Top with omega-3 rich anti-inflammatory

ground flaxseeds, and you have a delicious and healthy fiber-filled spin on a crowd favorite.

‣ For a spread that's appealing to both the eyes and the belly, arrange a platter of my Blanched Sea Salt Almonds (page 142) and Maple Sriracha Roasted Pecans (page 142) with an assortment of organic sulfur-free unsweetened dried fruits (figs, dried pears, and apricots are particularly decadent holiday choices).

‣ Some of my other favorite holiday-spirited starters include: Grilled Kale and Sweet Potato "Grain-Free Bruschetta" with Sunflower Seed Drizzle (page 180), Simply Sweet Maple Roasted Chickpea Croutons (page 144), and Sweet Pea Crostini with Dairy-Free Creamy Cashew Cheese (page 308).

Side Dishes

‣ **VEGGIES:** Vegetables make for safe side dishes that are perfect for serving at your holiday table. Roast, puree, steam, smash, sauté, or serve au naturel. Roasted root vegetables are a great way to incorporate hearty, caramelized flavors. Check out my Rosemary Roasted Carrots and Beets (page 278) and Abundant Roasted Winter Veggies with Cannellini Beans (page 251). Simply drizzling a combination of whisked balsamic vinegar and Dijon mustard on any veggie adds a delightfully complex (but easy-to-achieve) flavor. You can also try my Presto Pesto Drizzle (page 261), Almond Walnut Dipping Sauce (page 151), and other dressings or sauces like my Romesco Sauce (page 266), Ecstatic Grape Sauce (page 323), or Creamy Tahini Tzatziki (page 303).

‣ **SWEET POTATOES AND PUMPKIN:** For a healthy alternative to mashed white potatoes, try my Homemade Pumpkin Puree (page 123) instead. Add chopped apples, freshly squeezed orange juice, and coconut oil in place of the refined sugar and dairy-filled butter found in traditional recipes. Not a pumpkin fan? Opt for mashed yams or sweet potatoes with a drizzle of honey and a sprinkle of ground cinnamon. For the creamy taste that no one can refuse, add a splash of culinary coconut milk.

▸ **CAULIFLOWER:** This versatile veggie can be chopped into florets, roasted, and then tossed with a mixture of gluten-free whole-grain pasta, anti-inflammatory turmeric, fresh rosemary, sea salt, pepper, and extra-virgin olive oil for an aromatic and hearty side dish. Try my Unbelievable Cauliflower Parm (page 267) or my Grilled Cauliflower Bites with Romesco Sauce (page 266). Yearning for something even more decadent? Add my dairy-free nut cheeses, like Peppy No-Cheese Parmesan topping (page 307), Dairy-Free Brazil Nut Parm Cheese (page 308), Dairy-Free Creamy Cashew Cheese (page 308), or Dairy-Free Sunshine Macadamia "Cream" Cheese (page 310).

▸ **GREEN VEGGIES:** Try broccoli rabe, Brussels sprouts, green beans, Swiss chard, and asparagus, which turn out lovely when sautéed with extra-virgin olive oil and fresh lemon juice. Or roast 'em up in the oven, like I did with my Warm Hearted Swiss Chard Lentil Bake (page 243). For a quick recipe, try my Exciting Green Bean Chips (page 153); they're a fun finger food for kids, too!

▸ **SATISFYING SOUPS:** Try my Roasted Butternut Squash Soup with Poppy Seed Polka Dots and Maple Balsamic Drizzle (page 184) or my Curried Lentil Soup (page 186).

▸ **GRAIN-FREE CRACKERS:** Enjoy my protein-packed grain-free crackers (pages 156–162) in lieu of a nutrient-void dinner roll, or as an appetizer with my Peppery Sunflower Pesto (page 321), Dairy-Free Raw Macadamia Nut "Ricotta" Cheese (page 309), or Dairy-Free Creamy Cashew Cheese (page 308). Drizzle on some leftover Easy Cranberry Sauce on top (page 323) for a sweet treat.

MAINS

▸ **GLUTEN-FREE HOLIDAY STUFFING:** Creating a gluten-free, dairy-free, and soy-free stuffing is easier than you think. Simply toss together brown rice, quinoa, millet, roasted vegetables (like carrots and celery), unsweetened dried cranberries, fresh herbs, extra-virgin olive oil, apple cider vinegar, and my Super Soft Caramelized Red Onions (page 272).

---

how to explain your clean eating to family and friends

At this point, anyone I spend time with knows the drill: Chances are, when we're out, Amie probably can't eat it. I join in for the company and fun, not the food. I make sure to always let people know why I'm not eating so everyone is comfortable.

Trust your friends and family to respect your changes. They'll see you are putting yourself first, listening to your body, and getting healthier. But don't expect anyone to go out of their way to understand your clean eating needs or accommodate you. My goal is to inspire and empower you to make clean choices without feeling guilty about hurting people's feelings.

Get creative and serve my Flavored Sea Salts (page 325) on the side.

▸ **ADD GLUTEN-FREE WHOLE GRAINS:** Tossing your favorite whole grains with savory and sweet ingredients makes for a satisfying main dish for guests. See page 102 for more ideas on whole-grain recipes. Try my Ultimate Quinoa, Cherry, and Pecan Salad (page 217) or my Essential Picnic Basil Millet (page 212).

DESSERTS

▸ **FRUIT:** Focus on in-season fruits like pumpkin, apples, fresh cranberries, peaches, and pears to create crumbles, cobblers, and crisps. Add in a sprinkle of ground cinnamon, pumpkin pie spice, and nutmeg. Or try my Macadamia Nut, Carrot, and Zucchini Oat Breadless "Bread" Pudding (page 363) and Perfect Pumpkin Gelato (page 332).

▸ **CHOCOLATE:** Have a hankering for chocolate? Scratch the itch with my Hempy Cocoa Coconut Truffles (page 351), Gianduja Classic Chocolate Hazelnut Spread (page 368), or Delightful Almond Butter Cups (page 354).

HOW TO BE A GREAT GUEST

Inviting someone with food intolerances to dinner can be intimidating and scary for hosts, especially when they have to rule out gluten, dairy, soy, corn, eggs, peanuts, and refined sugar. People probably get migraines just thinking about my "Amie-Cannot-Eat-This List." But with a few considerations, you can save both you and your host a heck of a lot of stress.

▸ **CALL AHEAD:** Ask what you can bring. Make it clear you are not expecting them to create an entire menu just for you. Offer to contribute an appetizer and main dish you can enjoy, along with seltzer, fresh lemons, limes, and your handy-dandy sea salt.

▸ **BRING YOUR OWN:** I bring my own food and have the host grill or roast it along with whatever they're making. Then they bring it out with everyone else's meal. It's much easier and less stressful for both of us.

▸ **PREPARE YOURSELF:** Don't show up hungry! Eat before you go, and bring my grain-free crackers (pages 156–162) or any of my roasted nuts (pages 140–142), in case you need them.

YOU CAN LIVE A PERFECTLY NORMAL LIFE

It's easier than you think to live a "normal" life when you have to avoid certain foods, chemicals, and additives. Is it a little bit more work? Yes, but it's worth it. I'd rather spend the extra time prepping than landing in bed with a bellyache and swollen body.

You'll see how easy it can be to live this way. If I can do it in a tiny apartment in a crazy city like New York, then you can do it where you live, too. The best part is how amazing you're going to feel.

Buy a little cooler for your trips, sit down with your family and friends to tell them about your new lifestyle, and jump on over to my recipes to razzle dazzle your taste buds—they'll be pleasantly surprised. Give yourself a little pom-pom shake to celebrate all you're doing.

I think we've covered food pretty well, but unfortunately, it's not the only source of toxins creeping into your fabulous life. Believe it or not, you're likely absorbing them from your makeup, deodorant, and body lotion, too.

Let's take a peek at what's lurking in your pretty jar of perfume, bottle of shampoo, and bar of soap. Remember, this is about progress, not perfection, so take a deep breath before you start to audit your bathroom cabinets, makeup bag, and shower.

detox your personal care products

With just a few changes to your daily habits, you can gain the power to be your healthiest self ever. When I started eating clean, I didn't understand that my skin was my largest organ and that toxins could actually be entering my body from the creams and lotions I was slathering on it. I was later shocked to realize that manufacturers can use almost any ingredient they want in their formulations. According to the law, "Cosmetic products and ingredients are not subject to FDA premarket approval authority, with the exception of color additives."

Turns out many of the "clean" products I was using were filled with a number of chemicals that can disrupt health and well-being. I thought I was using the best brands available, but little did I know that they contained potentially toxic ingredients. I was using Neutrogena sunscreen, for example, because I thought it was a safer and cleaner choice than Coppertone. I was brushing my teeth with Colgate because I didn't know any better. I was washing my face with Cetaphil or whatever was on sale at the drugstore down the street because that's all I knew. I was wearing expensive makeup from high-end Manhattan department stores, thinking that was the best of the best.

I learned that all these products contain heavy metals, toxic chemicals, and other toxins that were getting into my body through my skin. Even though I was eating a fabulously delicious organic diet, I was still absorbing toxins every day. Of all the things I learned in school, college, and corporate America, no one ever educated me on this. I had no idea toxins could be present in everyday items I touched or applied to my body.

Did you?

After years of research, reading more detox books than I can count, and speaking with Integrative medical doctors—as well as keeping up with the latest research—I realized there was a missing link in my illness. My skin was absorbing toxins and making me sick. The more I learned, the more I realized how many potentially toxic ingredients exist in our personal care products, and how we all deserve the right to know what we're being exposed to in these seemingly harmless bottles of potions.

To put this into perspective, the last time Congress passed a major law regulating the cosmetics and skin care industry was 1938, and the law hasn't been updated since. Yikes! The FDA leaves it up to companies to decide what to put in their products and has no ability to take action, restrict, or ban harmful ingredients used by the beauty industry.

Most of us don't know we could be putting ourselves at risk. A product may contain only a small amount of a potentially toxic ingredient, so we're not likely to notice any effects right away (unless we have sensitive or reactive skin). After we use a product a couple times a day for several years (like body lotion or lip balm), however, we can create a buildup in the body that does cause us problems.

The Centers for Disease Control and Prevention (CDC) found through urine tests on study participants that things like phthalates (plasticizers linked with asthma, diabetes, infertility, and more) and parabens (preservatives linked to hormone disruption) are widespread in the U.S. population. Both of these ingredients, along with a number of other toxins, are in most of the personal care products we use every day.

Essentially, these companies are experimenting on us. We deserve better; wouldn't you say? We can't control everything we're exposed to, but we definitely have a choice about the products we put on our bodies.

After I completed my pantry makeover, I dove into a heavy-duty bathroom, closet, and medicine cabinet detox, tossing just about everything and restocking it with organic, nontoxic ingredients. My favorite, most versatile one? Organic coconut oil. Trust me. Google the ways to use coconut oil and you'll be amazed! No more body lotion needed. It works as an amazing eye makeup remover, and it's also an awesome moisturizing bath soak.

Now, it's your turn. Cozy on up in your bathrobe, get comfy, and read on for ways you can start detoxing your personal care items.

P.S. Don't get overwhelmed. Start by tossing out one toxic item in your beauty cabinet or linen closet this week.

QUESTIONNAIRE: ARE YOUR BEAUTY PRODUCTS TOXIC?

‣ Do you use commercial deodorant or antiperspirant?

‣ Do you dye or bleach your hair?

‣ Do you use cologne or perfume?

‣ Do you wash and condition your hair with regular drugstore shampoos and conditioners?

‣ Do you use standard styling products like mousses, gels, hair sprays, texturizing balms, temporary colorants, and more?

‣ Do you bathe with soap and/or typical body washes, like those made by Suave, Dial, Dove, and other drugstore brands?

‣ Do you slather moisturizing creams and lotions that you bought from your local discount store?

- Do you use chemical sunscreens that contain oxybenzone and octinoxate?

- Do you brush your teeth with standard toothpaste like Crest or Colgate?

- Do you use makeup products made by popular brands like Maybelline, L'Oréal, and Revlon?

- Do you use alcohol-based mouthwash or aftershave?

You know the drill by now. The more times you answered "yes" to these questions, the more likely it is that you're using toxic beauty products. It's time to toss those chemical-laden products in the trash and move on.

ASSESS YOUR MEDICINE CABINET

The first step in detoxing your personal care products is to take an assessment of what you already have. Unfortunately, things aren't as straightforward as you might think. The simple word "fragrance" could mean that the product contains over a hundred different chemicals that together create that fragrance! Remember, the longer these chemicals stay on your skin (such as in moisturizers and makeup), the more likely they'll find their way into your body.

The chart on the opposite page is my list for "never use" ingredients. These rate high on the "toxic scale" and simply just aren't worth putting onto your body. They have been linked with hormone disruption, allergies, dermatitis, inflammation, developmental problems, and more.

To find out how your products rate, turn them over and read the ingredient lists on the back. If you find any of the following chemicals, don't buy that product again. (I'd actually recommend you toss it in the trash, but it's up to you.) It's important to look behind the marketing, because even terms like "pure," "green," "natural," "hypoallergenic," and "botanical" are unregulated and don't mean a darn thing. Even if a product includes organic ingredients, it may be packaged with toxic preservatives. Your best bet for determining what's really in the product is to study the ingredient list, always.

What if the packaging fails to list the ingredients? If it has only one ingredient (like coconut oil, for example), then you know it's safe. Other than that, if the ingredients are not listed, go online and look up the product. The Environmental Working Group (EWG) has a handy reference tool called the Skin Deep Database (ewg.org/skindeep), which rates all ingredients found in thousands of products from one to ten. The higher the number, the more hazardous the ingredient and the more potential health problems it may cause over time.

For a list of my favorite nontoxic personal care brands, see pages 74–75.

AMIE'S LIST OF 10 NEVER-USE INGREDIENTS

Take a moment right now to go through your personal care and beauty products. Get a piece of paper and a pen, look at the ingredient list on the back of each product, and write down each product that has at least one of the following ten never-use ingredients in it.

If you find that most of your products have one or more of these ingredients, don't panic; I have the solutions for you coming up. You can replace these toxic products with cleaner alternatives like those on pages 74–75 or make your own from my beauty recipes on pages 76–77. If most of your products failed to list any of these ingredients, that's a good thing, but it doesn't mean those products are completely safe. Other ingredients may be linked to health problems, or at the very least are likely to do little to truly nourish your skin and hair.

Fragrance is a good example. Most products have synthetic fragrances that contain unknown

harmful ingredient	purpose	uses	dangerous properties
Phthalates (look for anything with the word "phthalate" in it, plus abbreviations MMP, MEP, MiBP, DMP, DEP, and DiBP)	‣ lubricant ‣ solvent ‣ strengthens plastics	‣ perfume ‣ nail polish ‣ other beauty products	‣ endocrine disruptor ‣ allergen ‣ asthma and lung irritation
Parabens (look for anything with the word "paraben" in it, including methylparaben, propylparaben, butylparaben, etc.)	‣ preservative	‣ most personal care and makeup products	‣ preliminary studies note a potential link with cancer—more studies need to be done ‣ hormone disruptor ‣ allergies
Amines (look for diethanolamine, triethanolamine, monoethanolamine, MEA, DEA, TEA)	‣ balances pH ‣ provides a foaming action ‣ preserves shelf life	‣ shampoos and conditioners ‣ cosmetics ‣ hair dyes ‣ lotions ‣ shave creams	‣ when mixed with nitrates, can form carcinogenic compounds ‣ skin irritation
Sulfates (look for sodium lauryl sulfate and sodium laureth sulfate)	‣ harsh detergents ‣ used for foaming	‣ shampoo ‣ soaps ‣ body washes	‣ dry, flaky skin and hair ‣ skin rashes ‣ premature aging ‣ allergic reactions
Formaldehyde (look for formaldehyde-releasing preservatives like quaternium-15, DMDM hydantoin, imidazolidinyl urea, diazolidinyl urea, sodium hydroxymethylglycinate, 2-bromo-2-nitropropane-1, 3-diol)	‣ acts as a preservative	‣ nail polish ‣ shampoos and gels ‣ liquid baby soaps ‣ eyelash glue	‣ allergic reactions ‣ carcinogenic effects

harmful ingredient	purpose	uses	dangerous properties
Mercury (look for thimerosal)	‣ restricted to low levels in U.S., but makes its way into our make-up from overseas ‣ acts as a preservative	‣ face/skin care products (anti-aging and skin lightening products) ‣ some mascaras ‣ some eye makeup removers	‣ toxic to human organs ‣ accumulates in the environment
Retinyl palmitate, retinal acetate, retinoic acid, retinol	‣ used in anti-aging products to smooth appearance of fine lines and wrinkles	‣ skin and lip care products	‣ encourages production of free radicals, which can actually accelerate aging ‣ animal studies have shown a link to cancerous tumors
Benzene	‣ used as a solvent	‣ perfumes ‣ colognes ‣ nail polishes	‣ skin and eye irritation ‣ organ toxicity ‣ respiratory problems ‣ known human carcinogen
Toluene	‣ used as a solvent	‣ nail polishes and other nail products	‣ reproductive and organ toxin ‣ skin irritation ‣ lung irritation ‣ dampens immune system
1,4-dioxane (look for sodium myreth sulfate, PEG, oxynol, ceteareth, oleth, and polyethylene)	‣ by-product of ethoxylation process in cosmetics manufacturing	‣ shampoo ‣ bubble bath ‣ body wash ‣ other sudsing products ‣ hair relaxers	‣ skin and lung irritation ‣ organ toxicity ‣ possible human carcinogen

chemicals—sometimes many are mixed together to create the right scent. Companies don't have to reveal these chemicals because their fragrances are protected as "trade secrets." I recommend that you avoid anything with the word "fragrance" in it and choose either fragrance-free products or those scented with plant-based ingredients or Aura Cacia organic essential oils.

Sadly, companies can slap the word "organic" on their packages when the product may be full of synthetic chemicals found in conventional products. If you see an organic beauty product, check the ingredient list to ensure my "10 Never-Use" ingredients are nowhere to be found on the label. As you get used to the idea of shopping for nontoxic products, you'll find that many personal care and beauty products are not organic but still contain safe ingredients that you can feel good about using. Check out the list on pages 74–75 for brands I love.

Cutting back on the toxins you apply to your skin decreases your overall toxic exposure, and reduces the burden your body has to fight off every day. While eating clean detoxifies the body from the inside out, applying clean products to your skin ensures that you're not undoing the progress you've already made with your diet. This double-duty detox ensures your body is clean inside and out! It may take some time and money in the short term, but you'll thank yourself later.

THE DETOX SOLUTION

The good news is that many people are discovering the links between toxic exposures in personal care products and health issues. They're demanding safer personal care products, which means you'll see more "clean" products popping up on the shelves as time goes on.

SWAP THIS FOR THAT

If you discovered that you have a virtual chemical cornucopia in your medicine cabinet, there's an easy solution. Toss it in the trash. Once you eliminate products that contain my "10 Never-Use" ingredients and begin to shop for safer brands (or make your own DIY beauty products from my recipes on pages 76–77), you're well on your way to enjoying clean personal care. The chart on the next page will assist you further—I've included items that often harbor harmful toxins and have listed safer alternatives.

truth in labeling?

Just because a personal care product contains organic, natural, or plant-based ingredients doesn't mean it's free of toxic chemicals, soy, or gluten. Always keep in mind that natural or organic ingredients do not imply the product is safe. Be your best advocate by playing detective: Make a list for yourself before you get to the store, being mindful of ingredients you never want to put on or in your body. Scan the ingredient list to be sure the product does not contain any of my "10 Never-Use" ingredients.

product	common toxic ingredients	possible health issues	what to look for in clean products	favorite clean brands
Sunscreen	› Phthalates › Parabens › Estrogenlike compounds › Carcinogens › SPF >50 › Retinyl palmitate › Aerosols › Octinoxate › Oxybenzone › Nano-particles	› Hormone disruption › Reproductive health issues › Cancer › Allergens › Respiratory complications	› Fewer ingredients › Zinc oxide › Titanium dioxide › SPF between 30 to 50	› Raw Elements › Badger › Beautycounter › Erbaviva
Shampoo	› Formaldehyde › DEA › Artificial "fragrance" › Polyethylene glycol › Sodium lauryl sulfate › Sodium laureth sulfate › Coal tar › Polysorbate 60 and 80 › Quaterium 15 › Coloring agents (blue 1, red dye) › Parabens › Ethoxylates	› Rashes › Dermatitis › Birth defects › Allergens › Skin irritations › Endocrine disruptors › Infertility	› Essential oils	› Rahua › Acure Organics › Beautycounter
Mouth Care	› Fluoride › Triclosan › Sulfates › Titanium dioxide › Propylene glycol › Coloring agents (blue 1) › Flavorings (aspartame)	› Hormone disruption › Developmental defects › Liver toxicity › Respiratory problems › Allergens	› Baking soda (limited use) › Sea salt (antibacterial) › Essential oils	› Barlean's Organic Virgin Coconut Oil
Deodorant	› Aluminum › Parabens › Propylene glycol › Phthalates › Triclosan › Artificial fragrance	› Potential increased cancer risk › Hormone disruptors › Birth defects › Nervous system damage › Organ toxicity	› Essential oils › Witch hazel › Mineral salts › Baking soda	› The Crystal › Erbaviva

product	common toxic ingredients	possible health issues	what to look for in clean products	favorite clean brands
Feminine Hygiene	‣ Bleach ‣ Viscose rayon ‣ Dioxins ‣ Color additives ‣ Artificial "fragrance" ‣ Parabens ‣ Benzethonium chloride ‣ Benzocaine	‣ Hormone disruptors ‣ Organ toxicity ‣ Increased cancer risk ‣ Allergens/sensitivity	‣ Organic	‣ Natracare
Lip Care	‣ Lead ‣ Gluten ‣ Artificial "fragrance" ‣ Preservatives ‣ Parabens ‣ Heavy metals ‣ Petrochemicals ‣ Carmine	‣ Cancer-causing ‣ Allergens/sensitivity ‣ Hormone disruptors ‣ Accumulations of toxins	‣ Gluten-free ‣ Animal-cruelty free ‣ Cocoa butter ‣ Beeswax	‣ Intelligent Nutrients ‣ Badger
Hand Sanitizer/ Cleaner	‣ Triclosan ‣ Ethyl alcohol ‣ Artificial "fragrance" ‣ Sulfates ‣ Parabens ‣ DEA ‣ 1,4-Dioxane	‣ Absorption into bloodstream ‣ Organ toxicity ‣ Toxic to wildlife and environment ‣ Hormone disruptors ‣ Creates "superbugs"	‣ Food-grade ingredients ‣ No preservatives or fragrances (besides essential oils) ‣ Free of synthetic chemicals	‣ EO Products ‣ Intelligent Nutrients ‣ Branch Basics ‣ CleanWell
Moisturizer	‣ Coal tar ‣ DEA ‣ Formaldehyde ‣ Artificial "fragrance" ‣ Parabens ‣ Polyethylene glycol ‣ Sulfates	‣ Harmful to wildlife and environment ‣ Hormone disruptors ‣ Reproductive toxins ‣ Allergens/ sensitivities	‣ Shea butter ‣ Coconut oil ‣ Argan oil ‣ Jojoba oil	‣ Intelligent Nutrients ‣ CV Skinlabs ‣ Odacite ‣ Beautycounter

DIY: HOMEMADE PERSONAL CARE RECIPES

Did you know that your kitchen may contain a lot of the supplies you need for smooth, radiant skin and hair? You can also buy basic supplies like oils to use as moisturizers and redness soothers (think jojoba, olive, and coconut).

If you'd like to try your hand at mixing up some homemade personal care products, here are some solutions.

When I was growing up, my grandmother swore by using the inside of a banana peel to moisturize her skin. That's why smearing a little coconut oil on my eyes, using coconut oil and tea tree oil for toothpaste, or slathering a little avocado on my face for a hydrating mask never seemed strange to me.

What's really strange is buying a beauty product with unlisted or unpronounceable ingredients and putting them all over your body! That's why I love to make my own products, when I have the time to do so. It ends up being cheaper because I can make things in larger quantities than I would buy, and I have the benefit of knowing the ingredients.

CAUTION: Whenever making your own beauty products, do a patch test on your skin before using to make sure you don't have an allergy to any one ingredient.

AMIE'S DIY BEAUTY PRODUCTS

beauty product ›	*replacement*	*recipe/ratio*
Toothpaste ›	Coconut and tea tree oil paste	Mix organic coconut oil with tea tree oil or oregano oil and spread a small amount onto your toothbrush. Brush as usual.
Lip Balm ›	Coconut honey lip balm	Mix 1 tablespoon coconut oil with 1 tablespoon extra-virgin olive oil, plus 1½ teaspoons honey for the perfect moisturizing lip balm.
Toner ›	Cucumber juice and lavender oil	Combine these two ingredients in equal parts and pour into a spray bottle or directly onto an organic cotton ball.
Acne Cream ›	Raw honey, tea tree oil, apple cider vinegar, or lavender oil	Using an organic cotton ball, apply your ingredient of choice directly onto the pimple or blackhead.
Hair Buildup Cleanser ›	Apple cider vinegar mask	Mix 2 teaspoons apple cider vinegar into 1 cup purified water, and then pour this solution over your hair in the shower. Comb through and rinse out with cold water.
Shampoo ›	Coconut milk castile shampoo	Combine ⅓ cup liquid castile soap (like Dr. Bronner's) with ¼ cup coconut milk and 15 drops of your favorite organic essential oil (I use peppermint), plus a drop of vitamin E oil (optional).

beauty product ›	*replacement*	*recipe/ratio*
Face Mask ›	Avocado almond mask	Combine 1 ripe avocado with gluten-free oats and unsweetened almond milk for a hydrating face mask.
Skin Scrub ›	All-natural exfoliator	Gluten-free oats, sea salt, organic coffee, lemon juice, raw organic sugar, and honey are all wonderful ingredients to exfoliate your skin. Make your own combination of your favorites.
Body Scrub ›	Coconut oil scrub	Mix coconut oil with sea salt and exfoliate your skin all over. (For sensitive skin, mix with raw organic sugar instead of salt.)
First-Aid Cream ›	Fresh aloe vera gel	This natural wonder helps soothe minor cuts and scrapes, burns, sunburn, and other skin irritations.
Makeup Remover ›	Favorite natural product	Chamomile tea, cucumber juice, rose water, lemon juice and apple cider vinegar all work to gently remove makeup.
Eye Makeup Remover ›	Organic virgin coconut oil	Use coconut oil on a tissue to gently remove eye makeup.
Teeth Whitener ›	Baking soda or activated charcoal	Mix either baking soda or activated charcoal with organic essential oils and apply directly on teeth for a nontoxic teeth whitening solution.
Nourishing Hair Mask ›	Everything-but-the-kitchen-sink hair mask	Mash avocado, honey, apple cider vinegar, lemon juice, banana, almond oil, and extra-virgin olive oil or raw egg together and work through hair; let sit for 10 to 20 minutes before rinsing.
Astringent ›	Apple cider vinegar	Use just as you'd use a store-bought astringent with an organic cotton ball.
Burn First-Aid Cream ›	Raw honey	Slather raw, organic honey generously on minor burns. (If a burn is blistered, it is a second-degree burn and may need medical attention. If you are unsure of the severity of your burn, always seek medical attention.)
Flyaway/Split-End Treatment ›	Organic essential oils	Rub a very small amount of your chosen organic essential oil in your hands so that your fingers are evenly covered. Run over split ends and flyaway hairs.

I love this beauty scrub recipe because it combines my favorite scents—almond and lavender—into an invigorating scrub that is a great way to start or end the day.

- 2 cups sea salt
- 3 cups almond oil
- 45 drops lavender oil

Mix and apply to your wet body, massage, and then rinse and towel dry.

THE VIRTUE OF OILS

Skip the toxic, processed body oils and lotions and use organic oils (such as jojoba, macadamia, sweet almond, argan, and rosehip) to moisturize your skin after you shower. Apply them immediately when your skin is still moist—that's when it's most absorbent. Add a few drops of organic essential oils to create a unique scent that you truly love, thereby replacing your conventional perfume, as well.

Try the following, and then have fun coming up with your favorite combinations:

- **ORGANIC ALMOND OIL.** Evens out skin tone. Use along with liquid vitamin E.

- **EXTRA-VIRGIN OLIVE OIL.** Packed with anti-aging antioxidants, it's hydrating and rich in vitamins E and A.

- **COCONUT OIL.** Reduces age marks and stretch marks and clears the complexion. It can also be used as a moisturizer, lip balm, cuticle cream, nail growth stimulator, defrizzer for your hair, and soothing balm for irritated skin. It even fights athlete's foot and low-level fungal infections.

- **COCOA BUTTER.** This antioxidant-rich butter isn't an oil, but a fabulous creamy butter that makes your skin super soft. It's derived from the cacao bean and rich in vitamin E.

- **ORGANIC ESSENTIAL OILS.** Add a few drops of these beautifully scented oils to your bath and shower for an incredibly relaxing scent. You can also add them to another oil listed here and rub onto your skin for a sweet scent.

- **JOJOBA OIL.** Great pore cleanser and softens and soothes skin.

- **ARGAN OIL.** Contains essential fatty acids to brighten hair and skin.

BEYOND YOUR EVERYDAY PRODUCTS

Your nail beds and scalp are highly permeable areas of your body. They soak up chemicals like a sponge. As a general rule, avoid acrylic nails, tanning beds, keratin hair straighteners, gel nails, and hair coloring from nonorganic ingredients. Chemicals in conventional nail polish like toluene, dibutyl phthalate (an endocrine disruptor), acetone, and formaldehyde (a carcinogen) are incredibly harmful to breathe, and can get into your bloodstream.

I like to bring my own bottles of nail polish and polish removers to the spa, and soak my hands in organic almond oil followed by an organic coconut oil lather to prep them for color. Or just skip the nail polish all together. The natural look, as long as hands are nicely moisturized, always looks nice.

As you now know, your home can be another potent spot for toxins. From the sunscreen you put on for the beach to the toothpaste you use twice a day, you can expose yourself to thousands of chemicals that interfere with your body's chemical operations, throwing off your hormonal system, detoxification, and much more.

Have no fear. You can start tossing a few of these products today. This will make a huge difference on your internal toxic load. Start small and create a strategy based on my above suggestions, and you'll be well on your way to clean living.

detox your home and office

You may have already heard about detoxing to eliminate harmful ingredients from your body, but did you ever look around your home or office and think you needed to do a detox in those spaces, as well?

I never thought about that. Growing up, I was a Clorox Wipes and Windex kinda gal. I didn't know a thing about the toxins in common cleaning products, or the potentially harmful chemicals that could be trapped in my living and working environments.

I live in Manhattan, folks, so there are toxins all over the place. The bad news is that most of them are hidden. We're unable to see, taste, or smell them. Super fun, right? Makes it even more exciting to deal with them when you don't even notice them.

How well you tolerate these chemicals depends on your genetics, your current nutrition levels, and your previous contact with other chemicals. Sadly, many of the products we use to clean our furniture, windows, bathrooms, cars, and more are filled with potentially dangerous toxins. Most of them don't even appear on the labels.

Do me a little favor and take a good look around your home—toss those plastic products, make your own cleaning products (see my homemade recipes on page 83), dust often, use a HEPA-filter vacuum, and avoid excess moisture, which encourages the growth of mildew and mold.

If you're going to paint, use low-VOC, low-odor latex (water-based) products, and check for carbon monoxide leaks. Replace your toxic lawn and garden pesticides and herbicides with natural ones, and avoid furniture, carpets, and clothing with stain guards and fire retardants.

These are just a few little tips. Read on for more information on detoxing your home and office. And please—don't freak out and go running around trying to make everything perfect right now. This takes time; it took me two years. You'll get there.

IS YOUR HOME OR OFFICE TOXIC?

Most of us spend the majority of our lives at home (or for some of us, at work). Usually our homes are safe places where we can relax and renew. But unfortunately, work and home environments can both be filled with toxic ingredients that add to our overall toxic load—without us even knowing it.

I know we can't get rid of every single toxin in these spaces, but we can slowly replace the most egregious items with things that are friendlier to our bodies. If you're not sure how toxic your home or working environment might be, answer these questions:

‣ Do you use commercial household cleaners?

‣ Do you have wall-to-wall carpet in your home or office?

‣ Do you use store-bought air fresheners?

‣ Do you wear dry-cleaned clothes?

‣ Do you work in an office with fluorescent lights?

‣ Do you get more than two colds per year?

‣ Are your nails weak? Do they often split and break?

‣ Do you have strong-smelling urine?

‣ Do you have bad breath or a metallic taste in your mouth?

The more times you answered yes to these questions, the more likely it is that you are living in a toxic environment.

LET'S START WITH THE KITCHEN

Since this is a cookbook, let's start detoxing the home with the kitchen. Even if you are eating clean and buy organic, it's important to assess your kitchen as a whole.

Examine your pots and pans, and how you store food. Take a look at any hidden plastics, such as on your electric teapot, which could leach chemicals into your water. Use a water filter on your kitchen sink faucet so that you're not ingesting chemicals from tap water. Notice if you put wooden cutting boards in the dishwasher—a big no-no. When you start to observe these things, you might find that it's easier than you think to replace toxic items with safer alternatives.

POTS AND PANS

Teflon-coated nonstick pans can release small chemical toxins into the air when the pans are heated, contributing to indoor air pollution. They also have PFCs, short for "perfluorochemicals," which are used to coat carpets, clothes, furniture, and food packaging, among other things. They persist in the environment as well as in the human body and have been associated with lower birth weight for babies, cancer, infertility, elevated cholesterol, and liver problems.

To reduce your toxic exposure here, upgrade your pots and pans. The best ones to use are glass, ceramic, cast iron, and stainless steel. A cast-iron skillet evenly distributes heat and a bit of iron into your food, and stainless steel is lighter. They may not be cheap, but they don't present any dangers to your health.

You don't have to buy new cookware all at once. Pick the one or two pieces of cookware you use the most and replace those first—and consider it an investment in your health. It's especially important to do this if nonstick surfaces are scarred or peeling. Look for ceramic pots such as Le Creuset, stainless-steel pots and pans such as All-Clad, and glass bakeware such as Pyrex.

Storage Sense

With curious eyes, look around your kitchen. Do you store food in plastics? Go through them and look at the recycling numbers on the bottom. Toss anything bearing the code 3, 6, or 7, as these plastics contain BPA. Actually, I'd recommend eventually tossing all your plastic containers and bowls. That's what I did. You're better off with glass, because who knows what those plastic manufacturers are replacing BPA with, right? Not good.

Whatever you decide, never heat food in any plastic. Use glass, ceramic, or stainless steel instead. And remember—your glass containers don't have to be fancy. Used (and washed) spaghetti jars and salsa jars work just fine! Here are a few tips for keeping your kitchen clean and safe from bacteria, mold, plastics, and other harmful ingredients such as BPA.

▸ Replace plastic containers with glass mason jars and glass containers—glassware is the safest.

▸ Limit (and try to avoid) canned food, since many aluminum cans are lined with polycarbonate plastic, which contains BPA. If you are making a recipe that calls for culinary coconut milk, you can choose one from a BPA-free can.

▸ Use parchment paper instead of cling wrap, which often is made with PVC. This comes from petroleum, which is not renewable and releases chemicals like dioxin and benzene. The chemicals in plastic can also leach into your food and drink.

▸ Select unbleached paper products, including baking cups, cheesecloth, coffee filters, waxed paper, and parchment paper.

▸ Don't let your fruit and veggies wilt in the fridge; eat them within two to three days or freeze them to prevent bacteria and mold overgrowth.

▸ Cool hot leftovers to room temperature before storing in glass containers in the fridge or freezer to prevent cracking.

▸ After removing food from the freezer, allow it to thaw in the refrigerator.

▸ Freeze leftovers to prevent bacteria and mold overgrowth.

▸ Label each glass container with the name of the food and the date stored so everyone knows what's inside. Pull out containers that have been in there the longest.

▸ Transfer any dry goods like rice and oats into glass containers so they're not prone to mold. Do this immediately when unloading from the grocery store.

▸ Use a distilled white vinegar and water solution to clean fruits and veggies (it helps remove bacteria and mold). Measure half white vinegar and half water into a spray bottle; wipe and clean. Use the same solution to clean out your fridge once a week.

▸ Many foods like berries and grapes often have mold in their bags before you even get them home. Wash them well and do not put them in the bin with other fruits and veggies, as they could contaminate them. Wash fruit with tough skins like watermelons, pears, and oranges to remove mold and bacteria before you put them into the fridge.

▸ Throw out any expired food and condiments like cocktail sauce or ketchup.

HOUSEHOLD CLEANERS

Home and office cleaners, ironically, can be some of the most toxic items around, filled with harsh, carcinogenic, and hormone-disrupting chemicals.

Antibacterial cleaners? Even worse. It's almost as though they are working to undermine our immune systems.

Don't be fooled by certified green products, either, because label claims are not always true. A product that says "eco-friendly" or "natural" might contain a handful of yucky chemicals. And beware of marketing ploys. Look for products with specific information, such as "free from petroleum-based solvents, perfumes, acids, dyes" or "no solvents or phosphates." The more detailed, the better.

Fortunately, there are plenty of affordable nontoxic organic cleaners on the shelves today, and you can replace your window cleaner, toilet bowl scrubber, surface cleaner, laundry and dishwasher detergents, dish soap, and more with safe and effective products from brands I trust. See page 381 for the list.

SWAP THIS FOR THAT

In addition to replacing standard cleaners with more natural, safe options, you can further detox your home or office environment by making your own cleaning products. Start by removing the toxic items listed below and replacing them with some basic, all-purpose nontoxic ones. Then, you can use some basic ingredients to create economical and safe cleaning products.

REMOVE:

Bleach	Glass cleaner
Carpet cleaner	Metal cleaner
Dishwashing detergent	Liquid dishwashing soap
Deodorizer	Oven cleaner
All-purpose cleaners	Scouring cleaner
Disinfecting wipes	Silver polish
Drain cleaner	Stain stick
Floor-mopping detergent	Tile cleaner
Floor wax	Toilet cleaner
Furniture polish	

USE INSTEAD:

All-purpose, nontoxic cleaner	Nontoxic dishwashing detergent
Baking soda	Distilled white vinegar
Castile soap	Organic essential oils
Borax	Nontoxic liquid dishwashing soap

DIY CLEANING INGREDIENTS

Stores are loaded with all kinds of fancy and overpriced concoctions of baking soda and white vinegar, so put your wallet away and take a trip to your kitchen cupboard. I guarantee you've got the goods to begin your very own cleaning arsenal.

› **ORANGE RIND:** The oil in orange rind contains d-Limonene, a natural solvent that can cut through grease.

› **FRESH LEMONS:** One of the strongest food acids, lemon is effective against most household bacteria.

› **TEA TREE OIL:** This powerful antibacterial agent is great for use in the bathroom and kitchen.

› **BAKING SODA:** Baking soda cleans, deodorizes, and scours. It softens water and neutralizes minerals, helping soap clean better. It also absorbs odors and can be used daily.

› **LIQUID CASTILE SOAP:** Unscented soap in liquid form, flakes, powders, or bars is biodegradable and will clean just about anything. Avoid using soaps that contain sodium lauryl sulfate, phosphates, and petroleum distillates.

› **DISTILLED WHITE VINEGAR:** Vinegar is naturally antibacterial and cuts through grease, making it a good all-purpose cleaner for toilets, baths, table tops, countertops, and more. Don't use vinegar on marble surfaces, though, as they're porous and vinegar may stain them.

DIY Cleaning Products

Using the ingredients listed on the opposite page, you can make most of your cleaning supplies.

▸ **CLEAR YOUR DRAIN:** Pour 1 cup baking soda down the drain, followed by 1 cup distilled white vinegar. It will bubble; when the solution has stopped bubbling, add 3 cups boiling water to unclog your drain naturally.

▸ **CLEAN YOUR CAST-IRON PAN:** Using salt and olive oil, you'll get the pan clean and help condition the surface.

▸ **MAKE A SCRUB:** 1 cup baking soda plus liquid soap along with 15 drops organic eucalyptus essential oil makes a soft scrub. Or, dip a sponge in a mixture of ½ cup baking soda with 1 cup liquid soap and 20 drops organic lavender essential oil.

▸ **CLEAN YOUR SINK:** Use distilled white vinegar to dissolve soap scum and buildup from minerals, and to kill bacteria.

▸ **CLEAN YOUR MIRROR:** Use a 1:2 ratio of white distilled vinegar to water. Organic essential oils like lavender and eucalyptus add fragrance and boost antibacterial properties.

▸ **POLISH YOUR FURNITURE:** 1 cup olive oil plus ½ cup fresh lemon juice on a rag does the trick!

▸ **MAKE AN ALL-PURPOSE CLEANER:** Peel 3 large oranges and place the orange peels in a quart-size mason jar. Fill the jar three-quarters full with distilled white vinegar; put the lid on and let sit for two weeks. Then pour the mixture into a spray bottle or dip your towel into the liquid and use it to clean. Your house will smell amazing.

▸ **FRESHEN THE AIR:** Add your favorite combination of cinnamon, cloves, citrus peel, essential oils, and flower petals to water on the stovetop and simmer for a nontoxic air freshener.

TIPS ON HOUSECLEANING

▸ Open your windows when cleaning so you don't trap anything inside.

▸ Dust often, as dust can contribute to asthma and allergies and encourages mold growth.

▸ Use organic cotton gloves.

▸ Use chemical-free microfiber cloths that cling to dust and lint until they're washed.

safe cleaning tools

▸ Chemical-free microfiber cloths

▸ Scrub brush

▸ Glass spray bottles

▸ Glass jars and lids

▸ Measuring cups and spoons

▸ An old toothbrush—great for grout

▸ HEPA-filtered vacuum to clean carpet and upholstery

▸ Rags made from old T-shirts or towels

- Avoid antibacterial products because they are filled with chemicals that seep into your skin. Opt for natural antibacterial products like witch hazel.

- Dispose of old toxic chemical cleaners safely by taking them to your local hazardous waste facility. Do not pour them down the drain.

- Always remove your shoes when entering your home. Dirt, bacteria, feces, lead dust, chemicals, pesticides, animal dander, allergenic dust, and other things that are carried on your shoes can come into your home—and carpets trap chemicals. This is especially dangerous in homes with children and pets that play on the floor.

- If you are allergic or sensitive to any ingredients, you shouldn't have it in your cleaning supplies. If you have celiac disease or you're sensitive to gluten, avoid household products that contain gluten. If you are allergic to thyme or rosemary, avoid those ingredients in your cleaning supplies.

- Donate and recycle old clothing, furniture, and clutter.

CARPETS

Carpets contain harmful chemicals, including volatile organic compounds (VOCs), flame retardants, anti-stain ingredients, and the toxic chemicals in glue binders and rubber cushioning, all of which can release fumes into the air for months. That new carpet smell comes from a carcinogen called p-Dichlorobenzene, derived from 4-Phenylcyclohexene, which also gives off-gas fumes.

This doesn't mean you have to go without carpet, however. Try taking the following steps to reduce toxic exposure from the fibers under your feet.

- Look for carpets and rugs made of natural fibers like hemp, jute, or wool. Bonus: Natural fibers help absorb toxins in the air.

- Buy from eco-conscious companies that have reduced chemicals in their products.

- Watch out for the carpet pad, too—it contains just as many chemicals.

- Deodorize carpets with baking soda and let sit for forty minutes before vacuuming. You could add eucalyptus, lavender, and rosewood essential oils; mix and put on carpet for twenty minutes, and then vacuum up for a fragrant fix.

- Rent a steam cleaner and steam carpets at least twice a year.

- Use a dehumidifier in a damp room to prevent the growth of mildew.

- For food and wine spills, use cold water, seltzer, and salt on a towel; remember to blot, not rub.

- For grease stains on carpeting, use boiling water, and then sprinkle with baking soda.

LAUNDRY

There are many harmful chemicals in laundry products. Detergent can contain phosphates, chlorine, synthetic dyes and fragrances, and petroleum products. Dryer sheets use synthetic fragrances that contain benzyl acetate, benzyl alcohol, and terpines, all of which are toxic. (Some are even carcinogenic.)

I know you're all familiar with the "fresh" scent of Snuggle coming out of your washer and dryer, but I'm sorry to say that's toxic, folks. The fragrance in laundry detergent is made to cling to clothes. Your pants and shirts and other items absorb these harmful chemicals and then deposit them on your skin. Reduce your toxic exposure with these healthier alternatives:

- Use nontoxic laundry liquid. See page 381 for brands.

- Use ½ cup baking soda per load of wash—it acts as a natural fabric softener.

▸ Instead of bleach (it is harmful when inhaled and can react with water to form toxic by-products), use a cup of distilled white vinegar to whiten whites and brighten colors.

▸ Make your own dryer sheets with sponges, small pieces of towel, or wool balls that can be purchased from Molly's Suds. (See page 381 for more information.)

▸ Scale down your dry cleaning by washing your delicate clothing using a nontoxic cleaner at home. If you do dry clean, go organic, or go to a green dry cleaner and try wet cleaning. I send my clothes out to an organic cleaner in New York City. If your items come home with plastic bags, remove them outside or in the garage. If you use traditional dry-cleaning methods, let the clothes air out for three days before placing them in your closet.

▸ Change bed linens weekly. Wash sheets in hot water and dry on high to kill dust mites.

UNWANTED PESTS

We're surrounded by microorganisms every day. These include bacteria, viruses, fungi, and more. Our homes are also warm and comfy places for insects that carry diseases with them. Give them an inch and they'll take a mile, as the saying goes, so it's important to take precautions to make sure they don't gain a foothold strong enough to make you sick.

Clean up food and drinks as soon as possible. Seal up your food and store it within an hour of cooking. Throw out makeup and skin-care products that have passed their expiration dates, or that you've had for more than three to six months. (No more than ninety days for eye products like mascara and liner.)

Remove clutter, and get into the cracks and crevices where these little bugs hide. Use mattress and pillow encasings that keep dust mites out, and avoid feather pillows and comforters. For your closets and drawers where you store clothing, use cedar chips instead of mothballs. Use organic peppermint essential oil for rodents and ants: combine 1 cup water with 1 tablespoon organic peppermint oil, and spray where ants are getting in. Cedar oil also works great as a nontoxic pest repellant.

BASEMENT AND GARAGE

These areas can be full of potentially toxic things like antifreeze, old batteries, cleaning chemicals, old paint, stains and varnishes, motor oil, herbicides, pesticides, insecticides, glues, gasoline, and more. Get rid of the products you no longer need (be sure to dispose of them properly), and store the rest out of reach of children and pets. Do your best to seal them so the fumes aren't seeping into your lungs when you breathe.

BEDDING MATERIALS

Many sheets, blankets, comforters, and pillows are made with synthetic chemicals in their material and dyes. Wrinkle-free sheets contain perfluorinated chemicals (PFCs). Bedspreads, comforters, sheets, and blankets may contain stain-resistant water-repellent finishes. Sheets may also contain flame retardants, which have been linked to neurological damage, endocrine disruption, and even cancer. Other toxins may be added to make sheets softer, and these can emit formaldehyde gas. Long-term exposure to formaldehyde can cause neurotoxicity, cancer, and liver toxicity.

Nonorganic cotton sheets and towels are made with conventional cotton, which is a crop that accounts for a ton of insecticide use, including some of the planet's most hazardous chemicals. Manufacturers often use dyes derived from petroleum in a highly polluting process that leaves chemicals gushing into waterways and habitats, and clinging to you and your products.

Replace towels, sheets, and bedding with organic options. Look for unbleached, untreated, 100 percent organic cotton, linen, hemp, and bamboo, which are eco-friendly. For pillows, use wool, buckwheat, or organic cotton fillers. At the end of the day, remove the chemicals from your body by showering before you get into bed because everything that touches your skin during the day is transferred to your pillow and sheets.

Here are some good go-to companies that provide organic home goods. You can find more on page 380.

▸ **SHEETS AND COMFORTERS:** The Company Store, West Elm, Plover Organic, Pure Rest, CB2, Anna Sova, and Coyuchi. TheUltimateGreenStore.com and NoFeathersPlease.com also have great selections.

▸ **MATTRESSES:** Pure Rest, Savvy Rest, White Lotus, Cozy Pure, Heart of Vermont, Keetsa, and Hastens are great eco-friendly mattress sources.

▸ **TOWELS:** Coyuchi, Gaiam, and Pottery Barn are all great choices.

PAINT

Adding color to your walls? Many paints contain VOCs that may have an adverse effect on your health. Conventional paints also produce fumes that pollute indoor air and contribute to outdoor air pollution.

To reduce your exposure, remodel with nontoxic, low- or no-VOC paint. Many home supply stores carry a wide selection of options, such as the Benjamin Moore nontoxic line, Natura. You can find other options online.

SHOWER CURTAINS

Vinyl shower curtains are made with polyvinyl chloride (PVC), otherwise known as plastic number 3 or vinyl, a plastic that can release hormone-disrupting phthalates into the air. These gases can linger in your home for up to four months.

The solution is easy—simply avoid PVC shower curtains, and use hemp or organic cotton shower curtains instead. Brands such as Pottery Barn, Coyuchi, and Gaiam have linen or hemp curtains and liners, too.

keep your home smelling fresh

Slice 2 large lemons. Add 3 sprigs fresh rosemary and 1 teaspoon pure vanilla extract in 2 quarts water in a saucepan on the stovetop. Bring to a boil and then simmer. As the water evaporates, add more to keep the lemons and rosemary covered at all times. This will make your home smell beautiful.

In winter, simmer orange slices, cinnamon sticks, and allspice in fresh orange juice. Bonus: You can drink it, too! Save the peels from oranges you eat to simmer in the water.

THE AIR YOU BREATHE

You may be inhaling toxins in your home without even knowing it. Cigarette smoke, dust, pet dander, lead, off-gassing from carpets, formaldehyde from particle board, chemicals in aerosol sprays, unclean air ducts, fumes from cleaning products, benzene, carbon monoxide, asbestos, flame retardants, and more can all contribute to air that's unhealthy to breathe.

The Environmental Protection Agency (EPA) states that indoor levels of pollutants can be two to five times higher than outdoor air pollutants. These pollutants can cause side effects like watery eyes, brain fog, lethargy, headaches, rashes, and skin irritation. They can even damage the body's defense functions.

Most of these chemicals come from human sources and are the result of heavy industry, car exhaust, wood- and coal burning, paints, and plastic. Not only will you feel the pollutants in your lungs, but they can also disrupt your cellular metabolic function and harm your ability to handle reactions.

‣ Consider investing in an air filter and/or air purifier, especially if you live in an urban area or in a region where you know the air quality is poor. See page 380 for my suggested brand.

‣ Clean air ducts, vents, and filters frequently.

‣ Allow your home to breathe by opening windows and creating ventilation.

‣ Houseplants are great toxin fighters. Invest in several and place them around your home and office. (See sidebar below.)

‣ Dust often, and regularly clean window treatments and coverings.

‣ Eliminate insults to indoor air quality—which means no smoking indoors.

‣ Never char food inside—invest in an outdoor grill, and don't grill your food until it's blackened. That creates carcinogenic chemicals that you then absorb when you eat the blackened part.

‣ Replace all your toxic candles—which can emit toxic fumes—with natural beeswax candles.

‣ Avoid synthetic air fresheners—they emit toxic fumes—and use essential oils instead.

---

detoxifying houseplants

If you can't afford an air purifier, a couple of houseplants can work wonders. The following are known for their ability to clean indoor air:

‣ English Ivy	‣ Spider Plant	‣ Chinese Evergreen
‣ Gerbera Daisy	‣ Bamboo Plant	
‣ Peace Lily	‣ Weeping Fig	

---

hidden heavy metals

I've been dealing with toxic levels of heavy metals in my body for years, but it wasn't until I started working with Functional Medicine doctors that I realized it. A few years ago, I was tested for metals, and found my levels were sky-high due to chemicals in our water supply, conventional food, and air. That was the day I went 100 percent organic, cleaned out my home, and started using a water and air filter.

Take a look at the chart below to see how you can start to reduce your exposure to heavy metals. No need to be overwhelmed, but you can make small changes starting today. Look for aluminum-free deodorants and cookware, for example, and get a quality water filter for your kitchen sink and shower. In a year, you'll have removed many of these toxic sources from your life. For those heavy metals that are already inside you (we all have some!), you'll find solutions on page 31 to help flush them out.

COMMON SOURCES OF HEAVY METALS

heavy metal ▸	*how we are exposed to them*
Aluminum* ▸	antacids, antiperspirants, aluminum cookware, automobile exhaust, tobacco smoke, dental amalgams, baking powder, foil, cooking utensils
Arsenic ▸	air pollution, wood preservatives in lumber and playgrounds, wallpaper dye and plaster, colored chalk, herbicides, cereals, auto exhaust, fruit juice (apple, pear), grains (rice)
Cadmium ▸	Teflon, tap water, cigarettes, batteries, ceramic glazes, art supplies, fungicides, plastic, paint pigments, processed food, soft drinks, refined wheat flour
Chromium ▸	stainless-steel cookware, tobacco smoke
Copper ▸	copper pipes, dental alloys, insecticides, swimming pools, chocolate, soy products, gold dental fillings and crowns, some cooking utensils
Lead ▸	auto exhaust, canned fruits and juices, tobacco smoke, cosmetics, household dust, lead-glazed pottery, paint, pesticides, PVC plastics, toys, candy, old paint, tap water, candle wicks, toothpaste, stained glass
Mercury ▸	seafood, dental amalgams, some vaccines and medicine, fungicides, old paint, pesticides, wood preservatives, air conditioner filters, felt, cosmetics, fabric softener, skin creams, tattoos, batteries
Nickel ▸	tobacco smoke, auto exhaust, oysters, stainless-steel cookware, tea, nuts, vegetable shortening, chocolate, hair spray, batteries, hydrogenated oils, coins, jewelry

*Aluminum is not a heavy metal, but it is a metal we are commonly exposed to that can increase the risk of health problems.

FURNITURE

Inexpensive particleboard, aka pressed wood, is often made from isocyanate glues and formaldehyde. Both are toxic and release potentially dangerous fumes. Upholstered furniture made with polyurethane foam often has brominated and chlorinated flame retardants. These have been linked with fertility problems, learning disabilities, obesity, autism, and even cancer.

Increasingly, industrial production depends upon VOCs. These compounds, such as formaldehyde, are found in many glues, vinyl products, paints, fuels, carpet, and plastics. For instance, furniture made of particleboard often contains formaldehyde in the glue, while the "new car smell" is actually that of volatile organic compounds in the paint, leather, carpet, and glue.

VOCs can produce a host of allergic symptoms, such as itchy throat, headaches, brain fog, and confusion. At higher concentrations, it is especially harmful to human health. To reduce your exposure, avoid buying cheap particleboard furniture. If new furniture is too expensive, spend some time at your local thrift store or garage sale (but be sure to check for mold). You might be surprised at the high-quality things you can find.

MOLD

Mold is common in any damp area in the home, such as bathrooms and basements.

People who are sensitive to it may experience eye and skin irritation, nasal stuffiness, wheezing, rashes, and asthma. Some molds produce toxic substances that can cause immune problems or serious infections.

While black mold is visible to the eye, many other forms of mold are not as easy to spot and will build up in humid areas. Mold can also be ingested when we eat certain foods, such as peanuts, pistachios, dried fruits, mushrooms, and moldy cheese (like Roquefort blue cheese and Brie). Mold-sensitive individuals should avoid these.

Clean up mold growth with tea tree oil, grapefruit extract, and distilled white vinegar, and prevent further growth by putting moisture absorbers or dehumidifiers in all damp areas of your home.

CROSS-CHECK YOUR LIFESTYLE

Detoxing your home and your lifestyle takes time. It's taken me many years. Yes, years.

It doesn't have to be scary or alarming, so don't go running through your home in panic mode. That'll just mess with your adrenals and cortisol, which isn't going to do your detox organs any good, now, is it?

Over the past few years, I've kicked an ever-growing list of toxic products from my home and educated myself on what's safe. I've used the Environmental Working Group's (EWG) Guide to Healthy Cleaning and their Skin Deep Cosmetics Database (ewg.org) to help me make smart choices and toss the majority of the products that missed the mark.

Detoxing your life does require that you take a good look at not just what you're eating, but how you're living. Nontoxic personal care and cleaning products, a clean living space, and a clean working space can go a long way toward diffusing any symptoms you may be experiencing and helping you to feel more energy and vitality. Plus, you'll be lessening your toxic load, which can have positive effects on your long-term health.

simple detox strategies that work

‣ Lower your pesticide, herbicide, antibiotic, and growth hormone intake by eating certified organic.

‣ Have a bowel movement in the morning; drink hot water with fresh lemon and dandelion root tea to help stimulate your digestive system and liver.

‣ Take high-quality multistrain probiotics (see page 380 for brand suggestions).

‣ Eat more fiber from whole foods like fresh fruits and veggies. We all need real fiber (not the fake, factory-made fiber you'll find in a Fiber One bar) for optimum detox. Fiber helps prevent reabsorption of toxins (and hormones) while ushering them through your bowels and out of your body.

‣ Eat more prebiotic-rich foods (see page 20 for examples). Add fermented foods (probiotic-rich foods) such as kimchi, chickpea miso, my easy No-Soy Chickpea Miso Soup (page 187), and sauerkraut.

‣ Create a routine so your body has a natural rhythm.

‣ Pay attention to your eating habits, and change them according to how you feel.

‣ Eat every three to four hours with healthy snacks (page 139) to keep your blood sugar in balance. You need healthy fats (avocado), protein (beans), healthy carbohydrates (gluten-free whole grains), and fiber (vegetables) at every meal.

‣ Use a calendar on your phone or computer to remind you when to eat, drink, stretch, and take your supplements.

‣ Light a beeswax candle, close your eyes, and sit in stillness for a few minutes before bed or upon rising.

‣ Try a few yoga poses in the morning and evening.

how to
PREP IT, COOK IT,
AND MAKE IT TASTE
(really) GOOD

For many of you, "cooking" is synonymous with "changing the oil in your car" or "filing your taxes." It may sound boring, tedious, and really, really hard, but it doesn't have to be that way!

You can create delicious, satisfying meals without having to go to culinary school. Plus, you can have fun while doing it. All you need are a few simple skills and rules of thumb, and you'll be well on your way to creating flavorful and nourishing food that you'd be hard-pressed to find in any store or restaurant.

GETTING STARTED

Before you turn on the oven or whip out your cutting board, skim through the following tips. They'll come in handy as you navigate the kitchen. A few things to remember:

▸ **FORGET THAT COOKING SHOULD BE FANCY.** Less is always more. Start with fresh whole foods and then build on those flavors with pantry staples like raw nuts, seeds, olive or coconut oils, vinegars, herbs, and spices. Or just keep it simple with sea salt and freshly ground black pepper. The better the quality of the ingredients you use, the less you'll need to jazz them up to make them taste amazing.

▸ **LEARN TO COOK SEASONALLY.** Fresh fruits and veggies picked at their peak are tasty and economical. Become a regular at your farmers' market or shop in the local organic produce aisle at your grocery store. Trust me: Your dishes will look and taste ten times better.

▸ **GOING GLUTEN-FREE, REFINED SUGAR–FREE, DAIRY-FREE, SOY-FREE, CORN-FREE, EGG-FREE, AND PROCESSED FOOD–FREE ISN'T AS HARD AS YOU THINK!** Take inventory of the foods you'll miss most, and then find new foods or ingredients that will scratch that itch. Since many "whatever-free" products in the stores contain additives and fillers that cause inflammation and might bother you just as much as the classic triggers (gluten, dairy, etc.), your best bet is to learn how to whip up tasty substitutes at home. This book is brimming with ideas for new, healthy versions of your old standbys. And remember: The best anti-inflammatory foods are the ones that are naturally free of all the junk and "sawdust," as I call it.

▸ **CUSTOMIZATION IS KEY.** Feel free to swap ingredients. Don't like arugula? Add finely chopped dandelion leaves. Not interested in Swiss chard? Add collard greens. Not only is everyone's digestive system unique enough to require special care, but our taste buds differ as well.

▸ **BECOME YOUR OWN CHEF.** Just as no two blueberries taste alike, your kale or spinach may not taste like mine, and that's okay. Produce can vary in flavor, size, color, sweetness, and bitterness. For this reason, as well as variations in altitude, moisture content of food, and, of course, the difference in cooking tools in the kitchen, no two dishes come out exactly the same. Always taste your recipe as you go along and don't be afraid to make adjustments. Your balsamic vinegar may be thicker or stronger than mine, and your cashews may not have much flavor to them while mine were incredibly fresh and flavorful. Tweak your recipes based on your needs and you'll be much happier in the kitchen.

KEEP IT CLEAN

To prep your produce and make sure your kitchen surfaces and utensils stay clean during and after meal preparation, you can easily make your own homemade kitchen cleaners. They're less expensive than store-bought versions and contain none of those icky ingredients.

My favorite cleaning "recipes" that are easy on the wallet and the environment are listed on the next page. If you don't want to go the DIY route, check out page 381 for a list of brands that make high-quality, nontoxic cleaning products. I've also got tips for detoxing your cleaning supplies on page 82.

For Leafy Greens and Fresh Herbs

1   cup distilled white vinegar

3   cups cold purified water, plus more for rinsing

Combine the vinegar and water in a large bowl. Add your greens or herbs to the bowl and allow them to sit for 5 to 10 minutes, depending on how dirty or sandy they are. Rinse with a bit more purified water and pat dry with an organic cotton towel.

For Fruit and Veggies

1   tablespoon freshly squeezed lemon juice

2   tablespoons distilled white vinegar

1   cup cold purified water, plus more for rinsing

2   tablespoons sea salt

A few drops of grapefruit seed extract (optional, but great for candida)

Add all the ingredients to a glass spray bottle, shake, and spray on produce. Then rinse with purified water.

Easy All-Purpose Cleaner

1   cup water

2   teaspoons castile soap, such as Dr. Bronner's

15 drops organic essential oil, such as those made by the Aura Cacia brand; lemongrass, lavender, and lemon are great for grease in the kitchen—I also love to use pine, tea tree, eucalyptus, rosemary, and grapefruit

Mix all the ingredients in a glass spray bottle and store in a cool, dark place so the essential oils don't oxidize in the sunlight. Shake well before using.

Simple Vinegar Cleaner

½   cup water

½   cup organic apple cider vinegar or distilled white vinegar

15 drops organic essential oil (see recipe above for my recommendations)

Mix all the ingredients in a glass spray bottle and store in a cool, dark place so the essential oils don't oxidize in the sunlight. Shake well before using.

PREP WITHOUT STRESS

Changing your lifestyle may seem pretty drastic, but trust me when I say revamping your pantry, your meals, and your environment will lead to a much richer life experience. Start by turning your obstacles into opportunities and create your own shortcuts for how you want to prep your weekly meals and snacks.

▸ **PREPARE YOUR GRAINS:** Make a batch of gluten-free grains on Sunday night to use throughout the week. See page 102 for serving suggestions.

> ▸ Reheat a few scoops of any grain in a cast-iron skillet with olive oil, sea salt, freshly ground black pepper, and herbs for an easy 5 minute meal.

> ▸ Make a comforting bowl of breakfast cereal by warming up leftover rice, millet, quinoa, or other grains (on page 100) in a pot on the stovetop with my nut and seed "mylks" (page 290) and cinnamon. (See Overnight Black Rice and Berry Breakfast Bowl, page 138.) Serve with fresh fruit, honey, or maple syrup.

> ▸ Toss your grains with beans, lentils, my hummus recipes (pages 301–303), diced veggies, olives, or my dairy-free nut cheeses (pages 307–310). Serve chilled as a cold grain salad or warm as a pilaf. See my unique Serving Ideas for Cooked Gluten-Free Whole Grains (page 102) to spark your imagination.

▸ **FLAVOR IT UP:** Sauté a batch of Super Soft Caramelized Red Onions (page 272) or my Easy No-Foil Roasted Garlic (page 329) for quick flavors that can be added to almost any savory meal.

▸ **TOSS IT UP QUICK:** Grab a bag of prewashed organic salad greens for a quick meal starter. Add legumes or beans, whole grains, and a few of my tasty toppings (like my Gluten-Free Herbed Croutons, page 190) for an easy, last-minute meal.

▸ **BRING ON THE BEANS:** Cook a batch of beans and legumes on Sunday night so you have them prepped for the week. I cook beans from scratch and try to avoid cans because of my heavy-metal accumulation, but I know many of my clients enjoy a quick meal using canned beans. Just make sure you purchase BPA-free cans (see page 381 for brands). All you have to do—whether preparing the beans yourself or buying them canned—is heap them onto dark leafy green salads, add them to soups, toss them with veggies, or serve them mixed with grains sprinkled with sea salt, pepper, lemon zest, nuts or seeds, spices, herbs—and a drizzle of olive oil. See my chart on page 99 for how to cook beans.

▸ **THINK AHEAD:** When preparing your breakfast, lunch, and dinner, think ahead to what you can make for your next meal or the next day to save you time. Leave grains, nuts, and beans to soak, or prep some chopped veggies and store in glass jars in your fridge. See my meal plan (page 371) to make your weekly meals run smoothly.

▸ **LAY ON THE SAUCES:** Keep homemade marinades, salad dressings, dips, and sauces in the fridge. They come in handy for assembling quick meals. Check out Dip It, Spread It, Dress It (page 300) to create condiments to complement tonight's dinner.

▸ **MAKE YOUR OWN TOMATO SAUCE:** It's not as hard as you think to make a pot of tomato sauce (see my Heirloom Tomato Sauce on page 318 and my Sun-Dried Tomato Sauce on page 320), and it's so much better for you than the store-bought options that are loaded with added refined sugar and other gross ingredients. Make a big pot of sauce regularly and keep leftovers in the freezer. All you'll need to do is thaw it and toss with gluten-free pasta, veggies, or whole grains.

▸ **ROAST THOSE VEGGIES:** Roasting a bunch of cruciferous veggies like Brussels sprouts, cauliflower, and broccoli along with root veggies like sweet potatoes, parsnips, and rutabagas will provide you with a snack, side dish, or even an entrée at a moment's notice. Plus, having leftovers on hand to toss into my salads (pages 199–217) is a great idea. Try my Rosemary Roasted Carrots and Beets (page 278).

▸ **MAKE ONE THE STAR:** Build a meal around one star dish, not several. All the main recipes in this book—like my Big Broccoli Rabe Veggie Pasta (page 219) or Spring Veggie Paella (page 221)—are hearty enough to be a whole meal. You can also pair them with a basic salad like my Simple Life Cucumber Summer Herb Salad (page 203).

▸ **BE A WEEKEND WARRIOR:** Use your Sundays to make versatile, high-flavor components to simplify your weekday cooking. Try my Oven-Roasted Cherry Tomatoes with Poppy Seeds (page 283) and Grain-Free Protein-Packed Breadcrumbs (page 283), or my roasted nut recipes (pages 140–142).

▸ **KEEP IT HANDY:** Make Amie's Grain-Free Granola (page 121) and store in mason jars with a scoop. You can use it anytime for a quick protein boost when you're short on time for a snack or breakfast.

▸ **BE READY FOR UNEXPECTED GUESTS:** Make my Happy Lemon Coconut Balls (page 351) and Delightful Almond Butter Cups (page 354) once a month and store them in airtight containers in the freezer. Defrost them when you need a sweet fix or last-minute treat for unexpected company.

▸ **TRY THIS NO-COOK COOKING METHOD FOR KALE:** It's called "massaging." Strip the leaves from the stems and reserve the stems for another recipe. Slice the leaves by stacking them, rolling them tightly into a burrito shape, and then thinly slicing from one end (also known as a chiffonade). Add the sliced leaves to a mixing bowl, drizzle with extra-virgin olive oil, and then massage the kale as though you were kneading bread. Massage for 1 to 2 minutes or until the kale deepens in color and gets silky in texture.

SAVE YOUR SCRAPS

As you're cooking, the parts of the veggies you're likely to toss away can be as tasty and nutritious as the ones you're already eating. Putting everything to use helps you get the biggest bang for your buck (which goes a long way when you're eating organic). Try these tips for making good use of your scraps.

▸ **SWISS CHARD STEMS:** These are loaded with gluta-mine, an amino acid that helps the immune system. Tie the stems in bundles of 8 to 10 with kitchen twine, and braise them in my Cleansing Detox Veggie Broth (page 194) with honey and raw garlic for 30 minutes.

▸ **CELERY LEAVES:** These have five times more magnesium and calcium than the stalks. They're also a rich source of vitamin C and antioxidants. Finely chop the leaves with parsley and stir into salsa, or use as a garnish for pasta and whole-grain dishes. Add to my Cleansing Detox Veggie Broth (page 194).

▸ **ORANGE PEEL:** The peel contains over four times the fiber of the fruit inside. Grate and sprinkle the zest on veggies, green salads, or whole grains.

▸ **LEMON PEEL:** If a recipe calls for just the juice, save the peel and chop it up to add to marinades, or dry it out for a few days and then use it in your tea. Simmer peels with olive oil in a saucepan for an infused olive oil, and then transfer to a glass jar and store it in your fridge for up to a week. Drizzle over salads or vegetable dishes.

▸ **BROCCOLI LEAVES:** These babies deliver a boat-load of vitamin A. Don't toss them into the trash! Cook the leaves as you would spinach. Blanch them in boiling water, and then sauté them with extra-virgin olive oil, minced garlic, and sea salt.

▸ **BROCCOLI STEMS:** These taste like mild broccoli with a slight cabbage flavor. Add them to salads and stir-fries for a little crunch, or slow cook them in my Heirloom Tomato Sauce (page 318) to bring out their sweet flavors.

▸ **RADISH GREENS:** These taste like a pungent spinach or Swiss chard. Sauté them with extra-virgin olive oil and minced garlic for an easy side dish, add them to pasta, or top pizza with them.

▸ **CARROT TOPS:** These taste like peppery parsley. Chop them up and sprinkle on soups, salads, or grilled veggies as a garnish, or perk up your pesto by using them in place of basil.

▸ **ONION SKINS:** The papery wrapping contains more antioxidants than the onion itself. Simmer white and red onion skins in stocks, soups, and stews for flavor, and then discard them before serving. Try them in my Cleansing Detox Veggie Broth (page 194).

▸ **FRESH HERBS:** All too often recipes call for a tablespoon of this herb or a few sprigs of that herb, leaving the rest to turn brown in your fridge. Get out those ice cube trays and make flavored cubes with extra-virgin olive oil (see pages 293–296). Freeze and then use the frozen cubes to toss into stir-fries for flavor.

▸ **VEGGIE BROTH:** Freeze leftover broth in ice cube trays and transfer to a sealed container. When you're making a pot of rice or grains, pop in a cube or two for a flavor boost. You can also add the cubes to a hot skillet when making sautéed greens or mashed sweet potatoes.

▸ **BLANCHING OR STEAMING LIQUID:** This flavor- and nutrient-rich liquid that's left over from blanching or steaming veggies is great to reuse for cooking beans and grains. Store in a sealed container in the fridge, or sip on it served warm in a mug with a dash of sea salt and pepper.

LOVE YOUR LEFTOVERS

When you invest in quality, organic food, you'll want to get the most mileage out of your ingredients. Here's how to give new life to those leftovers:

▸ For soup: Allow it to cool, and then transfer to large (half-quart or one-quart) glass mason jars and either store in the fridge for up to five days, or in the freezer. If you freeze the soup, leave 2 to 3 inches at the top to avoid cracking before adding the lid. To defrost, fill a bowl with warm water and place your jar in the water to defrost. No need for a microwave—the food will defrost in 15 minutes.

▸ Create "everything-but-the-kitchen-sink" meals. Save money by using up what's in the fridge to make burritos, tacos, DIY Buddha bowls (like my Humble Sriracha Roasted Wild Rice Buddha Bowl on page 253), salads, and soups.

▸ Make tomorrow's lunch with tonight's leftovers. Turn leftovers into a quick salad, stir-fry, wrap, or sandwich. Layer them in large mason jars by placing ingredients like quinoa and veggies in the jar, but leave out the dressing. Cut a piece of parchment paper about 8 inches square and place it over the mouth of the jar. Push down the middle to form a little cup. Making sure the edges of the parchment don't fall into the jar, pour the dressing into the cup, and twist on the jar's lid. When it's time to eat, pour the dressing into a bowl along with the salad ingredients. Toss and enjoy.

five-minute salads

Healthy, gluten-free, whole-grain salads are easy to freestyle. Use these tips to build your own bowl of goodness with what you have on hand in your pantry and fridge. All you have to do is add your desired ingredients, season with sea salt and freshly ground black pepper, taste, and adjust the seasonings. See Serving Ideas for Cooked Gluten-Free Whole Grains (page 102) for more inspiration.

▸ Layer crisp, raw veggies with cooked ones. Shave some veggies thinly (like carrots), grate others, and try some chopped. Veggie variety, different textures and colors make the best salad combos!

▸ Use fresh herbs like chives, parsley, dill, and cilantro to add color and flavor.

▸ Add toasted nuts and seeds for a crunch (page 108).

▸ Make a simple dressing using freshly squeezed lemon juice, extra-virgin olive oil, sea salt, pepper, and apple cider vinegar. Brighten things up with freshly grated lemon zest.

▸ Throw in a theme—use shredded red cabbage, lime wedges, scallions, and sliced radishes for a Mexican vibe, or use olives, spinach, my dairy-free nut cheeses (pages 307–310), and extra-virgin olive oil for a Mediterranean feel.

SOAKING AND COOKING BEANS, GLUTEN-FREE WHOLE GRAINS, NUTS, AND SEEDS

Do you know how to soak nuts, seeds, beans, and grains? It's a fantastic skill to have when you want to eat clean; the benefits are amazing. Soaking activates nutrients in foods, which means all those vitamins and live enzymes are easier for your body to digest and use. It also encourages the growth of friendly bacteria in your gut, which boosts immunity (because almost 80 percent of your immune system is in your gut).

Soaking reduces cooking time for grains and beans. It also makes nuts and seeds easier to blend to a creamy consistency, which is perfect for your smoothies, my fresh nut and seed "mylks" (page 290), dairy-free nut cheeses (pages 307–310), desserts (page 330), soups, salads, and sauces.

For more specific soaking guidelines for nuts, grains, and beans see pages 108, 101, and 98. In the meantime, here are a few handy-dandy tips to get you started:

▸ **USE THEM RIGHT AWAY:** Soaked nuts, seeds, beans, and grains need to be used immediately in recipes such as soups, milks, smoothies, dairy-free nut cheeses, desserts, and creams.

▸ **MEASURE THE LIQUID:** Most soaked grains only need a 1:1 water or broth ratio when cooking because the grain will fill with water from the soaking process.

▸ **START A PRE-BEDTIME SOAKING ROUTINE:** I do most of my soaking before I go to bed so everything's ready to go in the morning. Just place everything in a glass jar or bowl and cover with water, and then let it sit overnight. In the morning, drain well and give a quick but thorough rinse.

▸ **THE SHORT SOAK:** If you're short on time and don't have hours to soak, you can put your nuts, seeds, grains, or beans in a bowl of boiling water (enough to cover) and let them soak for 15 to 20 minutes. Drain and rinse a few times. This won't give you the nutritional benefit of soaking for hours because the hot water will destroy the live enzymes, but it will soften them up enough so they are ready for immediate use in recipes.

BEANS

Most people keep canned beans on hand because they're convenient, but many come in BPA-laden cans—yuck. I personally avoid canned beans because of the heavy metals that leach into the food.

Instead, I highly recommend using dried beans. It's a great way to sidestep the can, plus you'll save money, reduce your sodium intake, and get a lot more flavor. Try to use homemade cooked beans (they're easier than you think) for any recipe that calls for beans, and then freeze leftovers to use later in salads, dips, and soups.

My recipes using beans are measured in cups to suggest using fresh beans instead of canned beans, however, if you need to use canned beans, please purchase BPA-free cans. The measurement below will help you know how many cans to purchase at the grocery store:

1 (15.5-ounce) can of rinsed and drained beans is equal to 1½ cups of cooked beans.

Beans are high in indigestible sugars, so they are often known as a "gassy" food. If you cook them correctly, though—by adding a bay leaf, for example, a few strips of kombu (seaweed), or spices such as cumin during the cooking process—you can help break down those sugars.

Say adios to your bloated belly. Soaking is another great way to de-bloat, in addition to helping beans cook more quickly and evenly.

There are three methods for soaking beans:

1. Long-soak

2. Quick-soak

3. No-soak

As I mentioned, I highly recommend the long-soak method because it makes beans easier to digest. The other two methods are great if you're short on time.

1. **LONG-SOAK METHOD:** Rinse the beans and place them in a large glass bowl. Add enough cold water to cover by at least four inches. Leave them to soak at room temperature or in the fridge for at least six to eight hours or overnight. Add more water as necessary to keep the beans covered. Remove any beans that float to the top and do not add salt—salting beans before they are ready to cook will make them tough. When you're finished soaking, drain and rinse the beans, and then proceed with your recipe.

2. **QUICK-SOAK METHOD:** Rinse the beans and place them in a large pot. Add enough cold water to cover by at least four inches. Bring the water to a simmer over medium-high heat for three minutes but do not boil. Remove the pot from the heat, cover, and set aside for at least two hours. Drain, rinse, and then proceed with your recipe.

3. **NO-SOAK METHOD:** Rinse the beans and add them to boiling salted water (use sea salt). Allow the water to return to a boil, and then lower the heat to low and cover the pot. Cook the beans until tender. Add more water as needed to keep them covered. Test for doneness—they'll take approximately 40 minutes longer than the soaked bean cooking times (see chart on opposite page). Remove the beans from the heat and serve.

HOW TO COOK SOAKED BEANS AND LEGUMES

After soaking, rinse the beans and then place them in a large pot with enough cold water or organic vegetable broth to cover by at least four inches. You can also add flavor by tossing in one peeled and diced small white onion, one chopped garlic clove, two tablespoons finely chopped herbs, or any spices you like. (I love to add a pinch of ground cumin, a bay leaf, or a stick of cinnamon.)

I also love adding a few pinches of sea salt to the water to add flavor and minerals. You can add a 1-inch piece of kombu seaweed, which will help make the beans more digestible and will release into the cooking water.

To cook, make sure you use filtered water and not tap water; this will affect the cooking time. Please note that cooking times can vary drastically depending on the age of the beans or legumes. Bring the beans or legumes to a boil over high heat and skim off any foam or debris that rises to the top. Reduce the heat to low and partially cover the pot. The water should be at a simmer—boiling the beans will cause the skins to split.

Check the liquid every 30 minutes, adding more liquid if necessary to keep the beans or legumes fully covered by a couple inches. As they reach the end of their cooking time (see chart on the opposite page), test for doneness. They should be tender, but not mushy, and retain their shape.

Remove the pot from the heat and proceed with your recipe. Once cooked, eat beans within two days or freeze for up to three months. To store in the freezer, divide them up into batches and then defrost in the refrigerator.

NOTE: It's important to cool your beans completely before storing them so they don't grow bad bacteria in the container as it cools.

COOKING TIMES FOR SOAKED BEANS AND LEGUMES

dry beans and legumes	*amount* (Measured before soaking— yields 2½ to 3 cups when cooked)	*cooking time* (For soaked dried beans)
Black Beans	1 cup	30 minutes to 1 hour
Chickpeas (Garbanzo Beans)	1 cup	1½ to 2 hours
Cannellini Beans	1 cup	1 to 1½ hours
Fava Beans	1 cup	2½ to 3 hours
Great Northern Beans	1 cup	1 to 1½ hours
Kidney Beans	1 cup	1 to 1½ hours
Green or Brown Lentils	1 cup	No soaking required. 15 to 40 minutes
Red or Yellow Lentils	1 cup	No soaking required. 20 minutes
Lima Beans	1 cup	1 to 1½ hours
Navy Beans	1 cup	1½ to 2 hours
Split Peas	1 cup	No soaking required. 35 minutes to 1 hour

GLUTEN-FREE WHOLE GRAINS

To cook the most nutritious bowl of gluten-free grains, start by soaking them.

Like you, I don't have time to soak grains every day, so I'll soak them on Saturdays overnight and then cook them up on Sundays. If you don't have time to soak, don't fret. You don't have to. It's a personal preference, but it will speed up your cooking time; give you plumper, more evenly cooked grains; and help release all the enzymes and nutrients that aid digestion and gut healing.

Simply place the grains in a large bowl and cover with warm purified water (about a 2:1 ratio with ½ teaspoon sea salt). Cover with a light cloth for your desired soaking time, and then rinse thoroughly and drain well.

To help break the grains down further before cooking, soak them in an acidic solution (¼ teaspoon sea salt, or 1 tablespoon fresh lemon juice, apple cider vinegar, or coconut kefir per cup of water). For even more flavor and an extra antioxidant boost, consider adding ground spices like coriander, cumin, turmeric, or curry powder to the soaking liquid.

After soaking, draining, and rinsing well, transfer the grains to a large pot and add water (see chart on pages 104–107). You can add flavoring elements like the spices listed above to the cooking water, along with ½ tablespoon extra-virgin olive oil or organic coconut oil per cup of grains, or ¼ to ½ teaspoon sea salt per cup of grains.

Bring the water to a boil, reduce the heat to low, and cover. Allow the grains to simmer until tender, stirring often, until all the water has been absorbed. Remove the pot from the heat and let sit, covered, for 15 minutes. Remove the lid, fluff with a fork, and serve!

Types of Gluten-Free Whole Grains

If you're avoiding gluten, that doesn't mean you can't enjoy the gluten-free whole grains below and on pages 104–107. These gluten-free grains are delicious served hot, cold, or at room temperature. Check out my Serving Ideas for Cooked Gluten-Free Grains on page 102.

▸ **AMARANTH** is a tiny grain that can be enjoyed savory or sweet and even popped like popcorn (without the corn). See page 256 for my Perfectly Popped Amaranth Salad with Carrot Ginger Dressing. It has a mild peppery taste and is high in protein. (It's a complete protein, which means it contains all of the essential amino acids.) Serve it as a side dish mixed with fresh herbs and olive oil, as a warm porridge with Homemade Almond Mylk (page 290) and fresh berries or as a snack with Energizing Maple Cranberry Amaranth "Granola" (page 122).

▸ **BLACK RICE** is black in color and high in nutrients and antioxidants. It has a mild, nutty taste like wild rice and a similar fiber content. It turns a deep purple color when cooked and adds a beautiful pop of color to a dish. It's great for making a sweet morning porridge with cinnamon and almond milk, or for tossing into savory salads, burgers (check out my Mini Black Rice and Almond Sliders in Radicchio Cups on page 225), and pilafs. It has a rougher texture than brown rice, so don't expect a soft 'n' tender grain. Try my Overnight Black Rice and Berry Breakfast Bowl (page 138).

▸ **BROWN RICE** comes in short-, medium-, and long-grain varieties. It's more nutritious than white rice and is just as delicious on its own as it is mixed with fresh or dried fruits, fresh herbs, and veggies (with extra-virgin olive oil). It also adds heartiness to soups!

▸ **GLUTEN-FREE OATS** are a high-fiber whole grain that can be used for breakfast (see my Breadless Coconut Vanilla French Toast, page 129), desserts, stuffing recipes, and smoothies. If you are sensitive to gluten, it's important to find certified gluten-free oats to avoid cross-contamination. There are many types of oats, but my favorite are steel-cut oats, extra-thick rolled oats, and whole oats (groats). Steer clear of instant oatmeal, which often contains salt, sugar, and other additives. You can easily make your own oat flour (see page 39) for use in many of my desserts, like my Morning Glory Carrot Muffins (page 127).

▸ **MILLET** is a tiny, round, gluten-free grain that has a slightly grassy taste, sort of like quinoa. It can be white, gray, yellow, or red, and it reminds me of mashed potatoes! It's so easy to make and doesn't require presoaking. You can toast it first in a dry skillet for four minutes, tossing often, or just cook it as is. You can use less water for a fluffy grain, or more for a creamy porridge. Use millet for holiday stuffings, baked goods, or in place of mashed white potatoes! My Millet 'n' Veggie Breakfast Tacos: Two Ways (page 130) is a great way to introduce millet to your family.

▸ **QUINOA** is a small seed that's loaded with protein (it's another complete protein). It comes in white, red, and black varieties, which vary slightly in flavor. (I think red and black pack a little more punch, but all three are earthy and delicious!) Quinoa is naturally coated with a bitter substance called saponin, which keeps animals and birds from eating it while it's growing. That's why it's important to rinse quinoa well before cooking (at least one minute under running water). You'll actually see the saponin washing off in what looks like soapy bubbles. To serve cooked quinoa, simply combine with extra-virgin olive oil, veggies, and fresh herbs like basil for dinner, or make a savory porridge for breakfast with my Homemade Almond Mylk (page 290), toasted sesame seeds, and sliced avocado, or go sweet with dried fruit, cashews, and cinnamon.

▸ **TEFF** is a tiny grain (think the size of poppy seeds). You can find it in colors ranging from reddish brown to ivory. It's gluten-free and has a moist, melt-in-your-mouth texture that's both bitter and sweet. The ivory variety is a bit milder in flavor than the brown. Enjoy this grain as a porridge for breakfast with pure maple syrup, or add it to soup. I like serving teff with extra-virgin olive oil and fresh herbs, or tossing a few spoonfuls in my pancake or waffle batter for a nutrient boost.

▸ **WILD RICE** is actually a grass and takes longer to cook than white rice. It's delightfully chewy after cooking and has a distinct nutty flavor that I love. Pair wild rice with quinoa and serve it as a pilaf, stuff it into mushroom caps for an easy holiday appetizer, add it to soups, or toss it with chopped kale, fresh fruit, and toasted walnuts. Check out my Antioxidant Wild Rice Flatbread with Glorious Chickpea Garlic Sauce (page 227) for a creative new way to use wild rice instead of flours.

TIPS FOR COOKING GLUTEN-FREE WHOLE GRAINS

▸ **IN GENERAL:** The directions on pages 104–107 are all for cooking 1 cup of grains. Every brand of grain, pot size, and stovetop heat will differ, so if you need to add a little more water during the cooking time, you can add it anytime. Always add ¼ teaspoon sea salt toward the end of the cooking time. Check grains for doneness by cutting a few of the grains in half: they should be one color throughout. Always let grains steam for 10 minutes

after cooking. When using a strainer, let the grains sit in the strainer for five minutes before serving.

▸ **WHICH GRAINS TO SOAK:** Quick-cooking grains like millet and quinoa do not have to be soaked. Slow-cooking grains such as whole gluten-free oats and rice benefit from soaking. They cook more evenly, making them more plump and tender. Soaking can also reduce cooking time and aid digestion. If you forget to soak or have no time, you can cook the grains a little longer, or use the quick-soak method that is also used for beans: Put the grains in a pot, cover with an inch of water, and bring to a boil. Cook for two minutes, remove from the heat, cover, and let stand for one hour. Drain and cook as directed in the recipe.

▸ **HOW TO SOAK:** Combine the grains and full amount of warm water along with an acid, such as kombucha, raw unfiltered apple cider vinegar, or fresh lemon juice. Use 1 tablespoon of the acid per cup of liquid. Start the soaking the night before, so the grains will soak for at least eight hours. After the soaking time has passed, begin the cooking process. If you can't soak overnight, even a three-hour soak will be beneficial.

▸ **SOAKING TIME:** I always recommend soaking overnight, which could mean anything between 8 and 12 hours. If you don't have time to cook the grains right away, just leave them in their soaking water in the fridge for up to 24 hours. Do not oversoak beyond 48 hours. Overnight soaking works best.

▸ **WATCH WHILE COOKING:** No two grain kernels are alike, so use common sense and watch your grains. Just like with beans, different varieties and freshness affect cooking time. Since you don't know how old your grains are, allow for some flexibility. Check occasionally and cook a bit longer, adding a little more water to your pot if necessary. Or drain excess liquid if grains are cooked before all the water is absorbed.

serving ideas for cooked gluten-free whole grains

The next time you're stumped on what to do with your big ol' pot of cooked grains, try one of my fun flavor combos! Add the ingredients listed below to 2 cups of your favorite cooked gluten-free grain.

▸ **APRICOT PECAN ORANGE TRIO:** Toss whole grains with 1 cup chopped dried apricots, ⅓ cup chopped toasted pecans, 3 tablespoons freshly squeezed orange juice, 2 tablespoons extra-virgin olive oil, and sea salt and pepper to taste.

▸ **COCONUT LIME CILANTRO:** Toss whole grains with ¼ cup finely chopped fresh cilantro, 1 teaspoon toasted unsweetened coconut flakes, 2 sliced scallions, juice of 1 lime (about 2 tablespoons), 2 tablespoons extra-virgin olive oil, and sea salt and pepper to taste.

▸ **HERBES DE PROVENCE AND DAIRY-FREE CREAMY CASHEW CHEESE:** Toss whole grains with my Dairy-Free Creamy Cashew Cheese (page 308), ½ teaspoon herbes de Provence, 2 tablespoons extra-virgin olive oil, and sea salt and pepper to taste.

▸ **DAIRY-FREE RAW MACADAMIA NUT "RICOTTA" CHEESE AND MARJORAM:** Toss whole grains with my Dairy-Free Raw Macadamia Nut "Ricotta" Cheese (page 309), 2 tablespoons extra-virgin olive oil, 2 tablespoons finely chopped fresh marjoram, 4 sliced fresh chives, a pinch of chili powder, and sea salt and pepper to taste.

▸ **DAIRY-FREE CREAMY CASHEW CHEESE WITH CHERRIES AND DILL:** Toss whole grains with 2 tablespoons finely chopped fresh dill, my Dairy-Free Creamy Cashew Cheese (page 308), ½ small diced shallot, ¼ cup chopped fresh (or dried) cherries, 2 tablespoons extra-virgin olive oil, and sea salt and pepper to taste.

▸ **LEMONY PEA:** Toss whole grains with 1 cup green peas, 1 cup halved cherry tomatoes, ¼ cup finely chopped fresh curly parsley, 2 tablespoons extra-virgin olive oil, juice of 1 lemon (about ¼ cup), ¼ teaspoon freshly grated lemon zest, and sea salt and pepper to taste.

▸ **TARRAGON DRIED CRANBERRY:** Toss whole grains with 2 tablespoons finely chopped fresh tarragon, 3 tablespoons chopped pecans, ⅓ cup unsweetened dried cranberries, 2 tablespoons extra-virgin olive oil, and sea salt and pepper to taste.

▸ **ADDING SEA SALT:** It seems that grains behave very much like beans. If I add sea salt too early, it toughens the grain and then the water can't penetrate for even cooking. Always add sea salt toward the end of cooking.

▸ **STEAM AFTER COOKING:** All grains benefit from steaming after cooking. Grains will absorb any remaining liquid and plump up.

▸ **STORING:** Cooked grains will keep in the refrigerator for five days (in a sealed container). Chilling can make them hard and clumpy, but that is not a problem—just separate them with a wooden spoon before cooking. The grains will soften when they reheat. You can also freeze your grains for three months. To reheat grains from the refrigerator, place them in a saucepan with about one-quarter inch of vegetable broth or water, cover, and heat on medium-low until they are softened and warmed through.

SPECIFIC GRAIN CHART NOTES

There are two ways to toast grains before cooking. Toast until the grains show some color and smell toasty and nutty. Some grains take longer, some shorter, depending on the oven and stovetop flame, age of the grain, and relative dryness. It's best to go by doneness signs and just use timing as guidance.

▸ **STOVETOP METHOD** (quicker): Toast dry grains over medium heat in a large, dry skillet for 3 to 5 minutes, shaking and stirring regularly. Be sure to add only a small amount of the dry grain so that each grain gets toasted. Crowding the skillet with a large amount of grain will not work. Start with 1 tablespoon of the grain at a time in the skillet until it's toasted, then remove the toasted grains and add more to the skillet. Repeat until all grains are toasted. When done, the grains should smell nutty.

▸ **OVEN METHOD** (slower but less risk of burning): Spread dry grains on a rimmed baking sheet in a single layer, and toast at 350°F for 15 to 20 minutes or until golden brown and fragrant. Stir halfway through cooking time to allow for even toasting.

HOW TO COOK GLUTEN-FREE GRAINS

gluten-free grain	water needed for cooking	yield	amie's notes
1 cup Quinoa	2½ cups water	3 cups	Toast before cooking to bring out flavor. (See page 103 for instructions.) Avoid constant stirring while cooking, as stirring can cause stickiness.
1 cup Millet	2½ cups water	4 cups	Toast before cooking to bring out flavor. (See page 103 for instructions.) Millet tends to cook unevenly, with some grains very soft and others slightly crunchy. This gives it a nice textural variation. Millet dries out as it cools, so it's not suited for a room-temperature salad. For added flavor, cook in vegetable broth instead of water.
1 cup Gluten-Free Whole Oats (Groats)	3 cups water	3 cups	Toast before cooking to bring out flavor. (See page 103 for instructions.)
1 cup Gluten-Free Steel-Cut Oats	3 cups water	3⅓ cups	Soaking the oats before cooking is not necessary but will greatly reduce the cooking time, to about 5 minutes.
1 cup Gluten-Free Extra-Thick Rolled Oats	2 cups water	1¾ cups	Toast before cooking, 5 to 7 minutes in a dry skillet, to bring out flavor.

how to know when the grain is done/cooked	*method* (without soaking)	*cooking time* (without soaking)	*method* (with soaking)
Done when you no longer see a white dot of starch in the center. You still want a little crunch in the texture. Some or all of the germ will release from the seeds and unfurl; this is a sign that the grain is done.	Rinse quinoa until water runs clear. Add water and quinoa to a pot and bring to a boil. Reduce heat and simmer, uncovered. Toward the end of cooking time, add sea salt.	15 minutes	Not necessary (unless specified in the recipe).
Check a few grains of millet: they should be one color throughout.	Add water and millet to a pot and bring to a boil. Reduce heat to a simmer and cover. Toward the end of cooking time, add sea salt.	15 to 20 minutes	Not necessary.
Done when oats are chewy throughout and are no longer white in the center.	Bring water to a boil in a pot and add oats. Reduce heat, and simmer, covered, for 50 to 60 minutes. Remove from heat and let stand for 10 minutes. Toward the end of cooking time, add sea salt.	50 to 60 minutes	Soak for 8 to 12 hours. After soaking, cook for 35 to 40 minutes in 2½ cups water.
Done when oats are thick, chewy, and porridgelike.	Bring water to a boil in a pot and add oats. Reduce heat and simmer, covered. Stir every few minutes. Toward the end of cooking time, add sea salt.	25 to 30 minutes	To soak: Bring 4 cups water to a boil, stir in oats, turn off the heat, cover, and let sit overnight in the refrigerator. The next morning, stir well, add more water if needed, and cook over low heat until oats are tender, about 5 minutes.
Done when oats are thick, chewy, and porridgelike.	Add water to a pot and bring to a slow boil. Add oats and stir to incorporate them in liquid. Cover pot and turn off the heat. Let sit on the burner for 7 minutes. Toward the end of cooking time, add sea salt.	10 to 20 minutes (depending on desired consistency)	Not necessary.

HOW TO COOK GLUTEN-FREE GRAINS

gluten-free grain	water needed for cooking	yield	amie's notes
1 cup Amaranth	1 cup water (dry results); 2 cups water (polenta-like consistency); 3 cups water (porridge results)	2 cups (dry); 3 cups (polenta-like consistency); 4 cups (porridge)	Virtually impossible to overcook. It will always maintain some crunch. The grain also releases a starch that makes it slippery and silky. Don't add salt to the cooking water until the very end: the amaranth will take longer to cook or never reach full tenderness.
1 cup Teff	1 cup water (poppy seed–like consistency); 3 cups water (polenta-like consistency)	1 cup (poppy seed–like consistency); 3 cups (polenta-like consistency)	Toast before cooking to bring out flavor. (See page 103 for instructions.)
1 cup Brown Rice	2 cups water (for short- and long-grain rice)	2 cups (short grain); 3 cups (long grain)	Soak overnight for better results.
1 cup Black (Forbidden) Rice	1¾ cups water	1¾ cups	Rice bleeds beet-red when you rinse it.
1 cup Wild Rice	2 cups water	3 cups	Do not soak or toast. Soaking and toasting creates mushy rice that loses its sleek shape.

how to know when the grain is done/cooked	method (without soaking)	cooking time (without soaking)	method (with soaking)
Done when amaranth looks pearlescent. The grains will be tender with a slight crunch.	Toast amaranth in a large, dry pan (2 teaspoons at a time) until it begins to pop and smell toasty, 2 to 4 minutes. Transfer to a pot, add water, and bring water to a boil, cover, reduce heat, and simmer. Toward the end of cooking time, add sea salt.	15 minutes (dry); 7 to 9 minutes (polenta); 20 to 22 minutes (porridge)	Not necessary.
Done when all the water is absorbed. Depending on your preference, teff should have a poppy seed–like or sticky texture.	Add water and teff to a pot and bring to a boil. Reduce heat and simmer, covered. Toward the end of cooking time, add sea salt.	6 to 7 minutes (poppy seed–like consistency); 15 to 20 minutes (polenta). Stir, turn off the heat, cover again, and let it sit for 10 minutes before serving.	Not necessary.
Done when rice is tender throughout and there is no white spot in the center of each grain.	Add water and rice to a pot and bring to a boil. Reduce heat to a simmer and cover. Toward the end of cooking time, add sea salt.	45 to 50 minutes	Soak overnight: 8 to 12 hours for best results. If you don't have time to soak overnight, soaking for a quick 30 minutes before cooking will be beneficial. After soaking, cook for 35 to 40 minutes in 1½ cups water.
Done when rice holds its shape well and is chewy. Turns a deep burgundy color when cooked.	Add water and rice to a pot and bring to a boil. Reduce heat, simmer, and cover. Toward the end of cooking time, add sea salt.	30 to 35 minutes	Soak overnight: 8 to 12 hours. After soaking, cook for 25 to 30 minutes in 1½ cups of water.
Done when rice is tender and chewy; some pieces will burst open. If the pieces curl, they are overcooked.	Add water and rice to a pot and bring to a boil. Reduce heat to a simmer and cover. Toward the end of cooking time, add sea salt.	35 to 45 minutes	Not necessary.

NUTS AND SEEDS

Soaking nuts and seeds makes them more nutritious and easy to blend into a creamy consistency for making dairy-free nut cheeses (pages 307–310) and nut and seed "mylks" (page 290).

To soak nuts and seeds, add them to a glass bowl with enough warm, purified water to cover. Add a pinch of sea salt and, optionally, a splash of acid—such as raw unfiltered apple cider vinegar or fresh lemon juice—to help soften harder nuts. (I add ¼ teaspoon sea salt with ½ teaspoon apple cider vinegar to 2 cups water when I soak 1 cup raw nuts.)

Cover the bowl with a dish towel, leave to soak at room temperature (see chart below), drain, and then rinse well with water in a colander; then use immediately. Always use raw, salt-free, no-oil, unroasted seeds and nuts for soaking.

DRY ROASTING AND TOASTING

To roast and toast nuts and seeds, you can use the oven or stovetop. Watch closely so they don't burn.

OVEN METHOD FOR NUTS: Spread raw nuts in a single layer on a rimmed baking sheet. Bake at 325°F, stirring occasionally, until nuts are fragrant and golden brown, 10 to 20 minutes.

STOVETOP METHOD FOR NUTS: Place raw nuts in a large, dry sauté pan over medium heat. Shake until fragrant and golden brown.

OVEN METHOD FOR SEEDS: Place raw seeds in a shallow baking dish. Bake at 350°F for 5 to 10 minutes or until fragrant and golden brown.

STOVETOP METHOD FOR SEEDS: Place raw seeds in a large, dry skillet over medium heat, stirring until fragrant and golden brown, 3 to 5 minutes.

HOW TO SOAK NUTS AND SEEDS

raw nut/seed	soaking time
1 cup Almonds	8 to 12 hours
1 cup Cashews	2 to 4 hours
1 cup Hazelnuts	8 to 12 hours
1 cup Hemp seeds	No soak
1 cup Macadamia nuts	2 hours
1 cup Sesame seeds	8 hours
1 cup Sunflower seeds	8 hours
1 cup Brazil nuts	3 hours
1 cup Pumpkin seeds	8 hours
1 cup Pecans	6 hours
1 cup Walnuts	4 hours

delicious,
DELECTABLE
DETOX RECIPES

If you've ever seen a Manhattan apartment, you can probably guess that whoever designed them pretty much assumed no one would be cooking in them. Except I do—every single day. I'm a rare breed, since most people in the city dine out daily. My point being: If I can make fresh, delicious, clean food daily, so can you. It's not exhausting. It's not rocket science. And the payoff is well worth it.

On my blog, The Healthy Apple (TheHealthy Apple.com), and in this book, I've given you glimpses of my life, my kitchen, and my health crusade.

A decade of chronic illness in my 20s was the start to this incredible journey. Eating clean allowed me to take control of my years of debilitating pain, fight inflammation, and reset my body while giving me back my life. I had no idea food could help heal me and have such a profound impact on my entire life. I've learned there's a rainbow in every storm cloud, and these recipes are the rainbow that pulled me out of ten years of storm clouds. They're life-changing and I'm living proof. My insight, my true voice, my authentic self, my healing hugs, and my love that I'm sharing with all of you in this book is what makes these recipes so unique and special. The transparency through my work comes from my heart as I share my journey to wellness with you.

I know that cutting out foods or trying to eat clean may seem challenging, frustrating, or isolating. But you're not alone. You're not alone in the process of wellness and self-growth. Developing these recipes forced me to be brave and feel the freedom and peace of knowing that I helped heal myself and I can help others who feel stuck, are struggling, or are just sick 'n' tired of food that does nothing but create inflammation. I'm not perfect, but these recipes are close to it. Creating these fabulously delicious recipes helped me to know myself better and realize life is a lot simpler when you make choices for your own well-being and eat what works for you—not what works for everyone else.

My goal is to empower you to make changes that will have you feeling healthier than ever before.

The key is to find your own style. It's not about what foods you should eat, or whose diet you should copy, but what you enjoy and, most important, what makes you feel good. For me, that means leafy greens, ribbons of zucchini, jeweled fruit tossed with quinoa, and fresh beds of arugula with basil and scallions. But you may have entirely different favorites.

I've developed more than two hundred brand-new recipes with you (and your health) in mind to transform your relationship with food. I've selected them based on what's easy, what's delicious, and what can be improvised or switched out to make it your own. **Every single recipe is detox-approved and is free of animal protein, gluten, dairy, soy, peanuts, eggs, corn, eggplant, white flour, and refined sugar—nothing from a box.**

Whether you're battling inflammation and food sensitivities, want to overhaul your lifestyle or are looking for new ideas to try out in the kitchen, consider these recipes as a way to begin. The everyday practice of simple cooking with whole foods—and the sheer pleasure of eating them—are two amazing gifts, and I hope you treasure them as much as I do. To do that, you've got to get into your kitchen.

I've broken down my recipes into the basics: Breakfast and Brunch; Small Bites; Appetizers and Soups; Timeless Salads; The Main Dish; More Than Just a Side; Refreshing and Restoring Sippers; Dip It, Spread It, Dress It; and Refined Sugar–Free Sweets and Treats. You don't have to get all fancy-pants—keep it simple, and follow your instincts. These recipes are mere guidelines; they're what I've found that works for me, but you may find a better way.

No more frustration, boredom, or teary-eyed angst that there's nothing you can eat, because it simply isn't true. No more feeling stuck with steamed peas while everyone else is eating the good stuff. I'm going to blow your mind with a world of flavors you've never tasted or even considered before.

So let's get cooking!

good morning: breakfast and brunch

My journey through chronic illness has led me to discover myself, in my 5x5-foot kitchen, in the center of the craziest city in the world. I started creating breakfast recipes to nourish my body because I felt so sick, exhausted, numb, and blah in my corporate jobs that sucked the very life out of me. This chapter is the beginning of my personal eating-clean journey. I can still remember waking up at 5 a.m. for my corporate jobs, bloated, tired, and "not right" and just tossing something in my mouth to hold me over until lunch. Those days are long gone. Breakfast, to me, is the greatest part of my day. It's when I relax, enjoy the morning sunshine, and relish the moment with gratitude that I'm waking up without chronic pain—as I did for over 10 years. I think every morning should be like Sunday morning—easy, relaxed, and restorative. Fortunately, it can be when you love breakfast!

Here's my unique collection of fresh, flavorful breakfast recipes. Some are great for run-out-the-door convenience, some can be prepared the night before so you can shave minutes off your morning routine, and others are perfect for enjoying on a weekend morning, when you've got nothing but time.

Forget heavy bagels and cakey doughnuts masquerading as breakfast. So long, chalky-tasting breakfast shakes and boxes of sugary processed cereal. Armed with a nutritious and satisfying morning meal, you'll give your body the fuel it needs to get through the first part of your day without suffering hunger pangs or energy shortages. Finally—junk-free breakfasts worth waking up for!

creamy
BREAKFAST CHIA PUDDING

For a grain-free breakfast packed with anti-inflammatory omega-3 fatty acids and protein, you can't beat chia. This makes an easy, no-cook breakfast for a weekday morning.

¼ cup chia seeds

1½ cups water

⅔ cup raw cashews

6 large dates, pitted, soaked in water overnight, and drained

½ teaspoon ground cinnamon

½ teaspoon pure vanilla extract

Pinch sea salt

OPTIONAL TOPPINGS

1 cup fresh berries, chopped pineapple, or sliced bananas

2 tablespoons unsweetened cocoa powder or ground cinnamon

Handful Amie's Grain-Free Granola (page 121) or another granola (pages 118 and 122)

In a small bowl, combine the chia seeds and water; set aside until the mixture forms a gel, about 20 minutes.

Combine the cashews, dates, cinnamon, vanilla, salt, and half of the chia gel in a high-speed blender. Puree until smooth. Transfer the pureed mixture to a medium bowl and stir in the remaining chia gel. Serve immediately, topped with one or more of the optional toppings, if desired, or store in the refrigerator until ready to serve.

SERVES 4

cozy
BAKED "COCONUT APPLE" OATMEAL

This is the perfect breakfast for a cozy autumn or winter morning. It's jam-packed with fiber 'n' flavor and smells amazing. Leftovers are great reheated in the oven, too!

Coconut oil, for coating pan

2 tablespoons chia seeds

¼ cup water

2 cups gluten-free rolled oats

2 large apples, finely diced

3 tablespoons unsweetened coconut flakes, toasted (see below)

½ cup dried cranberries

1 teaspoon aluminum-free baking powder

1 tablespoon ground cinnamon

½ teaspoon ground cardamom

¼ teaspoon sea salt

2¼ cups unsweetened almond milk

2 tablespoons pure maple syrup

2 teaspoons pure vanilla extract

Blissful Dessert Cashew Cream (page 365), optional

Preheat the oven to 375°F. Lightly coat an 8x8-inch baking dish with coconut oil.

In a small bowl, combine the chia seeds and water; set aside until the mixture forms a gel, about 5 minutes. Then mix well and set aside.

In a large bowl, combine the oats, apples, coconut flakes, cranberries, baking powder, cinnamon, cardamom, and salt. In a small bowl, whisk together the almond milk, maple syrup, vanilla, and chia mixture. Fold the wet ingredients into the oat mixture and transfer to the prepared baking dish.

Bake for 45 minutes, or until golden brown. Remove from the oven and allow to cool for at least 10 minutes. Top with a dollop of the Blissful Dessert Cashew Cream, if desired, and serve.

SERVES 6

HOW TO TOAST COCONUT FLAKES In a small dry skillet or pan on the stovetop, toast coconut flakes over medium heat until golden brown and fragrant. Keep an eye on the pan and give it a few shakes to prevent the flakes from sticking and burning. Remove from the heat and transfer the coconut flakes to a small bowl until ready to use.

plentiful
COCONUT GRANOLA WITH PEACHES

This is a lovely snack or decadent breakfast served over coconut or almond yogurt, sprinkled on gluten-free oatmeal, or even used to top off a smoothie. It can also be made with raspberries instead of peaches.

½ cup slivered raw almonds

½ cup gluten-free rolled oats

⅓ cup unsweetened coconut flakes

½ cup pitted Medjool dates

¼ cup dried blueberries, cranberries, golden raisins, or a combination, chopped

2 tablespoons pure maple syrup

¼ teaspoon ground cinnamon

¼ teaspoon sea salt

4 large peaches, pitted and diced, for serving

Blissful Dessert Cashew Cream (page 365), for serving

Preheat the oven to 350°F.

Spread the almonds, oats, and coconut flakes in a thin layer on a rimmed baking sheet and toast in the oven, stirring occasionally, until they turn tan and smell nutty, about 8 minutes. (Keep an eye on it as the coconut browns quickly.) Transfer the mixture to a food processor and add the dates, blueberries, maple syrup, cinnamon, and salt; pulse until coarsely ground.

Divide the peaches among four serving bowls and top with a dollop of the Blissful Dessert Cashew Cream, then a spoonful of the granola. Serve immediately. Store leftover granola in a sealed container in the refrigerator for up to 5 days.

SERVES 4

MUSHROOM, KALE, AND CARAMELIZED ONION SAVORY OATS

I'm not sure why oatmeal is almost always prepared as a sweet food, when oats actually lend themselves so well to savory flavors. The highlight of this oatmeal is my caramelized onions, which impart richness to the whole dish.

2	cups plus 2 tablespoons water, divided
1	cup gluten-free rolled oats
¼	teaspoon sea salt, plus more for serving
3	tablespoons quinoa, rinsed
⅓	cup chopped raw cashews
1	small portobello mushroom, sliced
2	tablespoons extra-virgin olive oil, divided
½	teaspoon fresh thyme leaves
1	cup finely chopped kale leaves
2	tablespoons Super Soft Caramelized Red Onions (page 272)
4	fresh chives, thinly sliced
	Freshly ground black pepper

In a small saucepan, combine 2 cups of the water, the oats, and the salt and cook over medium heat until the oats reach the desired consistency.

While the oats are cooking, place the quinoa and cashews in a dry skillet and toast over medium heat for 2 to 3 minutes, or until golden brown. Transfer to a small bowl.

Place the mushroom, 1 tablespoon of the oil, and the thyme in the same skillet. Cook over medium heat until the mushroom is tender, 3 to 4 minutes (cover if it appears to be drying out, or add the remaining 1 tablespoon oil). Add the kale and the remaining 2 tablespoons of water. Cover and cook for 3 minutes more, or until the kale is bright green and wilted. Stir in the Super Soft Caramelized Red Onions and remove from the heat.

To serve, divide the oats between two bowls. Top with the mushroom and kale mixture, and then sprinkle with the toasted quinoa and cashews. Garnish with the chives and season with salt and pepper to taste.

SERVES 2

STARTING OFF YOUR REFINED SUGAR-FREE DAY If you start your day with loads of refined sugar from boxed cereal or other processed foods, you'll send your blood sugar soaring, only to crash a few hours later. Your energy will drop and you'll crave more sugar—it's a constant cycle and it will make you feel horrible. So what to do? Start your day with meals that include quality carbohydrates (gluten-free whole grains), healthy fats (nuts, seeds), fiber (fruits, veggies), and protein (beans). If you're in a rush, even a simple apple with nut butter will do.

honey cinnamon
QUINOA GRANOLA

This simple recipe is a favorite in my cooking classes, and you don't actually need to cook the quinoa before making the granola! Quinoa gives this mixture a nutty, toasty flavor that's distinctly different from traditional granola made with oats. I make this recipe with dried cherries, but dried cranberries, dried blueberries, or dried apricots work well, too.

1	cup quinoa
½	cup raw almonds, roughly chopped
½	cup raw pecans, walnuts, or cashews, roughly chopped
3	tablespoons raw honey
2	tablespoons extra-virgin olive oil
½	teaspoon ground cinnamon
½	teaspoon sea salt
½	cup dried cherries, chopped
	Unsweetened almond milk, optional
	Fresh berries, optional

Preheat the oven to 350°F.

Rinse the quinoa until the water runs clear. Spread it out in a single layer on a sheet of parchment paper to dry for at least 1 hour. Make sure the quinoa is completely dry before proceeding.

In a large bowl, combine the quinoa, almonds, pecans, honey, oil, cinnamon, and salt. Mix until the quinoa is well coated. Spread the mixture in a single layer on a rimmed baking sheet lined with clean parchment paper. Bake for 20 to 25 minutes, or until golden brown. Remove the granola from the oven, stir in the dried cherries, and set aside to cool for 20 minutes. Use your hands to break up the granola chunks into small pieces. Serve granola dry or in a bowl with almond milk and fresh berries, if desired. Store in a sealed container for up to 5 days.

MAKES ABOUT 2½ CUPS

amie's
GRAIN-FREE GRANOLA

If you're not a grain eater, this granola's for you. It's a simple blend of raw nuts, seeds, sulfur-free dried fruit, and unsweetened shredded coconut—so easy to make a kid could do it (and, in fact, it's a great recipe to have kids help you with). Be sure to make enough for the week— you'll go through a batch of this in no time!
The other thing to know about this recipe is that you can adjust the flavors according to the seasons. This version works well for spring/summer; to make a fall/winter blend, replace the cherries with cranberries, pecans with walnuts, apricots with golden raisins, and sunflower seeds with pumpkin seeds. Replace the ground cinnamon with pumpkin pie spice and use pure maple syrup in place of the honey. This granola makes a great holiday gift offered up in glass jars tied with festive ribbon.

1½	cups raw almonds, chopped
1½	cups unsweetened shredded coconut
1	cup raw pecans, chopped
1	cup raw Brazil nuts, chopped
1	cup shelled raw sunflower seeds
1	teaspoon ground cinnamon
	Pinch sea salt
¼	cup melted coconut oil
¼	cup raw honey or pure maple syrup
3	tablespoons water
1½	teaspoons pure almond extract
1	cup chopped dried apricots
½	cup chopped dried cherries

Preheat the oven to 325°F. Line a rimmed baking sheet with parchment paper.

In a large bowl, combine the almonds, coconut, pecans, Brazil nuts, sunflower seeds, cinnamon, and salt. In a small bowl, whisk together the oil, honey, water, and almond extract. Add the wet ingredients to the nut mixture and toss to coat.

Spread the granola on the prepared baking sheet in a single layer and bake for 25 to 30 minutes, or until golden brown, stirring halfway through. Remove the granola from the oven and stir in the dried apricots and cherries. Set aside to cool for 15 minutes before serving. Store in a sealed container in the refrigerator for 3 to 5 days.

MAKES 8 CUPS

MAPLE CRANBERRY AMARANTH "GRANOLA"

*Amaranth pops just like popcorn and is easy to make on your stovetop. This "granola" is perfect
on its own as a cereal or as a topping for almond or coconut yogurt, my dairy-free ice creams
(pages 334–339), fresh berries, or gluten-free oatmeal. You can even get a little fancy and serve this
"granola" over grilled or poached fruit. If you like, change it up by varying the nuts you use
and adding dried cherries or golden raisins in place of the cranberries.*

½	cup amaranth
½	cup raw cashews
¼	cup dried cranberries, finely chopped
¼	cup chopped raw almonds
¼	cup chopped raw walnuts
2½	tablespoons pure maple syrup
2	tablespoons extra-virgin olive oil
½	teaspoon ground cinnamon
½	teaspoon sea salt

Preheat the oven to 350°F. Line a rimmed baking sheet with parchment paper.

Heat a large, high-sided pan over high heat for at least 5 minutes or until the pan is very hot. Add 2 teaspoons of the amaranth and let it pop, about 15 seconds, until all the amaranth has popped. Popping will start after 15 to 20 seconds, depending on how hot your pan is. Be sure not to crowd the pan with too much amaranth or it won't pop. Wait until all the amaranth has popped before starting the next batch. Place the popped amaranth in a large bowl. Repeat with the remaining amaranth, 2 teaspoons at a time.

Add the cashews, cranberries, almonds, walnuts, maple syrup, oil, cinnamon, and salt to the popped amaranth and toss to combine. Transfer the mixture to the prepared baking sheet and press down hard to create a ½-inch-thick layer. Bake for 12 to 14 minutes. Let cool for at least 10 minutes before serving. Store in a sealed container in the refrigerator for up to 5 days.

MAKES 2½ CUPS

SPLENDID MACADAMIA OATMEAL SKILLET

Pumpkin starts showing up in the fall, but I love it year-round. This hearty oatmeal dish looks beautiful served up right in the skillet (especially if you have a cast-iron one). This skillet is great to prepare for Sunday brunch; use leftovers for an easy weekday on-the-go breakfast.

1½	tablespoons melted coconut oil, divided
2	tablespoons ground flaxseeds
⅓	cup water
2	cups gluten-free rolled oats
½	cup dried cherries, finely chopped
1	tablespoon pumpkin pie spice
1	teaspoon ground cinnamon
1	teaspoon aluminum-free baking powder
½	teaspoon sea salt
2	cups unsweetened almond milk
1	cup pumpkin puree (see below)
¼	cup pure maple syrup, divided
2	teaspoons pure vanilla extract
1	cup finely chopped raw macadamia nuts

Preheat the oven to 375°F. Lightly coat a medium, oven-safe skillet with 1 teaspoon of the oil.

Place the flaxseeds in a small bowl and add the water. Set aside for 5 minutes to form a gel. Then mix well.

In a medium bowl, combine the oats, cherries, pumpkin pie spice, cinnamon, baking powder, and salt. In a separate medium bowl, place the almond milk, pumpkin puree, 2 tablespoons of the maple syrup, the vanilla, and the flaxseed mixture. Whisk to combine. Stir the almond milk mixture into the oat mixture and mix well. Spoon into the prepared skillet.

In a small bowl, combine the macadamia nuts, the remaining 2 tablespoons maple syrup, and the remaining oil. Sprinkle over the mixture in the skillet. Bake for 30 minutes, or until golden brown. Remove from the oven and set aside for at least 10 minutes to cool slightly before serving. Serve warm.

SERVES 4 TO 6

HOMEMADE PUMPKIN PUREE For pumpkin puree you can enjoy throughout the season, take an edible variety of pumpkin and cut it in half. Remove the seeds and roast them in the oven later, if desired. Arrange the pumpkin halves cut-side down and roast at 350°F for 1 hour, or until the skin gives with the back of a wooden spoon. (If using a large pumpkin, cut into wide slices and arrange on a rimmed baking sheet. Roast for 45 minutes, or until the flesh yields to the back of a wooden spoon.) Set aside to cool. When cool enough to handle, scrape out the pumpkin flesh into a food processor. Process until smooth. To store, measure out 15-ounce or 1½-cup portions and spoon into freezer bags. Lay the bags flat in the freezer and use as needed throughout the year.

sunday morning
BLUEBERRY PEAR OATMEAL BAKE

Something as simple as baking oatmeal in the oven instead of cooking it on the stovetop changes it completely, giving it a thicker and chewier texture. Be sure to let the baked oatmeal rest for 15 minutes before serving. If you serve it directly out of the oven, it will crumble! This is an easy recipe to prepare for a weekend brunch; serve leftovers for a quick weekday breakfast.

3	tablespoons melted coconut oil, divided
1	tablespoon chia seeds
3	tablespoons water
2	cups gluten-free rolled oats
½	cup chopped raw pecans
1½	teaspoons ground cinnamon
1	teaspoon aluminum-free baking powder
½	teaspoon ground ginger
¼	teaspoon ground cardamom
	Large pinch sea salt
1¾	cups unsweetened almond milk
¼	cup pure maple syrup
1	tablespoon pure vanilla extract
½	large pear, cored and thinly sliced
1	cup fresh blueberries
	Butter Me Up Honey-Almond Nut Butter (page 307) or other nut butter, optional

Preheat the oven to 350°F. Coat a large cast-iron skillet with 1 tablespoon of the oil and set aside.

Place the chia seeds in a small bowl and add the water. Set aside for 5 minutes to form a gel. Then mix well.

In a large bowl, combine the oats, pecans, cinnamon, baking powder, ginger, cardamom, and salt. In a small bowl, whisk together the almond milk, maple syrup, vanilla, the remaining 2 tablespoons oil, and the chia gel mixture. Fold the wet ingredients into the dry ingredients and stir until well combined.

Place the sliced pear in a single layer on the bottom of the skillet. Pour the oatmeal mixture over the pear slices and top with the blueberries. Bake for 30 minutes, or until golden brown. Remove from the oven and let the oatmeal set for 15 minutes before serving. Drizzle with the Butter Me Up Honey-Almond Nut Butter, if desired, and serve.

SERVES 6 TO 8

charismatic
CRANBERRY SPICE QUINOA BAKE

---

*This light and fluffy dish reminds me of baked oatmeal, but the quinoa—super high in protein—
makes it so much more nutritious. For added richness, add a dash of almond milk before serving.
If you have leftovers, reheat by placing the desired amount on a rimmed baking sheet lined
with parchment paper and heating for 5 minutes in a 350°F oven. Add an extra pinch of sea salt
to leftovers to bring out the flavors!*

1	teaspoon melted coconut oil
2	tablespoons ground flaxseeds
6	tablespoons water
½	cup white quinoa, rinsed
½	cup red quinoa, rinsed
2½	teaspoons ground cinnamon, divided
½	teaspoon ground nutmeg
½	teaspoon ground cardamom
½	teaspoon ground ginger
	Small pinch ground cloves
	Sea salt
2	large ripe bananas, thinly sliced
1	pear, cored and cut into ¼-inch cubes
½	cup dried cranberries
2	cups unsweetened almond milk
3	tablespoons pure maple syrup
1½	teaspoons pure vanilla extract
½	cup slivered raw almonds

Preheat the oven to 350°F. Lightly coat an 8x8-inch baking dish with the oil.

Place the flaxseeds in a small bowl and add the water. Set aside for 5 minutes to form a gel. Then mix well.

In a large bowl, combine the white and red quinoa, 2 teaspoons of the cinnamon, the nutmeg, cardamom, ginger, cloves, and small pinch of salt; mix well. Transfer to the prepared baking dish. Place the banana slices and pear cubes on top of the quinoa mixture, followed by the cranberries.

In a small bowl, whisk together the almond milk, maple syrup, vanilla, and flaxseed mixture. Pour the almond milk mixture over the banana, pear, and cranberries. Sprinkle the almonds and the remaining ½ teaspoon cinnamon on top.

Bake for 50 to 55 minutes. Remove from the oven and set aside to cool (mixture will still be watery) for 30 minutes or until all liquid is absorbed. Serve warm and scoop onto serving plates or place in the refrigerator overnight. Add additional salt, to taste, if needed.

SERVES 4 TO 6

morning glory
CARROT MUFFINS

These are the only muffins in this entire book, and you don't wanna miss them!
They're a tasty combination of carrot cake, zucchini muffins, and banana bread. If you like,
get a little fancy and serve them with my Blissful Dessert Cashew Cream (page 365)
dolloped on top for a healthy afternoon snack or dessert.

3	tablespoons extra-virgin olive oil, plus more for coating muffin tin
2	tablespoons chia seeds
6	tablespoons water
1	large ripe banana, mashed
¼	cup unsweetened applesauce
3½	tablespoons pure maple syrup
2	large carrots, peeled and grated
1	large zucchini, grated
1½	cups gluten-free oat flour, store-bought or homemade (see page 39)
¼	cup slivered raw almonds
½	cup dried cranberries
¼	cup gluten-free dairy-free semisweet chocolate chips, optional
1	teaspoon aluminum-free baking powder
1½	teaspoons ground cinnamon
½	teaspoon baking soda
¼	teaspoon sea salt
½	teaspoon ground ginger
	Pinch ground allspice
	Blissful Dessert Cashew Cream (page 365), for topping, optional

Preheat the oven to 350°F. Prepare a 12-cup muffin tin with oil or paper liners.

In a small bowl, combine the chia seeds and water; set aside until the mixture forms a gel, about 5 minutes. Then mix well.

Place the banana, applesauce, maple syrup, oil, and chia gel in a medium bowl. Whisk until well combined. Fold in the carrots and zucchini.

In a medium bowl, combine the oat flour, almonds, cranberries, chocolate chips (if using), baking powder, cinnamon, baking soda, salt, ginger, and allspice. Add the banana mixture to the dry ingredients and gently stir to combine; do not overmix.

Spoon the batter into the prepared muffin tin, filling each cup three-quarters of the way. Bake for 20 minutes, or until golden brown and set. Remove from oven and set aside to cool for 10 minutes before serving, then top each muffin with a dollop of the Blissful Dessert Cashew Cream, if desired. Store the muffins and the cream in seperate sealed containers in the refrigerator.

MAKES 12 MUFFINS

BREADLESS COCONUT VANILLA FRENCH TOAST

French toast without bread? It can be done! Soaking oats overnight creates a delicious breadlike cake that can be cut into strips, and then Frenchified. If you don't care for gluten-free bread, this recipe will be a revelation. To ensure the oats have enough time to soak, start this recipe the night before. Leaving it uncovered is the secret to stiffening the "bread."

OVERNIGHT "BREAD"

Coconut oil, for coating dish

2¼ cups water

1½ cups gluten-free rolled oats

1½ teaspoons ground cinnamon

1 teaspoon pure vanilla extract

¼ teaspoon sea salt

BATTER

1 tablespoon ground flaxseeds

3 tablespoons water

⅔ cup well-shaken full-fat culinary coconut milk

2 tablespoons raw honey

1 tablespoon unsweetened shredded coconut

1 tablespoon pure vanilla extract

2 teaspoons ground cinnamon

¼ teaspoon ground allspice

Coconut oil, for coating skillet

TOPPINGS (OPTIONAL)

Pure maple syrup

Fresh berries

Dollop Totally Whipped Coconut Whippy Cream (page 364)

MAKE THE "BREAD": Lightly coat an 8x8-inch baking dish with the oil.

Bring the water to a boil in a large saucepan. Add the oats, cinnamon, vanilla, and salt. Cook over medium heat until the oats are cooked through, but not mushy. Transfer to the prepared baking dish. Refrigerate overnight, uncovered, to set.

Remove the oats from the refrigerator and cut them into 2x2-inch squares.

MAKE THE BATTER: Place the flaxseeds in a small bowl and add the water. Set aside for 5 minutes to form a gel. Then mix well.

In a large bowl, combine the remaining batter ingredients except the coconut oil; mix well. Stir in the flaxseed mixture, and then pour the batter into a 10x10- or 9x13-inch baking dish. Dip the oat squares into the batter to coat and let soak for 3 minutes on each side. Make sure each square is coated with the batter. Use a spoon to completely coat each piece, if needed.

Melt 1 teaspoon of the oil in a large skillet over low heat. Place 3 squares of the "bread" in the skillet at a time and cook until golden brown, 4 to 5 minutes per side. Repeat with the remaining squares, using 1 teaspoon of oil per batch. Serve warm on its own or with toppings. Tip: To keep the French toast warm before serving, place squares on a baking sheet in a single layer in a 200°F oven.

SERVES 4

MILLET 'n' VEGGIE BREAKFAST TACOS: TWO WAYS

This filling combination of whole grains and veggies will keep you satisfied long until your next meal.

1½   cups cooked millet (see page 104)

¼   cup finely chopped fresh cilantro

1   tablespoon freshly squeezed lime juice

¼   teaspoon sea salt

8   gluten-free whole-grain tortillas (corn-free)

1   recipe Butternut Squash and Swiss Chard or Portobello Mushroom and Red Pepper mixture (see opposite)

1   cup shredded red cabbage

1   large ripe avocado, pitted, peeled, and thinly sliced

4   scallions, thinly sliced

Sea salt and freshly ground black pepper

Cumin Cashew Cream Sauce (page 230), optional

Seriously Sensational Sriracha Sauce (page 318), optional

In a small bowl, combine the millet, cilantro, lime juice, and salt. Stir to combine and set aside.

Make one (or both) of the Flavor Options.

To assemble, warm the tortillas on a baking sheet in a 350°F oven or in a dry skillet on the stovetop over medium heat. Place the warm tortillas on a platter or on individual plates. Divide the millet among the tortillas. Top each with either the Butternut Squash and Swiss Chard or the Portobello Mushroom and Red Pepper mixture. Top with the cabbage, avocado slices, scallions, and salt and pepper to taste. Finish with a dollop of the Cumin Cashew Cream Sauce and/or a drizzle of the Seriously Sensational Sriracha Sauce, if desired.

FLAVOR OPTIONS:

BUTTERNUT SQUASH AND SWISS CHARD

2   tablespoons coconut oil

4   cups peeled, seeded, and diced butternut squash (¼-inch cubes)

½   bunch Swiss chard, finely chopped

½   teaspoon chili powder

¼   teaspoon sea salt

¼   teaspoon freshly ground black pepper

In a large skillet, heat the oil over medium-high heat. Add the squash and sauté for 7 to 8 minutes. Add the remaining ingredients and cook until the chard has wilted, about 2 minutes. Keep warm.

PORTOBELLO MUSHROOM AND RED PEPPER

2 to 3 tablespoons extra-virgin olive oil

1   large portobello mushroom, cut into 8 slices

1   large red bell pepper, cut into long strips

¼   teaspoon ground cumin

¼   teaspoon sea salt

¼   teaspoon freshly ground black pepper

Pinch chipotle powder

¼   cup thinly sliced radish, for garnish

In a medium skillet, heat 2 tablespoons of the oil over medium heat. Add the mushrooms in a single layer. Cover and cook for 4 minutes, then flip and cook for 2 minutes more. Add the bell pepper, cumin, salt, black pepper, chipotle powder, and remaining oil, if needed. Cook for 5 minutes or until vegetables are cooked through, stirring often. Garnish with the radish. Keep warm.

SERVES 4

graceful
BANANA ALMOND PANCAKES

Instead of all-purpose flour, these pancakes are made with gluten-free oat flour and almond flour. You can buy oat flour and almond flour, or make them yourself (page 39). I urge you to make extra so that you always have them on hand. Tip: To keep the pancakes warm before serving, place them in a single layer on a baking sheet in a 200°F oven.

1	tablespoon ground flaxseeds
3	tablespoons water
1	cup gluten-free oat flour, store-bought or homemade (see page 39)
½	cup almond flour, store-bought or homemade (see page 39)
1	tablespoon aluminum-free baking powder
½	teaspoon ground cinnamon
¼	teaspoon sea salt
¼	teaspoon ground cardamom
1	large ripe banana
1	cup unsweetened almond milk
1	tablespoon raw honey
1	teaspoon pure vanilla extract
3	teaspoons melted coconut oil, plus more if needed for coating the skillet
	Sliced fresh stone fruit, berries, or oranges for topping, optional

Place the flaxseeds in a small bowl and add the water. Set aside for 5 minutes to form a gel. Then mix well.

In a medium bowl, combine the oat flour, almond flour, baking powder, cinnamon, salt, and cardamom; mix well to combine. In a small bowl, mash the banana, and then add the almond milk, honey, vanilla, and flaxseed mixture; whisk well to combine. Fold the banana mixture into the dry ingredients and gently stir to combine.

Add ½ teaspoon of the oil to a large skillet over medium-low heat. Ladle in 3 ounces (about ⅜ cup) of pancake batter into the middle of the skillet and cook until the pancake bubbles on top—about 3 minutes. Flip with a spatula and cook the other side until golden brown, 1 to 2 minutes. Transfer the pancake to a plate and repeat using the remaining batter and oil. Serve warm with fresh fruit, if desired.

MAKES 6 PANCAKES

OTHER OPTIONAL PANCAKE TOPPINGS

› Drizzle of honey

› Dollop Totally Whipped Coconut Whippy Cream (page 364)

› Sliced ripe bananas

› Dollop Toasted Coconut Macadamia Nut Butter Drizzle with Stone Fruit (page 335)

long weekend
CHICKPEA SPINACH SCRAMBLE

I've always wanted to find an alternative to scrambled eggs, and I'm so glad I have. You can enjoy this scramble on its own, use it as a filling for tacos and burritos, or serve it on top of gluten-free whole-grain toast with sautéed veggies. Garnish with fresh herbs, if desired.

1	tablespoon coconut oil
4	cups cooked chickpeas (see page 99)
¼	teaspoon ground cumin
¼	teaspoon chili powder
¼	teaspoon sea salt
¼	teaspoon freshly ground black pepper
4	cups baby spinach
¼	cup water
2	large ripe avocados, pitted, peeled, and thinly sliced
8	fresh chives, thinly sliced
1	tablespoon sesame seeds

Heat the oil in a medium skillet over medium heat. Place the chickpeas in the skillet and mash half of them with the back of a fork. Stir in the cumin, chili powder, salt, and pepper and cook for 2 minutes, stirring often. Add the spinach and water and continue cooking until tender and soft, about 2 minutes. Remove from the heat and garnish with the avocado slices, chives, and sesame seeds. Serve immediately.

SERVES 4

egg-free
HUEVOS RANCHEROS

Huevos lovers, rejoice! You can enjoy this Mexican favorite even if you don't eat eggs; I've replaced eggs with my Chickpea Spinach Scramble. What's more, these huevos rancheros are so easy to make you can whip them up on a weekday morning and still be out the door in time for work.

8	gluten-free whole-grain tortillas (corn-free)
1	recipe Long Weekend Chickpea Spinach Scramble (opposite)
1	recipe Perfect Pico de Gallo (page 242)
1	large ripe avocado, pitted, peeled, and thinly sliced
2	scallions, thinly sliced
	Handful finely chopped fresh cilantro
	Sea salt and freshly ground black pepper
1	lime, cut into wedges

Warm the tortillas on a baking sheet in a 350°F oven or in a dry skillet on the stovetop over medium heat. Place the warmed tortillas on a platter or on individual plates. Divide the Long Weekend Chickpea Spinach Scramble among the tortillas, and then top each with a spoonful of the Perfect Pico de Gallo, the avocado slices, scallions, and cilantro. Season with salt and pepper to taste. Squeeze some lime juice on top and serve immediately.

SERVES 4

MANGO AND COCONUT CREAM PARFAIT

*After I stopped eating dairy, I had to amend my definition of a parfait. Turns out, you don't need
ice cream or yogurt to create this layered dish. Here, I use a sauce of mango puree to heighten
the flavor of oranges and nuts. This recipe makes a lovely brunch dish. For maximum visual impact,
serve it in small parfait or juice glasses (though bowls will also do just fine).*

1   large ripe mango, peeled, pitted, and diced

2   tablespoons melted coconut oil

2   medium navel oranges, peeled, seeded, and segmented

½   cup slivered raw almonds

2   tablespoons unsweetened coconut flakes

¼   cup chopped raw walnuts

2   teaspoons finely chopped fresh mint

Peeled grapefruit segments, for serving, optional

Puree the mango and coconut oil in a blender or food processor.

Divide the oranges between two serving bowls, and then top with the mango mixture. Place the bowls in the refrigerator for 30 minutes.

While the parfaits are chilling, place the almonds in a small, dry skillet on the stovetop and toast over medium heat for 2 minutes. Transfer to a plate. Add the coconut flakes to the skillet and lightly toast for 2 minutes.

To serve the parfaits, top each bowl with half of the toasted almonds, toasted coconut flakes, walnuts, mint, and grapefruit segments, if desired. Serve immediately.

SERVES 2

RAW PECAN WALNUT PLUM CRUMBLE

I confess: I almost put this recipe in the dessert section. It's decadent, but not overly so—that's why I settled on putting it here. Just know, though, that if you decide to serve it for dessert at your next dinner party, no one will suspect you pulled it from the breakfast chapter!

¾ cup pitted Medjool dates

½ cup raw pecans

½ cup raw walnuts

2 tablespoons shelled raw hemp seeds

¼ teaspoon pure vanilla extract

Pinch ground cinnamon, plus more for garnish

Pinch sea salt

5 plums, pitted and diced or sliced

2 tablespoons raw honey

Blissful Dessert Cashew Cream (page 365), for serving

Combine the dates, pecans, walnuts, hemp seeds, vanilla, cinnamon, and salt in a food processor; pulse until crumbs form. Transfer the mixture to a small bowl; if using immediately, set aside. (You can make the crumble a day in advance and store in a sealed container in the refrigerator until ready to serve.)

Place the plums in a medium bowl, drizzle with the honey, and then divide them among four bowls. Spoon the crumb mixture on top. Finish with a dollop of the Blissful Dessert Cashew Cream and a sprinkle of cinnamon. Serve immediately.

SERVES 4

no-bake
FUEL UP BARS

When I've got a long flight from Manhattan to LA, I whip up a batch of these before I go and munch away on the plane. They're so much "cleaner" than the processed bars sold in the airport and food stores. Of course, they're also great to have around when you're sticking close to home.

1	cup gluten-free rolled oats
½	cup unsweetened coconut flakes, toasted (see page 114)
½	cup dried cranberries
⅓	cup gluten-free oat flour, store-bought or homemade (page 39)
¼	cup shelled raw sunflower seeds
2	tablespoons chia seeds
¼	teaspoon sea salt
½	cup almond butter
2	tablespoons melted coconut oil
2	tablespoons raw honey
1	teaspoon pure vanilla extract

Line an 8x8-inch baking dish or 8-inch tart pan with parchment paper.

In a medium bowl, combine the oats, coconut flakes, cranberries, oat flour, sunflower seeds, chia seeds, and salt; mix well. In a small bowl, whisk together the almond butter, oil, honey, and vanilla. Fold the almond butter mixture into the oat mixture and mix well. Spoon the batter into the prepared baking dish and refrigerate for 2 to 3 hours, or until set. Slice into 8 bars and serve.

MAKES 8 BARS

overnight
BLACK RICE AND BERRY BREAKFAST BOWL

This make-ahead recipe is a great change of pace from the usual bowl of store-bought processed cereal. I like to eat it with a dollop of coconut or almond yogurt and a pinch of finely chopped fresh mint. You can also serve it topped with any fresh berries you like, diced peaches, and my grain-free granola.

1	cup black rice
1	cup well-shaken full-fat culinary coconut milk
2	tablespoons pure maple syrup, plus more if needed
2	tablespoons unsweetened shredded coconut
½	teaspoon sea salt
½	teaspoon pure vanilla extract
1	cup fresh berries
1	peach, pitted and diced
½	cup Amie's Grain-Free Granola (page 121), for topping
	Large pinch ground cinnamon

Cook the rice in a medium saucepan according to the chart (page 106) until tender (add more water if needed). Add the coconut milk, maple syrup, shredded coconut, salt, and vanilla to the saucepan. Cook over medium heat until the mixture reaches a puddinglike consistency, 8 to 10 minutes. Remove from the heat and set aside to cool. When cool, transfer to a sealed container and place in the refrigerator. Serve the next morning, chilled, at room temperature, or reheated on the stovetop, and top with the berries, peach, Amie's Grain-Free Granola, and cinnamon.

SERVES 4

small bites

One of my favorite things to do is snack. Anyone who knows me will tell you that my bag is always packed with enough food to cover anything from a blood sugar crash to several days hunkered down in a bomb shelter. And if it's finger food, it's for me—I'd rather not bother with utensils if I don't have to.

If there's one thing my clients and readers are always asking me for, it's snack ideas. Breakfast, check. Lunch, check. Dinner, check. But snacks? They're stumped for anything outside of a vending machine. And we all know that manufacturers of packaged, processed foods may have cornered the market on snacks, but their products are designed to fuel their bottom lines more than our bodies.

I'm no different than you—I grew up in the era of Fruit Roll-Ups. I lived on all that stuff. Combos and Dunkaroos; yep, those too! But we all need more to get us through the day (and keep us healthy).

I've got it here for you.

The key is to kick up the flavor profile for your workday (and weekend) snacks: think Grain-Free Lemon Peppered Almond Crackers (page 162), Freckled Sesame Almond Clusters (page 140), and Divine Paprika Chickpea Croutons (page 144). I know you've done carrots and packaged hummus to the hilt—which is why you'll love my fresh, homemade hummus recipes (pages 301–303) with sliced raw veggies, or my Butter Me Up Honey-Almond Nut Butter (page 307) with apple slices and clementine segments. Sprinkle on toasted coconut flakes (see How to Toast Coconut Flakes, page 114) and a dash of ground cinnamon and you're set.

These snacks are super easy and not intimidating at all. Make a few this weekend and enjoy them all week long. Happy snacking!

PERFECT PARTY NUTS THREE WAYS

Satisfying and protein-packed homemade roasted nuts taste better when they're not dumped straight out of a bag of store-bought nuts, which are usually made from inflammatory (and sneaky) ingredients such as canola oil, refined table salt, refined sugar, MSG, and other additives.

FRECKLED SESAME ALMOND CLUSTERS

Summertime brings out my freckles. When I developed this recipe, all I could think about was how these little almonds took a "summer vacation" in my oven and popped out with freckles! Black sesame seeds get their striking black hue from phytochemicals (nutritious plant chemicals). They're fun and look so pretty on these almonds, but you can use brown or tan, if you prefer.

2	tablespoons raw honey
2½	cups raw almonds
3	tablespoons black or white sesame seeds
¼	teaspoon sea salt
¼	teaspoon ground allspice

Preheat the oven to 350°F. Line a rimmed baking sheet with parchment paper.

In a small saucepan, heat the honey over medium-low heat for 20 seconds. Remove from the heat and immediately add the remaining ingredients and mix well to coat the almonds. Test to see if they need more seasonings and add to taste.

Spread the coated almonds on the prepared baking sheet and bake for 12 to 15 minutes, or until golden brown. Set aside to cool. Break into clusters before serving or storing. Store in a sealed container in the refrigerator for up to 5 days.

NOTE: These clusters are a little sticky; break them apart with your hands after roasting for a sweet dessert or afternoon nibble.

MAKES 2½ CUPS

BLANCHED SEA SALT ALMONDS

Serve these crunchy almonds for an appetizer or afternoon snack. Add your favorite spices, if desired. A pinch of cayenne pepper adds a touch of heat, but for a real kick, add two pinches!

2   cups raw almonds
1   teaspoon extra-virgin olive oil
½   teaspoon sea salt
½   teaspoon freshly ground black pepper
    Pinch cayenne pepper

To blanch the almonds, drop them into a pan of boiling water for 1 minute, and then remove them with a slotted spoon. When cool enough to handle, pinch off the skins (they should slip off very easily; if they don't, put them back in the boiling water for another minute). Be careful not to soak the almonds for too long or they'll become soggy and waterlogged.

Preheat the oven to 350°F. Line a rimmed baking sheet with parchment paper.

Toss the almonds with the oil and place on the prepared baking sheet. Bake for 20 minutes, or until golden brown, stirring halfway through. Remove from the oven and sprinkle the baked almonds with the salt, black pepper, and cayenne pepper; toss to coat. Test to see if they need more seasoning and add to taste. Store in a sealed container in the refrigerator for up to 5 days.

MAKES 2 CUPS

MAPLE SRIRACHA ROASTED PECANS

These pecans are perfect for guests to nibble on at a dinner party before the main dish is served. If you want a spicier nut, add more sriracha sauce, but be careful—the heat intensifies as they roast!

2   cups raw pecans
3   tablespoons pure maple syrup
2   tablespoons Seriously Sensational Sriracha Sauce (page 318)
    Sea salt

Preheat the oven to 325°F. Line a rimmed baking sheet with parchment paper.

In a medium bowl, toss the pecans with the maple syrup, Seriously Sensational Sriracha Sauce, and salt to taste. Spread the pecans on the prepared baking sheet and roast for 15 minutes, or until starting to brown. Remove from the oven and cool for 15 minutes. Serve immediately, or store in a sealed container for up to 3 days.

MAKES 2 CUPS

TRANSFORMED CRUNCHY BREADSTICKS
(with chocolate drizzle option for a mock biscotti)

Serve these breadsticks with soups, or salads, or use as a "breadstick" to dip into my salsa recipes (pages 230 and 305–306) or hummus recipes (pages 301–303). Shelled raw pumpkin or sunflower seeds can be substituted for the almonds. For a sweet alternative, use gluten-free cinnamon-raisin bread in place of the whole-grain bread.

BREADSTICKS

6   slices gluten-free whole-grain bread, cut into ¾-inch-wide sticks

3   tablespoons raw honey, plus more if needed

3   tablespoons thinly sliced raw almonds

Sea salt and freshly ground black pepper

Ground cinnamon, optional

CHOCOLATE DRIZZLE (OPTIONAL)

½   cup gluten-free, dairy-free semisweet or bittersweet chocolate chips

MAKE THE BREADSTICKS: Preheat the oven to 400°F. Line a rimmed baking sheet with parchment paper.

Place the breadsticks on the prepared baking sheet in a single layer. Using a small brush, brush the honey onto one side of the breadsticks. Immediately top the sticky honey side of the bread with the almonds—don't allow the honey time to soak into the bread. If you do, the almonds won't stick to the breadsticks. Add more honey if needed. Season with salt, pepper, and cinnamon to taste, if desired.

Bake the breadsticks for 15 minutes, or until golden brown. Using a spatula, immediately transfer the breadsticks to a plate and serve warm or at room temperature. (If any almonds fell off during cooking, save them to add to salads or soups.)

MAKE THE CHOCOLATE DRIZZLE: In a double-boiler over medium-low heat, melt the chocolate chips, about 10 minutes. Drizzle the baked breadsticks with the melted chocolate. Lay the breadsticks on a rimmed baking sheet lined with parchment paper and place in the refrigerator until the chocolate hardens, 10 to 15 minutes.

SERVES 6

simply sweet
MAPLE ROASTED CHICKPEA CROUTONS

Sometimes I want a handful of something sweet when I am out running errands. My body cannot digest processed food, so I'm happy to create my own nibbles. To make sure I don't get hungry when I'm out of the house, I like to keep a parchment-paper baggie full of roasted chickpeas in my purse. These are a great protein-packed snack or salad topping.

1½	cups cooked chickpeas (see page 99), dried with a towel
1	tablespoon melted coconut oil
1	teaspoon ground cinnamon
1	teaspoon pure maple syrup
½	teaspoon sea salt
½	teaspoon freshly ground black pepper

Preheat the oven to 400°F. Line a rimmed baking sheet with parchment paper.

In a large bowl, combine all the ingredients; toss to coat the chickpeas. Transfer to the prepared baking sheet and arrange in a single layer. Bake for 20 minutes, or until the chickpeas are crispy but not burnt, stirring halfway through. Remove from the oven, shake the pan, and set aside to cool for 15 to 20 minutes before serving.

MAKES 1 CUP

divine
PAPRIKA CHICKPEA CROUTONS

Everyone loves the crunch of croutons when they're eating a softer meal, but store-bought croutons made from gluten-free white bread are rather empty in terms of nutrients. Chickpeas are high in fiber and protein, which will help keep you satisfied, so they won't leave you scavenging the cabinets later. I enjoy these croutons alone as a snack, and kids do, too!

1½	cups cooked chickpeas (see page 99), dried with a towel
1	tablespoon melted coconut oil
1	teaspoon paprika
1	teaspoon ground coriander
½	teaspoon sea salt
½	teaspoon freshly ground black pepper

Preheat the oven to 400°F. Line a rimmed baking sheet with parchment paper.

In a large bowl, combine all the ingredients; toss to coat the chickpeas. Transfer to the prepared baking sheet and arrange in a single layer. Bake for 20 minutes, or until chickpeas are crispy but not burnt, stirring halfway through. Remove from the oven, shake the pan, and set aside to cool for 15 to 20 minutes before serving.

MAKES 1 CUP

HAZELNUT OREGANO "SPRINKLES"

Enjoy all the crouton crunch without any gluten or bread in sight. These baked hazelnuts are an easy way to add a dose of protein to your salads, whole grains, or veggies. Toss these "sprinkles" into my soups (pages 181–198) and salads (pages 199–217), or serve them with my Vegetarian Antipasto Platter (page 64).

1   cup raw hazelnuts

1   tablespoon extra-virgin olive oil

¼   teaspoon freshly grated lemon zest

¼   teaspoon dried oregano

       Sea salt and freshly ground black pepper, to taste

Preheat the oven to 350°F. Line a rimmed baking sheet with parchment paper.

Arrange the hazelnuts on the prepared baking sheet and bake for 12 to 14 minutes, or until golden brown. Keep the oven on, but remove the hazelnuts from the oven and let them cool for 5 minutes, then rub them between your hands to remove the skins.

Combine the hazelnuts with the remaining ingredients in a large bowl and toss to coat. Transfer to the prepared baking sheet and arrrange in a single layer. Bake for 3 minutes more. Remove from the oven and cool for at least 15 to 20 minutes before serving. Adjust seasoning to taste.

MAKES 1 CUP

ABUNDANT MANGO CARDAMOM WALNUT BARS

*These delicious and healthy bars won't last long! They're filled with orange zest and mango—
a fun and brightly colored combo. They're also naturally sweet without any refined sugar. You've never
had a bar like these. Trust me. Take one look at the ingredients—you won't find bars like this in the food
store, that's for sure! For a more exotic flavor, make a batch and substitute finely chopped dried pineapple for
the raisins, or roll the dough into balls and then coat with the coconut. They're a great on-the-go snack and
will work for breakfast, too. Wrap them in parchment paper if traveling.*

3	cups raw walnuts, soaked in water for 4 hours, drained, and rinsed
3	cups chopped dried mango
3	cups golden raisins
¾	teaspoon ground cinnamon
¾	teaspoon ground cardamom
¾	teaspoon freshly grated orange zest
¾	teaspoon sea salt
	Coconut oil, for coating hands
1½	cups unsweetened shredded coconut

Place the walnuts in a food processor and pulse until they become small chunks; don't overprocess (you don't want the mixture to form a nut butter). Transfer to a small bowl.

Place the mango, raisins, cinnamon, cardamom, orange zest, and salt in the food processor and process until well mixed. Add the processed walnuts and pulse until combined.

Coat the palms of your hands with the oil and form the mixture into a large ball. Place the ball between two large sheets of parchment paper and, using a rolling pin, roll it out to a ½-inch-thick 12x9-inch rectangle. Transfer the rectangle to a cutting board and place in the refrigerator for at least 3 hours. Slice into eighteen 2x3-inch bars and place one bar at a time in a large bowl. Add the shredded coconut and toss to coat all sides of the bars. Store the bars in an airtight container in the refrigerator for up to 1 week.

MAKES 18

delightful dairy-free
NUT CHEESE AND BERRIES ON TOAST

*This snack is gorgeously vibrant and perfect for when your belly starts rumbling. Whip up my Dairy-Free Creamy Cashew Cheese (page 308) or Dairy-Free Raw Macadamia Nut "Ricotta" Cheese (page 309) on Sunday night and enjoy it all week with this recipe. Toss leftover nut cheeses into my Nuts About Butternut Squash and Kale Salad (page 210). I suggest heating the berries in a pan with honey and lemon juice until the berries burst and turn into a lovely berry compote. These berries still have their volume—they're not like a jam. You actually want them to retain some of their shape, as that will make for a stunning topping on the dairy-free nut cheese. For a grain-free version of this dish, use ¼-inch slices of zucchini rounds sliced on a diagonal instead of the bread.
Note: The honey is optional, so if your berries are very sweet, you won't need it.*

2	cups mixed fresh berries (blueberries, raspberries, blackberries, or strawberries)
1	tablespoon freshly squeezed lemon juice
1	tablespoon raw honey, plus more for drizzling, optional
4	slices gluten-free whole-grain Italian bread, sliced on a diagonal and toasted
¼	cup Dairy-Free Creamy Cashew Cheese (page 308) or Dairy-Free Raw Macadamia Nut "Ricotta" Cheese (page 309)
2	tablespoons sliced raw almonds
¼	teaspoon sea salt
¼	teaspoon freshly ground black pepper

Toss the berries in a large bowl with the lemon juice and honey, if using. Transfer to a medium saucepan and slowly simmer over medium heat until some of the berries burst open with their juices running out, about 5 minutes.

Spread each slice of bread with 1 tablespoon of the Dairy-Free Creamy Cashew Cheese or Dairy-Free Raw Macadamia Nut "Ricotta" Cheese and divide the berry mixture among the slices of bread. Drizzle with honey and sprinkle with the almonds, salt, and pepper before serving.

SERVES 4

inspiring
RAW LAYERED OAT SQUARES

When you taste how delicious these homemade squares are, you're never going to want to buy another packaged bar again. That means you might be spending more time in the kitchen, but believe me, it'll be worth it! These are soft and chewy and great for a snack or dessert. Store these squares in the refrigerator until ready to serve; otherwise, the coconut oil will melt and make them goopy.

SQUARES

³⁄₄ cup dates, pitted and chopped

½ cup gluten-free rolled oats

¼ cup shelled raw hemp seeds

2 tablespoons almond butter

1 tablespoon pure maple syrup

1 tablespoon melted coconut oil

1 tablespoon chia seeds

1 tablespoon almond flour, store-bought or homemade (see page 39)

1½ teaspoons pure vanilla extract

1 teaspoon ground cinnamon

¼ teaspoon sea salt

TOPPING

2 tablespoons melted coconut oil

1½ tablespoons unsweetened cocoa powder

2 teaspoons raw honey

Pinch sea salt

1 tablespoon sesame seeds, for topping

MAKE THE SQUARES: Line an 8x8-inch baking dish with parchment paper and set aside.

Place the dates and oats in a food processor and process until well combined. Add the remaining ingredients for the squares and pulse until well combined.

Using your hands, press the mixture into the prepared baking dish and set aside.

MAKE THE TOPPING: In a small saucepan over the lowest heat setting, slowly whisk together the oil, cocoa powder, honey, and salt until well combined. Pour the warm coconut-cocoa mixture over the pressed squares in the prepared baking dish and sprinkle with the sesame seeds. Chill in the refrigerator for at least 5 hours or overnight. Before serving, cut into 9 squares. Store in the refrigerator for up to 4 days.

MAKES 9 SQUARES

RAW ROMAINE SUMMER ROLLS
with almond walnut dipping sauce

I've always loved Asian spring rolls, but that isn't to say they couldn't use an update for those of us with food sensitivities. Like a traditional roll, these are filled with vegetables, but lettuce leaves replace the traditional rice wrapper and each roll gets a dollop of my Almond Walnut Dipping Sauce. I've swapped the usual peanut dipping sauce for an almond and walnut variation. You'll likely have leftover filling; just toss it into a salad the next day. Serve leftover sauce with raw veggies as a dip.

ALMOND WALNUT DIPPING SAUCE

¼   cup raw almonds

¼   cup roughly chopped raw walnuts

1   medium English cucumber, diced

½   medium orange bell pepper, diced

1   roasted garlic clove (see page 329)

1   tablespoon raw honey

1   teaspoon freshly squeezed lemon juice, plus more to taste

    Pinch crushed red pepper flakes

    Sea salt and freshly ground black pepper, to taste

RAW ROMAINE SUMMER ROLLS

4 to 6   large romaine leaves

2   carrots, peeled and julienned

2   stalks celery, thinly sliced

1   cup grape tomatoes, quartered

2   scallions or 4 fresh chives, thinly sliced

2   tablespoons finely chopped fresh curly parsley

MAKE THE SAUCE: Combine the almonds and walnuts in a blender and blend until finely ground. Add the remaining ingredients and puree until the consistency is smooth and creamy. Chill in the refrigerator for 10 minutes. Mix well before serving.

MAKE THE SUMMER ROLLS: Lay the romaine leaves on a flat surface. Layer the carrots, celery, grape tomatoes, scallions, and parsley on top.

Drizzle the summer rolls with the Almond Walnut Dipping Sauce and roll up like a burrito.

SERVES 2; MAKES 1 CUP SAUCE

courageous
BRUSSELS SPROUT CHIPS

When I first started on my path to wellness, my days were consumed with doctor appointments and stints in the sterile labyrinth that is the cancer hospital. The snacks offered in these locations were unhealthy at best; at worst, they were, ironically, stuffed with chemicals. I quickly learned to bring my own treats to perk up my blood sugar and my spirits, like these simple chips made from Brussels sprouts.
Soon I found myself bringing enough to share with the nurses—that's how good they are! Once you start whipping these up, you won't miss the starchy, less wholesome alternatives (aka white potato chips).
If you want to get fancy for entertaining or a dinner party, these are great as a garnish for soups or gluten-free whole-grain dishes (like quinoa salads). You can also turn them into a side dish with roasted veggies. If you have flavored olive oil, you can use lemon or blood orange olive oil in this recipe in place of the olive oil.

24 medium Brussels sprouts, ends trimmed
1   tablespoon extra-virgin olive oil
    Sea salt and freshly ground black pepper

Preheat the oven to 325°F.

Remove 10 to 12 leaves from each Brussels sprout and place the leaves in a large bowl. (Be sure that you've trimmed the ends of the sprouts so that the leaves come off easily.) Add the oil and salt and pepper to taste; toss to coat.

Arrange the leaves on a rimmed baking sheet in a single layer. Bake for 12 minutes, and then shake the baking sheet and stir the sprouts with a spatula to ensure even roasting. Bake for another 6 to 8 minutes, or until the leaves are crisp. Serve immediately.

SERVES 4

HAVE A HEART   After making this dish, you can turn the inner "hearts" of the sprouts (about 2 cups total) into a tasty side dish or toss them into salads. Cut these inner sprouts in half, place on a rimmed baking sheet, and toss with 1 tablespoon extra-virgin olive oil. Season with sea salt and pepper, to taste. Roast at 350°F for 20 to 25 minutes.

GREEN BEAN CHIPS

My family loves snacking on these for movie night instead of bagged chips or pretzels. They've got the crisp of a chip without the inflammatory oils and additives. If you want a different flavor, add a pinch of celery salt after you take them out of the oven.

1   cup green beans, ends trimmed
1   tablespoon extra-virgin olive oil
    Sea salt and freshly ground black pepper

Preheat the oven to 400°F.

Spread the green beans on a rimmed baking sheet and toss with the oil and salt and pepper to taste. Bake for 20 to 25 minutes, or until very crispy and golden brown. Remove from the oven and season with more salt and pepper, if needed, and let cool for 5 to 10 minutes before serving.

MAKES 1 CUP

irresistible
CHIPOTLE "FRIED" GREEN TOMATOES

These "fried" green tomatoes aren't fried at all, and they're loaded with healthy protein and omega-3s. Serve them for a weeknight appetizer or side dish. Be sure to line your baking sheet with parchment paper—the acid of the tomatoes can react with metal pans, giving tomatoes an unpleasant taste.

½   cup ground flaxseeds
¼   cup chia seeds
¼   cup shelled raw hemp seeds
1   teaspoon chili powder
½   teaspoon sea salt
½   teaspoon freshly ground black pepper
½   teaspoon chipotle powder
3   large green tomatoes, cut crosswise into ½-inch slices (about 12 slices)
¼   cup extra-virgin olive oil

Preheat the oven to 425°F. Line a rimmed baking sheet with parchment paper.

In a food processor, combine the flaxseeds, chia seeds, hemp seeds, chili powder, salt, pepper, and chipotle powder. Pulse until the mixture is finely ground, resembling cornmeal. Transfer to a plate.

Using a pastry brush, brush the tomatoes with the oil, and then gently press each side of the tomato into the flax mixture. Place the tomatoes on the prepared baking sheet and repeat with the remaining slices. Bake for 15 minutes. Flip the tomatoes and bake for 10 minutes more, or until golden brown. Remove from the oven and serve warm.

SERVES 4 TO 6

MAGNIFICENT MAPLE SQUASH TARTINES
with caramelized red onions

Ever since I was a young girl, I've loved caramelized onions. Once I found out restaurants use pro-inflammatory canola oil, refined sugar, and other yucky ingredients to make them, though, I opted for developing my own. The sweet red onion is roasted with fresh orange juice, extra-virgin olive oil, fresh thyme, and sea salt; they're the perfect touch to add to my Magnificent Maple Squash Tartines. I am a butternut squash fanatic, and when you top my grain-free crackers (pages 156–162) with a spread of Dairy-Free Creamy Cashew Cheese (page 308) and a spoonful of this warm squash, you'll never want to make another snack (or appetizer) ever again. This is also a great party dish to serve when entertaining.

1	large butternut squash, peeled, seeded, and halved lengthwise
1	large red onion, thinly sliced
2	tablespoons extra-virgin olive oil, divided
2	tablespoons freshly squeezed orange juice
½	teaspoon finely chopped fresh thyme leaves
	Sea salt
2	teaspoons pure maple syrup
2	teaspoons apple cider vinegar
	Large pinch chili powder
	Large dollop Dairy-Free Creamy Cashew Cheese (page 308), optional
1	recipe grain-free crackers (pages 156–162) or gluten-free whole-grain crackers
¼	teaspoon freshly grated orange zest

Preheat the oven to 350°F.

Cut the squash into 1-inch cubes and place in a large bowl. Add the onion, 1 tablespoon of the oil, the orange juice, thyme, and salt to taste. Arrange on a large rimmed baking sheet in a single layer and bake for about 35 minutes, or until both the squash and onion are tender and easily pierced with a knife. Transfer to a food processor or blender and add the remaining 1 tablespoon oil, the maple syrup, and the vinegar. Pulse until smooth. Add the chili powder and, if desired, more salt, and then pulse again to combine.

To serve, spread the Dairy-Free Creamy Cashew Cheese on the crackers, if desired, and top with the maple squash mixture. If not using the nut cheese, simply spread the squash mixture on the crackers. Garnish with the orange zest. Serve warm.

MAKES 4 SERVINGS

REINVENTED GRAIN-FREE CRACKERS

These six grain-free cracker recipes are showstoppers. I love to make two batches of each recipe, put them in the middle of the table, and let people serve themselves with a cracker bar, tapas style, that includes my Super Soft Caramelized Red Onions (page 272), Sun-Dried Tomato Sauce (page 320), Seriously Sensational Sriracha Sauce (page 318), Kalamata Olive and Cashew Tapenade (page 304), and a variety of hummus recipes (pages 301–303). Speaking of tapas, check out my tapas serving suggestions on page 64. These gluten-free crackers also make a great snack when topped with my Butter Me Up Honey-Almond Nut Butter (page 307) or paired with my Easy No-Foil Roasted Garlic (page 329), as well as my healthy salads for a main meal; simply crush them and use in place of croutons for a crunchy bite.

grain-free
PERFECT PARSLEY SUNFLOWER CRACKERS

These savory crackers are hard, crunchy, and herbaceous. They pair well with any of my spreads (like my dairy-free nut cheeses, pages 307–310, or my hummus recipes, pages 301–303), topped with julienned veggies or microgreens. They're also fabulous on their own.

1¼	cups shelled raw sunflower seeds, toasted (see page 108)
¾	cup sesame seeds
⅓	cup chopped red onion
¼	cup finely chopped fresh flat-leaf parsley
2	tablespoons water, plus more if needed
1	teaspoon dried rosemary
¾	teaspoon sea salt
½	teaspoon freshly ground black pepper

Preheat the oven to 350°F. Line a baking sheet with parchment paper.

In a food processor, pulse the sunflower and sesame seeds until finely crumbled. Add the remaining ingredients and process until the mixture resembles a nut butter paste.

Transfer the mixture to the prepared baking sheet and slightly flatten with the back of a spoon. Top with another piece of parchment paper and, using a rolling pin, flatten the mixture into a ¼-inch-thick rectangle. Remove the top sheet of parchment paper and score (indent with your knife, but don't cut through) 12 squares.

Bake for 15 to 18 minutes, or until the edges are golden brown, reversing the baking sheet halfway through cooking. Remove from the oven and let cool completely, and then break into pieces or cut along the scored lines with a knife before serving or storing. Store in a sealed container in the refrigerator for up to 1 week.

MAKES 12 (2X2-INCH) SQUARES

CLOCKWISE FROM TOP LEFT:
GRAIN-FREE PERFECT PARSLEY SUNFLOWER CRACKERS
GRAIN-FREE GRACIOUS HEMPY SEEDY ROUNDS. (PAGE 160)
GRAIN-FREE LEMON PEPPERED ALMOND CRACKERS. (PAGE 162)

CLOCKWISE TOP FROM RIGHT:
HAPPY HEMP SEED, CHICKPEA MISO, AND CRANBERRY GRAIN-FREE CRACKERS.
GRAIN-FREE GOLDEN HERBES DE PROVENCE CRACKERS. (PAGE 161)
GRAIN-FREE MULTI-SEED CRACKERS. (PAGE 162)

HAPPY HEMP SEED, CHICKPEA MISO, AND CRANBERRY GRAIN-FREE CRACKERS

Beyond tasting amazing, these crackers are packed with protein (and fiber) and they're completely grain-free. Their flavor is unexpected: the combination of tomatoes and chickpea miso paste has lots of umami, one of the five basic tastes that make food so irresistible. You'll want to bring these crackers with you to restaurants when dining out so you can enjoy your own grain-free "bread" while everyone else digs into the gluten-filled bread basket.

1	cup cherry tomatoes, diced
⅓	cup dried cranberries
1	tablespoon chickpea miso paste
2	cups finely chopped red onion
¾	cup ground flaxseeds
1	garlic clove, minced
¼	teaspoon dried rosemary
½	cup shelled raw hemp seeds
2	tablespoons chia seeds
¼	teaspoon sea salt
¼	teaspoon freshly ground black pepper

Preheat the oven to 250°F. Line a baking sheet with parchment paper.

In a food processor, combine the tomatoes, cranberries, and miso; process until smooth. Add the onion, flaxseeds, garlic, and rosemary; process until smooth. Transfer to a large bowl, add the hemp seeds, chia seeds, salt, and pepper, and mix well to combine.

Transfer the mixture to the prepared baking sheet and flatten with a spatula into an even ¼-inch-thick layer. Place a piece of parchment paper on top of the mixture.

Bake for 1 hour, and then reverse the baking sheet and remove the parchment paper. Bake for about another hour, or until golden brown. Remove from the oven and let cool completely, about 15 minutes, and then break into pieces or cut with a knife before serving or storing. Store in a sealed container for up to 4 days.

MAKES 8 SERVINGS (ABOUT 20 CRACKERS)

grain-free
GRACIOUS HEMPY SEEDY ROUNDS

These delicate round crackers are light and chewy with a touch of spice. They pair well with any of my spreads or dips, especially my dairy-free nut cheeses (pages 307–310) and my salsas (pages 230 and 305–306), but they're equally great served on their own.

½ cup shelled raw pumpkin seeds, finely ground (see Note)

¼ cup almond flour, store-bought or homemade (see page 39)

¼ cup ground flaxseeds

¼ cup shelled raw hemp seeds

1 teaspoon chili powder

1 teaspoon dried oregano

¼ teaspoon sea salt

Pinch cayenne pepper

¼ cup water

1 tablespoon extra-virgin olive oil

1 teaspoon freshly grated orange zest

Preheat the oven to 350°F. Line a baking sheet with parchment paper.

In a medium bowl, combine the ground pumpkin seeds, almond flour, flaxseeds, hemp seeds, chili powder, oregano, salt, and cayenne pepper. Add the water, oil, and orange zest; mix well to combine. You should end up with a slightly wet, sticky mixture.

Either use a ½-teaspoon measure to drop the dough onto the prepared baking sheet and flatten with the back of a spoon to no more than ⅛ inch thick or top with another piece of parchment paper and use a rolling pin to flatten the entire piece of dough to ⅛-inch thick and use a small, round cookie cutter to make the crackers. Make sure the rounds are even and flat. Bake for 15 minutes, or until crisp and golden brown. Remove from the oven and let cool completely before serving or storing. Store in a sealed container in the refrigerator for up to 1 week.

NOTE: You can use a mini food processor to finely grind the pumpkin seeds.

MAKES 12 CRACKERS

grain-free
GOLDEN HERBES DE PROVENCE CRACKERS

These crackers are made with chia seeds, which makes them a bit spongier and bendable. Serve them alone or with any of my spreads (hummus, pages 301–303, or Kalamata Olive and Cashew Tapenade, page 304). They make a great addition to my Vegetarian Antipasto Platter (page 64).

1	cup ground flaxseeds
½	cup shelled raw sunflower seeds, toasted (see page 108)
½	cup chia seeds
¼	cup raw pine nuts, toasted (see page 108)
1	tablespoon coconut flour
1	teaspoon herbes de Provence
1	teaspoon freshly grated lemon zest
½	teaspoon freshly ground black pepper
1	teaspoon sea salt
	Pinch cayenne pepper
1	cup water

Preheat the oven to 350°F. Line a baking sheet with parchment paper.

In a medium bowl, combine all the ingredients except the water, until blended well. Add the water and mix well.

Transfer the mixture to the prepared baking sheet and slightly flatten with the back of a spoon. Top with another piece of parchment paper and, using a rolling pin, flatten into a ¼-inch-thick rectangle. Remove the top sheet of parchment paper and score (indent with your knife, but don't cut through) into 16 squares.

Bake for 25 minutes, or until the edges are golden brown. Reverse the baking sheet halfway through baking. Remove from the oven and let cool completely, at least 15 to 20 minutes, and then break into pieces or cut with a knife along the scored lines before serving or storing. Store in a sealed container in the refrigerator for up to 1 week.

MAKES 16 (2X2-INCH) SQUARES

grain-free
LEMON PEPPERED ALMOND CRACKERS

These crunchy, thick crackers have a mild flavor that can be served alone or paired with any of my spreads, such as my dairy-free nut cheeses (pages 307–310) or Kalamata Olive and Cashew Tapenade (page 304).

1¼ cups almond flour, store-bought or homemade (see page 39)

¼ cup shelled raw sunflower seeds

1 tablespoon ground flaxseeds

½ teaspoon sea salt

½ teaspoon freshly grated lemon zest

½ teaspoon freshly ground black pepper

3 tablespoons water

Preheat the oven to 350°F. Line a baking sheet with parchment paper.

Place all the ingredients except the water in a food processor; pulse until crumbly. With the motor running, in a steady stream, add the water until the mixture starts to come together.

Transfer the dough to the prepared baking sheet. Top with another piece of parchment paper and, using a rolling pin, flatten into a ¼-inch-thick rectangle. Remove the top sheet of parchment paper and score into 24 squares.

Bake for 15 minutes, or until the crackers are lightly browned on the edges. Let cool completely and then break into pieces or cut with a knife along the scored lines before serving or storing. Store in a sealed container in the refrigerator for up to 1 week.

MAKES 24 (2X2-INCH) SQUARES

grain-free
MULTI-SEED CRACKERS

These flaxy, soft, and chewy crackers pair well with my hummus recipes (pages 301–303). You can serve these in lieu of the glutenous bread basket before dinner so you don't feel deprived.

½ cup raw walnuts

1 cup shelled raw pumpkin seeds, toasted (see page 108)

½ cup ground flaxseeds

½ teaspoon ground cumin

½ teaspoon sea salt

½ teaspoon freshly ground black pepper

Pinch crushed red pepper flakes

½ cup water

Preheat the oven to 350°F. Line a baking sheet with parchment paper.

Place the walnuts in a food processor and process until finely ground. Add the remaining ingredients except the water and pulse to combine. In a steady stream, add the water and pulse a few times. The mixture will be very wet.

Transfer to the prepared baking sheet and, using a spatula, flatten into a ¼-inch-thick rectangle. Let the mixture sit for 12 minutes, and then bake for 20 minutes. Score the crackers with a butter knife and then rotate the baking sheet and bake for another 15 minutes, or until golden brown. Let cool completely and then break into pieces or cut with a knife along the scored lines before serving or storing. Store in a sealed container in the refrigerator for up to 1 week.

MAKES 20 CRACKERS

appetizers and soups

Light fare? Maybe. But don't underestimate soups and appetizers! These aren't one-trick ponies. Sure, they make great party food and tasty starters for dinner, but they also hold up very well on their own.

The misconception about cooking for your health is that one meal is supposed to contain at least a third of your daily nutritional intake. In reality, it's easier to fulfill your dietary needs by eating a variety of things over the course of the day, and my appetizers are the perfect way to do this!

Honestly, sometimes appetizers can be served as a main meal. I turn my kitchen into a DIY tapas restaurant, nibbling on a range of starter-type dishes that work well together, complementing each other in terms of both flavor profile and nutrition. However you decide to eat them, these tasty appetizers are a great way to start eating clean.

A Word about Soups

Nothing says comfort food like a big, warm bowl of soup. And really, nothing's easier, especially for a hot meal that transports easily. I'm totally bringing back the 1980s thermos—I tote my soups all around town, and I urge you to do the same.

As you can imagine, I'm not a fan of canned soups—they're not only loaded with sodium, added sugar, fillers, and preservatives, but they're canned, and that means chemicals used to preserve the food and line the can, as well as BPA and yucky heavy metals like aluminum leach into your food...yum.

What about those soup bars at restaurants and delis? Puh-leeeease. You never really know what's in them (doubt that anyone does), and if you're sensitive to any ingredients like I am, they could spell trouble for you. Once you go the homemade route, it's really hard to go back to those tin-can, salty excuses for soup.

Every soup recipe you'll find in this book is, of course, gluten-, dairy-, soy-, corn-, egg-, and peanut-free. Nothing's from a can or a box, and there's no refined sugar. In fact, many of the soups I create are just a mixed-up jumble of fresh ingredients and veggies in my pantry and fridge. Once you know what you like, you really can improvise! If you're not there yet, these recipes will serve as a simple guide; feel free to divert from them however you please.

Best part: They smell delicious on the stove and taste amazing.

HOMEMADE TORTILLA PARTY BOWL

Your Super Bowl will never be the same after you dig into this power bowl. While everyone else is chowing down on Buffalo wings filled with high-fructose corn syrup and chips made from ingredients you can't pronounce, why not toss together this easy-peasy party bowl for yourself? It's my go-to appetizer for tailgate parties, summer block parties, and watching sports games (though, of course, you can serve it for friends anytime).

1½   cups cooked cannellini beans (see page 99)

1½   cups cooked black beans (see page 99)

1   teaspoon chili powder

1   teaspoon ground cumin

    Sea salt and freshly ground black pepper

1   (16-ounce) bag gluten-free whole-grain (corn-free) tortilla chips

2   large ripe avocados, pitted, peeled, and diced

1   pint cherry tomatoes, halved

1½   cups Perfect Pico de Gallo (page 242) or your favorite store-bought salsa

1   cup Dairy-Free Creamy Cashew Cheese (page 308)

½   cup finely chopped fresh cilantro

4   scallions, white and light green parts, thinly sliced

Preheat the broiler to high.

In a medium bowl, combine both of the beans, chili powder, cumin, and salt and pepper to taste. Layer a 9x14-inch rimmed baking dish with the tortilla chips and top with the bean mixture. Broil the beans and tortilla chips for 5 minutes on the middle rack (or, if you have a separate broiler, 6 inches from the heat source). Remove from the oven and top with the avocado, tomatoes, Perfect Pico de Gallo, Dairy-Free Creamy Cashew Cheese, cilantro, and scallions. Serve warm with cocktail napkins so guests can eat with their hands.

SERVES 6 TO 8

vivacious
ZUCCHINI AND GINGER CASHEW PESTO
ON ZUCCHINI LOGS

*At the height of summer when zucchini is spilling over the edges of grocers' tables
(or monopolizing your garden), you don't want to run out of ways to capitalize on the wealth of green.
This dish is easy to make, yet very impressive. This also makes a beautiful party appetizer.*

1	small zucchini, ends trimmed
2	tablespoons extra-virgin olive oil, plus more for brushing zucchini
	Sea salt and freshly ground black pepper
½	cup raw cashews
¼	cup peeled and diced cucumber
1	tablespoon finely chopped fresh basil
1	tablespoon peeled minced fresh ginger
1	teaspoon ground ginger
1	teaspoon finely chopped lemongrass
1	small garlic clove
1	cup arugula
1	tablespoon sesame seeds, toasted (see page 108), for serving

Preheat the oven to 350°F. Line a rimmed baking sheet with parchment paper.

Slice the zucchini lengthwise into ¼-inch slices and place on the prepared baking sheet. Using a pastry brush, brush each side of the zucchini with oil and sprinkle with a dash of salt and pepper to taste. Bake for 10 minutes, flip the slices, and bake for another 5 minutes, or until the zucchini is tender. Transfer to a serving plate.

In a food processor, combine the cashews, cucumber, basil, gingers, 2 tablespoons oil, lemongrass, garlic, and salt and pepper to taste. Puree until smooth, about 2 minutes. Scrape down the sides and let the food processor run for 1 to 2 minutes more, or until the pesto is smooth.

Spread the pesto down the center of each slice of zucchini and top each with arugula. Sprinkle with the toasted sesame seeds and serve whole or sliced into 1-inch pieces and serve with toothpicks.

SERVES 2

SUNRISE NORI WRAPS
with spicy tahini drizzle

If you like California rolls, you'll love these nori wraps (though personally, I think they're so much better!). The tahini dressing is truly addictive—you're going to want to dress everything in it—and the cabbage provides a nice crunch. If possible, use a food processor to slice the cabbage so you can get it super thin. Also, make sure the vegetable strips are all the same width and length so that they don't hang over the edges of the nori sheets; this will make rolling up the wraps easier. Use leftover tahini drizzle as a dressing for salads or a dip for crudités.

SPICY TAHINI DRIZZLE

2	tablespoons freshly squeezed lemon juice
1¼	tablespoons chickpea miso paste
1	tablespoon tahini (see Note, page 301)
2	Medjool dates, pitted
1	garlic clove, minced
¼	teaspoon crushed red pepper flakes
	Water, as needed

SUNRISE NORI WRAPS

4	nori seaweed sheets
¼	small head red cabbage, very thinly sliced
1	large carrot, peeled and julienned
1	small yellow summer squash, julienned
1	small cucumber, julienned
1	large ripe avocado, pitted, peeled, and sliced

MAKE THE TAHINI DRIZZLE: Combine all the drizzle ingredients except the water in a blender. Blend, adding water 1 teaspoon at a time as you go, until the mixture becomes a thin sauce.

MAKE THE NORI WRAPS: Place the nori sheets on a flat surface. Divide the cabbage, carrot, squash, cucumber, and avocado among the sheets.

Top each pile of vegetables with a heaping tablespoon of the Spicy Tahini Drizzle, and then roll up the nori sheets into a tube shape and serve immediately.

NOTE: You can also make these into a fun appetizer size by cutting each piece of nori into quarters and topping with a teaspoon of the drizzle as shown.

SERVES 4; MAKES ⅓ CUP SAUCE

RAW JICAMA ROMAINE WRAPS
with dilly lime drizzle

Jicama has long been relegated to Mexican dishes, but it's such a wonderful vegetable—light, crunchy, distinctly flavored—that we should all use it more often. Here, I envelop jicama in romaine leaves, a great alternative to the usual processed grain–based wraps. The romaine is sturdy enough to hold the wrap ingredients in, but soft enough to bite into.

3	tablespoons shelled raw pumpkin seeds
2	tablespoons freshly squeezed lime juice
1	tablespoon finely chopped fresh dill or basil
1½	teaspoons white sesame seeds
	Pinch crushed red pepper flakes
	Sea salt and freshly ground black pepper
8	large romaine lettuce leaves
½	cup Oil-Free Traditional Hummus (page 301)
2	large carrots, peeled and finely grated
1	medium jicama, peeled and finely grated, shredded, or diced
2	cups finely shredded red cabbage
1	cup diced English cucumber
	Sprouts or microgreens, for topping, optional

In a small bowl, combine the pumpkin seeds, lime juice, dill, sesame seeds, red pepper flakes, and salt and pepper to taste.

Place the romaine leaves on a flat surface. Spread 2 tablespoons of Oil-Free Traditional Hummus on each leaf, and then layer the carrot, jicama, cabbage, and cucumber on top. Sprinkle with the pumpkin seed mixture and, if desired, top with sprouts or microgreens. Roll the romaine leaves up lengthwise. Serve immediately.

SERVES 4

HERBED AVOCADOS
with caramelized lemon drizzle

When I first made this dish, I couldn't get over how a handful of simple ingredients could be so flavorful. I love how the charred lemon brings out the creamy, smoky flavors of the warmed avocado. Then, just when you thought it couldn't get any better, the tomato-basil mixture takes you to another level.

10	grape tomatoes, halved
¼	cup slivered raw almonds, toasted (see page 108)
1	tablespoon finely chopped fresh basil
2	teaspoons extra-virgin olive oil, plus more for grilling
	Sea salt and freshly ground black pepper
2	large ripe avocados, halved, pitted, and peeled
1	large lemon, halved
4	fresh chives, thinly sliced

Preheat a grill to medium.

In a small bowl, combine the tomatoes, almonds, basil, oil, and salt and pepper to taste.

Lightly coat the cut side of the avocado and lemon halves with oil. Place them on the grill cut-side down for 8 minutes, or until the avocados have grill marks and the lemons are lightly charred and caramelized. Transfer to a serving plate.

Top the avocado halves with the tomato-basil mixture. Sprinkle with the chives and drizzle with juice from the caramelized lemon. Serve immediately.

SERVES 4

GRILLED GREEN BEANS, SHALLOTS 'N' SCALLIONS
with romesco sauce

Shallots are one of the great unsung members of the onion family. Milder than onions, they're particularly tasty on the grill. Here, I combine them with scallions and green beans, and then serve the whole mess o' veggies on a big platter, drizzled with Romesco Sauce and garnished with hazelnuts and parsley.

1	tablespoon extra-virgin olive oil, plus more for coating grill basket
2	cups green beans, ends trimmed
8	large thick scallions
2	shallots, sliced in half lengthwise
¼	teaspoon sea salt
¼	teaspoon freshly ground black pepper
1½	cups Romesco Sauce (page 266)
¼	cup finely chopped fresh flat-leaf parsley
1	tablespoon chopped raw hazelnuts

Preheat a grill to medium. Lightly coat a grill basket with oil.

In a large bowl, combine the green beans, scallions, and shallots. Drizzle with the oil, salt, and pepper and toss to coat. Transfer to the grill basket.

Grill for 8 to 10 minutes, or until the vegetables are tender, tossing halfway through for even cooking. Transfer to a serving platter and drizzle the Romesco Sauce on top. Garnish with the parsley and hazelnuts. Serve warm.

SERVES 4 TO 6

GRILLED VIDALIA ONIONS
with blueberry tarragon dressing

Vidalia onions are so wonderfully sweet that they barely need any prep work. Simply grill them, drizzle a dressing on top, and you've got a lovely appetizer. Be aware that, for maximum flavor, it's best to make the dressing the day before and chill it overnight.

BLUEBERRY TARRAGON DRESSING

⅔ cup fresh blueberries

¼ cup apple cider vinegar

3 tablespoons extra-virgin olive oil

2 tablespoons raw honey

1 teaspoon finely chopped fresh tarragon

Sea salt and freshly ground black pepper, to taste

GRILLED VIDALIA ONIONS

3 tablespoons extra-virgin olive oil, plus more for coating grill basket

4 medium Vidalia onions, cut into ½-inch slices

Sea salt and freshly ground black pepper

MAKE THE DRESSING: Combine all the dressing ingredients in a blender and puree until smooth. Store in a sealed jar in the refrigerator overnight to let the flavors marry.

MAKE THE ONIONS: Preheat a grill to medium. Lightly coat a grill basket with oil.

Rub the oil over the onion slices and sprinkle with salt and pepper to taste. Place the onions in the grill basket and set on the grill. Cook for 10 minutes, or until tender and grill marks appear, flipping halfway through the cooking.

Transfer the onions to a serving platter. Drizzle with the Blueberry Tarragon Dressing and serve immediately. Keep additional dressing on the side, if needed.

SERVES 6 TO 8; MAKES ¾ CUP DRESSING

CHAR-TICHOKES (GRILLED ARTICHOKES)
with honey mint dipping sauce

I love artichokes every which way, but grilling them really takes these veggies to new heights—
as does the honey mint dipping sauce served alongside. Infused with fresh basil and citrus,
it complements the artichokes' earthy flavor (you'll never dip artichokes in butter again).

HONEY MINT DIPPING SAUCE

⅓ cup finely chopped fresh mint

2 tablespoons extra-virgin olive oil

2 tablespoons freshly squeezed lemon juice

1 tablespoon raw honey

1 tablespoon finely chopped fresh basil

Pinch sea salt

GRILLED ARTICHOKES

4 large artichokes, tops and leaves trimmed,
cut in half lengthwise (see Note)

2 tablespoons freshly squeezed lemon juice,
divided

3 tablespoons extra-virgin olive oil

Sea salt and freshly ground black pepper

MAKE THE SAUCE: In a small bowl, whisk together all of the sauce ingredients. Store the sauce in a sealed container in the refrigerator for 30 minutes or until ready to serve.

MAKE THE ARTICHOKES: Scoop out the choke of each artichoke and drizzle or brush 1 tablespoon of the lemon juice over the halves to prevent browning.

Place a steamer basket in a large pot filled with water up to the steamer's bottom. Place the artichokes in the steamer, cover, and steam over medium heat until tender, about 30 minutes.

Transfer to a serving platter and brush the cut sides of the artichoke halves with the oil and the remaining 1 tablespoon lemon juice. Sprinkle with salt and pepper to taste.

Preheat a grill to medium.

Place the steamed artichokes cut-side down on the grill and grill until charred, about 10 minutes.

Serve the artichokes with Honey Mint Dipping Sauce.

NOTE: To trim the tops and the leaves of the artichokes, cut about 1 inch off the top of each artichoke using a sharp knife. Remove tough, dry leaves around the stems and then trim ¼ inch off of the leaf tips.

SERVES 4; MAKES ABOUT ⅓ CUP SAUCE

SWEET PEA CROSTINI
with dairy-free creamy cashew cheese

Here, I pair cashew cheese with a lemony pea spread, which provides a nice tangy contrast to the richness of the cheese. Both also work well on their own—the pea spread served with gluten-free whole-grain bread or my grain-free crackers (pages 156–162), and the Dairy-Free Creamy Cashew Cheese (page 308) topped with sliced fruit or roasted bell peppers. If you're using frozen peas, remove them from the freezer, measure, and place in a strainer. Run cold water over the peas for one to two minutes or until thawed. Drain well.

1½ cups fresh or thawed frozen green peas

3 tablespoons finely chopped fresh mint

1 tablespoon freshly squeezed lemon juice

1 tablespoon extra-virgin olive oil

Pinch freshly grated lemon zest, plus more for garnish, optional

Sea salt and freshly ground black pepper

Dairy-Free Creamy Cashew Cheese (page 308)

Gluten-free whole-grain bread, toasted, or grain-free crackers (pages 156–162)

Fresh whole mint leaves, for garnish, optional

Place the peas, mint, lemon juice, and oil in a food processor. Process until smooth. Season with the lemon zest, if desired, and salt and pepper to taste; pulse to combine.

Spread the Dairy-Free Creamy Cashew Cheese on top of toast or crackers. Top with the pea spread and serve immediately. Garnish with lemon zest and mint leaves, if desired.

SERVES 4

SUMMER SQUASH CASHEW KALE BOATS

From the vitamin-packed dark green kale to the protein-rich macadamias, every crumb in this dish will contribute to your good health. These "boats" are also beautiful to look at—and a nice change from tossed vegetables. The herbs also help to turn plain squash into something fresh and vibrant. You can also add a sprinkling of pine nuts or chopped toasted almonds, if desired. In a pinch, you can always use my Dairy-Free Creamy Cashew Cheese (page 308) instead of the recommended Dairy-Free Sunshine Macadamia "Cream" Cheese (page 310).

2	medium yellow summer squash
1	tablespoon extra-virgin olive oil
1	large garlic clove, minced
1	cup orange or red grape tomatoes, quartered
⅓	cup chopped and stemmed dinosaur (lacinato) kale or Swiss chard
4	baby bella mushrooms, finely chopped
¼	cup finely chopped fresh flat-leaf parsley
	Sea salt
2	tablespoons Dairy-Free Sunshine Macadamia "Cream" Cheese (page 310), for serving, plus more if needed
4	fresh chives, thinly sliced, for garnish
	Few sprigs fresh mint or cilantro, finely chopped, for garnish

Preheat the oven to 350°F.

Place the squash on a rimmed baking sheet and bake until the flesh is tender and the skin is soft, 15 to 20 minutes. Remove from the oven, slice in half, and scoop out the flesh with a spoon, leaving a ⅓-inch shell and keeping the skin intact. Reserve the flesh.

In a large skillet, heat the oil over low heat and sauté the garlic for 30 seconds. Add the squash flesh, turn up the heat to medium, and cook until the squash is golden, about 5 minutes. Add the tomatoes, kale, and mushrooms and cook until the tomatoes release their juices and the kale is soft, about 5 minutes. Remove from the heat, stir in the parsley, and season with salt to taste.

Combine the Dairy-Free Sunshine Macadamia "Cream" Cheese with the kale mixture, and then stuff the mixture into the squash boats. Garnish with the chives and mint. Serve warm. Add more nut cheese, if desired.

SERVES 2

GRILLED PEACH AND DAIRY-FREE CASHEW CHEESE ZUCCHINI SPEARS
with honey chili sauce

As summer heats up, everyone always wants to know what meatless edibles I'm putting on the grill. Veggie burgers and grilled mushrooms are great, but I don't stop there. These grilled peach and zucchini rounds, souped up with my dairy-free cashew cheese and honey chili sauce, take the boredom out of vegetarian barbecuing—I promise you, even the carnivores will gobble them up. The sauce is also great paired with sweet potato fries, my dairy-free ice creams (pages 334–339), and brownies.

1½	tablespoons extra-virgin olive oil, divided, plus more for coating grill basket
3	tablespoons raw honey
½	teaspoon chili powder
2	large zucchini, cut into spears or ½-inch rounds
½	teaspoon smoked sea salt
¼	teaspoon freshly ground black pepper
2	slightly firm large peaches, cut in half and pitted
2	fresh basil leaves or chives, thinly sliced, for garnish
	Dairy-Free Creamy Cashew Cheese (page 308)

Preheat a grill to medium. Lightly coat a grill basket with oil.

In a small bowl, whisk together the honey and chili powder. Set aside.

In a large bowl, toss the zucchini with 1 tablespoon of the oil, the salt, and the pepper. Brush the cut side of the peaches with the remaining ½ tablespoon oil. Place the zucchini in the grill basket and the peach halves cut-side down directly on the grill. Grill the zucchini and peaches for 7 to 10 minutes, and then flip and continue to grill until golden brown with grill marks, about 5 minutes.

Transfer the zucchini and peaches to a serving plate and drizzle with the honey chili sauce. Garnish with the basil and serve warm with dollops of the Dairy-Free Creamy Cashew Cheese on top.

SERVES 6 TO 8

GRILLED KALE AND SWEET POTATO "GRAIN-FREE BRUSCHETTA"
with sunflower seed drizzle

Bruschetta, as you probably know, is an Italian recipe typically made with toasted bread. This breadless variation on the theme, using sweet potato as a base, is much more nutritious—and just as delish. While this dish is the perfect appetizer for a crowd (simply double and triple the recipe as needed), don't wait for a party: I've happily snacked on this bruschetta alone in my Manhattan apartment many times.

SUNFLOWER SEED DRIZZLE

½   cup shelled raw sunflower seeds

⅓   cup apple cider vinegar

¼   cup extra-virgin olive oil

3   tablespoons water

2   tablespoons raw honey or pure maple syrup

1   teaspoon Dijon mustard

¼   teaspoon horseradish

    Sea salt and freshly ground black pepper, to taste

GRAIN-FREE BRUSCHETTA

1   large sweet potato, peeled and cut into ½-inch rounds

    Freshly squeezed juice of 1 large lime

1   tablespoon extra-virgin olive oil

1   teaspoon coconut aminos

¼   teaspoon freshly ground black pepper

1   large bunch curly kale, stems removed and chopped

1½ cups sprouts, for garnish

4   fresh chives, thinly sliced, for garnish

1   tablespoon sesame seeds, for garnish

MAKE THE SUNFLOWER SEED DRIZZLE: Combine all the drizzle ingredients in a blender and process until smooth.

MAKE THE BRUSCHETTA: Place a steamer basket in a large pot filled with water up to the steamer's bottom. Place the sweet potatoes in the steamer, cover, and steam over medium heat until tender, about 7 minutes.

Preheat a grill to medium.

In a small bowl, whisk together the lime juice, oil, coconut aminos, and pepper.

In a large bowl, toss the kale with half of the lime juice dressing. Transfer the kale to a rimmed baking sheet, place the baking sheet on the grill, and grill until crispy, about 10 minutes.

Place the sweet potato rounds on a serving plate, drizzle with the remaining lime juice dressing, and top with some grilled kale and the Sunflower Seed Drizzle. Garnish with the sprouts, chives, and sesame seeds. Serve immediately.

SERVES 4; MAKES 1 CUP SAUCE

SUMMER ZUCCHINI AND FRESH BASIL SOUP

*In the early stages of my road to wellness, I couldn't tolerate any foods that weren't liquefied.
The Western medicine doctors I was seeing recommended that I try liquid meal replacements—you know,
those milk-shake-y kinds of drinks typically sold in drugstores—but I was shocked at how unwholesome they
were. I couldn't even pronounce the ingredients listed on their labels! How could doctors offer these
supplements to their patients as a viable alternative? Determined to find a better way, I began blending all
kinds of healthy foods together to make liquid meals of my own. It was during this experimentation phase
that I came up with this recipe, now one of my cold soup faves. Who knew zucchini would taste so fantastic
pureed? This soup makes a lovely summer weeknight meal or starter for a dinner party.*

4	cups low-sodium vegetable broth
¼	cup extra-virgin olive oil, plus more for drizzling
½	medium onion, diced
1	medium carrot, peeled and diced
1	small celery stalk, diced
7	medium zucchini, ends trimmed, seeded, and diced
	Sea salt and freshly ground black pepper
½	cup finely chopped fresh basil
1	cup Gluten-Free Herbed Croutons (page 190), for garnish
	Microgreens, for garnish
	Fresh basil leaves, cut into a chiffonade, for garnish

In a medium saucepan, bring the broth to a boil over high heat. Turn off the heat and set aside.

In a large pot, heat the oil over medium-high heat. Add the onion, carrot, and celery and cook until tender, about 4 minutes. Add one-third of the zucchini to the pot and season with salt and pepper to taste. Cook for 2 minutes and repeat with the remaining zucchini.

Add the broth to the pot, cover, and bring to a low boil. Cook until the zucchini is tender, about 8 minutes. Add the basil and cook until just wilted.

Let the soup cool slightly, and then, in batches, transfer to a blender and puree until smooth. If needed, pass the soup through a fine sieve. Taste and season with salt and pepper if necessary. Portion into serving bowls and garnish with the Gluten-Free Herbed Croutons, microgreens, and basil. Drizzle with oil and serve.

SERVES 6

GOLDEN BELL PEPPER SOUP

Dipping your spoon into this bell pepper–sweet potato combo is like dipping into a bowl of sunshine. It's stunning—and the perfect antidote to a gloomy winter's day. This soup also freezes well, so if you're not serving a crowd, store the leftovers for a later date. I like to enjoy this soup accompanied by my Massaged Kale Salad with Spicy Hazelnuts (page 201).

¼ cup extra-virgin olive oil

½ small onion, diced

2 medium carrots, peeled and diced

1 celery stalk, diced

Sea salt and freshly ground black pepper

8 yellow, red, and/or orange bell peppers, chopped

1 large sweet potato, peeled and chopped

4 cups low-sodium vegetable broth

1 tablespoon finely chopped fresh marjoram

Water, if needed

1 recipe Gluten-Free Herbed Croutons (page 190), for garnish

Sliced avocado, for garnish, optional

Finely chopped fresh cilantro, for garnish, optional

Seriously Sensational Sriracha Sauce (page 318), for garnish, optional

In a large pot, heat the oil over medium heat. Add the onion, carrots, celery, and a pinch of salt and black pepper. Cook until the vegetables are tender, about 4 minutes. Add the bell peppers and cook until soft, about 6 minutes. Add the sweet potatoes and broth. Season with salt and black pepper to taste, cover the pot, and bring to a boil. Lower the heat and add the marjoram. Simmer until the vegetables are tender, about 20 minutes.

Let the soup cool slightly, and then, in batches, transfer to a blender and puree until smooth. If needed, thin the soup with water. Taste and season with salt and black pepper if necessary. Return the soup to the pot to keep warm until serving. Serve garnished with the Gluten-Free Herbed Croutons and, if desired, the avocado and cilantro on top and a drizzle of the Seriously Sensational Sriracha Sauce, if desired.

SERVES 6 TO 8

ROASTED BUTTERNUT SQUASH SOUP
with poppy seed polka dots and
maple balsamic drizzle

*I decided to throw poppy seeds into this butternut squash soup recipe for a few reasons.
First, I'm a Jersey girl with a Manhattan heart, and true New Yorkers eat poppy seed bagels.
Obviously, that's not an option for me, but I love poppy seeds nevertheless, and I also happen to really like
polka dots. So what's better than poppy seeds in soup? It doesn't hurt that they also add a pleasant crunch
along with a dose of calcium, iron, zinc, plus the micronutrients folate and niacin. Bear in mind that
you can use apples instead of pears in this soup if you prefer. Just don't leave out the polka dots!*

1	large butternut squash
3½	cups low-sodium vegetable broth
3	large pears, cored and diced
¼	teaspoon ground ginger
¼	teaspoon sea salt
¼	teaspoon freshly ground black pepper
¼	teaspoon ground cinnamon
1	tablespoon balsamic vinegar
1	tablespoon pure maple syrup
1	tablespoon poppy seeds, for garnish
	Pinch ground nutmeg, for garnish

Preheat the oven to 350°F. Line a rimmed baking sheet with parchment paper.

Remove and discard the ends of the squash. Cut the squash in half lengthwise and remove all the seeds. Place the squash cut-side down on the prepared baking sheet. Bake for 45 minutes, or until the squash is tender. Set aside to cool.

Using a spoon, scoop out the flesh of the squash and place it in a large pot. Add the broth, pears, ginger, salt, pepper, and cinnamon. Cook over medium-high heat until heated through, 10 to 12 minutes.

In the meantime, whisk together the vinegar and maple syrup in a small bowl. Set aside.

Transfer the squash to a blender and puree until smooth. Add more salt if necessary.

Portion the soup into serving bowls and garnish with the poppy seeds, nutmeg, and a drizzle of the maple balsamic sauce. Serve immediately.

SERVES 4

"CREAMY" TARRAGON CAULIFLOWER SOUP
with chickpeas

You don't actually need a drop of cream to make a deliciously creamy soup. The proof: This super-easy, sauté-simmer-and-serve cauliflower dish. The trick I use here—adding cashews and legumes to give the soup a thick, velvety texture—can be used to make any soup heartier, no dairy required!

2	tablespoons extra-virgin olive oil
1	large leek, thinly sliced
3	celery stalks, sliced
1	large garlic clove, minced
1	large head cauliflower, cut into ½-inch florets
1	cup cooked chickpeas or cannellini beans (see page 99)
¼	teaspoon crushed red pepper flakes
	Sea salt and freshly ground black pepper
5½	cups low-sodium vegetable broth
¼	cup finely chopped fresh tarragon, plus more for garnish
4	fresh chives, thinly sliced, plus more for garnish
½	cup raw cashews
2	tablespoons water, if needed

In a large pot, heat the oil over medium heat. Add the leek and sauté for 3 minutes. Add the celery and garlic and sauté until the celery is soft, about 2 minutes. Add the cauliflower, chickpeas, red pepper flakes, and salt and black pepper to taste. Mix well, and then add the broth. Cover and cook until the cauliflower is soft, about 20 minutes. Turn off the heat and stir in the tarragon and chives.

Let the soup cool slightly, then, in batches, transfer to a blender and puree with the cashews until smooth. If needed, thin the soup with the water. Taste and season with salt and black pepper if necessary. Return the soup to the pot to keep warm until serving. Portion into serving bowls and serve garnished with additional tarragon and chives.

SERVES 4

BUILD A BETTER SOUP Toss gluten-free grains like cooked quinoa, teff, millet, brown rice, wild rice, black rice, or amaranth into your soup for a protein and fiber boost.

curried
LENTIL SOUP

*My father loves lentil soup, even the canned varieties that are packed with tons of sodium
(and who knows what else!). I created this recipe to wean him off the unhealthy stuff and get him
hooked on the real deal instead. And it worked—he's a fan. This soup is pureed, so it's not like the classic
soup with whole lentils, plus it has a lovely curry flavor that will wow your taste buds. It's perfect for
a chilly winter evening or afternoon served with my grain-free crackers (pages 156–162).*

1	tablespoon extra-virgin olive oil
¾	cup finely chopped white onion
1	garlic clove, minced
1	teaspoon peeled minced fresh ginger
2	teaspoons curry powder
¼	teaspoon sea salt
¼	teaspoon freshly ground black pepper
	Pinch crushed red pepper flakes
7	cups low-sodium vegetable broth
1½	cups dried green lentils
1½	cups baby kale
1	tablespoon balsamic vinegar
3	tablespoons finely chopped fresh cilantro, for garnish
2	tablespoons shelled raw pumpkin seeds, toasted (see page 108), for garnish

In a large saucepan, heat the oil over medium heat. Add the onion and sauté until translucent, about 3 minutes. Add the garlic and ginger and sauté for another minute. Add the curry powder, salt, black pepper, and red pepper flakes and cook for another 45 seconds. Add the broth, lentils, kale, and vinegar. Cover, increase the heat to high, and bring to a boil. Uncover, reduce the heat, and simmer until the lentils are fully cooked, about 15 minutes depending on type of lentils. Season to taste with salt.

Let the soup cool slightly, and then, in batches, transfer to a blender and puree until smooth. Return the soup to the pot to keep warm until serving. Portion into serving bowls and serve garnished with the cilantro and pumpkin seeds.

SERVES 4

no-soy
CHICKPEA MISO SOUP

As difficult as it is to give up foods you love due to sensitivities, inflammation, or other health concerns, take heart: I found that I could make delicious substitutes for almost every food I grew up loving. Among them is miso soup. Because of my hypothyroid condition, I avoid soy. But—eureka!—I found that it's possible to make miso out of chickpeas instead. This dish also calls for dulse and nori, two types of nourishing seaweed. If you can't find them, use a pinch of crushed red pepper instead. You'll note that this recipe serves one. That's because I love sipping on this a few times a week when I eat on my own.

1	cup water
1	small leek or 2 scallions, trimmed and very thinly sliced
1	large portobello mushroom, finely chopped
	Sea salt and freshly ground black pepper
2	teaspoons chickpea miso paste
1	teaspoon dulse flakes, or 1 piece dulse, torn into small pieces
1	nori sheet, torn into 1-inch pieces, optional
2	fresh chives, thinly sliced, for garnish
	Sesame seeds, for garnish

In a small saucepan, bring the water to a boil over high heat. Add the leek, mushroom, and salt and pepper to taste, and then lower to a simmer. Cook until the vegetables are tender, 10 to 12 minutes. Remove from the heat and add the miso; mix well until dissolved. Add the dulse and, if desired, the nori. Transfer to a bowl or mug and serve garnished with the chives and sesame seeds.

SERVES 1

FUN GARNISHES FOR YOUR SOUP

- thinly sliced napa or red cabbage
- sliced asparagus
- sliced fresh chives
- baby spinach
- cubed sweet potatoes
- sliced mushrooms
- snow peas

- snap peas
- sprouts
- sliced scallions
- sliced daikon radishes
- sliced carrots
- sliced radishes
- toasted sesame seeds

SPICY HONEYDEW MELON
AND CUCUMBER GAZPACHO

My favorite way to cool down on a hot day is with a cold soup, especially one that involves no cooking.
Even though this honeydew-cucumber combo is a bit spicy (courtesy of arugula and jalapeño),
it's still easy on the stomach. If you're entertaining guests, serve it in shooter cups.

1	English cucumber, peeled and diced
1	large green or yellow heirloom tomato, diced, plus more for garnish, optional
2	cups chopped honeydew melon
1	small sweet white onion, diced
2	celery stalks, chopped
1	cup packed arugula, plus a handful for garnish
1	jalapeño, seeded (less if you like it less spicy)
1	tablespoon finely chopped fresh mint
1	tablespoon extra-virgin olive oil
1	garlic clove, chopped
½	teaspoon sea salt
¼	teaspoon crushed red pepper flakes
1	large ripe avocado, pitted, peeled, and diced, for garnish

In a blender, combine the cucumber, tomato, melon, onion, celery, arugula, jalapeño, mint, oil, garlic, salt, and red pepper flakes. Puree until smooth, and then place the covered blender container in the refrigerator to chill for 1 hour or more.

When ready to serve, adjust the salt if necessary. Serve chilled, garnished with tomato, arugula, and avocado, if desired.

SERVES 4 TO 6

RAINY DAY ROASTED TOMATO BASIL SOUP
with gluten-free herbed croutons

This is one of my all-time favorite soups, made with tomatoes roasted to perfection alongside garlic and extra-virgin olive oil, and then topped off with my Gluten-Free Herbed Croutons. It's divine, if I do say so myself.

GLUTEN-FREE HERBED CROUTONS

2	tablespoons extra-virgin olive oil
1	teaspoon dried basil
1	teaspoon dried rosemary
1	teaspoon dried thyme
¼	teaspoon sea salt
¼	teaspoon freshly ground black pepper
6	slices gluten-free whole-grain bread, cut into ½-inch cubes
¼	cup Dairy-Free Brazil Nut Parm Cheese (page 308)

TOMATO BASIL SOUP

11	medium ripe tomatoes, quartered
¼	cup plus 2 tablespoons extra-virgin olive oil, divided
¼	cup balsamic vinegar
8	garlic cloves, minced
	Pinch chili powder
	Sea salt and freshly ground black pepper
1	medium red onion, chopped
1	medium sweet white onion, chopped
½	cup finely chopped fresh basil
¼	cup finely chopped fresh curly parsley
4	cups water

MAKE THE CROUTONS: Preheat the oven to 375°F. Line a large rimmed baking sheet with parchment paper.

In a medium bowl, combine the oil, basil, rosemary, thyme, salt, and pepper. Add the bread cubes and toss to coat. Sprinkle half the Dairy-Free Brazil Nut Parm Cheese over the croutons and toss. Repeat with the remaining cheese. Arrange the croutons in a single layer on the baking sheet and bake for 12 minutes, or until crispy and brown, giving the baking sheet a shake halfway through baking. Let cool completely before serving. Store in an airtight container at room temperature for up to 4 days.

MAKE THE SOUP: Preheat the oven to 500°F.

In a large bowl, combine the tomatoes, ¼ cup of the oil, the vinegar, garlic, chili powder, and salt and pepper to taste. Arrange the tomatoes in a single layer, skin-side down, in a roasting pan or rimmed baking sheet. Roast for 45 minutes, or until tender. Set aside to cool. Remove and discard the skins, retaining all the juice from the pan.

In a large heavy pot, heat the remaining 2 tablespoons oil over medium heat. Add the red and white onions and 1 teaspoon of salt and cook until the onions are golden brown and caramelized, about 40 minutes. Add the basil and parsley and sauté for 2 minutes. Add the roasted tomatoes, juice from the roasting pan, and water. Cover, bring to a boil, then reduce to a simmer. Cook, covered, for 35 minutes.

Serve the soup warm, topped with Gluten-Free Herbed Croutons, if desired.

SERVES 6; MAKES 3½ CUPS CROUTONS

CREAM OF BEET SOUP
with honey chili tortilla strips

If food is medicine, then this soup is like a well-stocked first-aid kit.
I highly recommend serving this soup in a white bowl—the color contrast makes for a stunning dish.
The fresher the beets, the easier they are to peel.

HONEY CHILI TORTILLA STRIPS

2	tablespoons extra-virgin olive oil
1	tablespoon raw honey
2	teaspoons chili powder
1	teaspoon sea salt
½	teaspoon freshly ground black pepper
8	(10-inch) gluten-free whole-grain (corn-free) tortillas
	Sea salt, for sprinkling

CREAM OF BEET SOUP

4	large beets, scrubbed and trimmed
2¼	cups water, divided
1	large ripe avocado
2	tablespoons freshly squeezed lime juice
2	tablespoons shelled raw hemp seeds
1	teaspoon sea salt
¼	teaspoon ground cumin
¼	teaspoon freshly ground black pepper
	Finely chopped fresh cilantro, for garnish
	Chia seeds, for garnish, optional
	Microgreens, for garnish, optional

MAKE THE TORTILLA STRIPS: Preheat the oven to 350°F.

In a small bowl, combine the oil, honey, chili powder, salt, and pepper. Using a pastry brush, brush both sides of the tortillas with the oil mixture. Stack the tortillas and cut them into ¼-inch strips.

Arrange the strips in a single layer on two large rimmed baking sheets, fluffing them up as you go. Bake for 20 to 25 minutes, or until golden brown and crispy. Remove from the oven and let cool, then sprinkle with salt. Store in an airtight container at room temperature for up to 1 week.

MAKE THE SOUP: Preheat the oven to 425°F.

Place the beets in a glass oven-proof dish that has a lid, add ¼ cup of the water, and cover. Roast for 45 minutes to 1 hour, until you can easily pierce the beets with a fork. Remove from the oven and let cool enough to touch.

Using a paper towel, rub the skins off the beets, and then roughly chop beets into 1-inch pieces. Peel and pit the avocado, and then chop it into 1-inch pieces. In a blender, combine the beets, the remaining 2 cups water, the avocado, lime juice, hemp seeds, salt, cumin, and pepper and puree until smooth.

Place the covered blender jar in the refrigerator until the soup is completely chilled, 3 to 4 hours. Portion into serving bowls. Sprinkle the soup with cilantro and, if desired, chia seeds and microgreens. Serve with the Honey Chili Tortilla Strips.

SERVES 4

cleansing
DETOX VEGGIE BROTH

This is the go-to vegetable broth that I use in place of store-bought varieties. Simple, delicious, and full of vitamins, it's incredibly satisfying. Since clear veggie broth requires no digestion in your stomach, it can be sipped in small amounts throughout the day, or eaten along with other cooked veggies at meals. Use this in any recipe that calls for broth, and as a base for stir-fries, pasta, risotto, and other soups. If you like a more complex flavor, add a small bulb of fennel, a stick of celery, half a leek, or some black peppercorns and bay leaves. Store the broth in small sealed containers in the freezer so you don't have to defrost a whole batch every time you want to use it.

6	large carrots, peeled and cut into large chunks
2	large parsnips, peeled and cut into large chunks
2	medium sweet potatoes, peeled and cut into large chunks
1	large red onion, skin on, cut into large chunks
1	large daikon radish, cut into large chunks
2	cups shiitake mushrooms
4	garlic cloves, skin on, crushed
2	tablespoons dulse flakes, optional
2	sprigs fresh thyme
4	sprigs fresh flat-leaf parsley
12	cups water
	Sea salt and freshly ground black pepper

In a large stockpot, combine the carrots, parsnips, sweet potatoes, onion, daikon radish, mushrooms, garlic, dulse (if desired), thyme, and parsley. Add the water and bring to a boil over high heat. Reduce the heat to low, cover loosely, and simmer for 2 to 3 hours. Strain through a fine-mesh sieve and season with salt and pepper to taste. Reserve vegetables to eat separately as is, or add them to other recipes for sauces and stews. Cool completely and store in a sealed jar in the refrigerator for up to 4 days or in the freezer for up to 3 months.

MAKES 3 QUARTS

TOSS-INS TO ADD FLAVOR TO BROTHS soy-free chickpea miso paste ‣ kombu seaweed ‣ dulse seaweed ‣ nori seaweed ‣ Himalayan pink salt, sea salt, or my Flavored Sea Salts (page 325) ‣ bean sprouts ‣ bok choy ‣ toasted sesame seeds ‣ leafy green carrot tops ‣ mushroom stems ‣ pulp from juicing carrots and green veggies such as celery

velvety
PEAR AND FENNEL SOUP

Fennel and pears are a match made in foodie heaven. It doesn't hurt that fennel brings a lot to the table: flavonoids, vitamin C, fiber, folate, and potassium, which make it an immune-, colon- and heart-healthy vegetable. Fennel has been my go-to for upset stomach relief when I don't feel well, so I paired it with sweet pears for a lovely, silky-smooth soup that's easy to digest. This is a great soup to take you into fall and pairs well with dishes that feature roasted chestnuts, brown rice, and other gluten-free hearty grains. Be sure to choose pears that are firm and not overly ripe. If you purchase a fennel bulb with the fronds attached, cut them off and save to garnish your soup.

1	tablespoon extra-virgin olive oil, plus extra for drizzling
1	medium sweet white onion, diced
1	garlic clove, chopped
½	teaspoon ground coriander
½	teaspoon ground cardamom
¼	teaspoon ground white peppercorns
1	bay leaf
2	medium fennel bulbs, trimmed and thinly sliced
4	cups low-sodium vegetable broth, divided
2	firm medium Bosc pears, peeled, cored, and diced
2	tablespoons finely chopped fresh flat-leaf parsley, for garnish
	Sea salt for garnish

In a large stockpot, heat the oil over medium heat. Add the onion and sauté until it begins to turn golden brown, 4 to 5 minutes. Add the garlic, coriander, cardamom, peppercorns, and bay leaf and stir for 30 seconds. Add the fennel and ½ cup of the broth and cook, uncovered, stirring frequently, for 7 minutes. Add the pears and the remaining 3½ cups broth. Cover, raise the heat, and bring to a boil. Lower the heat and simmer until the fennel is soft and tender, 35 to 40 minutes. Uncover, let cool, and remove the bay leaf.

In batches, transfer the soup to a blender and puree until smooth. Return the soup to the pot and keep warm until serving. Portion into serving bowls and garnish each bowl with a drizzle of oil, parsley, and salt to taste.

SERVES 4 TO 6

SPRING CILANTRO, LEEK, AND SWEET PEA SOUP

I wonder if, in a former life, I was a bunny? If you could see me plucking herbs from my tiny Manhattan-size window garden and munching on them raw, you'd wonder, too. I love, love, love fresh herbs! Which brings me to why I get so excited about this soup. It's full of cilantro, a great detox herb jam-packed with antioxidants that really punches up this soup's flavor. If you like herbs as much as I do, you may want to throw in a little tarragon or sage as well. I consider this a delicate soup that pairs well with other light main dishes. Don't skimp on the lemon zest—it's key for adding just the right finishing touch.

1	tablespoon extra-virgin olive oil
2	large leeks, white and light green parts only, thinly sliced
1	garlic clove, minced
¼	teaspoon ground coriander
	Sea salt and freshly ground black pepper
4	cups low-sodium vegetable broth
3	cups fresh or thawed frozen green peas
2	tablespoons finely chopped fresh cilantro
¼	cup julienned daikon radish, for garnish
1	teaspoon freshly grated lemon zest, for garnish
	Finishing salt such as fleur de sel or fine sea salt

In a large pot, heat the oil over medium heat. Add the leeks and sauté until tender, about 4 minutes. Add the garlic, coriander, salt, and pepper to taste, and cook for another minute. Add the broth and bring to a simmer. Cook for 20 minutes, then add the peas and cilantro; cook for another 2 minutes.

Let the soup cool slightly, and then, in batches, transfer to a blender and puree until smooth. Return the soup to the pot and keep warm until serving. Portion into serving bowls and top each bowl with the daikon, lemon zest, and a pinch of finishing salt.

SERVES 4 TO 6

HOW TO CLEAN LEEKS Because leeks are grown partly underground, dirt is often lodged between their leaves, so it's important to wash them thoroughly before cooking. Trim off the roots and the tough, dark green tops of the leaves. Peel away wilted layers. Halve the stalk lengthwise and rinse under cold running water, separating the layers and rubbing the leaves to remove dirt between them.

COCONUT CURRY CARROT SOUP

Coconut water in a soup? Yes, it can be done! Don't mistake coconut water for coconut milk in a can. Coconut water is found in small tetra packs in the food store (see details on page 40) and it adds a lovely touch to this vibrant (and heavenly) orange bowl of goodness.

2	tablespoons coconut oil
3	cups peeled and diced carrots
1	large sweet potato, peeled and diced
1	large Vidalia onion, chopped
¼	teaspoon sea salt
¼	teaspoon freshly ground black pepper
1	tablespoon peeled minced fresh ginger
3	cups low-sodium vegetable broth
2	cups coconut water
2	tablespoons freshly squeezed lime juice
1½	teaspoons curry powder
¼	teaspoon ground cardamom
¼	cup unsweetened coconut flakes, toasted (see page 114), for garnish

In a large stockpot, heat the oil over medium heat. Add the carrots, sweet potato, onion, salt, and pepper. Cover and cook, stirring occasionally, until the vegetables are soft, about 10 minutes. Add the ginger and cook for 30 seconds more. Add the broth, raise the heat, and bring to a low boil, about 3 minutes. Reduce the heat to a simmer and cook, covered, for 10 minutes more.

Let the soup cool slightly, and then, in batches, transfer to a blender and puree until smooth. Return the soup to the pot and add the coconut water, lime juice, curry, and cardamom; mix well to combine. Taste and season with salt and pepper if necessary. Portion into serving bowls and serve warm, garnished with the toasted coconut flakes.

SERVES 4 TO 6

EASY MOROCCAN WHITE BEAN CHILI

Don't let the long list of ingredients for this stew put you off: you mostly just have to throw them all into a pot and cook them up. In other words, it's super easy, the ideal busy weeknight meal. This is also a great one-pot meal that freezes well. You'll notice that I've made adding millet optional. If you like your chili thick, toss it in, but also feel free to leave it out if you don't have any on hand.

½ cup millet, optional

1 large white onion, diced

1 tablespoon extra-virgin olive oil

1 large red bell pepper, diced

2 garlic cloves, minced

Sea salt

½ teaspoon ground cinnamon

½ teaspoon ground cumin

½ teaspoon ground cardamom

4 cups cooked cannellini beans (see page 99)

3 cups low-sodium vegetable broth

2 large ripe heirloom or regular tomatoes, diced

1 cup golden raisins

Freshly ground black pepper

4 cups firmly packed baby spinach

½ cup finely chopped fresh cilantro

2 tablespoons shelled raw sunflower seeds, toasted (see page 108)

Crushed red pepper flakes, to taste

If using the millet, cook it according to the chart on page 104.

Heat a heavy pot over medium heat. When it's hot, add the onion and oil. Sauté until the onion is tender and translucent, about 5 minutes. Add the bell pepper and cook for 4 minutes more. Add the garlic, ½ teaspoon salt, cinnamon, cumin, and cardamom. Stir for 3 minutes, and then add the beans, broth, tomatoes, raisins, and black pepper to taste. Cover and simmer until the vegetables are tender, about 40 minutes.

Remove the chili from the heat and add the spinach, stirring until the spinach wilts. Taste and adjust the seasonings if necessary. Divide the cooked millet, if using, among six serving bowls. Top with the chili and garnish with the cilantro, sunflower seeds, and red pepper flakes. Serve immediately.

SERVES 6

timeless salads

Sorry, but your lunch is boring. You know it, and I know it. But there's simply no avoiding it—when lunchtime rolls around, you need to eat something, and the more processed it is, the worse you'll feel later.

I'm about to sucker punch your lunch. Forget your standard iceberg salad with a lump of canned tuna and mysterious, gloppy, fat-free dressings (yuck), or your sad sandwiches layered with processed meat. These big fresh bowls of deliciousness are filled with gluten-free whole grains, fresh fruits, veggies, beans, seeds, and nuts. No, it's not "health" food. It's real food. A tasty blend of comfort and clean food that fuels your day without making you feel bloated and tired. Great for lunch, a light dinner, a way to disguise and reuse last night's leftovers, or an impressive start to a meal if you're entertaining. Ripe, fresh, whole, seasonal.

I was never a "salad gal." I need real food, not just a few leaves scraped into a disposable bowl. So you can bet these are real meals, designed to satisfy. I've actually found salads really fun. Sometimes when I'm making one, I'll go right in there and get my hands dirty and mix it up. I consider salads—something I once made fun of—to be a kind of art form.

What you'll find here is a fabulous collection of seasonal, fresh, and flavorful whole-food salads with simple and irresistible homemade dressings that create bona fide, boredom-free meals. Plus, they're filled with fiber, protein, minerals, antioxidants, chlorophyll, healthy fats, phytochemicals, and vitamins. Consider these recipes suggestions—you can get creative and swap this in or that out. Don't have almonds? Try sunflower seeds. Not a fan of kale? Opt for baby spinach. Fine by me.

I know some of you may not care for fresh cilantro—okay, okay! Use basil leaves instead.

Here are a few tips to get you started:

▸ **SAVE SOME TIME:** Chop fresh veggies on Sunday nights and store them in airtight containers so you can create different salad combinations without having to drag yourself through the whole rigmarole every day. This way you can also create a fun mix 'n' match "salad bar" that you can use to change up your salads for the week. Same goes for dressings.

▸ **BUILD YOUR OWN DREAM BOWL:** Start with a base of raw veggies and greens (kale, dandelion, spinach, arugula, Swiss chard, you name it), and then add contrasting textures and flavors (think crunchy, creamy, sweet, smooth, tart, and salty). Add healthy fats from ripe avocados, crunchy raw nuts, and seeds. Oh, and I hope you don't love iceberg (does anyone?), because you won't find any here. It takes up too much precious salad real estate without offering much in return.

▸ **SKIP THE BOTTLED DRESSINGS:** I know it's tempting to reach for a processed salad dressing (since there are thousands to choose from), but honestly, they're lousy. A typical store-bought salad dressing is made from refined oil, refined salt, and refined sugar—enough to create a massive inflammatory response in your body. Not to mention they're filled with preservatives and long-lettered words with numbers in them…aka chemicals. Improve the nutrition profile of your lunch or dinner bowl by using my super-simple, timeless, (and fresh) salad dressings.

MASSAGED KALE SALAD
with spicy hazelnuts

Kale salads are a dime a dozen these days, but this one stands out for its combination of bright flavors (from the grapefruit and lime juice) and spice (from chili powder and cayenne). Raw curly kale can be a little tough, so look for flat dinosaur (lacinato) kale. A good massage will make the kale soft.

½ cup raw hazelnuts

2 tablespoons extra-virgin olive oil, divided

¼ teaspoon chili powder

Pinch cayenne pepper

1 large grapefruit

1 bunch dinosaur (lacinato) kale, stems removed and leaves chopped

2 tablespoons freshly squeezed lime juice

1 tablespoon balsamic vinegar

¼ teaspoon sea salt

Pinch freshly ground black pepper

½ medium ripe avocado, pitted, peeled, and thinly sliced

Preheat the oven to 350°F.

Arrange the hazelnuts in a single layer on a rimmed baking sheet. Bake for 12 to 14 minutes, or until golden brown. Let cool, and then rub them between your hands to remove the skins.

In a large skillet, heat 1 tablespoon of the oil over medium heat. Add the hazelnuts, chili powder, and cayenne pepper and cook for 1 to 2 minutes. Set aside.

Prepare the grapefruit by slicing off the top and bottom of the fruit. From there, carve away the peel, removing all the white membranes underneath. Cut between the white membranes to release the grapefruit segments.

In a large bowl, combine the kale, lime juice, the remaining 1 tablespoon oil, the vinegar, salt, and black pepper. Using your hands, massage the kale until the leaves soften, about 1 minute (see page 94 for how to massage kale). Top with the hazelnuts, grapefruit, and avocado slices. Gently toss to combine and serve.

SERVES 2

MAGICAL PEACH ARUGULA SALAD

magical
PEACH ARUGULA SALAD

Here's a dish that provides a big payoff for very little effort. It takes about five minutes to throw this salad together, and the combination of peppers, peaches, and arugula is simply beautiful. Serve it in a wide bowl to show off its good looks.

10	cups arugula
5	medium ripe peaches, pitted and diced
2	yellow or orange bell peppers, diced
⅓	cup finely chopped raw walnuts
2	tablespoons extra-virgin olive oil
2	tablespoons balsamic vinegar
1	tablespoon freshly squeezed lemon juice
¼	teaspoon freshly grated lemon zest
¼	teaspoon sea salt
¼	teaspoon freshly ground black pepper

In a large bowl, combine the arugula, peaches, bell peppers, and walnuts.

In a small bowl, whisk together the oil, vinegar, lemon juice, lemon zest, salt, and pepper.

Drizzle the dressing over the arugula mixture, toss, and serve.

SERVES 6 TO 8

simple lif
CUCUMBER SU HERB SALA

This modest but tasty salad takes no effort whatsoever and is a perfect side salad to any meal. It's also fun for kids to help make by tossing all the ingredients into a sealed container and shaking to combine the flavorful ingredients and dressing.

2	large cucumbers, peeled, seeded, and roughly chopped
3	tablespoons pine nuts, toasted (see page 108)
1	small shallot, thinly sliced
1	tablespoon freshly squeezed lemon juice
1	tablespoon extra-virgin olive oil
2	teaspoons apple cider vinegar
2	teaspoons finely chopped fresh mint
2	teaspoons finely chopped fresh basil
2	teaspoons thinly sliced fresh chives
¼	teaspoon freshly grated lemon zest
	Sea salt and freshly ground black pepper, to taste

Place all the ingredients in a medium container with a lid. Shake until well combined. Transfer to a bowl and serve.

SERVES 4

CRANBERRY CURRY WALDORF SALAD

This healthy spin on a traditional Waldorf salad—without the mayo and walnuts—is super easy to prepare. Besides the Bibb lettuce called for here, you can serve this salad over chopped romaine hearts, or other leafy greens, or spoon it into a gluten-free whole-grain tortilla wrap.

SALAD

1½	cups cooked chickpeas (see page 99)
2	celery stalks, thinly sliced
1	large carrot, peeled and shredded
1	red apple, cored and diced
¼	cup raw cashews, chopped and toasted (see page 108)
¼	cup dried cranberries
1½	tablespoons finely chopped fresh flat-leaf parsley

DRESSING

¼	cup almond butter
4½	tablespoons freshly squeezed lemon juice
1	teaspoon raw honey
¼	teaspoon curry powder
	Pinch ground cumin
	Sea salt and freshly ground black pepper
1	tablespoon water, plus more if needed

4 to 6 large Bibb lettuce leaves, for serving

MAKE THE SALAD: In a large bowl, combine the chickpeas, celery, carrot, apple, cashews, cranberries, and parsley.

MAKE THE DRESSING: In a small bowl, whisk together the almond butter, lemon juice, honey, curry powder, cumin, and salt and pepper to taste. To thin the dressing, add the water, a little at a time, until the dressing is thin enough to drizzle. Taste and season with salt and pepper if necessary.

To serve the salad as lettuce wraps, toss the chickpea mixture with the almond butter dressing and spoon into lettuce leaves. Alternatively, lay the lettuce leaves on a platter and serve the chickpea mixture with the almond butter dressing on top.

SERVES 4 TO 6

ROASTED ONION AND SWEET PEA SALAD
with fresh mint and creamy almond dressing

This is a picnic showstopper! The dressing is slightly sweet and gets its "creaminess" from almond butter. Toast the seeds in a dry skillet (see page 108) if you would like a nuttier flavor.

CREAMY ALMOND DRESSING

1½	tablespoons almond butter
2	tablespoons extra-virgin olive oil
1	tablespoon pure maple syrup
2	teaspoons freshly squeezed lime juice
¼	teaspoon sea salt
	Pinch chili powder
	Pinch freshly ground black pepper

ONION AND SWEET PEA SALAD

1	large red onion, cut into ¼-inch slices
2	tablespoons extra-virgin olive oil
	Sea salt and freshly ground black pepper, to taste
1	medium cucumber, diced
1	yellow bell pepper, diced
1	cup cooked black beans (see page 99)
1	cup fresh or thawed frozen green peas
3	tablespoons shelled raw sunflower seeds
3	tablespoons shelled raw pumpkin seeds
2	cups Bibb lettuce, torn
1	cup arugula
	Small bunch fresh chives, thinly sliced, for garnish
	Few sprigs fresh mint, finely chopped, for garnish

MAKE THE DRESSING: In a small bowl, whisk together all the dressing ingredients until smooth.

MAKE THE SALAD: Preheat the oven to 350°F.

In a medium bowl, toss the onion with the oil, salt, and black pepper. Transfer to a rimmed baking sheet and bake for about 30 minutes, stirring every 10 minutes to ensure even browning, until the onion is soft and caramelized.

In a large bowl, combine the roasted onions, cucumber, bell pepper, black beans, peas, sunflower seeds, and pumpkin seeds. Add the Creamy Almond Dressing and toss to combine. Add the lettuce and arugula and gently toss again. Garnish with the chives and mint. Serve immediately.

SERVES 2; MAKES 5 TABLESPOONS DRESSING

CRANBERRY KALE SALAD
smothered with walnuts and broccoli pesto

Pesto is traditionally made with cheese, but once you taste this dairy-free, broccoli variation, you'll see that you can get by very well without it—it's as heavenly as any Parmesan-based paste. Make extra and toss it with roasted vegetables later in the week, serve it as a snack alongside my grain-free crackers (pages 156–162), or add it to warm gluten-free whole-grain pasta for a simple weeknight meal.

SPEEDY BROCCOLI PESTO

2	cups chopped broccoli florets
1/3	cup shelled raw hemp seeds
1/3	cup finely chopped fresh basil
1	tablespoon freshly squeezed lemon juice
1	tablespoon extra-virgin olive oil
1	tablespoon water
1	garlic clove
1/2	teaspoon sea salt
1/4	teaspoon crushed red pepper flakes
1/4	teaspoon paprika

CRANBERRY KALE SALAD

1	large bunch kale, stems removed, leaves cut or torn into bite-size pieces
3	tablespoons freshly squeezed orange juice
2	tablespoons extra-virgin olive oil
1/4	teaspoon sea salt
1/4	teaspoon freshly ground black pepper
1	medium red apple, cored and diced
1/2	cup raw walnuts, roughly chopped
1/2	cup dried cranberries

MAKE THE PESTO: Place all the pesto ingredients in a food processor and process until smooth.

MAKE THE SALAD: Place the kale in a large bowl and, using your hands, massage the orange juice, oil, salt, and pepper into the leaves until the leaves have softened, about 3 minutes. Add the apple, walnuts, and cranberries to the bowl and toss to combine. Add the Speedy Broccoli Pesto to the salad and toss again. Serve immediately.

SERVES 4 AS A MAIN DISH; 6 AS A SIDE; MAKES 1 CUP PESTO

CREAMY CASHEW CAESAR SALAD
with kale

I find that one of the hardest dishes for people to give up is the beloved Caesar salad. This variation on the theme, though, may make you forget your old (and let's face it, far from healthy) Caesar. Made without dairy, eggs, or anchovies, it nonetheless has the same salty and satisfying tang as the traditional salad. And since kale doesn't wilt as easily as romaine, this salad keeps well throughout the afternoon for a picnic, luncheon, or barbecue.

CASHEW CAESAR DRESSING

¼	cup raw cashews
2	tablespoons apple cider vinegar
2	tablespoons freshly squeezed lemon juice
2	tablespoons dulse flakes
2	garlic cloves, minced
2	teaspoons chickpea miso paste
1	teaspoon Dijon mustard
	Pinch freshly ground black pepper
	Pinch chili powder
¼	cup extra-virgin olive oil
¼	cup water

SALAD

4	cups finely chopped baby kale
1	red bell pepper, diced
¼	cup finely chopped fresh flat-leaf parsley
¼	cup shelled raw hemp seeds
3	large scallions, thinly sliced

Gluten-Free Herbed Croutons (page 190), optional, for serving

MAKE THE DRESSING: In a blender, combine the cashews, vinegar, lemon juice, dulse, garlic, miso, mustard, pepper, and chili powder. Pulse, stopping before it turns into a paste. With the motor running, add the oil in a steady stream. When the mixture emulsifies, add the water 1 tablespoon at a time until the dressing reaches a pourable but not runny consistency.

MAKE THE SALAD: In a large bowl, combine the kale, bell pepper, parsley, hemp seeds, and scallions.

Add a handful of Gluten-Free Herbed Croutons to the salad, if desired, drizzle with the dressing, toss, and serve.

SERVES 4

nuts about

BUTTERNUT SQUASH AND KALE SALAD

The key to this recipe is cooking the squash just until the point of tenderness; if you cook it too long, it will go mushy. Be sure to check in on the squash as it cooks to make sure you get the right texture.

SQUASH

1	large butternut squash, peeled, seeded, and cut into 1-inch cubes
2	tablespoons extra-virgin olive oil
2	tablespoons raw honey
	Sea salt and freshly ground black pepper

DRESSING

1	small shallot, chopped
2	tablespoons plus 2 teaspoons extra-virgin olive oil, divided
3	tablespoons apple cider vinegar
1	teaspoon mustard powder
	Pinch ground nutmeg
	Sea salt and freshly ground black pepper

SALAD

2	bunches dinosaur (lacinato) kale, stems removed and leaves chopped
3/4	cup dried cranberries
3½	tablespoons Dairy-Free Creamy Cashew Cheese (page 308)
1/4	cup chopped raw walnuts, toasted (see page 108)

MAKE THE SQUASH: Preheat the oven to 350°F.

In a medium bowl, combine the squash with the oil, honey, and salt and pepper to taste. Toss to coat, and then transfer to a rimmed baking sheet. Bake for 20 minutes, or until tender, but not falling apart. Let cool to room temperature.

MAKE THE DRESSING: Heat a small sauté pan over medium-low heat. Add the shallot and 2 teaspoons of the oil and sauté until soft but not burned, about 3 minutes. Let cool. In a small bowl, whisk together the vinegar, the remaining 2 tablespoons of oil, and the shallot, mustard, and nutmeg. Season with salt and pepper to taste.

MAKE THE SALAD: In a large bowl, combine the kale, cranberries, and dressing. Using your hands, massage the dressing into the kale until the leaves soften, about 1 minute. Add the squash and gently toss to combine. Top with the Dairy-Free Creamy Cashew Cheese and toasted walnuts. Serve immediately.

SERVES 4

nourishing
NECTARINE AND BASIL MILLET TOSS

Millet is so tender—it reminds me of eating cous-cous when I was a kid back in my pre–gluten-free days. This is an incredibly fresh side dish that makes for an easy weeknight meal. If you don't have millet on hand, you can make this dish with quinoa. Likewise, you can substitute peaches for nectarines, and grapefruit juice for orange juice.

1	cup millet
1	large nectarine, pitted and diced
½	cup raw pecans, toasted (see page 108)
⅓	cup plus 1 tablespoon freshly squeezed orange juice
¼	cup chopped Vidalia onion
¼	cup finely chopped fresh basil
4	fresh chives, thinly sliced
2	tablespoons extra-virgin olive oil
1	tablespoon freshly grated orange zest, optional
⅛	teaspoon ground cinnamon
	Sea salt and freshly ground black pepper, to taste

Cook the millet according to the chart on page 104. Let cool for 15 minutes and fluff with a fork. Add the remaining ingredients, toss, and serve immediately.

SERVES 4

essential
PICNIC BASIL MILLET

Infused with sweet basil, this delectable picnic favorite also gets a bit of tang from apple cider vinegar and a nutty crunch from toasted pine nuts. It works well as a side dish, so you can tote it along for a picnic, or serve it as a weeknight salad and have the leftovers for a fun and flavorful lunch the next day.

1	cup millet
3	tablespoons extra-virgin olive oil, divided
3	tablespoons apple cider vinegar
	Sea salt and freshly ground black pepper, to taste
1	large heirloom tomato, diced
1	large cucumber, diced
½	small red onion, diced
¼	cup finely chopped fresh basil, plus a few whole leaves for garnish
¼	cup pine nuts, toasted (see page 108)

Cook the millet according to the chart on page 104. Let cool slightly and toss with 1 tablespoon of the oil.

In a small bowl, whisk together the vinegar, the remaining 2 tablespoons of oil, and salt and pepper to taste.

In a medium bowl, combine the cooked millet, tomato, cucumber, onion, and basil. Drizzle in the oil and vinegar mixture and add the pine nuts. Toss to combine. Taste and season with salt and pepper if necessary. Serve immediately or chilled.

SERVES 4

ESSENTIAL PICNIC BASIL MILLET

MARVELOUS MANGO SALAD
with raspberry ginger dressing and toasted sunflower seeds

If you're looking for a way to show yourself some love, this is it—it's colorful and zesty enough to brighten anyone's spirits. Plus, this combination of fruit and greens is super nutritious: the vitamin C in the mango helps you absorb the iron in the spinach. The raspberry ginger dressing can also be used to dress other salads. I particularly like serving leftover dressing with kale. In the summer, when stone fruit is in season, you may want to swap the mango for peaches.

MANGO SALAD

½	cup shelled raw sunflower seeds
	Pinch sea salt
3	large mangoes, peeled, pitted, and cut into 1-inch cubes
½	cup firmly packed fresh baby spinach
8	radishes, thinly sliced
3	scallions, thinly sliced
3	tablespoons finely chopped fresh cilantro
2	tablespoons finely chopped fresh flat-leaf parsley
2	tablespoons finely chopped fresh mint

RASPBERRY GINGER DRESSING

2	teaspoons coconut oil
1	cup fresh raspberries
2	tablespoons freshly squeezed lemon juice
1½	tablespoons extra-virgin olive oil
2	teaspoons raw honey or pure maple syrup
	¼-inch piece fresh ginger, peeled and grated
	Sea salt and freshly ground black pepper

MAKE THE SALAD: Place the sunflower seeds in a large skillet and toast over medium heat. Toast until fragrant, shaking often. Remove from the heat and add the salt.

MAKE THE DRESSING: In a medium saucepan, heat the coconut oil over medium heat. Add the raspberries and stir until they release their juices, about 1 minute. Transfer to a blender and add the lemon juice, olive oil, honey, and ginger. Blend until smooth. Season with salt and pepper to taste. Note: Coconut oil hardens at room temperature, so use dressing immediately.

In a large bowl, combine the mangoes, spinach, radishes, scallions, cilantro, parsley, and mint, and toss to combine. Drizzle with the Raspberry Ginger Dressing to taste and toss again. Garnish with the toasted sunflower seeds and serve immediately.

SERVES 4; MAKES 1 CUP DRESSING

OUTSTANDING MANGO GREEN DREAM SALAD
with gluten-free herbed croutons

Mango and fresh dill add up to a restorative, one-bowl meal for two—or for one, with leftovers for the next day. The lime juice keeps it fresh tasting so the salad will easily hold up for twenty-four hours.

1	large mango, peeled, pitted, and diced
1½	tablespoons extra-virgin olive oil
1	tablespoon freshly squeezed lime juice
1	tablespoon finely chopped fresh dill
1	small garlic clove, minced
	Pinch crushed red pepper flakes
2	cups fresh baby spinach
1	large red bell pepper, diced
1	medium ripe avocado, pitted, peeled, and diced
	Sea salt and freshly ground black pepper
	Handful Gluten-Free Herbed Croutons (page 190), optional

In a large bowl, combine the mango, oil, lime juice, dill, garlic, and red pepper flakes; toss to combine. Add the spinach, bell pepper, avocado, and salt and black pepper to taste and toss again. Serve with Gluten-Free Herbed Croutons, if desired.

SERVES 2

EAST COAST TARRAGON GRAPEFRUIT SALAD
with macadamia maple dressing

I serve this midsummer side salad to my family at the shore. It's easy to make and very refreshing. The ruby red grapefruit lends a touch of natural sweetness.

GRAPEFRUIT SALAD

2	cups baby spinach or arugula
2	large ruby red grapefruits, chilled, peeled, and segmented
¼	cup finely chopped red onion
¼	cup finely chopped fresh tarragon

MACADAMIA MAPLE DRESSING

¼	cup apple cider vinegar
⅓	cup pure maple syrup
	Sea salt and freshly ground black pepper
½	cup raw macadamia nuts, finely chopped
2	tablespoons finely chopped fresh tarragon

MAKE THE SALAD: Divide the spinach among four serving plates. Top with the grapefruit, onion, and tarragon.

MAKE THE DRESSING: In a small bowl, whisk together the vinegar, maple syrup, and salt and pepper to taste. Add the macadamia nuts and tarragon; stir to combine. Drizzle the salad with the Macadamia Maple Dressing and serve immediately. Store the leftover dressing in a sealed container in the refrigerator for up to 4 days.

SERVES 4; MAKES ¾ CUP DRESSING

the ultimate
QUINOA, CHERRY, AND PECAN SALAD

This sweet yet savory salad could be your main or side dish for dinner. You'll love the combo of cherries and honey paired with toasted pecans and fresh parsley. You can substitute dried cherries or grapes if you can't find fresh cherries in season. You can also use hazelnuts or almonds in place of the pecans here.

QUINOA SALAD

1½	cups quinoa, rinsed
2	cups fresh cherries, pitted and halved
3	small or 2 large celery stalks, diced
½	cup roughly chopped raw pecans, toasted (see page 108)
⅓	cup finely chopped fresh curly parsley

DRESSING

2	tablespoons plus 1 teaspoon freshly squeezed lemon juice
1	tablespoon Dijon mustard
1	tablespoon raw honey
	Sea salt and freshly ground black pepper
3	tablespoons extra-virgin olive oil

¼	cup thinly sliced scallions, for garnish
1	teaspoon freshly grated lemon zest, for garnish

MAKE THE SALAD: Cook the quinoa according to the chart on page 104. Let cool; fluff with a fork.

In a large bowl, combine the cooked quinoa, cherries, celery, pecans, and parsley. Let sit for 5 minutes to give the flavors a chance to marry.

MAKE THE DRESSING: In a small bowl, whisk together the lemon juice, mustard, honey, and salt and pepper to taste. Continue whisking as you slowly add the oil.

Drizzle the dressing over the quinoa and toss to coat. Garnish with the scallions and lemon zest. Serve immediately.

SERVES 4 TO 6

the main dish

If you're like me, you grew up eating vegetables that were overcooked, overboiled, and steamed within an inch of their lives. And that's a shame, because that means an entire food group left a bad taste in your mouth. I truly believe that veggies have been at the sidelines of the American meal for so long because few have been taught how to prepare them in a way that makes anyone want to eat them.

Until now!

Of course, I'm biased. Veggies and I have a long, illustrious relationship. I'm one of those rare people who gets stoked over Brussels sprouts, and who will keep a zucchini in my purse to nosh on, no joke. But I've also had my share of lousy vegetable dishes—which is why I've been dedicated to creating crave-able ones.

I'm not a vegan, but I truly believe veggies can hold their own at the center of a meal, and I'm going to show you how. Worried you'll still be hungry? Rest assured, these vegetable-based meals are packed with healthy carbohydrates, protein, fiber, and healthy fats to keep you satisfied. And flavor? I'm about to blow your mind. My gluten-free friends, my meatless pals, you're going to be pleasantly surprised that these dishes don't just check the veggie box; they're completely outside of it in a way that you, your families, and your friends will love.

All these recipes, by the way, are safe for supersensitive eaters, as they're made without eggs, corn, dairy, gluten, peanuts, soy, and refined sugar. Instead, you're going to explore ingredients that may be new to you, such as coconut oil, chickpea miso paste, millet, black rice, and coconut aminos—all of which can create a fabulous, feel-good meal.

Regardless of your skill level or experience, you can make these meals using what's in your kitchen drawers. It doesn't get much simpler than that, folks. And please, no fat phobia! I hereby forbid you to be scared of avocados, nuts, or seeds—these healthy fats can help you lose weight by providing protein and fiber to balance your blood sugar. Plus, your hormones need healthy fats to function properly, so no fat means no hormones, which is not fun (trust me)!

You'll sacrifice nothing, by the way—not in flavor, texture, or taste. Get ready for the fresh crunch of veggies cooked the way they should be; creamy sauces blended from raw nuts like cashews and almonds; and savory, spicy yumminess that you'll want to make over and over again.

Welcome to a whole new way of thinking about dinner!

BIG BROCCOLI RABE VEGGIE PASTA

The ratio of vegetables to pasta in this healthy dish skews heavily on the side of vegetables.
That keeps the pasta light, but filling.

12	ounces gluten-free whole-grain penne or spiral pasta
2	tablespoons extra-virgin olive oil, divided
1	shallot, diced
2	small portobello mushrooms, sliced
2	garlic cloves, minced
1	bunch broccoli rabe, ends trimmed, cut into 1-inch pieces
1	red bell pepper, diced
1	cup pitted black olives, halved
¼	teaspoon sea salt
¼	teaspoon freshly ground black pepper
3	tablespoons low-sodium vegetable broth
½	cup finely chopped fresh basil
	Pinch crushed red pepper flakes
1	recipe Sun-Dried Tomato Sauce (page 320), warmed, for topping
1 to 2	tablespoons Peppy No-Cheese Parmesan (page 307) or Dairy-Free Brazil Nut Parm Cheese (page 308), optional

Bring a large pot of water to a boil. Cook the pasta according to the package directions. Drain, rinse with cold water, and transfer to a large bowl. Stir in 2 teaspoons of the oil to prevent sticking.

Heat the remaining oil in a large skillet over medium-low heat. Add the shallot and mushrooms and cook until tender, about 3 minutes. Add the garlic and cook for another minute. Add the broccoli rabe, bell pepper, olives, salt, and black pepper; stir well. Add the broth and continue to cook, covered, until the vegetables are soft and tender, about 10 minutes, stirring halfway through cooking.

Combine the vegetable mixture with the cooked pasta and toss gently with the basil and red pepper flakes. Add the Sun-Dried Tomato Sauce, sprinkle with the Peppy No-Cheese Parmesan, if desired, and toss again. Serve immediately.

SERVES 4

bowl-half-full
SWISS CHARD GARDEN HERB PASTA

As a city dweller, I don't have my own garden, but I eat like I do. This gluten-free pasta is loaded with one of my favorite leafy greens, along with a few delicate herbs that make me smile every time I taste them. Creamy avocado, chickpea miso, and lime juice are a winning combo that add a nice touch of flavor.

SWISS CHARD PASTA

12	ounces gluten-free whole-grain penne pasta
1	bunch Swiss chard, stems removed, leaves finely chopped
¼	cup finely chopped fresh cilantro
¼	cup finely chopped fresh basil
6	fresh chives, finely chopped
1	large ripe avocado, pitted, peeled, and diced
1	teaspoon finely chopped fresh mint
	Pinch crushed red pepper flakes

SAUCE

2¼	tablespoons freshly squeezed lime juice
1	tablespoon extra-virgin olive oil
1	tablespoon chickpea miso paste
1	large garlic clove, minced
1	teaspoon peeled minced fresh ginger
1	teaspoon raw honey
	Sea salt

MAKE THE PASTA: Cook the pasta according to the package directions. Drain and set aside to cool. When cool, transfer to a large bowl and add the Swiss chard, cilantro, basil, chives, avocado, mint, and red pepper flakes. Gently toss.

MAKE THE SAUCE: In a small bowl, combine the lime juice, oil, miso, garlic, ginger, honey, and salt to taste; whisk to combine.

Drizzle the sauce over the pasta mixture and gently toss. Serve warm or at room temperature.

SERVES 4 TO 6

SPRING VEGGIE PAELLA

Eating paella is like traveling to another world and enjoying a different culture's cuisine. The other beauty of paella is that it has everything you need in one dish—which means that you'll only have one pot to wash after dinner. This is a light take on the Spanish mainstay, with spring asparagus and a combination of cannellini beans and chickpeas for protein.

2 tablespoons extra-virgin olive oil

1 large sweet white onion, chopped

1 pint cherry tomatoes, quartered

1 orange bell pepper, diced

1 garlic clove, minced

1 cup brown rice

1 teaspoon saffron threads

1 teaspoon chili powder

½ teaspoon smoked paprika

¼ teaspoon crushed red pepper flakes

¼ teaspoon sea salt, plus more if needed

¼ teaspoon freshly ground black pepper, plus more if needed

4 cups low-sodium vegetable broth

1 cup cooked cannellini beans (see page 99)

1 cup cooked chickpeas (see page 99)

1 cup frozen green peas

1 bunch asparagus, ends trimmed and cut into 1-inch pieces

3 tablespoons finely chopped fresh flat-leaf parsley, for garnish

3 tablespoons finely chopped fresh cilantro, for garnish

In a large skillet, heat the oil over medium heat. Add the onion and sauté until soft and translucent, about 5 minutes. Add the cherry tomatoes, bell pepper, and garlic and cook for another 2 minutes, stirring often. Add the rice, saffron, chili powder, paprika, red pepper flakes, salt, and black pepper and give the mixture a few stirs. Add the broth, cover, and bring it to a boil. Cook over medium heat at a simmer until the rice is fully cooked, 30 to 40 minutes. (To test if the rice is done, cut a grain in half to see if the color is the same throughout.)

Add the cannellini beans, chickpeas, peas, and asparagus to the skillet and mix well. Reduce the heat to low and cook until the dish is well heated throughout, 5 to 7 minutes. Set aside to cool for 5 minutes. Check the seasonings and add more salt and pepper if needed, garnish with the parsley and cilantro, and serve.

SERVES 4 TO 6

COASTAL CARROT "FETTUCCINE"
with sun-dried tomatoes and pumpkin seeds

*In this dish, the "fettuccine" is actually made from carrots shredded into ribbons with a vegetable peeler.
I think you'll be surprised at how much it tastes like the real thing. The sauce clings to the ribbons,
giving each bite a delectable, earthy flavor.*

2	tablespoons extra-virgin olive oil
1	garlic clove, minced
½	cup grape tomatoes, whole or quartered
2½	tablespoons finely julienned or chopped fresh basil, divided
3	large rainbow or orange carrots, peeled
1	cup Sun-Dried Tomato Sauce (page 320)
¼	teaspoon sweet paprika
¼	teaspoon sea salt
¼	teaspoon freshly ground black pepper
2	tablespoons shelled raw pumpkin seeds, toasted (see page 108), for garnish

In a large skillet, heat the oil over medium-low heat. Add the garlic and sauté until soft and fragrant, about 30 seconds. Add the tomatoes and 2 tablespoons of the basil and sauté until the tomatoes burst and release their juices, about 5 minutes. Meanwhile, slice the carrots into ribbons, using either a spiral slicer (spiralizer) or a vegetable peeler (this is easiest when you hold the carrot down on a flat surface).

Add the carrots, Sun-Dried Tomato Sauce, paprika, salt, and pepper to the skillet, and cook until the carrots are tender, about 10 minutes. Sprinkle with the remaining ½ tablespoon basil and the pumpkin seeds before serving.

SERVES 4

raw and grain-free
ZUCCHINI PAD THAI

No rice or wheat noodles here. Instead, zucchini takes center stage, making your taste buds dance. When I moved to Manhattan, my friends always raved about pad thai, but white rice noodles and tofu always gave me a belly ache. So I tossed the tofu and created my own no-cook version. If you want this dish spicier, increase the crushed red pepper flakes and ginger and use a full stalk of lemongrass. If you don't have a spiral slicer (spiralizer), cut the zucchini into thin matchsticks.

2	large zucchini, cut into thin strands with a vegetable peeler or spiralizer
1	large carrot, peeled and julienned or shredded
1	cup shredded red cabbage
2	thin asparagus stalks, ends trimmed, thinly sliced on the diagonal
1/3	cup raw cashews, soaked for 10 minutes in hot water, drained, and rinsed
3	large Medjool dates, pitted
2	garlic cloves, minced
2	tablespoons freshly squeezed lemon juice
1	tablespoon smooth almond butter
1	teaspoon freshly grated lemon zest
2	teaspoons peeled grated fresh ginger, plus more if needed
1	lemongrass stalk, finely chopped, plus more if needed
1/2	teaspoon crushed red pepper flakes, plus more if needed
	Sea salt
1/4	cup water
2	tablespoons finely chopped fresh cilantro, for garnish
2	tablespoons slivered raw almonds, toasted (see page 108), for garnish
4	fresh chives, minced, for garnish

In a large bowl, combine the zucchini, carrot, cabbage, and asparagus. Set aside.

Place the cashews in a blender with the dates, garlic, lemon juice, almond butter, lemon zest, ginger, lemongrass, red pepper flakes, and salt to taste. Blend, adding the water 1 tablespoon at a time until the sauce is smooth, but not thin and watery. Season with salt. Pour the sauce over the zucchini mixture and gently toss to coat. Garnish with the cilantro, almonds, and chives. Serve immediately.

SERVES 2

MINI BLACK RICE AND ALMOND SLIDERS
in radicchio cups

I have eaten more disappointing veggie burgers than I can recall. That's what led me to develop these sliders, a more satisfying alternative served in a delightful radicchio cup. Make sure to squeeze out all the moisture from the shredded carrots. If you purchase whole flaxseeds, grind them very finely. Otherwise, they won't turn gelatinous when mixed with the water. You can use a coffee grinder to do this.

½ cup black rice

1 cup plus 3 tablespoons water, divided

2 tablespoons extra-virgin olive oil, divided

3 large garlic cloves, minced

¼ teaspoon chili powder

¼ teaspoon ground coriander

½ medium red onion, diced

2 cups baby bella mushrooms, finely chopped

2 medium carrots, peeled and shredded

2 tablespoons freshly squeezed orange juice

¼ teaspoon freshly grated orange zest

¼ teaspoon dried basil

½ teaspoon sea salt

¼ teaspoon freshly ground black pepper

2 tablespoons very finely ground flaxseeds

1 cup almond flour, store-bought or homemade (see page 39)

⅓ cup finely chopped fresh cilantro

8 radicchio leaves, for serving

1 large ripe avocado, pitted, peeled, and thinly sliced

2 small red radishes, thinly sliced

½ cup finely chopped fresh basil
Seriously Sensational Sriracha Sauce (page 318), for serving

Cook the rice with 1 cup of water in a small pot. Bring to a boil, reduce to a simmer, and cover. Cook for 30 minutes until tender and all the water is absorbed. Let cool.

In a large skillet, heat 1 tablespoon of the oil over medium heat. Add the garlic, chili powder, and coriander and cook until the spices release their fragrance, about 30 seconds. Add the onion and cook until translucent, about 10 minutes. Add the mushrooms, carrots, orange juice, orange zest, dried basil, salt, and pepper and cook until the mixture has lost most of its moisture and the carrots are soft, 5 minutes. Let cool.

Combine the flaxseeds with 3 tablespoons water in a small bowl. Set aside until the mixture forms a gel, about 10 minutes.

In a large bowl, combine the rice and cooled onion mixture with the flaxseed mixture, almond flour, and cilantro. Shape into 8 burgers.

Heat 1 tablespoon oil in a large skillet. Cook the burgers over medium heat for 5 minutes on each side, or until golden brown.

Serve each slider in a radicchio leaf topped with avocado, radishes, basil, and salt and pepper if necessary. Drizzle with Seriously Sensational Sriracha Sauce. Stick a toothpick through the top of the radicchio leaf and into the slider. Serve warm.

MAKES 8 SLIDERS

SWISS CHARD-WRAPPED PORTOBELLO BURGERS
stuffed with dairy-free creamy cashew cheese

I'm obviously a fan of veggie burgers. But most veggie burgers require quite a few ingredients and, while they're not difficult to make, sometimes you just want to slap something on a "bun" and go. This portobello burger is the answer. All you have to do is season the mushrooms a bit, heat them in the oven, add a few top-pings, and you're ready to eat! If you have more time to spare, I recommend slow cooking the mushrooms at a low temp, which enhances their meaty flavor. Otherwise, twenty minutes in a 350°F oven is all you need.

1	tablespoon extra-virgin olive oil
1	tablespoon coconut aminos
4	large portobello mushrooms, stems removed
4	large Swiss chard leaves, stems removed
	Dairy-Free Creamy Cashew Cheese (page 308)
	Freshly ground black pepper, to taste
2	tablespoons finely chopped fresh flat-leaf parsley
2	tablespoons thinly sliced scallions
1	large tomato, sliced into 4 thick slices

Preheat the oven to 350°F.

In a small bowl, combine the oil and coconut aminos. Rub the mixture on each mushroom cap and lay the mushrooms stem-side down on a rimmed baking sheet. Bake for 20 minutes, or until tender all the way through. Remove from the oven and let cool slightly.

Place each mushroom on a leaf of Swiss chard. Spread each mushroom with a dollop of the Dairy-Free Creamy Cashew Cheese, and then sprinkle with pepper. Garnish with the parsley and scallions and top with a slice of tomato. Serve immediately.

SERVES 4

ANTIOXIDANT WILD RICE FLATBREAD
with glorious chickpea garlic sauce

If you like falafel, you'll love this savory flatbread, which is both crusty on the outside and moist on the inside. Its main ingredients, split peas and wild rice, may not sound sexy, but they work well as contrasting ingredients. Note: It's very important to not overcook the peas and rice; you want them to be cooked but not mushy and soggy! Serve leftover Glorious Chickpea Garlic Sauce with raw or cooked veggies.

WILD RICE FLATBREAD

1½	cups cooked split peas (see page 99), very well drained
1½	cups cooked wild rice (see page 106), very well drained
¼	cup coconut oil
1	teaspoon dried oregano
1	teaspoon dried thyme
1	teaspoon dried parsley
½	teaspoon sea salt
½	teaspoon freshly ground black pepper

GLORIOUS CHICKPEA GARLIC SAUCE

2	tablespoons extra-virgin olive oil
2	garlic cloves, crushed
1½	cups cooked chickpeas (see page 99)
1	cup low-sodium vegetable broth, plus more for thinning sauce
1	tablespoon freshly squeezed lemon juice
½	teaspoon chili powder
½	teaspoon ground cumin
	Sea salt and freshly ground black pepper

OTHER SERVING SUGGESTIONS

Hummus (pages 301–303), Heirloom Tomato Sauce (page 318), or any of the toppings on page 235

MAKE THE FLATBREAD: Preheat the oven to 350°F. Line a rimmed baking sheet with parchment paper.

Combine the split peas, rice, oil, oregano, thyme, parsley, salt, and pepper in a food processor and process until smooth. Transfer to the prepared baking sheet and use the back of a large spoon to spread the flatbread dough onto the parchment paper to create a ¼- to ½-inch-thick crust.

Bake for 55 to 60 minutes, depending on the thickness of your crust, or until the crust is golden brown. Remove from the oven and set aside to cool for 10 minutes. Cut the flatbread into rectangles.

MAKE THE SAUCE: In a medium skillet, heat the oil over medium heat. Add the garlic. When it has softened, add the chickpeas, broth, lemon juice, chili powder, and cumin; bring to a simmer. Simmer until the flavors blend, about 10 minutes. Season with salt and pepper to taste and transfer to a blender. Blend until the mixture coats the back of a spoon. If the mixture is too thick, add more broth until it reaches the desired consistency.

Drizzle the flatbread with the Glorious Chickpea Garlic Sauce or the topping of your choice. Serve warm or at room temperature.

SERVES 2; MAKES 2 CUPS SAUCE

FABULOUS LEMON BASIL MILLET BURGERS
with miraculous mango salsa

These fresh-tasting burgers make an easy weeknight meal. No buns here; you can serve these wrapped in romaine or Bibb lettuce leaves and eat them with your hands. Make sure your millet isn't too dry or the burgers won't stick together!

1	cup millet
½	teaspoon sea salt, plus a pinch
1	tablespoon ground flaxseeds
3	tablespoons water
1	large carrot, peeled and grated
4	scallions, thinly sliced
1	handful fresh basil leaves, finely chopped
2	tablespoons freshly squeezed lemon juice
2½	teaspoons freshly grated lemon zest
½	teaspoon freshly ground black pepper
3	tablespoons coconut oil
6	large romaine or Bibb lettuce leaves
	Miraculous Mango Salsa (page 230), for serving
	Cumin Cashew Cream Sauce (page 230), for serving

Cook the millet with a pinch of salt according to the chart on page 104. Set aside to cool.

While the millet is cooking, combine the flaxseeds and water in a small bowl; set aside until the mixture forms a gel, about 10 minutes. Then mix well.

Combine the carrots, scallions, basil, lemon juice, lemon zest, salt, and pepper in a large bowl. Once the millet is cool, add it to the bowl with the flaxseed-carrot mixture and mix well. Using your hands, shape the mixture into 6 burgers.

In a large skillet, heat the oil over medium heat. Place the burgers in the skillet and cook until golden brown, 7 to 8 minutes on each side. Serve warm, wrapped in lettuce leaves with a dollop of the Miraculous Mango Salsa and a drizzle of Cumin Cashew Cream Sauce on top. Uncooked burgers will keep for up to 4 days in the refrigerator or 1 month in the freezer, stored between pieces of parchment paper in a sealed container.

SERVES 6

miraculous
MANGO SALSA

This salsa is perfect for adding a boost of flavor to your salads, burgers, and tacos. I love to add a spoonful of this with a smear of my Dairy-Free Creamy Cashew Cheese (page 308) on my grain-free crackers (pages 156–162).

1   ripe mango, peeled, pitted, and finely diced
1   medium English cucumber, finely diced
3   tablespoons finely diced red onion
1   tablespoon finely chopped fresh cilantro
2   teaspoons freshly squeezed lime juice
    Sea salt and freshly ground black pepper, to taste

Combine all the ingredients in a large bowl; toss to combine. Add more red onion, if desired, for a spicier salsa. Serve immediately.

MAKES 1½ CUPS

cumin cashew
CREAM SAUCE

I love the flavor and consistency of this dairy-free cream sauce; it's velvety smooth and flavorful. You can also serve this sauce with leftover roasted veggies for an afternoon snack.

1   cup raw cashews
¾   cup water
¼   cup freshly squeezed lemon juice
½   teaspoon ground cumin
¼   teaspoon sea salt

Combine all the ingredients in a blender and blend until smooth. Serve chilled or at room temperature. Store leftover sauce in a sealed container in the refrigerator for up to 5 days.

MAKES 1½ CUPS

NO-EGGPLANT GARDEN HERB RATATOUILLE

Ratatouille, the delicious Provençal vegetable stew, generally calls for eggplant, but I think it tastes just as deliciously French with peppers, squash, and a few tomatoes. Leftovers are terrific tossed with gluten-free whole grains like millet or quinoa.

2	large zucchini, diced
2	large yellow squash, diced
1	red bell pepper, diced
1	yellow or orange bell pepper, diced
6	tablespoons extra-virgin olive oil, divided
	Sea salt and freshly ground black pepper
1	large white onion, diced
2	large garlic cloves, minced
1	pint grape tomatoes, halved
2½	tablespoons finely chopped fresh flat-leaf parsley
2	tablespoons finely chopped fresh thyme
2	tablespoons finely chopped fresh basil
1	tablespoon finely chopped fresh rosemary
1	tablespoon balsamic vinegar
	Peppy No-Cheese Parmesan (page 307), for topping, optional

Preheat the oven to 475°F. Line a rimmed baking sheet with parchment paper.

In a large bowl, toss the zucchini, squash, and bell peppers with 4 tablespoons of the oil. Season with salt and pepper to taste. Transfer the vegetables to the prepared baking sheet and roast for 20 to 25 minutes, or until golden brown, stirring halfway through. Remove from the oven and set aside.

In a large heavy pot, heat the remaining 2 tablespoons oil over medium heat. Add the onion and sauté until translucent, about 5 minutes. Add the garlic, cook for 30 seconds, and then add the tomatoes. Cook until the tomatoes are tender, 7 to 8 minutes more. Add the roasted vegetables, parsley, thyme, basil, rosemary, and vinegar; mix well. Season with salt and pepper to taste and, if desired, top with a sprinkle of the Peppy No-Cheese Parmesan. Serve immediately.

SERVES 4

HAPPY SWISS CHARD-WRAPPED VEGGIE BURGERS

Sweet potatoes and carrots form the base for these burgers—both are good sources of the antioxidant beta-carotene. Many veggie burgers require time in the food processor during preparation. Not this one, which saves you some dishwashing time.

1	cup millet
2	medium sweet potatoes, peeled and cut into ½-inch cubes
2	cups low-sodium vegetable broth
1	cup cooked chickpeas (see page 99)
1	cup peeled and grated carrots
5½	tablespoons ground flaxseeds
3½	teaspoons finely chopped fresh basil
½	cup shelled raw pumpkin seeds
1½	teaspoons sea salt
½	teaspoon freshly ground black pepper
½	teaspoon chili powder
½	teaspoon finely chopped fresh thyme
8	Swiss chard leaves, stems removed, for serving
2	large heirloom tomatoes, thinly sliced, for serving
	Cumin Cashew Cream Sauce (page 230), for serving
8	fresh basil leaves, for serving

Preheat the oven to 400°F. Line a rimmed baking sheet with parchment paper.

In a medium pot, combine the millet, sweet potatoes, and broth. Cover and bring to a boil, and then reduce the heat to a simmer and cook until the millet and sweet potatoes are tender, but not overcooked, about 20 minutes. Set aside to cool.

In a large bowl, combine the cooled millet with the sweet potatoes, chickpeas, carrots, flaxseeds, chopped basil, pumpkin seeds, salt, pepper, chili powder, and thyme. Using a potato masher or the back of a fork, mash the sweet potatoes and chickpeas, leaving some chunky pieces. Using your hands, shape the mixture into 8 burgers.

Lay the burgers on the prepared baking sheet. Bake for 15 minutes, then flip each burger and bake for another 10 minutes, or until golden brown.

Remove from the oven and allow the burgers to sit for 2 to 3 minutes, and then wrap each one in a Swiss chard leaf and top with a slice of tomato, a spoonful of Cumin Cashew Cream Sauce, and a basil leaf. Serve immediately.

SERVES 8

GRAIN-FREE BUTTERNUT SQUASH PIZZA CRUST
with carrot cashew herb sauce

This pizza's crust is surprisingly like a regular pizza crust. Imagine serving up a good ol' Manhattan pizza pie without the gluten! Serve leftover Carrot Cashew Herb Sauce spooned over any veggie, especially cauliflower, chickpeas, green beans, and avocados.

CARROT CASHEW HERB SAUCE

- 2 large carrots, peeled and chopped
- ¼ cup raw cashews
- ¼ cup finely chopped fresh basil
- ¼ cup finely chopped fresh flat-leaf parsley
- ¼ cup finely chopped spinach
- ½ cup extra-virgin olive oil
-   Freshly squeezed juice of 1 large lemon
- ½ teaspoon sea salt
- ¼ teaspoon freshly ground black pepper
-   Pinch chili powder, plus more to taste

SQUASH PIZZA CRUST

- 1 large butternut squash
- 3 tablespoons chia seeds, divided
- ¼ cup water plus 1 tablespoon
- 1¼ cups almond flour, store-bought or homemade (see page 39)
- 1 cup chickpea flour (garbanzo bean flour)
- 1 teaspoon dried parsley
- ½ teaspoon sea salt
- ½ teaspoon freshly ground black pepper
- 2 medium garlic cloves, minced
- ¾ cup diced grape tomatoes, for topping
- ¼ cup finely chopped fresh basil, for topping

MAKE THE SAUCE: Combine the carrots, cashews, basil, parsley, and spinach in a food processor and process until smooth. Add the oil, lemon juice, salt, pepper, and chili powder, and pulse to combine.

Add more chili powder if you like a hotter sauce.

MAKE THE CRUST: Preheat the oven to 350°F. Line 2 rimmed baking sheets with parchment paper.

Lay the whole squash on a prepared baking sheet and bake for 30 minutes. Remove from the oven and let cool enough to handle, about 10 minutes.

Raise the temperature to 400°F. Re-line the baking sheet with parchment paper.

Cut the squash in half lengthwise and scrape out the seeds. Place cut-side down on the baking sheet. Bake until soft and easily pierced with a fork, 25 to 30 minutes. Let cool. Using a spoon, scrape out the flesh from the squash and mash with a fork.

Meanwhile, in a small bowl, combine 2 tablespoons of the chia seeds with the water and set aside until the mixture forms a gel, 8 to 10 minutes.

Raise the temperature to 425°F.

In a medium bowl, combine the squash with the chia mixture, remaining chia seeds, flours, parsley, salt, pepper, and garlic; mix well. Transfer to a prepared baking sheet. Using a rolling pin, flatten into a ¼-inch-thick rectangle or square. Bake for 25 to 30 minutes, or until golden brown. Remove from the oven and top with the Carrot Cashew Herb Sauce and add the tomatoes and basil. Bake for 8 minutes more and serve. Refrigerate leftover sauce for up to 2 days.

SERVES 2; MAKES 1 CUP SAUCE

SUNSET SESAME AND POPPY SEED CAULIFLOWER PIZZA CRUST

Think of yourself as an artist and this grain-free pizza crust as your canvas, then go to town! I've suggested a variety of Dazzling Pizza Toppings below, but the choice is yours.

2	tablespoons ground flaxseeds
6	tablespoons water
1	medium head cauliflower, cut into florets
⅓	cup almond flour, store-bought or homemade (see page 39)
1	tablespoon chia seeds
1	garlic clove, minced
1	teaspoon sea salt
½	teaspoon dried oregano
½	teaspoon dried basil
¼	teaspoon freshly ground black pepper
1	tablespoon sesame seeds
1	tablespoon poppy seeds
	Your choice of toppings (see below)

OPTIONAL DAZZLING PIZZA TOPPPINGS

▸ Easy No-Foil Roasted Garlic (page 329)

▸ Sun-Dried Tomato Sauce (page 320)

▸ Big-Flavor Marinated Roasted Bell Peppers (page 278)

Preheat the oven to 350°F. Line a baking sheet with parchment paper.

In a small bowl, combine the flaxseeds and the water; set aside until the mixture forms a gel, at least 5 minutes, while you prepare the cauliflower.

Place the cauliflower in a food processor and pulse until finely ground; you should have about 2 cups. Transfer to the prepared baking sheet and bake for 30 minutes, stirring the cauliflower crumbs at least twice during baking. Transfer to a large bowl and let cool, about 10 minutes. Wrap the cauliflower in a double layer of cheesecloth and, using your hands, squeeze out as much excess water as possible. Discard the excess water.

In a large bowl, combine the cauliflower with the flaxseed mixture, almond flour, chia seeds, garlic, salt, oregano, basil, and pepper; mix well. Spoon the mixture onto a clean parchment paper–lined baking sheet, and then, using a spatula, shape it into a thin crust. Sprinkle with the sesame and poppy seeds. Bake until golden, about 30 minutes. Cover with another piece of parchment paper and flip the crust onto another baking sheet. Bake for 15 minutes more. Add your desired toppings and bake for an additional 10 minutes, or until the toppings are cooked through. Serve warm.

SERVES 2

BLISSFUL QUINOA PIZZA
with carrot ribbons and shallots

*Quinoa is a bit of a miracle seed (yes, it's a seed, although it's often referred to as a grain).
Besides earning our affection for its remarkable protein content, quinoa can hold together well enough
to create a pizza crust. As is, this recipe makes a fairly simple pizza; add one of my pesto recipes
on top if you'd like more complex flavors.*

CRUST

1	cup quinoa, soaked overnight, drained, and rinsed (see note)
¼	cup low-sodium vegetable broth
¼	teaspoon chili powder
¼	teaspoon sea salt, plus more as needed
¼	teaspoon freshly ground black pepper, plus more as needed
2	tablespoons extra-virgin olive oil, plus more for drizzling

TOPPINGS

¼	cup Heirloom Tomato Sauce (page 318)
2	large carrots, peeled and cut into thin ribbons with a vegetable peeler
⅓	cup finely chopped fresh basil
1	shallot, thinly sliced
1	cup Dairy-Free Creamy Cashew Cheese (page 308)

MAKE THE CRUST: Preheat the oven to 350°F.

Place the quinoa in a food processor with the broth, chili powder, salt, and pepper and process until smooth.

Heat a large cast-iron skillet in the oven for 5 minutes. Add the oil and swirl to coat the skillet, then heat for another 5 minutes. Add the quinoa mixture to the skillet and press it evenly into the bottom of the pan. Bake until set, about 15 minutes. Using a spatula, flip the crust over and bake until golden brown, another 12 to 15 minutes.

Spread the Heirloom Tomato Sauce on top of the crust and cover with the carrots, basil, and shallot. Bake for an additional 8 minutes. Remove from the oven and top with the Dairy-Free Creamy Cashew Cheese, a drizzle of oil, and, if desired, a sprinkle of salt and pepper. Serve warm.

NOTE: Even though the grain chart in this book says soaking isn't needed for quinoa, it is needed for this recipe; it will not work if the quinoa is not soaked overnight. If you want to prepare the crust in advance, remove it from the oven before adding any toppings and let cool. When ready to serve, preheat the oven, add toppings, and bake as instructed.

SERVES 2

MOROCCAN CHICKPEA SKILLET PIZZA

This grain-free pizza features a blend of savory Middle Eastern flavors. It's kind of like a deep-dish pizza—best enjoyed with a fork and knife. If you like, drizzle the finished pizza with your favorite pesto.

1	cup chickpea flour (garbanzo bean flour)
½	teaspoon aluminum-free baking powder
¼	teaspoon sea salt
¼	teaspoon freshly ground black pepper
¼	teaspoon ground cumin
¼	teaspoon ground coriander
1	cup low-sodium vegetable broth
1	tablespoon extra-virgin olive oil
¼	cup Heirloom Tomato Sauce (page 318)
1	cup finely chopped curly kale (stems removed)
½	cup thinly sliced button mushrooms
1	small scallion, very thinly sliced
¼	cup Carrot Cashew Herb Sauce (page 234)
	Crushed red pepper flakes, for garnish

MORE DAZZLING PIZZA TOPPING SUGGESTIONS

‣ Super Soft Caramelized Red Onions (page 272)

‣ Spectacular Salt 'n' Pepper Baked Shallots (page 272)

In a large bowl, combine the flour, baking powder, salt, black pepper, cumin, and coriander; mix well. Slowly whisk in the broth until the mixture is as smooth as pancake batter.

In a medium cast-iron skillet on the stovetop, heat the oil over medium-high heat. Add the flour mixture so that it completely coats the bottom of the skillet. Cook until the bottom is golden brown, about 5 minutes, and then flip and cook on the other side until golden brown, another 3 to 4 minutes.

Preheat the broiler.

Add the Heirloom Tomato Sauce, using the back of a large tablespoon to coat the entire surface of the crust, except for ½ inch around the edge. Top with the kale, mushrooms, and scallion, and then drizzle with the Carrot Cashew Herb Sauce. Place under the broiler until the kale turns crispy, 4 to 6 minutes. Sprinkle with red pepper flakes and serve warm.

SERVES 2

MINI BAKED CHICKPEA-FREE FALAFEL
with cannellini bean za'atar sauce

If you have ever taken a trip to New York City, you know full well that falafel is where it's at. Every other street corner smells like chickpeas! The only problem with traditional falafel is that it's fried. That's a lot of pro-inflammatory grease I don't need. To make my own, healthier version, I bake these chickpea-free falafel and stuff them with other yummy ingredients like mushrooms, nuts, and seeds. These mini falafels can be served on their own, or wrapped in my Savory Chickpea Flour Crepes (page 274) or Swiss chard leaves.

½ cup ground flaxseeds

⅓ cup sesame seeds

2 cups baby bella mushrooms, finely chopped

1 small sweet white onion, finely diced

2 tablespoons extra-virgin olive oil

1 garlic clove, minced

¼ teaspoon sea salt

¼ teaspoon freshly ground black pepper

1 large carrot, peeled and cut into 1-inch pieces

1 cup raw Brazil nuts

1 cup raw cashews

¾ cup shelled raw pumpkin seeds

2 tablespoons finely chopped fresh flat-leaf parsley

2 teaspoons freshly squeezed lemon juice

½ teaspoon ground cumin

6 to 8 Swiss chard leaves, stems removed, for serving, optional

1 cup chopped fresh spinach, for serving

1 cup arugula, for serving

Perfect Pico de Gallo (page 242)

⅓ cup finely chopped fresh cilantro, for serving

Cannellini Bean Za'atar Sauce (page 242)

Preheat the oven to 250°F.

In a medium bowl, combine the flaxseeds and sesame seeds.

In a large bowl, combine the mushrooms, onion, oil, garlic, salt, and pepper. Mix well.

Place the carrot, Brazil nuts, cashews, and pumpkin seeds in a food processor and process into a very fine crumble. Transfer to the bowl with the mushroom mixture. Add the parsley, lemon juice, and cumin and mix well.

Shape the mixture into 1½-inch balls. Roll the balls in the flax and sesame mixture until completely coated. Place on a large rimmed baking sheet and bake for about 30 minutes, until crisp on the outside, but still moist on the inside. Remove from the oven.

Place a few falafel balls on each Swiss chard leaf, if desired, and divide the spinach and arugula among them. Add a spoonful of the Perfect Pico de Gallo and a sprinkle of cilantro to each, and then drizzle with the Cannellini Bean Za'atar Sauce. Fold up the Swiss chard leaves and serve.

SERVES 6 TO 8

perfect
PICO DE GALLO

*Perfect is an understatement here.
Add a spoonful to my Mini Baked Chickpea-Free
Falafel (page 240) and you'll thank me later.*

1   pint cherry tomatoes, sliced into small rounds
½   small red onion, diced
3   tablespoons finely chopped fresh cilantro
2   teaspoons apple cider vinegar
1   garlic clove, minced
½   teaspoon extra-virgin olive oil
      Pinch chili powder
      Sea salt and freshly ground black pepper

In a medium bowl, combine the tomatoes, onion,
cilantro, vinegar, garlic, oil, and chili powder.
Season with salt and pepper to taste and serve.

MAKES 2 CUPS

cannellini bean
ZA'ATAR SAUCE

*This creamy, hummus-like sauce
is ideal for serving with my Mini Baked
Chickpea-Free Falafel (page 240)*

2   cups cooked cannellini beans (see page 99)
¼   cup extra-virgin olive oil, plus more for drizzling
2   tablespoons freshly squeezed lemon juice
2   tablespoons water
2   garlic cloves
2   teaspoons za'atar spices*
1   teaspoon sea salt
¼   teaspoon freshly ground black pepper

Combine all the ingredients in a food processor
and process until smooth. Taste and adjust the
seasoning if necessary. If desired, drizzle with more
oil and serve.

**Available in Middle Eastern markets and some well-
stocked grocery stores.*

MAKES 2¼ CUPS

warm hearted
SWISS CHARD LENTIL BAKE

For those of you craving a heartier dish, bake away! This luscious blend of lentils, sweet vidalia onions, carrots, sun-dried tomatoes, and fresh herbs is a wintertime staple in my home. Serve this recipe with my Mock Mashed Potatoes: Yellow Split Pea and Cilantro Puree (page 265).

1	teaspoon extra-virgin olive oil, plus more for coating pie pan
1	cup brown lentils
1	large Vidalia onion, thinly sliced
2	large carrots, peeled and shredded
2	garlic cloves, minced
¼	teaspoon ground cumin
¼	teaspoon chili powder
⅓	cup thinly sliced sun-dried tomatoes (not packed in oil)
	Sea salt and freshly ground black pepper, to taste
½	bunch Swiss chard, ends trimmed, leaves and stems finely chopped
¼	cup finely chopped fresh flat-leaf parsley
¼	cup finely chopped fresh cilantro

Preheat the oven to 350°F. Lightly coat a 10-inch pie pan with oil.

Cook the lentils according to the chart on page 99, or until tender.

Meanwhile, heat the oil over medium-high heat in a large skillet. Add the onion and cook until translucent, about 5 minutes. Add the carrots, garlic, cumin, and chili powder and cook for another 5 minutes. Add the cooked lentils, sun-dried tomatoes, salt, and pepper; mix well.

Spread about one-third of the lentil mixture on the bottom of the pie pan and top with half of the Swiss chard. Add another third of the lentil mixture, the rest of the Swiss chard, and finish with the remaining lentil mixture. Bake for about 30 minutes, or until hot all the way through. Remove from the oven and top with the parsley and cilantro and serve warm.

SERVES 4

BEAMING QUINOA TABBOULEH
with coconut chili cashews

Get ready for some serious flavor. This tabbouleh is out of this world; it'll knock your socks off when paired with my crunchy Coconut Chili Cashews. Luckily, this recipe uses only half the cashew yield—you'll have a cup leftover for snacks. I never go a day without a bag of these Coconut Chili Cashews.

COCONUT CHILI CASHEWS

2	cups raw cashews
¼	cup unsweetened shredded coconut
1	tablespoon pure maple syrup
1	teaspoon freshly squeezed lime juice
½	teaspoon chili powder
½	teaspoon sea salt

QUINOA TABBOULEH

1	cup red quinoa, rinsed
2½	tablespoons extra-virgin olive oil
1	tablespoon freshly squeezed lemon juice
1	large garlic clove, minced
¼	teaspoon sea salt
¼	teaspoon freshly ground black pepper
1	large cucumber, thinly sliced
1	pint grape tomatoes, halved
1	cup finely chopped fresh curly parsley
⅓	cup finely chopped fresh cilantro, optional
2	tablespoons finely chopped fresh chives

MAKE THE CASHEWS: Preheat the oven to 325°F. Line a rimmed baking sheet with parchment paper.

In a large bowl, combine the cashews, shredded coconut, maple syrup, lime juice, chili powder, and salt; mix well to coat the cashews. Arrange the cashews in a single layer on the prepared baking sheet. Bake for about 20 minutes, or until golden brown, stirring after the first 10 minutes. Set aside to cool.

MAKE THE TABBOULEH: While the cashews are baking, cook the quinoa according to the chart on page 104. Remove from the heat and transfer to a large bowl. When cool, fluff with a fork.

In a small bowl, whisk together the oil, lemon juice, garlic, salt, and pepper. Set aside.

Add the cucumber, tomatoes, parsley, cilantro (if using) and chives to the quinoa. Mix well. Drizzle with the dressing and toss to coat. Serve with 1 cup of the Coconut Chili Cashews on top. The remaining cashews can be stored in a sealed container for up to 5 days.

SERVES 6; MAKES 2 CUPS CASHEWS

ENLIVENED SUMMER PEACH, ROASTED FENNEL, AND QUINOA TACOS

These soft tacos capture the combination of Mexican and health-conscious influences that recall my summers in California. They're a great substitute for that California staple, the fish taco.

QUINOA TACOS

½	cup red quinoa, rinsed
2	large fennel bulbs, trimmed and thinly sliced lengthwise (save the fronds for another use)
2	tablespoons extra-virgin olive oil, divided
1	teaspoon freshly grated orange zest
¼	teaspoon sea salt
¼	teaspoon freshly ground black pepper
½	medium white onion, diced
½	teaspoon ground cumin
¼	teaspoon chili powder

GRATEFUL GUACAMOLE

2	ripe medium avocados, pitted, peeled, and diced (reserve 1 pit)
3	tablespoons plus 1 teaspoon freshly squeezed lime juice
2	scallions, white and light green parts, thinly sliced
2	tablespoons finely chopped fresh cilantro
	Sea salt, to taste
8	small gluten-free whole-grain (corn-free) soft taco shells or tortillas, for serving
2	large peaches or plums, pitted and sliced, for serving
1	cup Dairy-Free Creamy Cashew Cheese (page 308), for serving
	Drizzle Seriously Sensational Sriracha Sauce (page 318) or hot sauce, for serving
⅓	cup finely chopped fresh cilantro, for serving

MAKE THE TACOS: Cook the quinoa according to the chart on page 104.

Preheat the oven to 400°F.

Place the fennel on a rimmed baking sheet and drizzle with 1 tablespoon of the oil. Sprinkle with the orange zest and season with the salt and pepper. Roast for 10 minutes, or until tender.

In the meantime, heat the remaining 1 tablespoon oil in a large skillet over medium heat. Add the onion and sauté until translucent. Add the cooked quinoa, cumin, and chili powder; mix well until heated through. Remove from the heat and fluff with a fork.

MAKE THE GUACAMOLE: In a medium bowl, mash all the guacamole ingredients together with a fork. Taste and adjust the seasoning as needed. To prevent browning, place one of the pits in the bowl of guacamole until ready to serve.

Toast the soft taco shells one at a time in a large, dry skillet over medium heat for 10 to 15 seconds on each side.

To assemble the tacos, lay the shells on a flat surface. Layer the quinoa mixture, fennel, peaches, and Grateful Guacamole. Top with the Dairy-Free Creamy Cashew Cheese and Seriously Sensational Sriracha Sauce. Sprinkle with the cilantro and serve.

SERVES 4; MAKES ½ CUP GAUCAMOLE

OPEN-FACED PUMPKIN ENCHILADAS
with moo-free cashew sour cream

This recipe is quick and easy enough to make for a weeknight dinner. If you're partial to crunch, leave the peppers out of the cooked mixture and serve them raw on top of the enchiladas.

3 tablespoons extra-virgin olive oil, divided

1 cup cooked black beans (see page 99)

2 garlic cloves, minced

3 tablespoons water

1½ teaspoons ground cumin, divided

¼ teaspoon sea salt, plus more to taste

¼ teaspoon freshly ground black pepper, plus more to taste

½ cup finely chopped red onion

1 red bell pepper, thinly sliced

2 cups finely chopped stemmed dinosaur (lacinato) kale

1 cup pumpkin puree, store-bought or homemade (see page 123)

2 teaspoons chili powder

Pinch cayenne pepper

8 gluten-free whole-grain (corn-free) tortillas

GARNISHES

1 ripe avocado, pitted, peeled, and thinly sliced

1 cup cherry tomatoes, halved

¼ cup finely chopped fresh cilantro

3 scallions, white and light green parts only, thinly sliced

1 tablespoon sesame seeds

Lime wedges

Moo-Free Cashew Sour Cream (page 309)

In a large skillet, heat 1 tablespoon of the oil over medium heat. Add the beans, garlic, water, ½ teaspoon of the cumin, and the salt and black pepper. Cook until warm, about 3 minutes. Transfer to a medium bowl.

In the same skillet, heat the remaining 2 tablespoons oil over medium heat. Add the onion and sauté for 2 minutes. Add the bell pepper and cook until tender-crisp, 1 to 2 minutes. Add the bean mixture and kale to the skillet, cover, and turn off the heat. Allow the kale to wilt.

Meanwhile, in a blender or food processor, puree the pumpkin, chili powder, remaining 1 teaspoon cumin, the cayenne pepper, and salt and black pepper to taste until smooth. Adjust the salt and pepper if necessary. Transfer the pumpkin mixture to a small saucepan and keep warm over low heat.

Toast the tortillas in a large, dry skillet over medium heat for 1 minute on each side. Spread the pumpkin puree onto the tortillas, top with the black bean mixture, and garnish with sliced avocado, tomatoes, cilantro, scallions, sesame seeds, and a squeeze of lime juice. Top with a dollop of the Moo-Free Cashew Sour Cream.

NOTE: You can also warm up your tortillas by setting them in your oven drawer, if you have one.

SERVES 4

WARM ME UP SWEET BASIL CURRY
with brussels sprouts and millet

This nod to Thai curry has the spicy sweet flavor of ginger, fresh herbs, and coconut milk, with just the right amount of heat (courtesy of red pepper flakes). You can toss your rubbery macaroni and cheese—this is my idea of comfort food! If you'd like to switch up the flavors, use thyme and sage in place of cilantro and basil.

3	tablespoons coconut oil
2	large garlic cloves, minced
1½	teaspoons ground turmeric
1	teaspoon crushed red pepper flakes
¾	teaspoon curry powder
½	teaspoon ground ginger
3	large sweet potatoes, peeled and cut into ½-inch chunks
1	(13.5-ounce) BPA-free can full-fat coconut milk
1	cup water
4	cups halved trimmed Brussels sprouts
	Sea salt
½	cup finely chopped fresh basil, for garnish
⅓	cup finely chopped fresh cilantro, for garnish
	Freshly ground black pepper
2	cups cooked millet (see page 104), warmed

In a large heavy pot, heat the oil over medium heat. Add the garlic and sauté for 30 seconds, and then add the turmeric, red pepper flakes, curry powder, and ginger; mix well. Add the sweet potatoes to the pot and cook for 3 to 4 minutes.

Shake the coconut milk and add it along with the water to the pot. Cover and cook over medium heat until the sweet potatoes are tender, about 10 minutes. Add the Brussels sprouts and salt to taste; simmer for 10 minutes more, and then remove from the heat. Stir in the basil, cilantro, and black pepper to taste, and serve atop the warm millet.

SERVES 4

MUCHO BROCCOLI AND DELICATA SQUASH BOWL
with tahini dressing

A bowl of steamed and raw veggies? Not particularly interesting. A bowl of steamed and raw veggies bathed in a zesty tahini dressing? A whole other story. You'll love the combination of roasted and raw veggies in this dish. It's chock-full of fiber and tastes simply fabulous. You can use this dressing to take any veggies to another level.

BOWL

2	tablespoons extra-virgin olive oil, divided
2	medium heads broccoli, cut into florets
	Sea salt and freshly ground black pepper
1	medium delicata squash, halved, seeded, and cut into ½-inch slices
1	large carrot, peeled and cut on the diagonal
2	teaspoons peeled minced fresh ginger
2	tablespoons raw honey

TAHINI DRESSING

¾	cup water
½	cup tahini
1	tablespoon freshly squeezed lemon juice
1	tablespoon extra-virgin olive oil
1	teaspoon freshly grated lemon zest
1	minced garlic clove
¼	teaspoon paprika
	Pinch ground cumin
	Sea salt and freshly ground black pepper
2	cups shredded red cabbage, for serving
2	cups packed baby spinach, for serving
¼	cup thinly sliced red onion, for serving
	Shelled raw sunflower seeds, toasted (see page 108), for topping

MAKE THE BOWL: Preheat the oven to 450°F.

On a rimmed baking sheet, toss 1 tablespoon of the oil with the broccoli and sprinkle with salt and pepper to taste. On a separate rimmed baking sheet, toss the squash, carrots, and ginger with the honey, remaining 1 tablespoon oil, and salt and pepper to taste. Place both baking sheets (one on each rack) in the oven and roast for 15 to 20 minutes, or until the vegetables are tender.

MAKE THE DRESSING: Place all the dressing ingredients except the salt and pepper in a food processor and process until smooth. Transfer to a bowl and season with salt and pepper to taste, then mix well to combine.

To serve, mound the shredded cabbage in the middle of a large serving platter. Make a ring of spinach around the cabbage. Top the spinach with the roasted vegetables and red onion. Drizzle with some of the Tahini Dressing. Sprinkle the platter with sunflower seeds. Taste and season with salt and pepper if necessary. Serve with the remaining Tahini Dressing on the side. Store any leftover dressing in an airtight container in the refrigerator for up to 5 days.

SERVES 4; MAKES 1 CUP DRESSING

ABUNDANT ROASTED WINTER VEGGIES
with cannellini beans

This dish is made start to finish on a baking sheet. Now that's what I call an easy weeknight meal! As you slice the leeks, be careful not to pull them apart.

2 large leeks, white and light green parts, cut into ¼-inch rounds

12 Brussels sprouts, trimmed and halved

3 large parsnips, peeled and cut into ¼-inch rounds

3 large carrots, peeled and cut diagonally into ¼-inch slices

4 garlic cloves, minced

3 tablespoons extra-virgin olive oil

1 tablespoon balsamic vinegar

Sea salt and freshly ground black pepper

1½ cups cooked cannellini beans (see page 99)

3 tablespoons slivered raw almonds, toasted (see page 108)

Preheat the oven to 425°F.

In a large bowl, combine the leeks, Brussels sprouts, parsnips, carrots, garlic, oil, and vinegar; mix well. Spread the mixture in a single layer on a large rimmed baking sheet (use two baking sheets if needed). Season with salt and pepper to taste. Roast for 30 minutes, or until tender and golden brown, tossing halfway through the cooking time. Add the cannellini beans and return to the oven for another 7 to 8 minutes, or until warm and crisped. Serve warm, topped with the almonds.

SERVES 4 AS A MAIN; 6 TO 8 AS A SIDE

HUMBLE SRIRACHA ROASTED WILD RICE BUDDHA BOWL

Rice bowls are standard healthy fare these days—a big bowl of goodness and healing. But, to be honest, they are often bland, so even if you know they're good for you, you might be hesitant to come back for more. This Buddha bowl, though, is anything but bland. Spiced up with my Seriously Sensational Sriracha Sauce (page 318), it's positively addictive!

1	cup well-shaken light culinary coconut milk
½	cup wild rice
½	teaspoon sea salt, divided, plus more to taste
1	small head broccoli, cut into ½-inch florets
3	small purple potatoes, peeled and cut into ½-inch chunks
2	medium parsnips, peeled and shredded
2	medium carrots, peeled and shredded
3	tablespoons Seriously Sensational Sriracha Sauce (page 318), plus more for serving
2	tablespoons extra-virgin olive oil, divided
¼	teaspoon freshly ground black pepper, plus more to taste
1	small bunch kale, stems removed and leaves chopped
2	small garlic cloves, minced
½	cup finely chopped fresh cilantro
1	small ripe avocado, pitted, peeled, and diced
3	tablespoons unsweetened coconut flakes
1½	tablespoons freshly squeezed lime juice
1	lime, cut into wedges, for serving

Combine the coconut milk, rice, and ¼ teaspoon of the salt in a medium pot. Cook, uncovered, over medium-high heat, stirring occasionally so the coconut milk doesn't burn on the bottom of the pot. Once the rice comes to a low boil, reduce the heat to low, cover, and cook until tender, about 35 minutes.

While the rice cooks, preheat the oven to 325°F.

In a large bowl, toss the broccoli, potatoes, parsnips, carrots, Seriously Sensational Sriracha Sauce, 1 tablespoon of the oil, the remaining ¼ teaspoon salt, and the ¼ teaspoon pepper. Transfer to a large rimmed baking sheet and roast for 20 to 25 minutes, or until golden brown.

Place the kale in a medium bowl and, using your hands, massage the remaining 1 tablespoon oil and the garlic into the kale leaves until the leaves have softened. Fold in the cilantro and avocado and season with salt and pepper to taste.

Remove the rice from the heat and fluff with a fork. Arrange the rice in the middle of a large serving platter. Spoon the roasted veggies on one side and the kale salad on the other. Top with the coconut flakes and drizzle with lime juice. To serve, spoon the vegetables, rice, and kale into serving bowls. Serve with the lime wedges and additional Seriously Sensational Sriracha Sauce sauce on the side.

SERVES 2 TO 4

CAREFREE CARROT AND BRUSSELS SPROUTS MEDLEY
with maple cashew dressing

This dish is so popular among my clients that I often get requests to make it for their parties and family gatherings. I strongly suggest you make sure to save enough for leftovers! The dressing recipe alone is plentiful: you won't use all of it on the vegetables.

MAPLE CASHEW DRESSING

- ½   cups raw cashews, soaked for 10 minutes in hot water, drained, and rinsed
- ½   cup water
- ¼   cup finely chopped fresh flat-leaf parsley
- ¼   cup extra-virgin olive oil
-     Freshly grated zest of 1 large lemon
- 2½   tablespoons freshly squeezed lemon juice
- 1   tablespoon apple cider vinegar
- 1   large garlic clove
- 2   teaspoons pure maple syrup
-     Pinch cayenne pepper, optional
-     Sea salt and freshly ground black pepper, to taste

CARROT AND BRUSSELS SPROUTS MEDLEY

- 7½   cups halved trimmed Brussels sprouts
- 1   bunch asparagus, ends trimmed and cut into 1-inch pieces
- 2   large carrots, peeled and cut diagonally into 1-inch slices
- 3   tablespoons extra-virgin olive oil, plus more as needed
-     Sea salt and freshly ground black pepper
- 2   apples, cored and finely diced
- 3   red radishes, thinly sliced

MAKE THE DRESSING: Combine all the dressing ingredients in a blender and puree until smooth and creamy. Taste and adjust the seasoning with salt and black pepper.

MAKE THE MEDLEY: Preheat the oven to 400°F.

Toss the Brussels sprouts, asparagus, and carrots with the oil, and salt and pepper to taste. Arrange in a single layer on a large rimmed baking sheet and roast for 20 minutes, stirring after 10 minutes to ensure the vegetables don't burn.

In a large bowl, combine the roasted vegetables with the apples and radishes.

Gently toss the vegetable mixture with a few tablespoons of the dressing. Add a pinch of salt and toss again. Add more dressing if needed. Serve warm or at room temperature. You will have leftover dressing, which you can store in a sealed container in the refrigerator for up to 5 days.

SERVES 6; MAKES 1¼ CUPS DRESSING

SPICY CHILI LIME CHICKPEAS
with cauliflower "rice"

Grain-free cauliflower "rice" fills in for rice so wonderfully that you'll never miss the real thing (with this recipe, especially, since I add chickpeas to give the dish some protein). If you like, grate the cauliflower on a coarse grater before pulsing in the food processor. This will give the "rice" a coarser texture.

1	cup cooked chickpeas (see page 99)
¼	cup freshly squeezed lime juice
3	tablespoons extra-virgin olive oil, divided
1½	teaspoons chili powder
¼	teaspoon sea salt, plus more to taste
¼	teaspoon freshly ground black pepper, plus more to taste
1	large head cauliflower, cut into florets
1	tablespoon raw honey
2	firm plums, pitted and diced
1	large ripe avocado, pitted, peeled, and diced
4	fresh chives, thinly sliced
2	tablespoons finely chopped fresh cilantro, plus more for garnish
2	tablespoons finely chopped fresh flat-leaf parsley, plus more for garnish
2	tablespoons shelled raw hemp seeds
1¼	teaspoons freshly grated lime zest, for garnish

Preheat the oven to 375°F. Line a rimmed baking sheet with parchment paper.

In a large bowl, combine the chickpeas, lime juice, 1 tablespoon of the oil, the chili powder, salt, and pepper; gently toss to coat. Arrange the chickpeas in a single layer on the prepared baking sheet. Bake for 20 to 25 minutes, or until golden brown and crisp.

Working in two batches, place the cauliflower florets in a food processor and pulse until they resemble rice.

In a small bowl, whisk the remaining 2 tablespoons oil, the honey, and salt and pepper to taste.

Transfer the crispy chickpeas to a large bowl and add the cauliflower "rice," plums, avocado, chives, cilantro, parsley, and hemp seeds. Gently toss with the honey–olive oil dressing, and garnish with the lime zest and additional cilantro and parsley.

SERVES 4

PERFECTLY POPPED AMARANTH SALAD
with carrot ginger dressing

No corn in this cookbook, but who needs it? Popped amaranth is a gluten-free option that you can pop on the stovetop. You'll want to make this again and again. In this recipe, it's not finger food like traditional popcorn, but it has the same playful texture. Dig in!

½   cup amaranth

2   cups mixed greens

3   large carrots, peeled and shredded

1   red bell pepper, diced

1   large cucumber, diced

1   large ripe avocado, pitted, peeled, and thinly sliced

1   cup shredded red cabbage

2   large scallions, thinly sliced

¼   cup dried cranberries

2   tablespoons shelled raw sunflower seeds

½   cup apple cider vinegar

¼   cup extra-virgin olive oil

2   tablespoons freshly squeezed lime juice

1½ teaspoons finely grated fresh ginger

½   teaspoon poppy seeds

    Sea salt and freshly ground black pepper

Heat a large skillet over medium-high heat. Wait until the skillet is so hot that a drop of water evaporates immediately upon contact. Add 1 tablespoon of the amaranth. Shake the skillet to move the seeds until all the amaranth has popped, 15 to 20 seconds. Remove the popped seeds and repeat with the remaining amaranth, 1 tablespoon at a time.

In a large bowl, combine the popped amaranth, greens, carrots, bell pepper, cucumber, avocado, cabbage, scallions, cranberries, and sunflower seeds.

In a small bowl, whisk together the vinegar, oil, lime juice, ginger, poppy seeds, and salt and black pepper to taste. Drizzle over the salad and gently toss to combine. Serve immediately.

SERVES 4

plentiful
CHERRY TOMATO AND PORTOBELLO DHAL

If you've got thirty minutes, I've got the perfect dinner for you. Dhal, the Indian lentil dish, can be flavored any which way. Here, it features the flavors of cumin and mustard seeds with a touch of chili powder. I've added tomatoes and mushrooms to make it a more substantial meal.

2	tablespoons extra-virgin olive oil
1	large sweet white onion, diced
2	garlic cloves, thinly sliced
1	teaspoon dried basil
1	teaspoon dried parsley
1	bay leaf
½	teaspoon ground cumin
½	teaspoon yellow mustard seeds
¼	teaspoon ground turmeric
¼	teaspoon chili powder
2	cups sliced baby bella mushrooms
1	cup cherry tomatoes, quartered
1½	cups low-sodium vegetable broth, divided
2	cups cooked yellow lentils (see page 99)
1	cup chopped fresh cilantro
	Sea salt

In a large skillet, heat the oil over medium heat. Add the onion and garlic and sauté until the onion is soft and translucent, about 4 minutes. Add the basil, parsley, bay leaf, cumin, mustard seeds, turmeric, and chili powder and stir until fragrant.

Add the mushrooms, tomatoes, and 3 tablespoons of the broth. Cook until the liquid has been absorbed, and then add the lentils and the remaining broth. Cook until the flavors combine and the dhal has thickened, about 30 minutes. Remove the bay leaf and stir in the cilantro. Season to taste with salt. Serve warm.

SERVES 4

more than just a side

These dishes are my answer to traditional "filler" side dishes you grew up on. Just because they're not taking center stage on your plate doesn't mean they can't be the most popular items. Rather than gloppy, starchy, heavy sides steeped in butter and breading, these recipes will brighten your meal without weighing it (or you) down. Not only do the foods you'll find here not cause inflammation—they actually help prevent it.

I don't know about you, but I love to eat little bites, snacks, and mini meals throughout my day. Each of these dishes is light, fresh, and flavorful, featuring veggies, herbs, spices, grains, fruits, nuts, and more, all of which are bursting at the seams with healthy nutrients. They boost the flavor and nutrient profile to your main meal—plus, they serve as delicious stand-alone snacks!

I'll show you how to apply easy principles to these tasty numbers without sacrificing flavor or variety. You'll learn:

‣ Quick ways to whip up simple, versatile side dishes and mini meals.

‣ Easy shortcuts and time-savers.

‣ How to turn simple sides into elegant holiday additions.

‣ Simple ways to mix 'n' match sides to create a complete meal.

‣ How to prepare foods that make you feel normal and alive again!

Feel free to keep the portions small, or double them up to make a meal. Your side dishes will never be sidelined again!

celebration
DELICATA SQUASH

I love delicata squash because you don't have to peel it! Top these beautiful rings with my Ecstatic Grape Sauce (page 323) and Dukkah (page 326), or enjoy this dish served on its own.

2	delicata squash, halved crosswise
3	tablespoons extra-virgin olive oil
1½	tablespoons pure maple syrup
¼	teaspoon ground coriander
¼	teaspoon ground cumin, plus a pinch for squash seeds
¼	teaspoon sea salt, plus a pinch for squash seeds
¼	teaspoon freshly ground black pepper, plus a pinch for squash seeds
¼	cup finely chopped fresh cilantro or sage, optional

Preheat the oven to 400°F. Line 2 large rimmed baking sheets with parchment paper.

Scoop out the squash seeds and pulp. Discard the pulp, rinse the seeds, and set aside. Slice the squash halves into ½-inch rings.

In a large bowl, combine the squash, oil, maple syrup, coriander, cumin, salt, and pepper and toss to coat. Arrange on a prepared baking sheet and bake for 20 minutes, or until tender, flipping after 10 minutes.

Place the rinsed seeds on a prepared baking sheet and sprinkle with the pinches of cumin, salt, and pepper. Bake for 8 to 10 minutes, or until golden brown.

Transfer the squash and seeds to a serving platter. Sprinkle with the fresh herbs, if desired, and toasted seeds. Serve warm.

SERVES 4

ROASTED SWEET POTATO BITES
with presto pesto drizzle

This is one of the most popular recipes in my cooking classes. It makes a great afternoon snack as well as an excellent side dish. These bites are fabulous to add to salads, too!

SWEET POTATO BITES

2   large sweet potatoes or yams, peeled and cut into 1-inch cubes

2   tablespoons extra-virgin olive oil

1   tablespoon ground flaxseeds

     Sea salt and freshly ground black pepper

PRESTO PESTO DRIZZLE

4   fresh chives, sliced

3   tablespoons extra-virgin olive oil

2   tablespoons chopped fresh basil

2   tablespoons freshly squeezed lemon juice

2   tablespoons water

1   small garlic clove, minced

½   teaspoon raw honey

     Pinch freshly grated lemon zest

     Sea salt and freshly ground black pepper, to taste

MAKE THE SWEET POTATO BITES: Preheat the oven to 350°F.

In a large bowl, combine the sweet potato cubes, oil, flaxseeds, and salt and pepper to taste. Arrange the mixture in a single layer on a large rimmed baking sheet. Roast for 30 to 35 minutes, or until the potatoes are tender yet crispy, shaking the pan after 15 minutes.

Remove from the oven and let the sweet potatoes cool for 5 minutes.

MAKE THE PRESTO PESTO DRIZZLE: Combine all the drizzle ingredients in a food processor and pulse until well combined. Serve the Sweet Potato Bites warm, drizzled with the Presto Pesto Drizzle. Transfer leftover pesto to a sealed container and store in the refrigerator until ready to serve, or for up to 2 days.

NOTE: This Presto Pesto Drizzle makes a great dipping oil (it can replace dairy-laden butter on your dinner table), or serve as a flavorful drizzle over my gluten-free pizza crusts (pages 234, 235, and 236) and your favorite roasted veggies.

SERVES 4

CHIMICHURRI SWEET POTATO SALAD

This brightly colored salad gets its oomph from chimichurri, a garlicky parsley sauce that's also wonderful served alongside roasted sweet potatoes, spread on gluten-free whole-grain sandwiches, drizzled over grilled vegetables, and used as a dipping sauce for carrots and other crunchy veggies. Serve this potato salad as an appetizer or side dish in tiny glass mason jars to show off its dazzling hues.

CHIMICHURRI SAUCE

¾   cup finely chopped fresh flat-leaf parsley

¾   cup finely chopped fresh cilantro

¼   cup extra-virgin olive oil

3   tablespoons freshly squeezed lemon juice

6   fresh chives, thinly sliced

2   large garlic cloves, minced

    Pinch crushed red pepper flakes

    Sea salt and freshly ground black pepper, to taste

POTATO SALAD

    Sea salt

4   medium sweet potatoes, peeled and cut into 1-inch cubes

    Large handful green beans, ends trimmed

1   tablespoon coconut oil

1   shallot, minced

    Freshly ground black pepper, to taste

    Pinch chili powder

    Handful arugula, for garnish, optional

MAKE THE SAUCE: In a small bowl, whisk together all the sauce ingredients. Mix well, and then let sit for at least 20 minutes.

MAKE THE SALAD: Bring a large pot of salted water to a boil. Add the sweet potatoes and cook until tender, about 10 minutes. Drain.

In a separate medium pot, bring salted water to a boil and cook the green beans until tender, about 5 minutes. Drain.

In a large skillet, heat the oil over medium heat. Add the shallot and cook until translucent, about 2 minutes. Add the sweet potatoes and green beans and season with salt, pepper, and chili powder to taste. Continue to cook for 1 minute more and transfer to a serving platter.

Drizzle the Chimichurri Sauce over the sweet potatoes and green beans, garnish with arugula, if desired, and serve. Store any leftover sauce in a sealed container in the refrigerator for up to 4 days.

SERVES 4; MAKES 1 CUP SAUCE

not-your-grandma's
POTATO SALAD

It wouldn't be summer without potato salad. But who wants mayo, additives, and low-nutrient white pota-toes served up in a bowl? Not me! So here's my satisfying replacement. It allows you to enjoy a summer staple while still eating according to your health needs. Sweet potatoes, rich in fiber and beta-carotene, sub for white potatoes; nutritious green beans and sugar snap peas get thrown in; and the dressing is a simple vinaigrette—no mayonnaise needed.

2   large sweet potatoes, peeled and cut into 1-inch cubes

    Sea salt and freshly ground black pepper

3   cups green beans, ends trimmed and halved

2   cups sugar snap peas, ends trimmed

¼   cup finely chopped fresh flat-leaf parsley

3   tablespoons extra-virgin olive oil

2   tablespoons red wine vinegar

2   tablespoons whole-grain mustard

1   small red onion, thinly sliced

    Handful fresh herbs: chives, dill, oregano, flat-leaf parsley

Place the sweet potatoes in a medium pot and cover with water by a few inches. Salt the water generously. Bring to a boil over medium-high heat and boil until the potatoes are tender but not falling apart, about 15 minutes. Drain and rinse with cold water to stop the cooking process.

In the meantime, bring a separate medium pot of water to a boil. Add the green beans and sugar snap peas and blanch until tender but not overcooked, about 2 minutes. Drain and rinse with cool water to stop the cooking process.

In a small bowl, whisk together the parsley, oil, vinegar, mustard, and salt and pepper to taste.

In a large bowl, combine the sweet potatoes, green beans, sugar snap peas, and red onion. Drizzle with the dressing, add the fresh herbs, and gently toss to combine. Taste and season with salt and pepper if necessary. Chill in the refrigerator before serving, or serve at room temperature.

SERVES 6 TO 8

mock mashed potatoes:
YELLOW SPLIT PEA AND CILANTRO PUREE

This tasty puree has a fabulous texture similar to mashed potatoes, but there aren't any potatoes here! A hint of crushed red pepper at the end is particularly pleasing. Serve it as a side dish along with my Warm Hearted Swiss Chard Lentil Bake (page 243) or Plentiful Cherry Tomato and Portobello Dhal (page 258). You can use green split peas instead of yellow split peas, if desired, but the yellow split peas create a glorious golden puree, which looks sensational.

2	cups yellow or green split peas, rinsed
3	tablespoons extra-virgin olive oil, divided
1	cup thinly sliced shallots
	Sea salt, to taste
2	large garlic cloves, minced
1	tablespoon finely chopped fresh cilantro
1½	tablespoons freshly squeezed lemon juice
	Freshly ground black pepper, to taste
	Large pinch crushed red pepper flakes
	Pinch ground coriander, optional

Cook the peas according to the chart on page 99, or until very tender and soft. Drain.

In the meantime, heat 1 tablespoon of the oil in a medium skillet over medium low heat. Add the shallots and salt and cook, stirring often, until translucent, about 3 minutes. Add the garlic and cook for another 2 minutes, stirring often.

Combine the cooked split peas, shallot mixture, cilantro, lemon juice, black pepper, red pepper flakes, coriander (if using), and remaining 2 tablespoons of oil in a food processor and process until smooth. Taste and adjust the seasonings with salt and black pepper. Serve warm.

SERVES 2 TO 4

GRILLED CAULIFLOWER BITES
with romesco sauce

These cauliflower bites can be a fun appetizer or side dish for entertaining, or for a casual night at home with the family. While I prefer this dish grilled, you can also roast the cauliflower in the oven.

ROMESCO SAUCE

2	large red bell peppers, halved
1	large tomato, halved
3	small garlic cloves
⅓	cup extra-virgin olive oil, plus more for drizzling
⅓	cup pine nuts, toasted (see page 108)
2	tablespoons red wine vinegar
2	teaspoons smoked paprika
¼	teaspoon sea salt
	Pinch cayenne pepper

CAULIFLOWER BITES

2	tablespoons extra-virgin olive oil, plus more if roasting cauliflower
1	large head cauliflower, cut into bite-size florets
4	fresh chives, thinly sliced, for serving
2	tablespoons finely chopped fresh flat-leaf parsley, for serving

MAKE THE SAUCE: Preheat the broiler.

Lay the peppers flat on a rimmed baking sheet. Broil for 12 minutes, or until blackened. Let cool for 2 minutes, and then place the peppers in a brown paper bag. Secure the bag with a rubber band or twist tie and let the peppers steam for 10 minutes. Remove from the bag and rub the charred skin off with your fingers. Run the peppers under water to ensure all the skin is removed. Discard the seeds and dice the peppers.

Preheat the oven to 375°F. Line a rimmed baking sheet with parchment paper.

Place the tomato cut-side down on the prepared baking sheet. Scatter the garlic cloves on the baking sheet and drizzle the tomato and garlic with oil to coat. Roast for 40 minutes, and then increase the oven temperature to 400°F and roast for 20 minutes more. Remove from the oven and let cool for 10 minutes.

Process the bell peppers, tomato mixture, and remaining sauce ingredients in a food processor until smooth.

MAKE THE BITES: Preheat a grill to medium. Or, if using an oven, preheat to 450°F.

To grill: Drizzle the oil over the cauliflower florets and grill until tender and golden brown, about 5 minutes on each side. ***To roast:*** Drizzle the oil over the cauliflower and arrange it in a single layer on a rimmed baking sheet. Roast for 25 minutes, or until tender and golden brown. Baste the florets with more oil halfway through if they appear to be drying out. Transfer to a serving platter.

Spoon the Romesco Sauce over the Cauliflower Bites, garnish with the chives and parsley, and serve. Store the sauce in a sealed container in the refrigerator for up to 3 days.

SERVES 4; MAKES 1½ CUPS

unbelievable
CAULIFLOWER PARM

*This Cauliflower Parm, a modification to my family's Italian favorite, really does taste cheesy!
But of course it contains no dairy, just a creaminess imparted from the ground nut and seed mixture.
And it's easy enough for a weeknight dinner. You should have no problem slicing the cauliflower,
but if for some reason yours crumbles, that's okay—make Cauliflower Parm bites.*

¼ cup raw cashews

¼ cup shelled raw sunflower seeds

2 tablespoons ground flaxseeds

2 teaspoons dried thyme

½ teaspoon sea salt

Pinch freshly ground black or white pepper

1 large head cauliflower

3 tablespoons extra-virgin olive oil

Sun-Dried Tomato Sauce (page 320), for dipping

Preheat the oven to 400°F. Line a rimmed baking sheet with parchment paper.

In a food processor, pulse the cashews and sunflower seeds until finely ground. Transfer the mixture to a shallow baking dish, then stir in the flaxseeds, thyme, salt, and pepper; mix well.

Slice the cauliflower into 4 large, thick slices. (For easiest slicing, keep the stem intact, hold the head of cauliflower upright, and slice vertically.) Lay the cauliflower slices on the prepared baking sheet and, using a pastry brush, coat each side with the oil. Dredge each side of the slices in the flaxseed-cashew mixture, and then return them to the baking sheet. Bake for 35 to 40 minutes, or until golden brown and tender. Serve warm, with the Sun-Dried Tomato Sauce on the side for dipping. Leftover sauce can be stored in a sealed container in the refrigerator for up to 4 days.

SERVES 2

PANZANELLA
with gluten-free herbed croutons,
cherry tomatoes, and fresh herbs

*Panzanella (bread salad) in its traditional gluten-filled form is a no-no in my world. But panzanella
with Gluten-Free Herbed Croutons (page 190) instead of bread? Now that's something you can feel
comfortable eating all the time (and believe me, you will). This dish is simple to make and,
if you use jarred peppers, requires no cooking at all.*

2	large red bell peppers, or 2 roasted red bell peppers from a jar
2	cups grape tomatoes, halved
1	cup Gluten-Free Herbed Croutons (page 190)
½	cup arugula
⅓	cup finely chopped fresh basil
⅓	cup coarsely chopped fresh flat-leaf parsley
½	large cucumber, peeled, seeded, and diced, optional
3	tablespoons extra-virgin olive oil
2	tablespoons balsamic vinegar
2	tablespoons thinly sliced shallot
1	teaspoon minced garlic, plus more to taste
	Sea salt and freshly ground black pepper

Preheat the broiler.

If using fresh bell peppers, cut the bell peppers in half and lay them flat on a rimmed baking sheet. Broil for 12 minutes, or until blackened. Let cool for 2 minutes, and then place the peppers in a brown paper bag. Secure the bag with a rubber band or twist tie and let the peppers steam for 10 minutes. Remove from the bag and rub the charred skin off with your fingers. Run the peppers under water to ensure all the skin is removed. Discard the seeds and dice the peppers.

In a large bowl, combine the roasted peppers, tomatoes, Gluten-Free Herbed Croutons, arugula, basil, parsley, and cucumber, if using.

In a separate bowl, whisk together the oil, vinegar, shallot, garlic, and salt and black pepper to taste. Drizzle the dressing over the bell pepper mixture and gently toss to combine. Serve at room temperature.

SERVES 4

GRAIN-FREE BASIL AND MINT SUMMER SQUASH "NOODLES"

grain-free
BASIL AND MINT SUMMER SQUASH "NOODLES"

A terrific summertime staple that's full of flavor and fiber without any grains. Did you happen to notice the simple directions for this recipe? Combine ingredients and serve. Easy as it gets.

3	large yellow summer squash, cut into thin strands with a vegetable peeler or spiral slicer (spiralizer) or julienned
1	large celery stalk, thinly sliced
1	tablespoon finely chopped fresh basil
2	teaspoons extra-virgin olive oil
2	teaspoons freshly squeezed lemon juice
1	teaspoon finely chopped fresh mint
½	teaspoon freshly grated lemon zest
¼	teaspoon ground cumin
	Pinch crushed red pepper flakes
	Sea salt and freshly ground black pepper, to taste

In a large bowl, combine all the ingredients, toss to coat, and serve.

SERVES 2

purifying
RAW MINT ZUCCHINI "NOODLES"

Mint and zucchini are a match made in heaven. Zucchini fills in for noodles, creating a lighter than usual, but no less satisfying, "noodle." If you don't have a spiral slicer, use a peeler and shave the length of the zucchini to make pappardelle-style "pasta."

2	large zucchini, cut into thin strands with a vegetable peeler or spiral slicer (spiralizer)
½	bunch asparagus, ends trimmed and cut into 1-inch pieces
1	large ripe avocado, pitted, peeled, and diced
3	scallions, white and light green parts, thinly sliced
½	cup fresh or thawed frozen green peas
¼	cup finely chopped fresh mint
3	tablespoons extra-virgin olive oil
2	tablespoons freshly squeezed lemon juice
¼	teaspoon freshly grated lemon zest
¼	teaspoon sea salt
¼	teaspoon freshly ground black pepper
	Pinch crushed red pepper flakes
1	teaspoon sesame seeds

In a large bowl, combine the zucchini, asparagus, avocado, scallions, peas, and mint.

In a small bowl, combine the oil, lemon juice, lemon zest, salt, black pepper, and red pepper flakes. Drizzle this dressing over the zucchini noodles and gently toss to combine. Top with sesame seeds, adjust the seasoning with salt and pepper to taste, and serve.

SERVES 4 TO 6

super soft CARAMELIZED RED ONIONS

I'd put these onions on everything if I could. Actually, I think I already do! Serve them with salads, burgers, or gluten-free whole grains like wild rice, quinoa, and millet. You can also make this recipe with white, yellow, Vidalia, and other types of onions for different levels of sweetness and flavor.

2   tablespoons extra-virgin olive oil
2   large red onions, thinly sliced
    Sea salt and freshly ground black pepper

In a large skillet, heat the oil over medium-low heat. Add the onions and salt and pepper to taste. Cook, stirring often, until the onions are caramelized, about 45 minutes. Be careful not to burn the onions; adjust the heat if necessary. Adjust the salt and pepper to taste and serve warm.

SERVES 4

spectacular SALT 'N' PEPPER BAKED SHALLOTS

A super-simple recipe that creates so much flavor in any dish. I can easily find hundreds of uses for these flavorful shallots. Add them to my salads or enjoy them as a snack with my Dairy-Free Creamy Cashew Cheese (page 308) on my grain-free crackers (pages 156–162).

4   large shallots, halved
1   teaspoon extra-virgin olive oil
    Sea salt and freshly ground black pepper

Preheat the oven to 350°F.

In a small bowl, combine the shallots, oil, and salt and pepper to taste; toss to coat. Transfer to a rimmed baking sheet and bake for 20 minutes, shaking the pan after 10 minutes. Remove from the oven and let cool for 5 minutes before serving warm.

SERVES 4

THREE WAYS TO USE CARAMELIZED ONIONS

SANDWICHES: Spread caramelized onions on your favorite gluten-free sandwich or burgers instead of fried onions or processed mayo.

SALAD DRESSINGS: Whisk roughly chopped caramelized onions into vinaigrettes.

SIDE DISHES: Stir caramelized onions into cooked lentils or quinoa or toss with roasted veggies.

quick
BALSAMIC PORTOBELLO MUSHROOMS

These mushrooms make a tasty and rich-flavored topping (without cream or butter) for your favorite burgers, gluten-free whole-grain recipes, and other veggie dishes. Serve with my grain-free crackers (pages 156–162) and dairy-free nut cheese recipes (pages 307–310), too.

6   cups baby bella mushrooms, stems removed

1   tablespoon extra-virgin olive oil, plus more if needed

      Sea salt and freshly ground black pepper

3   tablespoons balsamic vinegar

2   tablespoons freshly grated lemon zest

1   teaspoon finely chopped fresh oregano or ½ teaspoon dried oregano

Cut the mushrooms in half. Leave any very small mushrooms whole.

In a large skillet, heat the oil over medium heat. Add the mushrooms and salt and pepper to taste, and cook until the mushrooms are tender and golden, about 10 minutes. If the skillet becomes too dry during cooking, add more oil. Add the vinegar, stir to combine, and then add the lemon zest and oregano. Mix well. Remove the mushrooms from the heat and serve. Store in a sealed container in the refrigerator for up to 2 days.

SERVES 4

recharging
CARROT GINGER SLAW

This is a fabulous quick-and-easy slaw that works well as a side dish or added to a whole-grain Buddha "bowl" meal with roasted beets, asparagus, pickled cucumber, and gluten-free whole grains like brown rice, quinoa, millet, or wild rice.

½   cup extra-virgin olive oil

2½   tablespoons chickpea miso paste

2   tablespoons apple cider vinegar

1   tablespoon coconut aminos

2   teaspoons freshly squeezed lemon juice

1   teaspoon peeled minced fresh ginger

¼   teaspoon sea salt, plus more if needed

¼   teaspoon freshly ground black pepper, plus more if needed

2   cups shredded red cabbage

1½   cups peeled and shredded carrots

¼   cup finely chopped scallions, white and light green parts

¼   cup fresh herbs of choice, such as cilantro, basil, flat-leaf parsley, or dill

In a small bowl, combine the oil, miso, vinegar, coconut aminos, lemon juice, ginger, salt, and pepper.

In a large bowl, combine the cabbage, carrots, and scallions with the dressing. Toss to coat. Gently stir in the fresh herbs and, if needed, adjust the salt and pepper. Chill until ready to serve.

SERVES 4

SAVORY CHICKPEA FLOUR CREPES

The great flavor and earthiness from the chickpeas is complemented by the use of coriander and cumin. Serve these crepes with any of my recipes; I love using them to wrap around the Mini Baked Chickpea-Free Falafel with Cannellini Bean Za'atar Sauce (page 240). These will fly off the table!

1	cup chickpea flour (garbanzo bean flour)
½	teaspoon sea salt
¼	teaspoon ground coriander
¼	teaspoon ground cumin
¼	teaspoon smoked paprika
	Pinch chili powder
1¼	cups water
2	tablespoons extra-virgin olive oil, plus more for coating pan

In a large bowl, combine the flour, salt, coriander, cumin, paprika, and chili powder. Slowly whisk in the water and oil. Beat the mixture with an electric mixer at medium speed until all the ingredients are incorporated and the batter is smooth.

Lightly coat the bottom of a cast-iron skillet with oil and heat over medium heat. When the pan is hot, ladle a thin layer of batter into the skillet and cook until the bottom side is golden brown, 3 to 4 minutes. Flip with a spatula and cook until golden brown, another 2 minutes. Repeat with the remaining batter, using more oil to coat the skillet if necessary. Stack the crepes on top of one another as you finish cooking them so they remain soft and bendable for serving. Serve immediately, or keep warm in a 200°F oven until ready to serve.

MAKES 4 (8-INCH) CREPES

PEPPERED ROSEMARY BASIL SOCCA

Ooooh, another hearty and filling recipe that you'll want to make a few times a week—load up on your chickpea flour now! It's addictive and so delicious. This socca is soft and thick, and great to eat plain or served warm with my Seriously Sensational Sriracha Sauce (page 318) or Dairy-Free Creamy Cashew Cheese (page 308). I also love to top this socca with pesto, arugula, and fresh herbs like parsley and cilantro.

1	cup chickpea flour (garbanzo bean flour)
½	teaspoon sea salt
⅛	teaspoon freshly ground black pepper
1¼	cups warm water
3	tablespoons plus 3 teaspoons extra-virgin olive oil, divided
1	tablespoon finely chopped fresh rosemary
1	tablespoon finely chopped fresh basil
½	teaspoon ground cumin
⅛	teaspoon crushed red pepper flakes

Sift the flour, salt, and black pepper into a large bowl. Whisk in the water and 3 tablespoons of the oil. Add the rosemary, basil, cumin, and red pepper flakes and whisk again until well combined. Set aside and cover for at least 45 minutes or up to 2 hours, then stir.

Preheat the oven to 170°F.

Heat a medium skillet on the stovetop over medium heat for 2 minutes or until hot. When the skillet is hot, add 1½ teaspoons of the remaining oil. Pour in half of the chickpea batter and cook over medium heat until the bottom is golden brown, about 10 minutes. Flip with an extra-wide spatula and cook until the bottom is golden brown, another 4 to 5 minutes. Place the socca in the oven wrapped in a cotton towel on a baking sheet to keep warm until ready to serve. Repeat with the remaining batter, using the remaining 1½ teaspoons oil to coat the skillet. Serve the socca warm.

MAKES 2

big-flavor
MARINATED ROASTED BELL PEPPERS

These babies are soft and tender; they're addictively delicious. Use the leftover garlic-basil oil to drizzle atop salads and whole-grain dishes for an instant flavor boost without butter or cream.

5	red bell peppers
1½	cups extra-virgin olive oil
14	large fresh basil leaves, finely chopped
4	garlic cloves, thinly sliced
	Sea salt
¼	teaspoon freshly ground black pepper

Place the bell peppers on the gas stovetop burner over a medium flame, or under a broiler. Using tongs, turn the peppers so that they char evenly, about 8 minutes. Transfer to a bowl and cover with a lid, or place in a brown paper bag and secure it with a rubber band or twist tie. Set aside for 30 minutes to steam.

Remove the peppers' charred skin by wiping with a clean towel; do not rinse the peppers with water. Remove the stems and seeds, cut the peppers in half lengthwise, and then slice them into thin strips. Place the strips in a clean quart-size mason jar with the oil, basil, garlic, salt (¼ to ½ teaspoon depending on how salty you like your food), and black pepper. Seal the jar and store in the refrigerator overnight. Drain the oil before serving. The peppers will keep for up to 2 weeks in reserved oil in the refrigerator.

MAKES 1 QUART

rosemary
ROASTED CARROTS AND BEETS

A very tasty dish filled with gorgeous fall colors, its combination of sweet and savory flavors makes it a star at any table. The golden raisins are a nice touch, so I encourage you to include them.

4	small beets, peeled and cut in half
5	medium carrots, peeled and cut in half lengthwise
¼	cup apple cider vinegar
3	tablespoons extra-virgin olive oil
2	tablespoons finely chopped fresh rosemary or 2 sprigs fresh rosemary
	Sea salt and freshly ground black pepper, to taste
2	tablespoons golden raisins, optional

Preheat the oven to 400°F.

Combine all ingredients except the raisins on a large rimmed baking sheet. Toss to coat vegetables. Roast for 30 minutes, or until tender, tossing after 15 minutes. Remove from the oven and, if using the rosemary sprigs, discard them. Transfer the beets and carrots to a serving bowl and, if desired, add the raisins. Serve warm.

SERVES 4

ROSEMARY ROASTED CARROTS AND BEETS

FIRE-ROASTED PEPPERS AND TOMATOES
with herbs

Let's just say this fresh bowl of goodness is my family's summer staple. It's a must-make when I get to the shore after a hot summer's week in Manhattan! But it's not just for summer; you can roast this dish anytime of the year when you're craving fresh flavors with minimal ingredients. Fresh thyme and tarragon can also be used in place of the basil here. You can serve this dish with my tasty Vegetarian Antipasto Platter (page 64); it's the perfect addition.

3	yellow bell peppers, halved lengthwise
1	red bell pepper, halved lengthwise
3	tablespoons extra-virgin olive oil, plus more for coating baking dish
3	pints cherry tomatoes, halved
½	cup finely chopped fresh flat-leaf parsley leaves
¾	teaspoon sea salt, plus more to taste
¼	teaspoon freshly ground black pepper, plus more to taste
2	tablespoons finely chopped fresh basil, thyme, or tarragon
1	garlic clove, minced

Preheat the broiler to high.

Remove and discard the seeds and membranes from the bell peppers. Lay the peppers flat on a rimmed baking sheet. Broil for 12 minutes, or until blackened. Let cool for 2 minutes, and then place the peppers in a brown paper bag. Secure the bag with a rubber band or twist tie and let the peppers steam for 10 minutes. Remove from the bag and rub the charred skin off with your fingers. Run the peppers under water to ensure all the skin is removed, and then cut them into ½-inch strips. Set aside.

Preheat the oven to 400°F. Lightly coat a 2-quart baking dish with a lid with oil.

In a large bowl, combine the tomatoes, parsley, salt, and black pepper.

In a small bowl, combine the oil, basil, and garlic, and season with salt and pepper to taste.

Place half the tomato mixture on the bottom of the prepared baking dish, and then top with half of the peppers. Add a layer of the garlic mixture and then repeat the three layers. Cover and bake for 25 to 30 minutes, or until tender. Remove from the oven. Let cool, cover, and refrigerate. Serve chilled.

SERVES 6 TO 8

GRILLED BOK CHOY
with creamy cumin tahini sauce

Spring isn't quite the same without this dish. Fire up your grill and you'll see what I mean. It takes less than ten minutes and you'll be thanking me. The simple ingredients of the lime drizzle bring out the sweetness of the bok choy. I love how the bok choy leaves become paper thin when grilled—and how they melt in your mouth. Adding the smokiness of the Creamy Cumin Tahini Sauce makes this a perfect side dish!

CREAMY CUMIN TAHINI SAUCE

1	cup tahini (see note, page 301)
1	cup water
¼	cup freshly squeezed lemon juice
3	garlic cloves, roughly chopped
½	teaspoon ground cumin
½	teaspoon ground coriander

BOK CHOY

2	tablespoons extra-virgin olive oil
2	tablespoons freshly squeezed lime juice
½	teaspoon sea salt
½	teaspoon freshly ground black pepper
2	heads bok choy, halved lengthwise

MAKE THE SAUCE: Combine all the sauce ingredients in a food processor and puree until smooth and creamy, about 2 minutes. Refrigerate in a sealed container until ready to serve. Store in the refrigerator for up to 4 days.

MAKE THE BOK CHOY: Preheat a grill to medium.

In a small bowl, whisk together the oil, lime juice, salt, and pepper. Arrange the bok choy in a shallow baking dish and drizzle the juice mixture on top. Flip and coat the other side. Let the bok choy sit for 5 minutes to marinate.

Place the bok choy on the grill and cook for 8 to 10 minutes, or until tender, flipping halfway if the bok choy is thick, so it will cook evenly. Remove from the grill and serve warm, drizzled with the Creamy Cumin Tahini Sauce.

SERVES 4; MAKES 2 CUPS SAUCE

OVEN-ROASTED CHERRY TOMATOES WITH POPPY SEEDS

OVEN-ROASTED CHERRY TOMATOES
with poppy seeds

I think poppy seeds are underrated. They add flavor and texture to soft roasted tomatoes, so I thought they would be a fun addition. They are often an afterthought, so I chose to make them the star here. Serve these alongside my Unbelievable Cauliflower Parm (page 267) for a delicious meal.

1	pint cherry tomatoes, halved lengthwise
2	tablespoons extra-virgin olive oil, plus more if needed
½	teaspoon poppy seeds
	Sea salt and freshly ground black pepper

Preheat the oven to 250°F. Line a rimmed baking sheet with parchment paper.

Arrange the tomatoes in a single layer on the prepared baking sheet. Drizzle with the oil and toss with your hands to ensure the tomatoes are coated. Sprinkle with the poppy seeds and salt and pepper to taste. Transfer to the oven and roast for about 2½ hours. Check every hour to make sure the tomatoes haven't dried out. Add more oil if needed. The tomatoes will be soft and wrinkled with a tender center when they are done. Let cool before serving.

MAKES ¾ CUP

grain-free PROTEIN-PACKED BREAD CRUMBS

Say good-bye to nutrient-devoid white gluten-free bread crumbs and hello to bread crumbs that actually contribute to your well-being. These also happen to be better tasting than the store-bought kind. Try these bread crumbs on vegetable gratins and to give dishes like sweet potato fries a crunchy coating. To flavor the crumbs, simply add a sprinkle of dried herbs—such as herbes de Provence, Italian seasoning, oregano, or rosemary—before using.

1	cup raw walnuts
1	cup raw almonds
1	cup shelled raw sunflower seeds
1	cup shelled raw pumpkin seeds
1	cup raw sesame seeds
1	cup ground flaxseeds

Combine the walnuts and almonds in a food processor. Pulse 3 or 4 times, and then add the sunflower and pumpkin seeds. Pulse 2 times. Add the sesame and flaxseeds and pulse until coarse. Continue to pulse until the mixture is finely ground and resembles bread crumbs, but do not overmix or you will end up with nut butter. Store in a sealed container in the refrigerator for up to 3 weeks.

MAKES 5 CUPS

BLACK RICE STUFFED COLLARDS
with white bean thyme tahini sauce

This fiber-rich favorite is perfect for a weeknight or weekend dinner. The tasty white bean sauce is filled with bright fresh thyme and calcium-rich tahini. If you can't find collard greens, use kale leaves instead.

RICE STUFFED COLLARDS

12	large collard green leaves
½	cup brown rice
¼	cup black rice
1½	cups low-sodium vegetable broth, divided
1	tablespoon extra-virgin olive oil
2	medium zucchini, finely chopped
½	small white onion, diced
2	garlic cloves, minced
½	cup finely chopped fresh basil
	Sea salt and freshly ground black pepper

WHITE BEAN THYME TAHINI SAUCE

2	cups cooked cannellini beans (see page 99)
¼	cup extra-virgin olive oil, plus more for drizzling
2	tablespoons freshly squeezed lemon juice
2	garlic cloves
2	tablespoons water
1	tablespoon tahini (see note, page 301)
	Leaves from 2 sprigs fresh thyme
1	teaspoon sea salt
¼	teaspoon chili powder, or more to taste
½	cup finely chopped raw almonds, toasted (see page 108)

MAKE THE COLLARDS: Bring a large pot of water to a boil. Fill a large bowl with ice water and set it nearby. Add the collard greens to the boiling water and blanch for 1 minute. Drain the collards and shock them in the ice water. Drain again, and then remove the thick ends of the stems.

In a small pot, combine the brown rice and 1 cup of the broth. In another small pot, combine the black rice and the remaining ½ cup of the broth. Bring both to a boil, reduce to a simmer, and cover. Cook until tender, about 30 minutes for the black rice, and 30 to 40 minutes for the brown rice.

In a large pot, heat the oil over medium heat. Add the zucchini, onion, garlic, and cooked brown and black rice. Cook until the zucchini is tender, 2 to 3 minutes. Add the basil, stir, and cook for another minute. Season with salt and pepper to taste.

MAKE THE SAUCE: Combine all the sauce ingredients in a food processor and process until completely smooth. Taste and adjust the seasonings if necessary. Add more chili powder if you like the sauce spicy. Drizzle with more oil to taste.

Lay the collard greens flat on a surface. Scoop some of the rice and zucchini mixture into the center of each leaf and top with the toasted almonds. Drizzle the White Bean Thyme Tahini Sauce on top and roll the leaves up widthwise, like a taco. Serve warm.

SERVES 4; MAKES 2¼ CUPS SAUCE

GRILLED YELLOW SQUASH AND ASPARAGUS
with garden dressing

So light. So perfect. So easy. This is another go-to recipe in my parents' home on summer nights. It's great for weeknight dinners or weekend lunches when grilling. The dressing is key to this recipe, along with the grilled flavor!

2	tablespoons extra-virgin olive oil, plus more for coating grill basket
3	tablespoons freshly squeezed lemon juice
3	tablespoons finely chopped fresh flat-leaf parsley
1	small garlic clove, minced
¼	teaspoon sea salt
¼	teaspoon freshly ground black pepper
1	large red onion, cut into 1-inch chunks
1	large yellow squash, sliced lengthwise into ¼-inch slices
1	bunch asparagus, ends trimmed
	Pinch chili powder
	Pinch paprika

Preheat a grill to medium. Coat a grill basket with oil.

In a small bowl, whisk together the oil, lemon juice, parsley, garlic, salt, and pepper.

Arrange the onion, squash, and asparagus on a platter and sprinkle with the chili powder and paprika. Using your fingers, gently coat the vegetables with the dressing. Reserve extra dressing for serving.

Place the onion in the grill basket and grill for 4 minutes. Flip the onions and add the squash to the basket. Cook for 4 minutes more. Flip the squash and add the asparagus to the basket. Cook for 4 minutes more. (Grilling times may vary based upon grill type.) Remove the vegetables from the basket once they are tender and have grill marks. Return the vegetables to the platter and drizzle with any remaining dressing. Serve warm.

SERVES 4

humble
PICKLED PEARS AND APPLES

When planning for this recipe, make sure you have a lidded mason jar, and set aside time to chill the dish overnight in the fridge. That will give the flavors adequate time to blend together. Serve at your holiday meals for a sweet 'n' savory pickled side dish condiment, or as a flavorful topping to my dairy-free nut cheeses (pages 307–310).

1   cup raw honey

⅓   cup apple cider vinegar

¼   cup balsamic vinegar

     1-inch piece fresh ginger, peeled and thinly sliced

2   cinnamon sticks

3   whole cloves

5   black peppercorns

3   Bosc pears, peeled, cored, and thinly sliced

2   red apples, peeled, cored, and thinly sliced

In a large saucepan, combine the honey, vinegars, ginger, cinnamon sticks, cloves, and peppercorns. Bring to a boil over medium heat. Add the pears and apples, cover, reduce the heat to low, and cook for 20 minutes. Turn off the heat and let the mixture rest for 10 minutes.

Remove the fruit with a slotted spoon and transfer it to an uncovered quart-size glass mason jar. Pour the honey mixture over the fruit (make sure the mixture isn't too hot or it will crack the glass), cover with the lid, and transfer to the refrigerator to chill overnight before serving. Serve chilled. Store in the refrigerator for up to 1 week.

MAKES 1 QUART

refreshing and restoring sippers

If there was a PhD for creative and nourishing drinks, I'd have one by now: Ten years ago, I had no idea what the heck turmeric was, let alone why I'd want to put it in a drink. But when you start exploring new ingredients and making your own "sippers," you'll never go back to commercial bottled drinks. These drinks are an attraction all their own, helping to hydrate, energize, and balance your body, and more—without the refined sugar and empty calories.

When I was going through detox, I had to train myself to drink more fluids and remove refined sugars. Growing up in the 80s, I drank sports drinks, unaware of their ingredients—I didn't know that they were considered harmful chemicals. Once I detoxed those processed sweeteners, I had to retrain my taste buds to enjoy real flavor and sweetness from fruits, honey, and maple syrup. That's when I started making my own nut and seed mylks (dairy-free, of course) and discovered herbal teas. I wanted to be like everyone else and just walk into the coffee shop for a chai tea, but after countless stomachaches, I started making everything from scratch. That's the inspiration behind every one of these sippers (and my cute little Sun Salutation Cubes). Have fun, make some mocktails, and get ready to treat your taste buds to real, whole ingredients.

These recipes are packed with a range of anti-inflammatory ingredients to support overall well-being and put out that fire of silent inflammation. They can also address a range of symptoms, from the common cold to belly aches 'n' pains.

detoxing
GREENY-LICIOUS JUICE

I like fresh green juices (as beverages, not as meal replacements) because they give my digestive tract a break from the fiber in smoothies and other foods. This green juice is simple, yet perfect for a morning sipper or an evening pick-me-up before dinner.

4	cups baby kale leaves
2	English cucumbers
2	green apples, cored
4	celery stalks
1	romaine heart
1	cup fresh cilantro
	Freshly squeezed juice of 1 lemon

Run all the ingredients except the lemon juice through a juicer. (If you don't have a juicer, see below.) Stir the lemon juice into the green juice and divide the mixture between two glasses. Serve immediately.

SERVES 2

caffeine-free
CHAI

This drink is similar to a chai tea but without the caffeine. It's especially good when served really cold. Try it served over ice on a hot summer day for a refreshing sipper that tastes so much healthier than those store-bought chais filled with cow's milk and caffeinated black tea.

2	cups unsweetened almond milk
1½	teaspoons pure vanilla extract
1	teaspoon freshly grated orange zest
1	teaspoon ground cinnamon
¼	teaspoon pure almond extract
	Pinch ground allspice
	Pinch sea salt

Combine all the ingredients in a blender and puree until very smooth. Transfer to a sealed container and chill for 2 hours before serving. Store in the refrigerator for up to 4 days.

SERVES 2

NO JUICER? NO PROBLEM. If you're in the mood to make my green juice recipe but you don't have a juicer, you can roughly chop ingredients and then place them in a blender and puree until smooth. Take a twenty-four-inch piece of cheesecloth, fold it in half four times, and use it to line a large bowl. Pour the puree into the center, gather the cloth together with one hand, and use your other hand to twist the cloth as you squeeze the juice from the pulp.

healthy homemade
DAIRY-FREE NUT (AND SEED) MYLKS

These mylks are the homemade version of your store-bought nut and seed milks (such as almond milk). I use the term "mylk" when I'm referring to homemade and "milk" for store-bought, but you can use either for all the recipes in this book that call for milk. You can use nut and seed mylks just as you would regular cow's milk. Pour these mylks on top of your favorite cereals; use them in gluten-free oatmeal; add them to smoothies, tea, and "mylk" shakes; or drink them on their own. It's very important to use a high-speed blender for these nut and seed mylks! Feel free to add more water if you like a thinner consistency.

1   cup raw nuts or seeds, such as cashews, almonds, hazelnuts, or hemp

7   cups water, divided

1   tablespoon pure maple syrup, optional

    Pinch sea salt, optional

½   teaspoon pure vanilla extract, optional

¼   teaspoon ground cinnamon, optional

In a medium bowl, combine the nuts with 4 cups of the water. Set aside and soak according to the chart on page 108.

Drain and rinse the soaked nuts well. Transfer them to a high-speed blender and add the remaining 3 cups water. Blend on high speed until the nuts are ground and the mylk is frothy white, about 1 minute.

Using a nut milk bag (see page 292), strain the mylk into a large bowl. Squeeze to extract as much of the mylk liquid into the bowl as possible. (Store the pulp in a container in the refrigerator for a few days and add it to coconut yogurt or oatmeal.) If you wish to sweeten or flavor the mylk, whisk in the maple syrup, salt, vanilla, and/or cinnamon. Mix well. Transfer the mylk to a sealed jar and store in the refrigerator for up to 4 days. Separation may occur, so shake well before using.

SERVES 4

NUT AND SEED MYLK FLAVOR OPTIONS

To add a touch of flavor to your unsweetened nut mylk, try these single-serving variations.

▸ **STRAWBERRY MYLK:** In a blender, combine the nut mylk with a few strawberries (fresh or frozen). Strain and discard the solids, or keep for an extra boost of fiber and flavor.

▸ **CHOCOLATE MYLK:** Stir in a pinch of unsweetened cocoa powder, a dash of pure vanilla extract, and a touch of honey.

▸ **TURMERIC HONEY MYLK:** Stir in a few dashes of ground turmeric and a touch of honey.

easy homemade
COCONUT MYLK

I like to have a little variety in my life, so I don't depend on only nut and seed mylks. I make coconut mylk at home, too. Save the leftover coconut pulp (it's light and fluffy) to sprinkle on smoothies, gluten-free oatmeal, or my dairy-free ice cream recipes (pages 334–339). Note that this mylk recipe isn't a substitute for the canned culinary coconut milk that I use for my other recipes; instead, use this coconut mylk as you would any type of nut mylk, i.e., stirred into gluten-free oatmeal, my granola recipes (pages 118–122), and my Overnight Black Rice and Berry Breakfast Bowl (page 138), or enjoyed alone in a glass.

1   cup unsweetened coconut flakes
1   cup water

In a small bowl, combine the coconut flakes and water. Let sit for 2 hours, or until the coconut flakes are soft. Transfer to a blender and puree until smooth. Pour into a double-sided cheesecloth or nut milk bag (see below) over a large bowl. Gather the cloth around the mylk and squeeze to extract as much of the liquid mylk as possible. Pour the mylk into a jar with a lid, cover, and store in the refrigerator for up to 3 days. Discard the leftover pulp or store in a sealed container in the refrigerator for up to 3 days.

MAKES 1 CUP

CHEESECLOTH OR NUT MILK BAG Use cheesecloth or a nut milk bag to strain nut milks and to make my Dairy-Free Sunshine Macadamia "Cream" Cheese (page 310). A nut milk bag (a small nylon bag) strains finer than cheesecloth and is also reusable, but if you'd rather use cheesecloth, just place it over a fine-mesh sieve and set in a large bowl.

frozen
HOT CHOCOLATE

When I make this recipe, I'm reminded of summer mornings at the shore with my family. We make decadent smoothies from whole foods (like the ones in this recipe) that cool us off and keep us satisfied for a day at the beach. Simple, flavorful, and not too thick, this one's a great energizer.

2	large frozen bananas
2	cups ice
¾	cup unsweetened almond milk
2	tablespoons almond butter
1½	tablespoons unsweetened cocoa powder
2	Medjool dates, pitted
½	teaspoon pure vanilla extract
	Pinch sea salt

Combine all the ingredients in a blender and blend until smooth. Divide between two glasses and serve.

SERVES 2

TO MAKE A NUT MYLK CUBE SMOOTHIE

In a blender, combine 4 or 5 flavored nut mylk cubes with ¾ cup nut mylk and honey or maple syrup to taste. Add flavoring, to taste, such as:

▸ Pure vanilla or almond extract

▸ Raw cacao powder or unsweetened cocoa powder

▸ Fresh berries or a small ripe banana

▸ Creamy almond butter

peaceful
NUT MYLK CUBES

These are fabulous in a smoothie (see below), or to add flavor and chill to my nut "mylks" (page 290).

OPTIONS
CINNAMON ALMOND CUBES

1	cup raw almonds
2½	cups unsweetened nut milk
¼	teaspoon ground cinnamon

CORIANDER CASHEW CUBES

1	cup raw cashews
2½	cups unsweetened nut milk
¼	teaspoon ground coriander

FENNEL ALMOND CUBES

1	cup raw almonds
2½	cups unsweetened nut milk
½	teaspoon ground fennel seeds

Choose an option. Soak the nuts according to the chart on page 108. Drain, rinse well, and add them to a blender with the nut milk and spice. Puree until smooth and creamy. Pour into ice cube trays. Cover and freeze until completely frozen, about 4 hours.

FILLS 1½ STANDARD ICE CUBE TRAYS (24 CUBES)

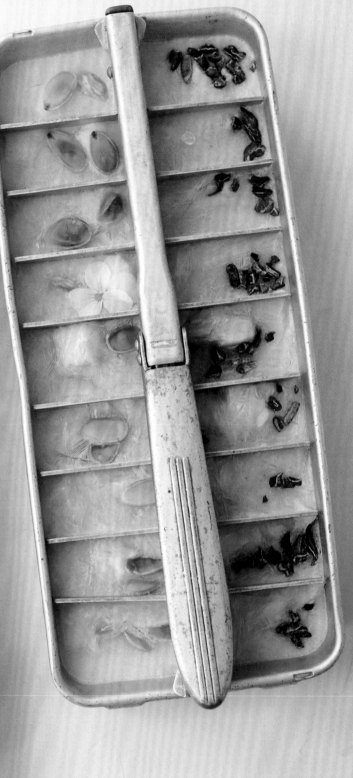

sun salutation
COOLING CUBES

Using flavored ice is fun and a great way to add a boost of antioxidants to your smoothie, seltzer, iced tea, or water. You can switch up these ingredients and add any of the below to mix 'n' match for flavored ice cubes. Try to keep it simple. If you choose to use fruit juices that are high in sugar, or culinary coconut milk (which has a high fat content), be prepared, because the ice will melt more quickly. That's why I choose to use unsweetened herbal teas or green teas (only choose green tea if you can handle caffeine). These ice cubes will keep in the freezer in a sealed container. I like to make four trays at a time so I have plenty when I'm having company over to entertain. You can also use these pretty little cubes in mocktails any time of the year.

LIQUID BASE OPTIONS

LIQUIDS: coconut water, green tea, herbal tea, nut milks, coconut milk, seed milks

JUICED VEGGIES: cucumbers, carrots, beets, fennel, celery

PUREED FRUITS: melon, pears, pomegranates, mangoes, pineapple, bananas, kiwis, berries, grapefruits, nectarines, limes, lemons, oranges, blood oranges, tangerines, clementines, grapes, apples, peaches

ADDITIONS

FINELY CHOPPED FRESH HERBS: mint, sage, rosemary, basil, cilantro, thyme, lavender, edible flowers

SPICES: ground ginger, ground cinnamon, ground fennel, ground cardamom

SWEETENERS: raw honey, pure maple syrup, raw cacao nibs, slivered almonds

In a small bowl, combine $1\frac{1}{3}$ cups liquid base and a combination of the additions. Stir, and then pour into a standard ice cube tray. Cover and freeze until the ice cubes are completely frozen, about 4 hours.

NOTE: See the next page for four flavored cooling cube recipes.

FILLS 1 STANDARD ICE CUBE TRAY (16 CUBES)

anti-inflammatory
CUCUMBER BASIL CUBES

1	cup peeled, seeded and diced cucumber
½	cup water
¼	cup finely chopped fresh basil
1½	tablespoons freshly squeezed lemon juice
½	teaspoon ground turmeric
	Pinch sea salt

Combine all the ingredients in a blender and puree until smooth. Pour into an ice cube tray, cover, and freeze until the ice cubes are completely frozen, about 4 hours.

FILLS 1 STANDARD ICE CUBE TRAY (16 CUBES)

minty melon
STRAWBERRY CUBES

1½	cups chopped honeydew melon or cantaloupe
½	cup fresh strawberries
6	fresh mint leaves
1	teaspoon freshly squeezed lime juice
	Pinch freshly grated lime zest

Combine all the ingredients in a blender and puree until smooth. Pour into an ice cube tray, cover, and freeze until the ice cubes are completely frozen, about 4 hours.

FILLS 1 STANDARD ICE CUBE TRAY (16 CUBES)

refreshing grapefruit
DETOX CUBES

1¼	cups freshly squeezed grapefruit juice
¼	cup finely chopped fresh cilantro
3	tablespoons freshly squeezed orange juice

In a medium bowl, combine all the ingredients; mix well. Pour into an ice cube tray, cover, and freeze until the ice cubes are completely frozen, about 4 hours.

FILLS 1 STANDARD ICE CUBE TRAY (16 CUBES)

cooling
WATERMELON CUBES

2	cups ½-inch cubes watermelon

Place the watermelon pieces in a blender and puree until smooth. Pour into an ice cube tray, cover, and freeze until the ice cubes are completely frozen, about 4 hours.

FILLS 1 STANDARD ICE CUBE TRAY (16 CUBES)

joyful HOT COCOA

Instead of those processed packets of store-bought powdered hot cocoa that are filled with chemicals, dairy, and refined sugar, try this version as a great alternative for yourself and your kids. It's also perfect after a brisk hike, playtime in the snow, or when you simply need the comfort of hot cocoa. Add my Totally Whipped Coconut Whippy Cream (page 364) for a special treat.

2¼   cups unsweetened almond milk

2½   tablespoons unsweetened cocoa powder

5   Medjool dates, pitted

1   tablespoon pure maple syrup

1   teaspoon pure vanilla extract

   Pinch ground cinnamon

   Dollop Totally Whipped Coconut Whippy Cream (page 364), optional

Combine all the ingredients except the Totally Whipped Coconut Whippy Cream in a small saucepan. Bring to a simmer, stirring constantly so that the almond milk doesn't stick to the bottom of the pan. Cook until warmed through, remove from the heat, and transfer to a blender. Blend until smooth. Divide between two mugs, top with the Totally Whipped Coconut Whippy Cream, and serve warm.

SERVES 2

grown-up ORANGE JUICE

Moms have been serving orange juice with breakfast forever. I feel good about this healthy version and I haven't met a child or adult who hasn't loved this recipe. If you don't like almonds, you can use any other dairy-free nut or seed "mylks" (page 290), or use your own rice or oat milk. Use chilled oranges and milk to make this extra refreshing.

½   cup unsweetened almond milk

¼   cup freshly squeezed orange juice

2   tablespoons shelled raw hemp seeds

1   tablespoon pure maple syrup

1   teaspoon pure vanilla extract

¼   teaspoon ground cinnamon

¼   teaspoon freshly grated orange zest

2   ice cubes, for serving

Combine all the ingredients except the ice cubes in a blender and puree until smooth. Place the ice cubes in a glass and pour in the orange juice. Serve immediately.

SERVES 1

healing
SORE THROAT SHOT

It's a spicy one and it burns going down, but boy o' boy is it a sore-throat saver as well as a gut healer! This has saved me many, many times. The garlic helps kill bad bacteria in your gut and turmeric helps fight inflammation. Take 2 teaspoons two times a day for a sore throat or tummy trouble.

1   garlic clove, crushed

1   teaspoon ground turmeric

2   tablespoons freshly squeezed lemon juice

2   tablespoons raw honey, plus more if needed

In a small bowl, combine the garlic and turmeric. Using a fork, mash to form a paste. Add the lemon juice and honey and mix well. Remove any leftover chunks of garlic. If the shot is too spicy or tart, add more honey. Serve immediately.

SERVES 1

cozy bellyache
GINGER TEA

This is my best bellyache remedy. Too many years of bellyaches when I was a young girl up until my thirties, made me a pro at finding a cure for the pain. This homemade elixir is my instant pick-me-upper. The freshly squeezed lemon juice is soothing and cleansing.

2   cups water

¾-inch piece fresh ginger, peeled and grated

1   tablespoon raw honey, plus more if needed

½   teaspoon freshly squeezed lemon juice

In a small saucepan, bring the water to a boil over medium-high heat. Place the ginger in a mug, and then fill the mug with the hot water. Steep for 5 to 7 minutes. Add the honey and lemon juice. If the tea is too tart, add more honey. Serve immediately.

SERVES 1

warm
CLEANSING TEA

This comforting tea feels like fall, though it can also be refreshing during summer heat waves if you serve it over ice cubes—lots of 'em! Add one of my dairy-free nut "mylks" (page 290) if you like your tea creamy, or toss in a few of my Sun Salutation cubes (page 295) for a pop of flavor and antioxidants.

4	cups water
2	teaspoons fennel seeds
1½	teaspoons cumin seeds
1½	teaspoons coriander seeds
	Honey, to taste, optional

In a small saucepan, bring the water to a boil over medium-high heat. Remove from the heat and add the fennel, cumin, and coriander seeds. Cover and let steep for 5 minutes. Strain through a fine-mesh sieve (or drink with the seeds whole) and add honey, if desired. Transfer to mugs and serve warm.

SERVES 2

dandelion
LIVER DETOX TEA

This tea has strong liver-cleansing powers and is perfect for detoxifying. Before my decade of chronic illness, I had no idea where my liver was in my body—nor did I have a clue as to what it actually did. After years of research, I learned how to support my liver daily to help remove toxins.

2	cups water
2	roasted dandelion root tea bags
½	teaspoon ground cardamom
1	cinnamon stick
	Freshly squeezed lemon juice, to taste, optional
	Honey, for serving, optional

Place the water, tea bags, cardamom, and cinnamon stick in a small saucepan. Cover and bring to a boil. Reduce the heat and simmer for 15 minutes. Pour into a large mug, add lemon juice and honey, if desired, and serve.

SERVES 1

dip it, spread it, dress it

Who doesn't want a little extra zing of flavor in their food? I do. Just because I eat clean doesn't mean I have boring taste buds. Hardly! But what I don't want to do is drown great food with refined sugars, inflammation-causing ingredients, and "sawdust."

The fact is, most of the dressings and sauces lining the aisles of your local grocery store are more filler than food, loaded up with chemicals, gums, added sugars, food dyes, and refined table salt. Gag. (Why else would they last for years on the shelf and in your fridge?) Seriously—take a look through the block of unpronounceable text on the back of that bottle of sauce, seasoning, or marinade in your kitchen. I challenge you to tell me what any of it even is! This stuff is practically embalmed.

You absolutely can create your own delicious homemade condiments without a whole lot of effort—even while watching *Friends* reruns in your pajamas, like I do! He-he. Start with some simple basics: quality sea salt, freshly ground black pepper, fresh and dried herbs, and freshly squeezed citrus juices.

I started experimenting with dips, dressings, and sauces when I had *C. diff* colitis, in which a form of bacteria (*C. difficile*—the name says it all, trust me) literally killed my poor little belly and put me at serious risk. My gut was shot—I could barely digest water! So I started using my food processor and blender for my meals, and got creative with seasonings and sauces since I couldn't eat any processed ingredients without doubling over in pain.

Once you taste the flavors of these DIY sauces, you're really never going to want to go back to bottled. From my Cumin Cashew Cream Sauce (page 230) to my Moo-Free Cashew Sour Cream (page 309) and Dairy-Free Raw Macadamia Nut "Ricotta" Cheese (page 309), I've got a topping or sauce for every taste and texture you crave. You can create infinite variations for the recipes you like most, to top your gluten-free whole-grain pasta, crackers, veggies, or fruits. Heck, you can even use as them as dips for my grain-free crackers (pages 156–162) and Transformed Crunchy Breadsticks (page 143). I have no doubt you'll get your fill of guilt-free flavor in every bite!

OIL-FREE TRADITIONAL HUMMUS

The varieties of hummus in the grocery store these days are mind-boggling. I'm partial to homemade, though, since it allows you to control the ingredients—plus it just tastes so wonderfully fresh. I made this hummus without oil and, as you'll see, it doesn't suffer a bit. In fact, it may be even more delicious! Serve as an appetizer or snack with my grain-free crackers (pages 156–162). For a pop of color, top with julienned veggies or microgreens.

2	cups cooked chickpeas (see page 99)
¼	cup (scant) freshly squeezed lemon juice
3	tablespoons tahini (see below)
1	small garlic clove
½	teaspoon sea salt
½	teaspoon freshly ground black pepper
½	teaspoon freshly grated lemon zest
	Pinch cayenne pepper
½	cup warm water, as needed

Combine all the ingredients except the water in a food processor and process, adding 1 tablespoon of water at a time, until the hummus is smooth and creamy. Store in a sealed container in the refrigerator for up to 4 days.

MAKES 1¾ CUPS

MAKE YOUR OWN TAHINI Did you forget tahini at the store? No worries—you can make your own! Use this recipe for any of my recipes that call for "tahini" instead of buying a jar. Preheat the oven to 350°F. Spread 1 pound white sesame seeds on a large rimmed baking sheet and toast for 15 to 20 minutes, or until golden brown, stirring every 3 minutes. Let cool for 40 minutes. Transfer to a food processor and process on low speed for 25 to 30 minutes. Scrape down the sides as needed. Add sea salt to taste, transfer to a glass container with a lid, and store in the refrigerator for up to 1 week.

oil-free
WHITE BEAN AND BASIL HUMMUS

This protein-packed, creamy bowl of love is one of my go-to filler-uppers. No oil? No problem. It's still delightfully rich and creamy. Adding a touch of balsamic vinegar heightens its savory flavor, and fresh basil adds a lovely sweet touch. Serve with my grain-free crackers (pages 156–162), or with gluten-free whole-grain toast, in place of mayo for a sandwich.

2	cups cooked cannellini beans (see page 99)
¼	cup finely chopped fresh basil
2½	tablespoons tahini (see note, page 301)
2	tablespoons freshly squeezed lemon juice
1½	tablespoons balsamic vinegar
1	small garlic clove
½	teaspoon sea salt
½	teaspoon freshly ground black pepper
	Water as needed

Combine all the ingredients except the water in a food processor and process until the hummus is smooth and creamy. If needed, add water, 1 teaspoon at a time. Store in a sealed container in the refrigerator for up to 4 days.

MAKES 1¾ CUPS

curried
MAPLE HUMMUS

I like to make this hummus on Sunday afternoons and use it for snacks and lunches throughout the week. I often place cooked and chilled quinoa on a bed of raw spinach, top it with veggies (like bell peppers, cucumbers, snap peas, and hearts of palm), and then add a dollop of this hummus as a finishing touch instead of a dressing—it's soaring with flavor and protein. Yum!

¼	cup freshly squeezed lemon juice, plus more if needed
3½	tablespoons tahini (see note, page 301)
2	tablespoons extra-virgin olive oil
2	teaspoons pure maple syrup
1	teaspoon ground cumin
½	teaspoon curry powder
½	teaspoon chili powder
½	teaspoon sea salt, plus more if needed
¼	teaspoon freshly grated lemon zest
¼	teaspoon freshly ground black pepper, plus more if needed
2	cups cooked chickpeas (see page 99)
	Water, if needed

Combine all the ingredients except the chickpeas and water in a food processor and pulse until smooth. Add the chickpeas and puree until smooth and creamy. For a thinner consistency, add water (or more lemon juice if you want a tarter hummus) 1 teaspoon at a time. Taste and season with salt and pepper if necessary. Store in a sealed container in the refrigerator for up to 4 days.

MAKES 2 CUPS

easy lentil
HERBED HUMMUS

Lentils take center stage here and you can flavor this hummus any way you like by using dill, tarragon, or basil. Serve a dollop with crackers or wrapped in kale and collard leaves. Roll up the leaves and when you reach the end, use some more of the hummus to create a seal. Try a dollop on top of baked sweet potatoes or my grain-free crackers (pages 156–162).

½   cup dried green lentils

¼   cup freshly squeezed lemon juice

2   tablespoons tahini (see note, page 301)

1   tablespoon minced shallots

1   small garlic clove

1   teaspoon extra-virgin olive oil

    Sea salt and freshly ground black pepper

¼   cup finely chopped fresh dill, tarragon, or basil

2   tablespoons finely chopped fresh flat-leaf parsley

Cook the lentils according to the package directions. Drain and let cool.

Combine the lentils, lemon juice, tahini, shallots, garlic, oil, and salt and pepper to taste in a food processor and process until smooth. Transfer to a serving bowl and fold in the dill and parsley. Serve immediately. Store leftovers in a sealed container in the refrigerator for up to 4 days.

MAKES 1 CUP

creamy
TAHINI TZATZIKI

The secret to a really good tzatziki—the garlicky Greek yogurt sauce—is to get the water out of the cucumbers. This recipe directs you to let the shredded cucumbers drain for a while; don't skip that part! I make this dairy-free tzatziki for an appetizer and serve it with raw veggies and my grain-free crackers (pages 156–162). Note: Use a box grater to easily shred the cucumber.

½   English cucumber, shredded

¼   teaspoon sea salt

⅓   cup tahini (see note, page 301)

3   tablespoons water

3   tablespoons freshly squeezed lemon juice

4   teaspoons finely chopped fresh dill

1   large garlic clove, minced

In a large bowl, combine the cucumber and salt; toss to coat. Cover the bowl and let sit for 5 minutes to draw out moisture from the cucumber.

In a blender, combine the tahini, water, lemon juice, dill, and garlic; blend until smooth. Transfer to a medium bowl.

Using your hands, squeeze water from the cucumber and drain. Discard liquid. Add the cucumber to the tahini mixture and stir to combine. Serve immediately.

MAKES ¾ CUP

KALAMATA OLIVE AND CASHEW TAPENADE

This tapenade has a distinctive flavor that's easy to fall in love with after one spoonful. Serve with my healthy Vegetarian Antipasto Platter (page 64) and my grain-free crackers (pages 156–162).

¾ cup raw cashews, soaked in water overnight, drained, rinsed, and dried

2½ cups pitted kalamata olives

¼ cup finely chopped fresh flat-leaf parsley

5 tablespoons freshly squeezed lemon juice

¼ cup extra-virgin olive oil

1¼ tablespoons raw honey

Pinch freshly grated lemon zest

In a dry skillet, toast the cashews over medium heat, shaking the pan occasionally to prevent burning, until the nuts are fragrant, 3 to 4 minutes. Transfer to a food processor and pulse until the nuts are ground. Add the remaining ingredients and pulse until smooth. Store in a sealed glass jar in the refrigerator for up to 4 days.

MAKES 2½ CUPS

SUN-DRIED TOMATO SUNFLOWER PÂTÉ

What makes pâté so delicious is the concentration of flavors. This vegetarian version is no less intense than traditional pâté. And 100 percent healthier! Serve with my grain-free crackers (pages 156–162).

5 cups water

1 cup shelled raw sunflower seeds

15 sun-dried tomatoes (not packed in oil)

½ cup sesame seeds

3½ tablespoons extra-virgin olive oil

2½ tablespoons freshly squeezed lemon juice

1 garlic clove, minced

1¼ teaspoons raw honey

1 teaspoon coconut aminos

¼ teaspoon sea salt

¼ teaspoon freshly ground black pepper

Pinch freshly grated lemon zest

Pinch ground coriander

Bring the water to a boil. In a small bowl, add 1 cup of the hot water to the sunflower seeds and blanch for 2 minutes. Drain and set aside.

Combine the remaining 4 cups hot water and the tomatoes. Let soak until the tomatoes are tender, about 30 minutes. Drain the tomatoes, reserving 1 cup of the soaking liquid.

In a food processor, pulse the sunflower seeds, tomatoes, and remaining ingredients until combined. Add 3 tablespoons of the soaking liquid. Add more 1 tablespoon at a time if needed. Serve immediately, or refrigerate for up to 1 week.

MAKES 2 CUPS

the easiest
GUACAMOLE

This guac is perfect on tacos, spooned on top of a salad, or spread on gluten-free whole-grain toast. And of course, it's a no-fail party dip— who doesn't love guacamole?

4	large very ripe avocados, pitted, peeled, and diced
1¼	cups quartered grape or cherry tomatoes
1	bunch fresh cilantro, finely chopped
½	small red onion, finely chopped
¼	cup plus 1 teaspoon freshly squeezed lime juice, plus more if needed
1¼	teaspoons very finely diced seeded jalapeño, optional
½	teaspoon sea salt, plus more if needed
	Freshly ground black pepper, to taste

In a large bowl, combine all the ingredients. Mash with a fork until smooth, but still chunky. Add more salt and lime juice, if desired. Serve immediately.

MAKES 4 CUPS

OPTIONAL GUACAMOLE ADD-INS

‣ Seriously Sensational Sriracha Sauce (page 318) or other hot sauce

‣ Chopped sun-dried tomatoes

‣ Chopped tomatillos

‣ Finely diced mango, chives, and scallions

peaceful
APRICOT SALSA

Fresh and simple, this vibrant and fruity salsa is good enough to eat alone with a spoon. It's lovely served with gluten-free whole-grain chips, and looks beautiful on top of salads, too.

2	large heirloom tomatoes, diced
1	cup diced red bell pepper
2	fresh medium apricots, pitted and diced
1	teaspoon extra-virgin olive oil
¼	cup diced Vidalia onion
½	teaspoon chili powder
¼	teaspoon ground cinnamon
¼	teaspoon sea salt, plus more if needed
¼	teaspoon freshly ground black pepper, plus more if needed
¼	cup finely chopped fresh cilantro
2	tablespoons plus ½ teaspoon freshly squeezed lime juice
1	scallion, thinly sliced, for serving

In a large bowl, combine the tomatoes, bell pepper, and apricots.

In a medium skillet, heat the oil over medium heat. Add the onion, chili powder, cinnamon, salt, and black pepper and cook for 7 minutes. Transfer the mixture to a food processor, add the tomato mixture, cilantro, and lime juice, and pulse until chunky. Taste and season with salt and black pepper if necessary. Chill for 2 hours before serving, then top with the scallion. Store in a sealed container in the refrigerator for up to 2 days.

MAKES 2½ CUPS

zippy
APPLE SALSA

Forget what you know about salsa—there's not a single tomato in here. Get creative and add this salsa to tacos, salads, berries, and gluten-free, whole-grain recipes for an easy boost of flavor. I know this dish will appear on your table every summer. It's surely on mine!

2	sweet crisp medium apples, such as Pink Lady or Fuji, cored and diced
½	cup finely chopped fresh cilantro
5	large scallions, white and light green parts, thinly sliced
3	tablespoons freshly squeezed lime juice
4	fresh chives, thinly sliced
	Pinch cayenne pepper, to taste
	Sea salt and freshly ground black pepper, to taste

In a medium bowl, combine all the ingredients; mix well. Taste and adjust the seasonings if needed. Transfer to the refrigerator and chill for 30 minutes before serving. Best served on the day it's made.

MAKES 3 CUPS

cheery
CHERRY SALSA

Besides serving the traditional way with chips, this salsa is delicious mixed with chilled quinoa. One recipe plus 1½ cups quinoa will make a side dish for four. As you process this salsa in the food processor, pay close attention. It can easily get watery if you process too long.

2	cups fresh cherries, pitted and halved
4	fresh chives, thinly sliced
¼	cup raw walnuts, soaked for 10 minutes in hot water, drained well, and finely chopped
¼	cup freshly squeezed orange juice, plus more as needed
¼	teaspoon freshly grated orange zest
	Pinch sea salt
	Pinch white pepper
	Pinch cayenne pepper
1	tablespoon chopped fresh mint, for serving

Combine half of the cherries, the chives, walnuts, orange juice, orange zest, salt, white pepper, and cayenne pepper in a food processor; pulse until chunky. Transfer to a medium bowl and add the remaining cherries. Add the mint, mix well, and serve.

MAKES 1½ CUPS

peppy
NO-CHEESE PARMESAN

You won't believe how much this tastes like real Parm! It's kind of a miracle of modern cooking. Keep a batch in the refrigerator and use just as you would traditional Parmesan. Note: Hemp seeds are delicate and can burn easily. Keep your eyes on these little morsels so they don't scorch.

2	tablespoons freshly squeezed lemon juice
2½	teaspoons chickpea miso paste
½	teaspoon sea salt
¼	teaspoon dried oregano
½	cup shelled raw hemp seeds

Preheat the oven to 325°F.

In a small bowl, whisk together the lemon juice, miso, salt, and oregano. Add the hemp seeds and stir to form a paste. Spread the paste in a thin, even layer onto the bottom of a 9x13-inch baking dish so there are no clumps. Bake for 15 minutes or until lightly golden, stirring every 5 minutes to prevent burning. Remove from the oven and let cool completely in the baking dish. Stir to break up clumps. Serve or store in a sealed container in the refrigerator for up to 5 days.

MAKES ½ CUP

butter me up
HONEY-ALMOND NUT BUTTER

If there is anything that can replace the classic peanut butter, this nut butter just might be it. The melted coconut oil helps make it super creamy and adds a touch of coconut flavor. Drizzle over my Grown-Up Grilled Bananas (page 359).

½	cup almond butter
2	tablespoons melted coconut oil
2	tablespoons honey
½	teaspoon pure vanilla extract

In a medium bowl, combine all the ingredients; mix well. Use immediately, or chill in the refrigerator for 2 hours, and then let sit at room temperature for 10 minutes before using. Store in a sealed container in the refrigerator for up to 1 week.

MAKES ½ CUP

JAZZ UP YOUR NUT BUTTERS For homemade nut butters, make your own mixture with raw cashews, almonds, Brazil nuts, pecans, walnuts, macadamia nuts, flaxseeds, hemp seeds, pumpkin seeds, and sunflower seeds. If you want an extra-creamy nut butter, add coconut oil or extra-virgin olive oil; start with 1 teaspoon and drizzle it into the food processor. After processing the nut butter, you can add organic sulfur-free dried fruit like cranberries or golden raisins along with pure maple syrup, honey, pure vanilla extract, cocoa or raw cacao powder, ground cardamom, and ground cinnamon.

dairy-free
CREAMY CASHEW CHEESE

There are about a hundred and one ways to use this dairy-free spreadable cheese. You'll see that it's called for in many of the recipes in this book, and you can use it as a substitute for regular cheese in almost any recipe that doesn't require melting.

1	cup raw cashews, quick soaked for 10 minutes in boiling water or soaked in water for 2 hours, drained, and rinsed
3	tablespoons freshly squeezed lemon juice
½	teaspoon sea salt
¼	teaspoon freshly ground black pepper
	Water, as needed
2	fresh chives, thinly sliced

Combine the cashews, lemon juice, salt, and pepper in a food processor and process until smooth. Add water, 1 teaspoon at a time, if needed to create a smooth texture.

Transfer to a bowl, stir in the chives, and mix well. Store in a sealed container in the refrigerator for up to 1 week.

MAKES 1 CUP

VARIATIONS: To make Cashew Dill "Havarti," add 1 tablespoon chopped fresh dill in place of the chives. To make an Herbed Cashew Cheese log, don't thin the nut cheese with water. Form into a log with parchment paper, roll in herbes de Provence, and slice in rounds.

dairy-free
BRAZIL NUT PARM CHEESE

As opposed to the Peppy No-Cheese Parmesan (page 307), which requires several ingredients, this dairy-free "Parm" is simply three ingredients (and only two if you forgo the pepper!). I like both cheeses equally; this one, though is a real time-saver.

½	cup raw Brazil nuts, soaked in hot water for 20 minutes, drained, and rinsed
½	teaspoon sea salt
	Pinch freshly ground black pepper, to taste, optional

Combine the Brazil nuts, salt, and, if desired, pepper in a food processor and pulse until the nuts are ground to a consistency like traditional Parmesan cheese, about 1 minute. Transfer to a sealed container and store in the refrigerator for up to 1 week.

MAKES ½ CUP

moo-free
CASHEW SOUR CREAM

*Tasty and tart! Who knew sour cream
could taste even better without the dairy?
Developing this recipe was life-changing for me.
I love serving a dollop of this with my
Open-Faced Pumpkin Enchiladas (page 248).*

1   cup raw cashews, soaked in water overnight, drained, and rinsed

2   tablespoons plus ¼ teaspoon freshly squeezed lemon juice

1   teaspoon apple cider vinegar

¼   teaspoon sea salt

     Pinch cayenne pepper, optional

10   tablespoons water, plus more if needed

In a blender, combine all the ingredients except the water and puree until smooth. While the blender is running, add 1 tablespoon of water at a time until the sour cream is smooth, silky, and slightly thick. Store in a sealed container in the refrigerator for up to 1 week.

MAKES 1½ CUPS

dairy-free
RAW MACADAMIA NUT "RICOTTA" CHEESE

*Another dairy-free cheese that's too good
to pass up. Serve anytime you'd normally serve
ricotta cheese—mixed into gluten-free whole-grain
pasta, added to roasted veggies, or spread
onto sliced strawberries with cinnamon.*

1   cup raw macadamia nuts

2   tablespoons extra-virgin olive oil

2   tablespoons freshly squeezed lemon juice

½   teaspoon sea salt

¼   cup water

3   tablespoons finely chopped fresh flat-leaf parsley, optional

Combine the macadamia nuts, oil, lemon juice, and salt in a food processor and pulse until the mixture starts to clump together. Add the water 1 tablespoon at a time until the mixture develops a ricotta cheese consistency. Transfer to a sealed container and store in the refrigerator for up to 1 week. If desired, garnish with the parsley before serving.

MAKES 1 CUP

dairy-free sunshine
MACADAMIA "CREAM" CHEESE

No cows were used in the making of this cheese—but it tastes terrific and the texture is very similar to the real thing. You can eat this cheese straight out of the oven or chilled, and there is no shortage of ways to change it up. You can top the disk with fresh thyme leaves, red pepper flakes, za'atar, sesame seeds, chopped nuts—anything that strikes your fancy. Once you know how to make this recipe, the sky's the limit.

¾ cup raw macadamia nuts, soaked in water for 12 hours, drained, and rinsed

4½ tablespoons coconut oil

Freshly squeezed juice of 1 large lemon

1 tablespoon sunflower seed butter, with no added salt or oil

1 teaspoon chopped fresh dill

⅛ teaspoon ground turmeric

¾ teaspoon sea salt

3 pieces cheesecloth (see page 292)

Freshly ground black pepper, for sprinkling

Combine the macadamia nuts, oil, lemon juice, sunflower seed butter, dill, turmeric, and salt in a food processor and process until smooth, about 5 minutes.

Place a large strainer over a large bowl and line it with two layers of cheesecloth, letting the ends hang over the sides of the strainer. Transfer the nut mixture to the strainer using a spoon, and then fold up the sides of the cheesecloth, twist them together tight against the cheese, and secure with a rubber band or tightly tied ribbon. Let sit for 10 to 12 hours at room temperature. Transfer to the refrigerator and chill for 1 hour.

Preheat the oven to 300°F. Line a rimmed baking sheet with parchment paper.

Remove the cheesecloth from the cheese and shape the cheese into a disk. Sprinkle it with the pepper. Wrap with a clean piece of cheesecloth and bake on the prepared baking sheet until the mixture is soft yet set on the outside, about 30 minutes, turning after 15 minutes of baking. Serve warm or set aside to cool, and then transfer to the refrigerator to chill. Store in a sealed container in the refrigerator for up to 1 week.

NOTE: You can freeze this nut cheese by preslicing it and storing in the freezer in a sealed container for up to 1 month. Defrost the slices as needed.

MAKES 1 (10-OUNCE) DISK

GET CREATIVE: MAKE YOUR OWN DAIRY-FREE NUT CHEESE PLATE

A cheese plate is the star of any gathering, especially when there's no gluten, dairy, or soy! Here are a few easy and fun ways to entertain even if you're only entertaining for one. I love serving my dairy-free nut cheeses (pages 307–310) on a wooden cutting board with small bowls and a cute wooden knife for spreading. Stack my grain-free crackers (pages 156–162) on the side and garnish with fresh herbs. Try these serving suggestions or pair my cheeses with raw olives, sulfur-free dried fruits, my roasted nut recipes (pages 140–142), and more.

HERE ARE SOME OPTIONS TO SERVE WITH MY NUT CHEESES:

▸ Served with figs and sprigs of fresh thyme, and drizzled with honey

▸ Topped with fresh blackberries, mint, and honey on my grain-free crackers (pages 156–162)

▸ Paired with roasted red grapes and a few sprigs of fresh thyme

▸ Topped with Oven-Roasted Cherry Tomatoes with Poppy Seeds (page 283)

▸ Teamed with grilled peaches, cherries, and fresh basil

▸ Served atop sliced zucchini and drizzled with Presto Pesto Drizzle (page 261)

▸ Accompanied by Super Soft Caramelized Red Onions (page 272)

▸ Enjoyed on top of grilled or toasted gluten-free whole-grain bread with fresh basil and roasted veggies

▸ Mixed into quinoa or another gluten-free whole grain (see Serving Ideas for Cooked Gluten-Free Whole Grains, page 102)

▸ Served on gluten-free whole-grain toast with The Easiest Guacamole (page 305)

▸ Spread on my grain-free crackers (pages 156–162) with Peaceful Apricot Salsa (page 305), Cheery Cherry Salsa (page 306), or Zippy Apple Salsa (page 306)

▸ Tossed into a leafy green salad like my Nuts about Butternut Squash and Kale Salad (page 210)

▸ Stuffed in endive leaves and drizzled with balsamic vinegar

▸ Wrapped like a burrito in Swiss chard leaves with chickpeas, fresh herbs, chili powder, and lemon zest

▸ Spread onto apple or pear slices and sprinkled with ground flaxseeds or hemp seeds

▸ Spread on my grain-free crackers (pages 156–162) with my Sun-Dried Tomato Sauce (page 320)

▸ Drizzled with honey, alongside toasted pine nuts, pitted Medjool dates or apricots

creamy
MOCK MAYO

*Homemade mayonnaise is so much better
than the bottled kind. This easy, egg-free version
is no exception. I love using this mayo
for sandwiches to add a boost of protein and
creaminess to every bite. Use it in potato salad
and other classic mayo-based dishes.*

1½	cups slivered raw almonds
¾	cup warm water
¼	cup apple cider vinegar
2	teaspoons freshly squeezed lemon juice
2	teaspoons Dijon mustard
½	teaspoon sea salt
½	teaspoon freshly ground black pepper
¼	teaspoon freshly grated lemon zest
½	cup extra-virgin olive oil

Combine all the ingredients except the oil in a
blender and blend until smooth. With the motor
running, slowly add the oil until emulsified and the
mixture is thick, about 1 minute. Store in a sealed
container in the refrigerator for up to 10 days.

MAKES 2 CUPS

surprisingly easy
MAKE-YOUR-OWN
MUSTARD

*If you know me, you know that I am a mustard
lover without compare. In fact, the entire door of
my refrigerator in Manhattan is loaded with
mustards. So I wouldn't steer you wrong. This
homemade version is delectable! Note: This mustard
needs to sit overnight in the fridge before serving.*

½	cup apple cider vinegar
3	tablespoons brown mustard seeds
1½	tablespoons yellow mustard seeds
1	teaspoon raw honey
½	teaspoon sea salt
1	small shallot, minced
	Pinch freshly ground black pepper

In a glass jar with a lid, combine all the ingredients
and mix well. Store in the refrigerator overnight,
which will allow the mustard seeds to soften and
absorb the sweet flavors. Transfer the mixture to a
blender and process until the mustard thickens and
the seeds break open. Store in a sealed container in
the refrigerator for up to 2 weeks.

MAKES ¾ CUP

CLOCKWISE:
CREAMY MOCK MAYO, (PAGE 313)
AMIE'S EASY HOME-STYLE SUN-DRIED TOMATO KETCHUP, (PAGE 315)
SWEET HOME HONEY MUSTARD, (PAGE 315),

sweet home
HONEY MUSTARD

*When I first moved to Manhattan, I used
bottles of processed honey mustard on everything—
yes everything. Then, after C-diff colitis, I started
to feel so sick every time I ate it. Turns out that
processed honey mustard was made with
high-frutose corn syrup. Ewww. I was destined
to find a healthier alternative. And this is it!
As a replacement for processed mustard or mayo,
this especially tasty spread is great on sandwiches
or in wraps. To vary its flavor, change
the type of honey you use.*

½   cup mustard powder

½   cup raw honey

2   tablespoons plus 2 teaspoons
     apple cider vinegar

1   tablespoon yellow mustard seeds

¼   teaspoon freshly ground black pepper

¼   teaspoon sea salt

1   tablespoon sesame seeds, toasted
     (see page 108)

In a medium saucepan, combine all the ingredients
except the sesame seeds and bring to a boil over
medium heat. Lower the heat and simmer until
the mixture thickens, about 5 minutes. Stir in the
sesame seeds and let cool. Store in the refrigerator
in a sealed container for up to 4 weeks.

MAKES 1 CUP

amie's easy home-style
SUN-DRIED TOMATO
KETCHUP

*Remember when you were a kid and you put
ketchup on everything? With my refined sugar–
free ketchup, you can feel like a kid again! Enjoy
with veggie burgers, my Long Weekend Chickpea
Spinach Scramble (page 133), and more. Sun-dried
tomatoes, fresh grape tomatoes, honey, and dates
add sweet touches while apple cider vinegar and
white onions round out the flavors. This yields a
lot of ketchup, so I recommend freezing half the
yield for up to three months. Note: It helps to have
a high-speed blender when making this recipe.*

1½   cups diced grape tomatoes

¾   cup sun-dried tomatoes (not packed in oil)

⅓   cup finely chopped sweet white onion

¼   cup extra-virgin olive oil

5   dates, pitted, soaked in hot water for
     10 minutes, and drained

2   tablespoons raw honey

1½   tablespoons apple cider vinegar

¼   teaspoon sea salt

Combine all the ingredients in a high-speed blender
and blend on low speed. As the mixture starts to get
smoother, turn the machine up to high speed and
puree until ultra-smooth and silky. Store in a sealed
container in the refrigerator for up to 3 weeks.

MAKES 1½ CUPS

HEALTHY SANDWICH IDEAS

Looking for a few ways to spruce up your lunchtime staple? These tasty ideas are perfect for a picnic or rejuvenating your brown bag lunch. Serve them open-faced if you desire.

▸ Sliced avocado, Dairy-Free Sunshine Macadamia "Cream" Cheese (page 310), sliced tomato, and sliced red onion or scallions

▸ Super Soft Caramelized Red Onions (page 272), arugula, and balsamic vinegar with Dairy-Free Creamy Cashew Cheese (page 308)

▸ Butter Me Up Honey-Almond Nut Butter (page 307) and Chia Seed Berry Jam (page 329)

▸ Oil-Free Traditional Hummus (page 301) with fresh bean sprouts and sliced carrots

▸ The Easiest Guacamole (page 305) with sliced heirloom tomatoes

▸ Sliced, roasted, golden beets with sliced pears atop Dairy-Free Creamy Cashew Cheese (page 308)

▸ Freshly chopped dill, Dairy-Free Creamy Cashew Cheese (page 308), Big-Flavor Marinated Roasted Bell Peppers (page 278), and Easy No-Foil Roasted Garlic (page 329)

▸ Mashed black beans, fresh sprouts, sliced cucumber, sliced tomato, and thinly sliced red onion

▸ Sautéed kale, sliced mushrooms, and Big-Flavor Roasted Bell Peppers (page 278) with Peppery Sunflower Pesto (page 321)

▸ Grilled Veggies (zucchini, yellow squash, and roasted red bell peppers), a drizzle of balsamic vinegar, Peppery Sunflower Pesto (page 321), and Kalamata Olive and Cashew Tapenade (page 304)

▸ Mini Baked Chickpea-Free Falafel with Cannellini Bean Za'atar Sauce (page 242) wrapped in my Savory Chickpea Flour Crepes (page 274) with leafy greens

NO MAYO? NO PROBLEM

Here are some gluten-free, dairy-free, egg-free, and soy-free alternatives to spread on gluten-free whole-grain toast, raw veggies, my grain-free crackers (pages 156–162), Savory Chickpea Flour Crepes (page 274), or any of my tasty burgers.

‣ Butter Me Up Honey-Almond Nut Butter (page 307)

‣ Hummus recipes (pages 301–303)

‣ Mashed extra-ripe avocado

‣ Homemade Pumpkin Puree (page 123) stirred into my Oil-Free Traditional Hummus (page 301)

‣ Sun-Dried Tomato Sauce (page 320)

‣ Sun-Dried Tomato Sunflower Pâté (page 304)

‣ Peppery Sunflower Pesto (page 321)

‣ The Easiest Guacamole (page 305)

‣ Creamy Mock Mayo (page 313)

‣ Moo-Free Cashew Sour Cream (page 309)

‣ Dairy-free nut cheeses (pages 307–310)

‣ Kalamata Olive and Cashew Tapenade (page 304)

‣ Zesty Orange Marmalade (page 328)

‣ Raw Strawberry Ginger Citrus Marmalade (page 327)

seriously sensational
SRIRACHA SAUCE

I like making my own condiments, and this Thai hot sauce is no exception. It has a pleasant mouth-numbing heat and sweetness, with a little afterburn, too. Stir sriracha into nut butters, hummus, and guacamole to create a dip for vegetables, or use it as a marinade for veggies before you grill or roast them. Note: This recipe takes 3 days to make. You'll also need a glass jar, a paper coffee filter, and a rubber band.

½   cup apple cider vinegar

6   serrano peppers, roughly chopped

2   tablespoons coconut aminos

2   tablespoons raw honey

2   large garlic cloves

¼   teaspoon sea salt
     Pinch chili powder
     Pinch crushed red pepper flakes

Combine all the ingredients in a food processor and pulse until the mixture reaches a chunky, salsa-like consistency. Transfer to a glass jar, cover with a paper coffee filter, and fasten with a rubber band to secure the filter on the jar (so it acts as the lid). Let sit on the counter at room temperature for 3 days.

Transfer the mixture to a blender and blend until smooth and silky. Serve or store in a sealed container in the refrigerator for up to 1 month.

MAKES ⅔ CUP

heirloom
TOMATO SAUCE

This tomato sauce is pure and sweet— it lets the tomatoes really shine. You can also add fresh parsley or leave out the basil, if desired. Serve this sauce on my gluten-free pizza crusts (pages 234, 235, and 236), with a bowl of gluten-free pasta and my Dairy-Free Brazil Nut Parm Cheese (page 308), or as a dipping sauce for my Transformed Crunchy Breadsticks (page 143) and grain-free crackers (156–162).

2   tablespoons extra-virgin olive oil

1   garlic clove, minced

3 to 4 large heirloom tomatoes (about 3 pounds), seeded

8   fresh basil leaves, cut into a chiffonade
     Sea salt and freshly ground black pepper, to taste

In a medium saucepan, heat the oil over medium heat. Add the garlic and sauté for 30 seconds. Add the tomatoes and basil and bring the sauce to a simmer. Cook, stirring often, until the liquid has been absorbed, about 15 minutes.

Remove and discard the basil leaves. Using a handheld blender, puree the sauce, and then return to the saucepan over medium heat. (If you don't have a handheld blender, transfer the sauce to a regular blender, allow to cool a bit, and then puree; return to the saucepan.) Season with salt and pepper. Serve warm.

MAKES 3 CUPS

HEIRLOOM TOMATO SAUCE

sun-dried
TOMATO SAUCE

There are so many ways to use this deeply flavored tomato sauce. Toss it into a cold, gluten-free whole-grain pasta salad, serve it over hot gluten-free whole-grain spaghetti, heap it on top of gluten-free whole-grain toast for bruschetta, or drizzle it over my Dairy-Free Creamy Cashew Cheese (page 308) and serve atop my grain-free crackers (pages 156–162). It's also a great sauce for gluten-free pizza; try it on top of my gluten-free pizza crusts (pages 234, 235, and 236).

1	large red bell pepper
3	cups water
½	cup sun-dried tomatoes (not packed in oil)
1½	cups diced grape tomatoes
⅓	cup chopped red onion
2	tablespoons finely chopped fresh basil
2	tablespoons finely chopped fresh flat-leaf parsley
1	tablespoon golden raisins
1	garlic clove
¼	teaspoon paprika
¼	teaspoon sea salt
¼	teaspoon freshly ground black pepper

TOMATO SAUCE TIP Less acid, more flavor: Tomato sauces can be a little too acidic for sensitive stomachs. To lower the acidity and add nutrients, add shredded carrots, zucchini, or chopped kale when sautéing onions in the beginning of the sauce-making. If needed, add a touch of honey, too, to even out the flavor.

Roast the bell pepper by holding it with tongs over a medium flame on a gas stovetop, rotating it for 7 minutes or until charred. Alternatively, cut the pepper in half, lay it on a large rimmed baking sheet, and smash it until flat. Broil on high for 7 minutes or until charred. Let cool for 2 minutes, and place the pepper in a brown paper bag, secure it with a rubber band or twist tie, and let the pepper steam for 10 minutes. Remove from the bag and rub the charred skin off with your fingers. Discard the seeds and chop the pepper into large chunks.

In a medium saucepan, combine the water and sun-dried tomatoes. Cover and bring to a steady simmer. Simmer for 20 minutes. Drain the tomatoes, reserving 1 cup of the soaking liquid.

In a food processor, combine the roasted pepper, soaked sun-dried tomatoes, grape tomatoes, onion, basil, parsley, raisins, garlic, paprika, salt, and black pepper; puree until smooth. Add ¼ cup of the reserved tomato soaking liquid to thin the sauce. If the sauce is still thicker than desired, add more soaking liquid 1 tablespoon at a time. Serve immediately or freeze in a sealed container for up to 1 month.

MAKES 2 CUPS

peppery
SUNFLOWER PESTO

Since watercress and arugula are both ideal for detox, I try to use them every way I can. Toss this pesto with gluten-free whole-grain pasta or quinoa (use ¼ cup per serving) or use as a topping for any of my gluten-free pizza crusts (pages 234, 235, and 236).

½ cup shelled raw sunflower seeds

2 cups watercress

2 cups arugula

⅓ cup extra-virgin olive oil

2½ tablespoons freshly squeezed lemon juice

2 small garlic cloves

Pinch crushed red pepper flakes

1½ tablespoons Dairy-Free Brazil Nut Parm Cheese (page 308)

Sea salt and freshly ground black pepper

In a large, dry skillet, toast the sunflower seeds over medium heat until golden brown, 2 to 4 minutes. Transfer to a food processor and pulse until crumbly. Add the watercress, arugula, oil, lemon juice, garlic, and red pepper flakes and process until smooth. Spoon the mixture into a small bowl and stir in the Dairy-Free Brazil Nut Parm Cheese and salt and pepper to taste. Serve immediately, or store in a sealed container in the freezer for up to 2 months.

MAKES 1 CUP

simple
SAGE SQUASH SAUCE

This savory sauce is an indispensable part of my fall and holiday cooking. It makes roasted veggies sing. You can also serve it on top of gluten-free whole-grain toast for a lovely snack or tossed into gluten-free whole-grain pasta for a simple meal.

3 cups peeled and diced butternut squash

½ teaspoon sea salt, divided

¼ cup low-sodium vegetable broth

2 tablespoons tahini (see note page 301)

1 tablespoon finely chopped fresh sage

Bring a large pot of water to a boil. Add the squash and ¼ teaspoon of the salt. Reduce the heat and simmer until the squash is tender, 8 to 10 minutes. Drain.

Transfer the squash to a food processor. Add the broth, tahini, sage, and remaining ¼ teaspoon salt. Process until smooth. Transfer to a sealed container and chill in the refrigerator overnight so flavors develop. Reheat on the stovetop over low heat and serve warm.

MAKES 2 CUPS

EASY CRANBERRY SAUCE

easy
CRANBERRY SAUCE

Thanksgiving isn't complete without cranberry sauce, but your typical cranberry sauce is awash in refined sugar. I'm sure you're not surprised that I've taken out the white sugar and replaced it with a moderate amount of pure maple syrup. This sauce has a bit of spice, too. And it's not only lovely on the Thanksgiving table; serve leftovers atop my grain-free crackers (pages 156–162), or alongside my dairy-free nut cheeses (pages 307–310).

2   teaspoons extra-virgin olive oil
1   small shallot, minced
2   large oranges
⅓   cup pure maple syrup
3   cups fresh cranberries
1   teaspoon chili powder
1   teaspoon ground cinnamon
     Sea salt

In a large skillet, heat the oil over medium heat. Add the shallot and cook until soft, about 3 minutes. Stir in the juice of 1 of the oranges (about ¼ cup) and the maple syrup. Bring to a simmer, add the cranberries, and cook until the cranberries have all popped and the mixture starts to reduce, about 5 minutes.

Peel the remaining orange and remove the segments from the membranes, reserving the juice. Add the segments and juice, chili powder, cinnamon, and salt to taste to the skillet and let the sauce thicken, about 20 minutes. Serve warm.

MAKES 2 CUPS

ecstatic
GRAPE SAUCE

The secret to this sweet sauce is rooibos tea, which has many health benefits and also creates a delicious and unique flavor you'll be ecstatic about. Trust me. Drizzle this sauce over my Celebration Delicata Squash (page 260) for an amazing holiday dish that all of your guests will love. This special sauce also pairs well with my Dukkah (page 326) on top of roasted veggies.

2   cups purple seedless grapes, halved
1   cup brewed rooibos tea
¼   cup balsamic vinegar
1   tablespoon extra-virgin olive oil
1½   teaspoons Dijon mustard

In a small saucepan, combine all of the ingredients and bring to a boil over medium-high heat. Boil until the mixture is thick, about 15 minutes.

Transfer half of the sauce to a blender, puree until smooth, and then return it to the pan. Cook until the sauce is thick, 2 to 4 minutes. Serve immediately. Store in a sealed container in the refrigerator for up to 3 days.

MAKES 1¾ CUPS

CREAMY CRANBERRY MAPLE DRESSING

Hazelnuts add a particular richness to this sweet salad dressing. It tastes like autumn in a jar! Delicious drizzled over acorn or delicata squash, kale salad, or roasted veggies.

⅓ cup raw hazelnuts

¼ cup plus 2 teaspoons extra-virgin olive oil, divided

½ small white onion, diced

1 cup fresh cranberries

⅓ cup freshly squeezed orange juice

2½ tablespoons balsamic vinegar

2 tablespoons pure maple syrup

¾ teaspoon freshly grated orange zest

¼ teaspoon sea salt

Preheat the oven to 350°F.

Spread the hazelnuts in a single layer on a rimmed baking sheet and toast in the oven for 15 minutes, or until fragrant. Let cool, then rub between your hands to remove the skins and chop the hazelnuts.

In a large skillet, heat 2 teaspoons of the oil over medium heat. Add the onion and sauté until soft, about 4 minutes. Add the cranberries and sauté until they're soft and popped, about 4 minutes.

Transfer the cranberry mixture to a blender and add the orange juice, vinegar, maple syrup, orange zest, and salt. With the motor running, slowly drizzle in the remaining ¼ cup oil. Puree until smooth and creamy. Transfer to a bowl and stir in the hazelnuts. Store in a sealed container in the refrigerator for up to 4 days.

MAKES 1¼ CUPS

FLAVORED SEA SALTS

Imagine: There once was a time when the only salt I knew about and used was refined, inflammatory table salt. Now, there are actually stores devoted to the myriad varieties of salt. The following three variations are just the tip of the iceberg. I encourage you to use your imagination to create your own favorites. These particular ones play nice with just about everything in your kitchen, and they make great gifts. For even more flavor, lightly toast the spices (i.e., fennel, cumin, or coriander seeds) by placing them in a dry skillet over medium heat and swirling for a few minutes until fragrant.

LEMON FENNEL SEA SALT

This salt has a lovely taste. It's perfect for desserts like truffles, brownies, ice cream, and cookies; tasty, too, on the rim of a mocktail glass.

¼   cup coarse Himalayan pink salt

1   teaspoon fennel seeds

1   teaspoon dried lemon peel

Combine all the ingredients in a container with a lid. Mix to combine. Cover and store at room temperature for up to 1 year.

MAKES ¼ CUP

SMOKED CUMIN SEA SALT

Serve this salt with savory dishes like avocado slices on gluten-free whole-grain toast, grilled veggies, and sliced heirloom tomatoes, and in soups and stews.

¼   cup coarse alderwood-smoked sea salt

1   teaspoon cumin seeds

Combine all the ingredients in a container with a lid. Mix to combine. Cover and store at room temperature for up to 1 year.

MAKES ¼ CUP

CORIANDER BLACK SEA SALT

This magical flavored sea salt is always tucked into a tiny container in my bag when I'm traveling or dining out. Why? Well, it's a lovely way to add a touch of natural flavor without relying on processed condiments, butter, and other inflammatory ingredients that make me sick when I eat out. The result? One heck of a party for your taste buds. Trust me on this: Add a pinch of this sweet and savory salt blend to your salads, roasted veggies, or gluten-free whole-grain dishes, and you'll be pleasantly surprised that you won't need any goopy dressings or sauces to go along with your meal.

½ cup coarse Hawaiian black sea salt

1 teaspoon coriander seeds

Combine all the ingredients in a container with a lid. Cover and store at room temperature for up to 1 year.

MAKES ¼ CUP

DUKKAH

This mix of ground nuts and seasonings, Egyptian in origin, can be sprinkled over food or served as a dip. If you're using it as a dip, serve it alongside a dish of extra-virgin olive oil; you can dip any of my grain-free crackers (pages 156–162) or vegetables into the oil, and then in the dukkah. This is also fun to serve with soups, salads, grilled veggies, or sprinkled over roasted veggies paired with my Ecstatic Grape Sauce (page 323).

½ cup raw almonds

½ cup raw pecans

¼ teaspoon coriander seeds

¼ teaspoon fennel seeds

¼ teaspoon ground cumin

½ teaspoon sea salt

Pinch freshly ground black pepper

In a dry skillet, toast the almonds and pecans over medium heat, shaking the pan occasionally to prevent burning, until the nuts are fragrant and lightly browned, about 4 minutes. Let cool.

In a separate dry skillet, toast the coriander and fennel seeds over medium heat, shaking the pan occasionally to prevent burning, about 3 minutes. Let cool.

Combine the toasted nuts and seeds with the cumin, salt, and pepper in a food processor and pulse until the mixture looks like bread crumbs. (Do not overprocess or it will turn into a nut butter.) Store in a sealed container at room temperature for up to 1 month.

MAKES 1¼ CUPS

pretty preserved
MEYER LEMONS

Preserved lemons are delicious minced or sliced into dressings, dips, pasta dishes, roasted veggies, salads, sauces, and whole-grain dishes or any other dish that calls for lemon—as well as those that don't. You've probably seen a ton of preserved lemon recipes in cookbooks and online, but this one has no added sugar, less salt than traditional recipes, and a whole lot of delicious flavor that makes it unique. Do not use cardamom pods, only whole cardamom seeds.

3	teaspoons sea salt
3	Meyer lemons, sliced vertically into 4 wedges
	Freshly squeezed juice of 4 Meyer lemons, divided
1	tablespoon cardamom seeds
3	bay leaves
2	cinnamon sticks

Sterilize a 1-quart mason jar in hot boiling water for 8 minutes.

Sprinkle the salt on the 12 lemon wedges, 1 teaspoon per lemon. Add 2 tablespoons of the lemon juice to the bottom of the sterilized jar. Add a layer of salted lemon wedge, and then a layer of the cardamom seeds, bay leaves, and cinnamon sticks. Repeat until all the ingredients are in the jar. Press down firmly on the lemons and spices to extract some of their juices and top off with the remaining lemon juice. Seal the jar with a lid and transfer to the refrigerator. Refrigerate for at least 5 days before using. Store any leftovers in the refrigerator submerged in the salty lemon juice for up to 2 months.

MAKES 12 PIECES

raw strawberry
GINGER CITRUS MARMALADE

Growing up in the '80s meant PB&J on stale bread at lunch. (My father called my mother's sandwiches "Wish Sandwiches" because he wished for something else.) This marmalade takes sandwiches (and snacks) to a whole new level. Add a dollop to my grain-free crackers (pages 156–162) or toasted gluten-free whole-grain bread with my Dairy-Free Creamy Cashew Cheese (page 308) for a pleasant surprise. Dates make a fun replacement for refined sugar; be sure to soak them in hot water first to ensure they whip up smoothly.

2	cups fresh strawberries, hulled and quartered
½	cup pitted Medjool dates, soaked in hot water for 10 minutes and drained
2	tablespoons minced orange peel
2	teaspoons peeled finely grated fresh ginger

Combine all the ingredients in a food processor and process until smooth. Store in a sealed container in the refrigerator for up to 2 days.

MAKES 2 CUPS

zesty
ORANGE MARMALADE

Adding vanilla extract to marmalade takes it from ordinary to extraordinary. You'll also taste the yummy difference when the refined sugar gets swapped out for honey. Serve over my grain-free crackers (pages 156–162) for a fun snack.

3	large oranges
½	cup freshly squeezed orange juice
½	cup honey
1	teaspoon pure vanilla extract

Peel the oranges and cut the peels into thin matchsticks. Cut away any remaining white membranes on the oranges and discard. Pull apart the orange segments and combine them with the matchstick peels and orange juice in a medium saucepan. Cover and bring the marmalade to a boil over medium-high heat. Reduce the heat and simmer for 15 minutes. Turn off the heat and, let the marmalade cool in the saucepan. Transfer to the refrigerator and chill, covered, for 8 hours or up to 1 day.

Remove the marmalade from the refrigerator and stir in the honey and vanilla. Bring to a boil over medium heat, stirring often. Cook until the marmalade thickens enough to coat the back of a wooden spoon, about 30 minutes. Let cool on the counter. Transfer to a glass jar with a lid and store in the refrigerator for up to 3 weeks.

MAKES 1 CUP

rosemary
PLUM JAM

This sweet jam has the consistency of apple butter and a surprising, palate-pleasing hint of rosemary and cardamom. Serve over gluten-free whole-grain toast or my grain-free crackers (pages 156–162).

1	cup dried plums
1	cup water
1	tablespoon balsamic vinegar
1	teaspoon freshly squeezed lemon juice
1	teaspoon finely chopped fresh rosemary
½	teaspoon ground cardamom
½	teaspoon freshly grated lemon zest
½	teaspoon pure maple syrup

In a medium saucepan, combine all the ingredients and bring to a boil over medium heat. Reduce the heat and simmer until the plums are very soft and tender, about 14 minutes.

Transfer the mixture to a blender and puree until smooth and creamy. Pour into a glass jar with a lid and chill in the refrigerator for at least 2 hours or overnight. Serve chilled. Keep for up to 2 weeks in the refrigerator.

MAKES 1 CUP

chia seed
BERRY JAM

As this jam sits in its jar for a couple of hours, the chia seeds will gel, thickening the ingredients into a spreadable mix. Serve with my dairy-free nut cheeses (pages 307–310) on top of gluten-free whole-grain toast.

1	cup frozen blackberries
½	cup frozen raspberries
2½	tablespoons raw honey, plus more as needed
2	tablespoons freshly squeezed lemon juice
1¾	tablespoons chia seeds

In a small saucepan over low heat, combine the blackberries, raspberries, honey, and lemon juice. Mix well, breaking up the berries with the back of a spoon as the mixture warms and becomes thicker, 12 to 15 minutes. Add more honey if the jam is too tart for your liking.

Stir in the chia seeds and continue to mix until fully incorporated, about 2 minutes. Let cool. Transfer the mixture to a large glass jar with a lid. Refrigerate for 2 hours or overnight. Store in the refrigerator for up to 2 weeks or until ready to serve.

MAKES ABOUT 1 CUP

easy no-foil
ROASTED GARLIC

Use these tender and flavorful roasted cloves spread on gluten-free whole-grain toast or my grain-free crackers (pages 156–162); added to mashed sweet potatoes, gluten-free whole-grain pasta, roasted veggies, or veggie burgers; served as a pizza topping for my gluten-free pizza crusts (pages 234, 235, and 236); or tossed into a salad and mixed with extra-virgin olive oil to create a flavorful garlic-infused oil.

2	heads garlic
1	tablespoon extra-virgin olive oil
¼	teaspoon sea salt
	Pinch dried rosemary

Preheat the oven to 400°F.

Slice the tops off each garlic head. Drizzle the oil onto the exposed cloves, and then sprinkle with the salt and rosemary. Roast for 20 to 25 minutes, or until golden brown and tender. Let cool for 5 minutes before serving warm.

MAKES 2 HEADS

sweets and treats

We could all do with a little less of the sweet stuff, but kicking your sugar cravings can be rough—especially if you don't have any healthy alternatives to satisfy your sweet tooth. Fortunately, there's a better way to do it than succumbing to sweetened sawdust treats that leave you slumped in a sugar coma.

Desserts are traditionally nutrient-deficient foods, filled with little more than flour, sugar, and dairy. I've designed every one of my desserts without all-purpose flour, white flour, refined sugar, high-fructose corn syrup, xanthan gum, guar gum, soy, gluten, dairy, eggs, preservatives, unhealthy fats, colorings, and any other fake ingredients. Instead, they contain nutrient-rich ingredients like almond flour, cacao powder, coconut, flaxseeds, chia seeds, and hemp seeds, which add flavor and texture.

No refined sugar means no sugar rush and no crash, making these must-have desserts perfect for an after-dinner treat. They also work great as crowd-pleasers at parties. (I always like to tell people what's not in these desserts after they've taken a bite—the looks on their faces are priceless!) If you're a real sugar hound, you can increase the sweetness using any of the approved sweeteners (see page 27), such as unsweetened cocoa powder, honey, pure maple syrup, fresh fruits, coconut, and fresh citrus juices.

That means the sweet ending to your meal won't leave you feeling full, bloated, and sleepy—in fact, it will contribute to the healthy nutritional profile of your meal. (Try doing that, store-bought cake!)

Rest assured, I've used only organic honey, dates, and pure maple syrup to sweeten up the recipes here. (They are detox approved—see page 27). These recipes contain lots of protein, fiber, and nutrients, so they're a lot better than what you'll find in a package—but still, I encourage you to eat them in moderation, not after every meal. (See page 25 to learn about the differences between naturally occurring sugars and added ones like high-fructose corn syrup.)

Before we get started, let me remind you of a few things.

SKIP THE "SUGAR-FREE" LABEL

If you're trying to ease off the sweets, avoid the siren call of "sugar-free" treats. Trust me here. This is not the way to go. Artificial sugars such as aspartame, saccharin, and sucralose are chemically manufactured science projects; they don't grow from the ground.

I was once a heavy user of those light blue, pretty pink, and buttercup yellow "fake" sugar packets, because I had no idea they were bad for me. I was sold by the ads ("made from real sugar!") and thought that if the government said it was safe to eat, it was.

That's a laugh! When a label reads "sugar-free," what it should say loud and clear is "chemical sweetener," because that's what it is. There are a range of conflicting reports on what these chemicals can do to us, but what I do know is that when your body craves something sweet and you fake it out with something synthetic, it's not falling for it, and your cravings actually get worse. My advice? Read the labels and avoid Splenda, NutraSweet, Equal, Sweet'N Low, and all the other lab-made sweeteners. They may not add calories, but calories are not evil. I'd rather have a little organic honey or pure maple syrup than a packet of chemicals (Note: Stevia, which is made from a plant and given the green light by lots of nutritionists and health experts, is also highly

processed in most cases—so bear that in mind. Only some products use pure stevia extract, therefore I did not use stevia in any of my recipes.) Don't be shy when cutting out sugar. Try these healthy sugar substitutes: unsweetened cocoa powder, fresh carrot juice, fresh citrus juices such as lemon, grapefruit, and orange, nut or seed butters, unsweetened coconut flakes, fresh coconut meat, rosewater, cacao powder, fruit purees and sulfur-free dried fruits such as dates, apricots, cranberries, and cherries.

THE LOWDOWN ON SUGAR

Even if you never touch a sugar bowl, you're likely taking in far more sugar than you realize in packaged processed products—everything from white flours, breads, and pastas to drinks (especially cocktails!), sauces, condiments, and anything else you get out of a bottle or box.

Highly refined sugars have an inflammatory effect on the body, and inflammation is the precursor to disease. They also feed the bad bacteria in your gut (and you already know almost 80 percent of your immune system is in your gut), so lay off the sugar for a healthy immune system. Not only will you pack on the pounds, but you can also disrupt and burden your body's organs and natural rhythm.

Fight sugar cravings with protein and healthy fats. Enjoy good fats—including raw nuts and seeds (which also contain protein), extra-virgin olive oil, full-fat coconut milk, coconut oil, and avocados—at each meal and snack. If you feel lousy when you go off sugar, it may be that you've formed a dependency on it or have a sensitivity to it that you never realized. Be patient with yourself. After a few days of eating clean, you'll feel more energized and alert. Don't forget: You created those cravings through habitual eating, and therefore, you can undo it.

For more helpful tips on how to detox your sugar intake and battle your cravings, see page 51.

IRRESISTIBLE DAIRY-FREE ICE CREAM RULES OF THUMB

› Before serving, remove the ice cream from the freezer and let it sit out for 5 minutes before scooping.

› To keep your ice cream really fresh and minimize freezer burn, add a layer of wax paper or parchment paper on top and cover before freezing.

› Important! Remember to put the ice cream machine bowl in the freezer the night before you make your ice cream. The ice cream base must be made at least 4 hours to 1 day before churning.

PERFECT PUMPKIN GELATO

This gelato tastes like a pumpkin pie—the flavor is spot on!

2	(13.5-ounce) BPA-free cans full-fat culinary coconut milk, well shaken and divided
½	cup honey
½	cup store-bought pureed pumpkin (from a BPA-free can)
1	tablespoon pure maple syrup
2	teaspoons pure vanilla extract
1½	teaspoons ground cinnamon
1½	teaspoons ground ginger
⅛	teaspoon ground allspice
⅛	teaspoon ground cloves
⅛	teaspoon ground nutmeg

At least 4 hours (or up to 1 day) before churning, make the ice cream base: Measure out ½ cup of the coconut milk and store for later use in another recipe or discard. In a large saucepan, whisk together the remaining coconut milk, honey, pumpkin, maple syrup, vanilla, cinnamon, ginger, allspice, cloves, and nutmeg.

Heat over medium-high heat, bringing the mixture to a low boil, stirring occasionally. Reduce the heat to medium-low and cook, stirring occasionally, until the mixture becomes thick enough to coat the back of a wooden spoon, 15 to 18 minutes. Transfer to a heatproof glass bowl and lay a piece of wax paper over the top to prevent a film from forming. Let the mixture cool on the countertop for 20 minutes. Transfer to the refrigerator and chill for 4 hours or overnight.

Remove the ice cream base from the refrigerator. The mixture should appear thick, like pudding. Pour the base into an ice cream maker and churn according to the manufacturer's instructions. Keep an eye on it! The ice cream is ready when it looks like soft-serve yogurt. Serve immediately, or store in a sealed container in the freezer for up to 1 week.

MAKES ABOUT 2½ CUPS

VANILLA BEAN COCONUT
ice cream

This vanilla bean ice cream is a great base for a variety of flavors. Stir in your favorite jam, dairy-free semisweet chocolate chips, unsweetened cocoa powder, Carefree Chocolate Sauce (page 367), or other dessert sauce or jam—any sweet ingredients or flavorings you like will work.

2   (13.5-ounce) BPA-free cans full-fat culinary coconut milk, well shaken

½   cup raw honey

1   teaspoon pure vanilla extract

1   vanilla bean, sliced in half, beans scraped out and pods reserved

At least 4 hours (or up to 1 day) before churning, make the ice cream base: In a large saucepan, whisk together the coconut milk, honey, vanilla extract, and vanilla bean seeds. Toss the vanilla bean pods into the mixture. Heat over medium-high heat and bring the mixture to a low boil, stirring occasionally. Reduce the heat to medium-low and cook, stirring occasionally, until the mixture becomes thick enough to coat the back of a wooden spoon, about 15 minutes. Transfer to a heatproof glass bowl and lay a piece of wax paper over the top to prevent a film from forming. Let the mixture cool on the countertop for 20 minutes. Transfer to the refrigerator and chill for 4 hours or overnight.

Remove the ice cream base from the refrigerator, discard the vanilla bean pod, and whisk a few times to blend. The mixture should appear thick, like a pudding. Pour the base into an ice cream maker and churn according to the manufacturer's instructions. Keep an eye on it! The ice cream is ready when it looks like soft-serve yogurt. If you're adding any flavorings, do so during the last 30 seconds of churning. Serve immediately, or store in a sealed container in the freezer for up to 1 week.

MAKES ABOUT 2½ CUPS

TOASTED COCONUT MACADAMIA
NUT BUTTER DRIZZLE
with stone fruit

This drizzle is a great alternative to peanut butter and can be served with fruits.
Try it with sliced apples or peaches on gluten-free whole-grain toast. You can change this recipe up,
too: nutmeg, cardamom, and allspice can all be substituted for cinnamon if you like.
Note: It's best to use a high-speed blender for this recipe.

3	cups unsweetened coconut flakes
¾	cup raw macadamia nuts
¼	teaspoon ground cinnamon
	Pinch sea salt
	Stone fruit, such as peaches, for serving
	Finely chopped fresh basil, for garnish, optional

In a large, dry pan, toast the coconut flakes over medium-low heat until fragrant and golden brown, 2 to 3 minutes. Transfer to a blender. Let the pan cool and, using a paper towel, wipe out any remaining coconut flakes.

In the same large pan, toast the macadamia nuts over medium-low heat until fragrant and golden brown, 4 to 5 minutes. Add the macadamia nuts, cinnamon, and salt to the blender. Cover and start blending on a low speed. Gradually increase the speed until the mixture is ultra-smooth, about 10 minutes. Stop the blender occasionally to stir and scrape down the sides. The drizzle will be done when thin and liquefied. Strain to remove any small bits.

Serve immediately over the stone fruit, garnished with basil, if desired. Store leftover drizzle in a sealed container at room temperature for up to 1 week (the mixture will separate; just stir before using).

MAKES ¾ TO 1 CUP

GORGEOUS GINGER ICE CREAM

Ginger lovers, you're in for a treat. Using a combination of fresh and dried ginger gives this ice cream an intense ginger flavor. The trick with this ice cream is letting the ginger steep to really extract the flavor for your ice cream base. This ice cream can be a summer cooler during hot nights, or pair it with your favorite pumpkin dessert to ring in the holidays. It's super creamy and I guarantee you won't miss the dairy.

2   (13.5-ounce) BPA-free cans full-fat culinary coconut milk, well shaken

½   cup raw honey

2   teaspoons ground ginger

1½   teaspoons pure vanilla extract

     4-inch piece fresh ginger, peeled and sliced

     Coconut flakes, toasted (see page 114), for garnish, optional

WET WALNUTS Goes well with any of my dairy-free ice creams (pages 334–339).

Makes ½ cup

¼   cup roughly chopped raw walnuts
¼   cup pure maple syrup

In a glass jar with a lid, combine the walnuts and maple syrup, stirring to coat. Set aside at room temperature for at least 1 hour before serving. Cover with the lid and store in the refrigerator for up to 3 weeks. Bring to room temperature before serving.

At least 4 hours (or up to 1 day) before churning, make the ice cream base: In a large saucepan, whisk together the coconut milk, honey, ground ginger, and vanilla. Add the sliced ginger and stir. Heat over medium-high heat, bringing the mixture to a low boil, stirring occasionally. Reduce the heat to medium-low and cook, stirring occasionally, until the mixture becomes thick enough to coat the back of a wooden spoon, about 15 minutes. Transfer to a heatproof glass bowl and lay a piece of wax paper over the top to prevent a film from forming. Let the mixture cool on the countertop for 20 minutes. Transfer to the refrigerator and chill for 4 hours or overnight.

Remove the ice cream base from the refrigerator, strain into a medium bowl, and discard the ginger slices. The mixture should appear thick, like pudding. Pour the base into an ice cream maker and churn according to the manufacturer's instructions. Keep an eye on it! The ice cream is ready when it looks like soft-serve yogurt. Serve immediately, with toasted coconut, if desired, or store in a sealed container in the freezer for up to 1 week.

MAKES ABOUT 2½ CUPS

BERRY CRUMBLE À LA MODE ICE CREAM

This tastes just like the kind of decadent sundae you'd get at a traditional ice cream shop. I make it in a terrine by layering the flavors so each scoop is a burst of flavor. The crumble topping—it's gluten-free—can be made up to three days in advance. The sauce, which contains no added sugar, can be made up to two days in advance.

Vanilla Bean Coconut Ice Cream (page 334)

BERRY-LICIOUS SAUCE

¼ cup blackberries

¼ cup raspberries

¼ cup dried currants

¼ cup water

BERRY CRUMBLE

2 tablespoons gluten-free oat flour, store-bought or homemade (see page 39)

2 tablespoons gluten-free rolled oats

½ teaspoon melted coconut oil

½ teaspoon raw honey

¼ teaspoon ground cinnamon

Pinch sea salt

HOW TO MELT COCONUT OIL

Coconut oil is solid at room temperature. It's possible to melt it in a warm spot on your kitchen counter or on top of your stove without turning on the heat or burner. If neither of those methods work, you can melt the coconut oil in a pot on the stovetop over low heat.

MAKE THE SAUCE: In a small saucepan, combine all the sauce ingredients and bring to a simmer over medium-low heat. While the berries are simmering, crush them using the back of a spoon. Cook until the sauce becomes thick enough to coat the back of a wooden spoon, about 15 minutes. Let cool. Transfer to a sealed container and refrigerate until completely chilled, about 4 hours.

MAKE THE BERRY CRUMBLE: Preheat the oven to 350°F. Line a rimmed baking sheet with parchment paper.

In a small bowl, combine the oat flour, oats, oil, honey, cinnamon, and salt; stir to combine. Spread the oat mixture on the prepared baking sheet and bake for 12 minutes or until light golden brown, stirring halfway through the baking. The mixture will feel wet coming out of the oven, but will harden when it cools. Let cool for 20 minutes. Transfer to a sealed container until ready to use.

Spoon a few tablespoons of the Berry-licious Sauce into the bottom of a quart-size, freezer-safe container. Top with a layer of the Vanilla Bean Coconut Ice Cream, sprinkle with a desired amount of the Berry Crumble, and repeat. Continue layering, using as much of the crumble mixture as you like (you'll use up all the sauce and ice cream, but you may have some of the crumble left over). Lay a sheet of wax paper or parchment paper on top and transfer the container to the freezer. Freeze for at least 4 hours before serving.

MAKES 2 CUPS; MAKES ABOUT 1 CUP SAUCE

west coast
VANILLA MANGO POPSICLES

These summertime pops are refreshing and colorful. Their natural sweetness is delicious.
If your mango is really ripe and sweet, you don't need to add the honey, but if your mango is tart,
drizzle in a bit of sweet honey to balance the flavors. You can omit the cinnamon and use lime juice
instead of lemon juice for a fun variation.

1½ cups chopped fresh mango

1 cup unsweetened almond milk

¼ cup freshly squeezed lemon juice

1 teaspoon pure vanilla extract

¼ teaspoon sea salt

Pinch ground cinnamon

Honey, optional

Combine all the ingredients except the honey, if using, in a blender, and puree until smooth. Taste for sweetness and add honey, if desired (start with 1 teaspoon). Pour into popsicle molds and freeze until set, at least 4 hours.

Remove from the freezer and run molds under warm water for 30 seconds to remove popsicles. Serve immediately.

MAKES 4 LARGE POPSICLES

coconut milk
RASPBERRY BASIL POPSICLES

Summer isn't the same without pretty popsicles. I loved popsicles as a child, but was shocked recently by the ingredient list on the box—so I started making my own! These are surprisingly delicious without being overly sweet. The basil almost makes them a little savory, but still super tasty.

1   (13.5-ounce) BPA-free can full-fat culinary coconut milk, well shaken

1   cup frozen raspberries

1   tablespoon finely chopped fresh basil

1   tablespoon plus ¼ teaspoon raw honey

Pinch sea salt

Combine all the ingredients in a blender and blend until very smooth. Divide the mixture among six popsicle molds, tapping the molds on the counter to remove any air bubbles. Freeze until solid, about 8 hours. Store any leftover mixture in a sealed container in the refrigerator for 3 days and refill the popsicle molds as needed.

Remove from the freezer and run the molds under warm water for 30 seconds to remove the popsicles. Serve immediately.

MAKES ABOUT 6 POPSICLES

HOW TO FREEZE BERRIES   Cranberries and blueberries can go in the freezer in a sealed jar. Delicate raspberries, blackberries, and hulled strawberries should be spread out in a single layer on a large rimmed baking sheet and then placed in the freezer. When frozen, transfer to sealed glass containers. If a recipe calls for thawed berries, you can have them sit out at room temperature for 45 minutes, and then transfer to a colander set over a bowl to drain; save the juice and use for flavoring seltzer water.

playful
OATY GRANOLA CLUSTERS

I thought I'd see if I could make a version of my favorite gluten-free oatmeal into a fun,
bite-size, protein-packed granola that's chunky and healthy to munch on as a snack or dessert.
You can travel with these clusters in a small container, or toss a few into a bowl of dairy-free ice cream
(pages 334–339) for a fun and crunchy fiber-rich topping!

2	teaspoons coconut oil
3¼	cups gluten-free rolled oats
1	cup almond butter
¾	cup dried cherries, chopped
½	cup raw walnuts, chopped and toasted (see page 108)
⅓	cup raw almonds, chopped and toasted (see page 108)
6	tablespoons pure maple syrup
	Pinch sea salt

Preheat the oven to 350°F. Coat two large rimmed baking sheets with the oil.

In a medium bowl, combine the oats, almond butter, cherries, walnuts, almonds, maple syrup, and salt. Mix well. Divide the mixture between the prepared baking sheets. Press down with your hands to create a flat layer.

Bake for 10 minutes. Lower the oven temperature to 325°F and bake for another 30 minutes, or until golden brown, stirring halfway through to ensure even browning. Remove from the oven and let cool for 15 to 20 minutes. Use your hands to break apart the oats into clusters. Keep the clusters in a sealed container for up to 5 days.

MAKES ABOUT 3½ CUPS

EASY RAW CHOCOLATE COCONUT BANANA TART
with amie's grain-free pie crust

Chocolate, coconut, and bananas like you've never seen them before. This is my favorite summer dessert that I serve to my family at the shore!

AMIE'S GRAIN-FREE PIE CRUST

2½	cups raw almonds
1	cup pitted Medjool dates
1	tablespoon water
1	teaspoon pure vanilla extract
	Pinch sea salt

COCONUT BANANA TART

5	ripe medium bananas, cut into ½-inch pieces
1	cup well-shaken full-fat culinary coconut milk
¼	cup unsweetened cocoa powder
1½	teaspoons pure vanilla extract
1	teaspoon raw honey
¼	cup chopped or slivered raw almonds
2	tablespoons raw cacao nibs

MAKE THE CRUST: Place the almonds in a food processor and process until coarsely chopped. With the machine still running, add the dates, water, vanilla, and salt until it forms a sticky dough. Stop the machine and scrape down the sides as needed to help the almond mixture process easily to form a doughlike consistency.

Firmly press the crust mixture into a parchment paper–lined 8x8-inch baking or tart pan to form a thick crust on the bottom and up the four sides of the pan.

MAKE THE TART: Combine the bananas, coconut milk, cocoa powder, vanilla, and honey in a blender; puree until smooth. Pour the mixture over the pie crust. Sprinkle with the almonds and cacao nibs. Cover with wax or parchment paper and freeze for at least 8 hours or overnight.

Thaw the tart on the counter until it's soft enough to cut into 9 squares, at least 45 minutes. Store leftover squares in a sealed container in the freezer for up to 4 days.

MAKES 9 SQUARES

lighthearted
RAW GRAIN-FREE FUDGY BROWNIES

Loaded with flavor, these brownies are soaring with protein! They're rich and delightful, so easy to make, and they pair well with my Blissful Dessert Cashew Cream (page 365), or my delicious dairy-free ice creams (pages 334–339).

1½	cups almond butter
½	cup unsweetened cocoa powder
½	cup pure maple syrup
5	tablespoons unsweetened almond milk
3	tablespoons melted coconut oil
1½	teaspoons pure vanilla or almond extract
¼	teaspoon sea salt
¼	teaspoon ground cinnamon
	Pinch cayenne pepper
2	tablespoons raw cacao nibs, for garnish
	Flaky sea salt, for garnish

Line an 8x8-inch baking dish with parchment paper.

Place all the ingredients except the cacao nibs and flaky sea salt in a food processor; process until the mixture is well combined and forms a dough. Spoon the mixture into the prepared baking dish. Top with the cacao nibs and flaky sea salt. Cover with wax paper and freeze until set, about 2 hours. Cut into 12 squares. Store in the freezer until ready to serve or for up to 4 days.

MAKES 12 SQUARES

EVERYTHING-BUT-THE-GLUTEN COOKIES

These cookies are crunchy, delicious, and toasty-tasting when baked, but they can also be eaten raw if you are in a rush. If you can't find cashew butter, you can use additional almond butter as a substitute.

½   cup gluten-free oat flour, store-bought or homemade (see page 39)

½   cup white sesame seeds

½   cup sliced raw almonds

¼   cup ground flaxseeds

3   tablespoons poppy seeds

1   tablespoon finely chopped fresh rosemary

1   teaspoon unsweetened shredded coconut, optional

¼   teaspoon ground cinnamon

¼   teaspoon sea salt

½   cup cashew butter

½   cup almond butter

½   cup pure maple syrup

In a large bowl, combine the oat flour, sesame seeds, almonds, flaxseeds, poppy seeds, rosemary, coconut (if using), cinnamon, and salt; mix well. Stir in the cashew butter, almond butter, and maple syrup. Transfer to the refrigerator and chill for 45 minutes.

Remove the cookie dough from the refrigerator and, using your hands, shape the mixture into 1½-inch round balls. Serve raw or bake in the oven. To serve these cookies raw, store in the fridge on two large rimmed baking sheets lined with parchment paper until ready to serve. To bake in the oven, preheat the oven to 350°F. Line two large rimmed baking sheets with parchment paper. Place the balls on the baking sheets 2 inches apart. Gently flatten by pressing down on each ball with the back of a fork. Bake for about 25 minutes, or until golden brown. Remove from the oven and let cool for at least 15 minutes before serving. Store leftover cookies in a sealed container in the refrigerator for up to 4 days.

MAKES 18 COOKIES

GOT A TUMMY ACHE? Wanna know why? Artificial sweeteners are often used in combination with sugar alcohols, such as sorbitol, mannitol, glycerol, maltitol, and others. These fake sweeteners don't get absorbed because they're not technically digested. That means they can sit in our digestive tract for a long time, causing tummy trouble. Better alternatives: Use natural forms of sweetness such as organic honey and pure maple syrup, in moderation.

authentic
CHOCOLATE ALMOND BUTTER BANANA COOKIES

Another protein-rich cookie that tastes more than good! This is an easy recipe to make on a weeknight when you want a little something sweet and delicious. The key to a good banana cookie is to let the bananas really ripen so they're 75 percent spotted or black. My friends beg me to make these every time we get together. I know you'll love them.

1	tablespoon ground flaxseeds
3	tablespoons water
2	large very ripe bananas
½	cup almond butter
2	tablespoons pure maple syrup
1	tablespoon melted coconut oil
1	teaspoon pure vanilla extract
2½	cups gluten-free rolled oats
½	cup gluten-free dairy-free semisweet chocolate chips
½	teaspoon aluminum-free baking powder
½	teaspoon ground cinnamon
¼	teaspoon ground cardamom
	Pinch sea salt

Preheat the oven to 350°F.

In a small bowl, combine the flaxseeds and water. Let sit for 5 minutes.

In a small bowl, mash the bananas with a fork. Stir in the almond butter, maple syrup, oil, and vanilla. Add the flaxseed mixture and mix well to combine.

In a medium bowl, combine the oats, chocolate chips, baking powder, cinnamon, cardamom, and salt. Fold the dry ingredients into the wet ingredients and gently stir until just combined (don't overmix).

Using a tablespoon, drop small mounds (about 2 tablespoons each) of cookie dough onto a rimmed baking sheet. Bake for 12 to 14 minutes, or until golden brown and set. Remove the cookies from the oven and let sit for 5 minutes. Transfer to a wire rack to cool before serving.

MAKES 20 COOKIES

hempy cocoa
COCONUT TRUFFLES

When a chocolate craving strikes, these bite-size treats make a fun snack or dessert. Protein, fiber, anti-inflammatory omega-3 fatty acids, and a whole lot more, whipped into a decadent truffle!

14	Medjool dates, pitted and diced
¼	cup shelled raw hemp seeds
¼	cup unsweetened shredded coconut
1	tablespoon unsweetened cocoa powder
¼	teaspoon Himalayan pink salt
	Pinch ground ginger

In a large bowl, combine all the ingredients. Using your hands, mix until the ingredients stick together like dough, about 2 minutes.

Wet your hands, pull off pieces of the dough, and roll them into 1-inch balls. Continue to wet your hands as needed to prevent sticking. Place in the refrigerator for at least 20 minutes or until ready to serve. Serve chilled.

MAKES 10 TRUFFLES

happy lemon
COCONUT BALLS

These irresistible treats are similar to truffles and make a fun protein snack or dessert. They're nice to serve with tea, for the holidays, and at small gatherings like bridal showers or luncheons.

1⅓	cups unsweetened coconut flakes
½	cup ground raw macadamia nuts
½	cup ground raw almonds
3	tablespoons coconut oil
3	tablespoons raw honey
3	tablespoons freshly squeezed lemon juice
½	teaspoon pure almond extract
¼	teaspoon sea salt

Combine all the ingredients in a food processor and pulse carefully. You want a smooth texture, but not a nut-butter consistency. Transfer to a large bowl. Using your hands, shape the dough into small ¾- to 1-inch balls. Let chill in the refrigerator for 1 hour or until ready to serve. Serve chilled.

MAKES 20 BALLS

mini raw and grain-free
RASPBERRY THUMBPRINT COOKIES

These are so pretty and can be played up in many ways with jam. The raspberry flavor reminds me of a linzer cookie, but you could use strawberry, apricot, or black currant jam, if desired. Serve these at a holiday party, or make them just to have as a healthier cookie alternative in your kitchen.

²/₃ cup raw cashews

3 tablespoons plus 1 teaspoon brewed rooibos tea

2 tablespoons melted coconut oil

2 Medjool dates, pitted

¼ teaspoon pure vanilla or almond extract

¼ teaspoon sea salt

¾ cup gluten-free rolled oats

Chia Seed Berry Jam (page 329)

Combine the cashews, tea, oil, dates, vanilla, and salt in a food processor and process until well mixed. Add the oats and process until it forms a dough. Using your hands, roll the dough into 14 tiny balls. Place them on a parchment paper–lined rimmed baking sheet and gently press your thumb in the center of each ball to make an indentation. Transfer to the refrigerator and chill for at least 3 hours, or until firm.

Remove the baking sheet from the refrigerator. Fill in the cookie indentations you made with your thumb with the Chia Seed Berry Jam. Store the cookies in a sealed container in the refrigerator for up to 4 days.

MAKES 14 COOKIES

delightful
ALMOND BUTTER CUPS

Better than a traditional peanut butter cup, these will truly satisfy your sweet tooth. Make sure to store these cups in the freezer until ready to serve because they will melt quickly. A few variations to try:
For a floral taste, top each cup with a few buds of dried lavender prior to freezing.
Substitute pure almond extract, orange blossom water, or rose water for the vanilla.
Play around with your gourmet salts and rather than mixing in the sea salt, add a sprinkle of flavored sea salt to the top of each cup. Try: fleur de sel or black sea salts.

½   cup melted coconut oil

½   cup almond butter

½   cup unsweetened cocoa powder

¼   cup raw honey

1½   teaspoons pure vanilla extract

     Pinch ground cinnamon

     Sea salt, to taste

Line a mini muffin tin with 20 mini paper muffin liners.

In a large bowl, whisk together all the ingredients until the mixture is smooth and thin. Pour the batter into the liners and place the tin in the freezer for 1 hour, or until set. Keep frozen until a few minutes before serving. To store, layer the cups with parchment paper in a sealed container and place in the freezer until ready to serve.

MAKES 20 MINI CUPS

BEST FRIEND BARS

By far one of my favorite recipes in this book! They're great to serve as granola bar snacks during the day, or for an after-dinner sweet treat. Chewy and wholesome, these babies are like my best friends—they make me smile. Wrap the bars in wax paper if packing these to go. To bring out more flavor, sprinkle a pinch of flaky sea salt on top before taking a bite.

2	cups gluten-free rolled oats
1	cup pitted Medjool dates, chopped
1	cup cashew butter
½	cup dried cherries, chopped
½	cup sliced raw almonds
½	cup shelled raw pumpkin seeds
1	tablespoon sesame seeds
1	teaspoon ground cinnamon
¼	teaspoon sea salt
½	cup raw honey
¼	cup coconut oil

Preheat the oven to 350°F. Line a rimmed baking sheet with parchment paper.

In a large bowl, combine the oats, dates, cashew butter, cherries, almonds, pumpkin seeds, sesame seeds, cinnamon, and salt.

In a small saucepan, heat the honey and oil over low heat until melted, about 1 minute. Pour over the oat mixture and mix well to combine. Transfer to the prepared baking sheet and use a spatula to flatten the mixture and give it a smooth surface. Bake for 20 minutes, or until golden brown.

Let cool for 20 minutes on the counter. Place in the refrigerator until firm, about 30 minutes. Slice into 24 bars and serve. Store leftover bars in a sealed container in the refrigerator for up to 1 week.

MAKES 24 BARS

grain-free
NUTTY APPLE PEAR CRUMBLE

*Diving into a delicious baked crumble without grains is a healthy and light way to end your day.
I like to use a variety of apples for the best flavor. You can try a mix of Granny Smith, Gala, and Honeycrisp
apples. Add a large dollop (or two) of my Lovely Cashew Almond Cream—proof positive
you don't need dairy or grains for a delectable dessert.*

2	tablespoons melted coconut oil, plus more for coating pie pan
4	apples, peeled, cored, and cut into ¼-inch slices
3	pears, peeled, cored, and cut into ¼-inch slices
¼	cup freshly squeezed orange juice
5	tablespoons raw honey, melted, divided
1	tablespoon pure maple syrup
2½	teaspoons ground cinnamon
	Pinch ground allspice
1	cup almond flour, store-bought or homemade (see page 39)
6	tablespoons finely chopped raw walnuts, divided
	Lovely Cashew Almond Cream (page 365)

Preheat the oven to 350°F. Lightly coat a 10-inch pie pan with oil.

In a large bowl, combine the apples, pears, orange juice, 2 tablespoons of the honey, the maple syrup, cinnamon, and allspice. Gently toss to coat the apples and pears with the liquid mixture. Transfer the mixture to the prepared pie pan and place on top of a large rimmed baking sheet to catch any drippings. Bake for 40 minutes or until golden brown.

Meanwhile, in a large bowl, combine the almond flour, 4 tablespoons of the walnuts, the remaining 3 tablespoons honey, and the oil; mix well. When the fruit mixture is done baking, crumble the almond flour mixture on top. Return the pie pan to the oven and bake for another 15 to 20 minutes, or until golden brown. Remove from the oven and top with a large dollop of the Lovely Cashew Almond Cream and the remaining 2 tablespoons walnuts. Serve warm.

SERVES 4

luxurious
CARDAMOM JASMINE RICE PUDDING

This is my heavenly dairy-free alternative to a classic dessert that I always wanted to eat during the holidays, but couldn't because it was full of cream. Serve warm or chilled.

3	cups unsweetened almond milk
1/3	cup jasmine or brown rice
	Pinch sea salt
1/2	cup pure maple syrup
1/2	cup dried cranberries or roughly chopped dried cherries, optional
1 1/2	teaspoons pure vanilla extract
1	teaspoon unsweetened coconut flakes
1	teaspoon ground cinnamon
1/4	teaspoon ground cardamom

In a small saucepan, bring the almond milk, rice, and salt to a boil over medium-high heat. Reduce the heat to a simmer and cook, uncovered, until the rice is tender, about 25 minutes; stir often.

Stir in the maple syrup, cranberries (if using), vanilla, coconut flakes, cinnamon, and cardamom. Cook, uncovered, until thick but not dried out, 5 to 7 minutes. Serve immediately, or cover and chill in the refrigerator for 4 hours. When storing, lay a piece of wax paper on top of the pudding to prevent a film from forming.

MAKES 2 CUPS

grown-up
GRILLED BANANAS

Ooh la la! If you add my Blissful Dessert Cashew Cream (page 365), Vanilla Bean Coconut Ice Cream (page 334), and fresh cherries, this could pass as a banana split!

2 1/2	tablespoons melted coconut oil
1	tablespoon unsweetened coconut flakes
1	tablespoon ground cinnamon
1/4	teaspoon ground coriander
4	large ripe bananas
2	tablespoons shaved gluten-free dairy-free dark chocolate, optional

Preheat a grill to medium.

Place the oil on a rimmed plate and combine the coconut flakes, cinnamon, and coriander on a separate plate. Roll the bananas in the oil to coat, then dip them into the dry coconut mixture. Transfer to the grill and cook for 3 to 4 minutes. Flip and cook until grill marks appear and the bananas are tender, about 3 minutes more. Remove the bananas from the grill, transfer to a serving dish, and sprinkle with the dark chocolate, if desired. Serve warm.

SERVES 4

GRILLED BOSC PEARS
with cardamom glaze

Decadent and simple! Here's a perfect way to use those pears sitting on your countertop. The presence of cardamom and honey gives this dessert a sweet touch of flavor, and the grilled pears are warm, soft, and tender. Add a pinch of finely chopped fresh basil on top for a pop of color, if desired. This glaze is incredible when used to coat raw nuts, too.

2   ripe Bosc pears, peeled, halved, and cored, stems left intact

½   teaspoon melted coconut oil

1   tablespoon raw honey

¼   teaspoon ground cardamom

Pinch ground cinnamon

Pinch sea salt

3   tablespoons finely chopped raw macadamia nuts, for garnish

Pinch finely chopped fresh basil, for garnish, optional

Preheat a grill to medium high.

Rub the pear halves with the oil and place cut-side down on the grill. Grill until tender and soft and grill marks appear, about 20 minutes. Transfer to a serving plate.

In a small bowl, combine the honey, cardamom, cinnamon, and salt; mix well. Drizzle over the pears. Garnish with the macadamia nuts and, if desired, basil. Serve warm.

SERVES 4

BANANA BREAD

This is a classic banana bread with a touch of flavor from cocoa powder, almonds, applesauce, and sunflower seeds. It's deliciously dense and filling. Serve each slice with a spread of creamy almond butter for breakfast, as a snack, or for dessert. This low-maintenance recipe will be your new go-to dessert.

¼	cup melted coconut oil, plus more for coating loaf pan
3	large ripe bananas, mashed
¼	cup unsweetened applesauce
3	tablespoons pure maple syrup
2	teaspoons pure vanilla extract
3	cups gluten-free oat flour, store-bought or homemade (see page 39)
½	cup slivered raw almonds
¼	cup shelled raw sunflower seeds
1½	teaspoons aluminum-free baking powder
1	teaspoon unsweetened cocoa powder
1½	teaspoons ground cinnamon
1	teaspoon baking soda
½	teaspoon sea salt
	Almond butter, for serving

Preheat the oven to 350°F. Coat a loaf pan with oil.

Combine the bananas, oil, applesauce, maple syrup, and vanilla in a food processor and process until well mixed. Transfer the mixture to a large bowl.

In a medium bowl, combine the oat flour, almonds, sunflower seeds, baking powder, cocoa powder, cinnamon, baking soda, and salt. Fold the dry ingredients into the wet ingredients and gently stir until just combined (don't overmix). Transfer to the prepared loaf pan and bake for 1 hour, or until golden brown and set. Remove from the oven and let cool for at least 20 minutes before serving. Serve each slice with a spread of almond butter.

MAKES 1 LOAF

macadamia nut, carrot, and zucchini oat
BREADLESS "BREAD" PUDDING

Veggies for dessert? There's no reason why not. The combination of soft textured oats and crisp, cool zucchini and carrots with hearty macadamia nuts and sweet dried cranberries makes this dish a winner! Serve leftovers for breakfast the next morning to get you out of bed on chilly mornings.

3	tablespoons melted coconut oil, plus more for coating baking dish
1	cup raw macadamia nuts
1	tablespoon ground flaxseeds
3	tablespoons water
3	large bananas
2	cups gluten-free rolled oats
2	teaspoons ground cinnamon
1	teaspoon aluminum-free baking powder
¼	teaspoon ground nutmeg
¼	teaspoon sea salt
1¼	cups unsweetened almond milk
¼	cup pure maple syrup
1½	teaspoons pure almond extract
2	large carrots, peeled and shredded
1	small zucchini, shredded
½	cup slivered raw almonds
⅓	cup dried cranberries
	Blissful Dessert Cashew Cream (page 365)

Preheat the oven to 350°F. Lightly coat an 8x8-inch baking dish with oil.

Place the macadamia nuts on a rimmed baking sheet and toast in the oven for 5 to 10 minutes, or until golden brown and "sweating" oils. Be careful not to burn them. Let cool. Once cooled, roughly chop the nuts.

In a small bowl, combine the flaxseeds and water. Set aside for 5 minutes to form a gel.

Place the bananas in the baking dish and mash with a fork to cover the entire surface of the dish.

In a large bowl, combine the chopped macadamia nuts, oats, cinnamon, baking powder, nutmeg, and salt.

In a medium bowl, whisk together the almond milk, maple syrup, oil, flaxseed mixture, and almond extract. Fold in the carrots, zucchini, almonds, and dried cranberries. Add the wet mixture to the dry oat mixture; mix well to combine.

Pour the batter over the mashed bananas in the baking dish. Place the baking dish on a large rimmed baking sheet, then transfer to the oven. Bake for 45 minutes, or until golden brown and set. Remove from the oven and let cool for at least 15 minutes before serving so the oats can absorb any remaining liquid. Serve warm with a dollop of the Blissful Dessert Cashew Cream.

SERVES 6 TO 8

totally whipped
COCONUT WHIPPY CREAM

A whipped cream recipe without dairy and refined sugar? Yes, it's possible, and it tastes amazing. This is a genius (and super-simple) way to make the whipped goodness of the dairy-filled whipped cream that you've been missing. No belly aches or bloating with this recipe! Use it as a fancy topping for all of your favorite desserts. Serve leftover whippy cream for breakfast on top of waffles or my Graceful Banana Almond Pancakes (page 132). It also tastes lovely when dolloped on top of my Joyful Hot Cocoa (page 297). Make sure to chill your BPA-free can of culinary coconut milk overnight (at least 12 hours) before you start this recipe; this is a critical step. I often keep a few cans of BPA-free culinary coconut milk in my fridge at all times so that I have them chilled and ready for use in recipes instead of waiting for the can to chill overnight.

1   (13.5-ounce) BPA-free can full-fat culinary coconut milk, refrigerated overnight

2   tablespoons raw honey

1½ teaspoons pure vanilla extract or a small drizzle of flavored extract, such as rose or orange water

½   vanilla bean, sliced in half, scraped out and pod discarded, optional

Pinch ground cinnamon

Pinch sea salt, optional

Place the whisk of an electric mixer and the mixer bowl (or a medium bowl if you're using a hand mixer) in the freezer for 15 minutes.

Remove the coconut milk can from the refrigerator. Scoop out the thick coconut cream layer at the top of the can and discard the coconut water below (or save for another use). Transfer the coconut cream to the chilled mixer bowl. Add the honey, vanilla extract, vanilla bean seeds, if using, and cinnamon and mix on high until soft peaks form, about 8 minutes. If desired, add the salt. Serve immediately, or store in a sealed container in the refrigerator for up to 4 days. This cream will harden in the fridge, so be sure to mix it well before serving after it's chilled.

MAKES 1 CUP

blissful
DESSERT CASHEW CREAM

Rich and creamy, this dairy-free cream pairs perfectly with my Grain-Free Nutty Apple Pear Crumble (page 358) and other roasted fruit desserts. Use this cream anywhere you'd ordinarily use whipped cream. I particularly recommend it as a topping for fresh fruit—it makes the ordinary extraordinary. To create a variety of flavors, add cocoa powder, cinnamon, or another favorite spice.

1	cup raw cashews, soaked in water for 4 hours or quick soaked for 10 minutes in hot water, drained, and rinsed
½	cup water
2	tablespoons raw honey
1¼	tablespoons melted coconut oil
1½	teaspoons pure vanilla extract
	Pinch flaked sea salt
	Pinch unsweetened cocoa powder or ground cinnamon, optional

Place all the ingredients in a food processor and process until smooth and thick. The mixture will become creamy after 3 to 4 minutes. Serve chilled. Store in a sealed container in the refrigerator for up to 4 days.

MAKES 1⅓ CUPS

lovely
CASHEW ALMOND CREAM

Serve this luscious, smooth, and creamy dairy-free topping in place of dairy-filled whipped cream. The beautiful creamy consistency pairs perfectly with fresh fruits and my Lighthearted Raw Grain-Free Fudgy Brownies (page 347). I love dipping fresh strawberries into this cream for a sweet summer treat. Note: A high-speed blender is a must for this recipe.

½	cup raw whole cashews, soaked in water overnight, drained, and rinsed
½	cup raw slivered almonds, soaked in water overnight, drained, and rinsed
1	cup unsweetened almond milk
½	tablespoon pure maple syrup
½	tablespoon raw honey
½	teaspoon pure vanilla extract
⅛	teaspoon ground cinnamon
	Pinch sea salt

Place the cashews and almonds in a high-speed blender and blend until ground. Add the remaining ingredients and blend until the mixture resembles a thick cream. Store in a sealed container in the refrigerator for up to 3 days.

MAKES 1½ CUPS

extra-thick
"CHEESECAKE" CREAM

If you miss the flavor of dairy-filled cheesecake, here's a raw, vegan, dairy-free, soy-free and gluten-free dessert that will bring your taste buds back to the days of real cheesecake without the bellyache. You can serve this cream atop my Grain-Free Nutty Apple Pear Crumble (page 358) with fresh fruit.

2½	cups raw cashews, soaked in water for 2 hours or overnight, drained, rinsed, and patted dry
1	cup water
½	cup raw honey
	Pinch freshly grated lemon zest
¼	cup freshly squeezed lemon juice
1½	teaspoons pure vanilla extract
	Pinch sea salt
¼	cup melted coconut oil

Combine the cashews, water, honey, lemon zest, lemon juice, vanilla, and salt in a food processor and process until smooth, 1 to 2 minutes. While the machine is running, slowly add the coconut oil and puree until smooth. Transfer to the refrigerator and chill for 1 hour before serving. Store leftovers in a sealed container in the refrigerator for up to 4 days.

MAKES 3⅓ CUPS

SOME OTHER SERVING IDEAS...

› Strawberry Cheesecake: strawberry jam + Extra Thick "Cheesecake" Cream

› Blueberry Cheesecake: blueberry preserves + Extra Thick "Cheesecake" Cream

› Chocolate Cheesecake: unsweetened cocoa powder + Extra Thick "Cheesecake" Cream

lemon cashew
DESSERT CREAM

A touch of lemon in a dairy-free "cream" that pairs especially well with fresh berries such as straw-berries, blueberries, and raspberries. This fluffy cloud of sweetness rivals those chemically processed whipped toppings in the freezer section. It's time to rely on cashews and lemon, not chemicals, for flavor and richness in your dessert topping.

1	cup raw cashews, soaked for 2 hours or overnight, drained, rinsed, and patted dry
½	cup water
1	teaspoon freshly grated lemon zest
2½	tablespoons freshly squeezed lemon juice
2	tablespoons raw honey

Place all the ingredients in a food processor and blend until smooth and creamy, 1 to 2 minutes. Serve chilled. Store leftovers in a sealed container in the refrigerator for up to 3 days.

MAKES 2⅓ CUPS

carefree
CHOCOLATE SAUCE

Coconut oil is magical! When it's used to make this easy chocolate sauce, it hardens over ice cream— just like the magic shell sauce, but with only four ingredients. Drizzle over fresh strawberries and pineapple slices. If you spoon it over my dairy-free ice creams (pages 334–339), let it sit for a minute or two and watch it harden over your ice cream.

⅓	cup coconut oil
6	tablespoons unsweetened cocoa powder
2½	tablespoons pure maple syrup
¼	teaspoon pure vanilla extract
	Pinch sea salt

In a small saucepan, melt the oil over low heat. Remove from the heat and whisk in the cocoa pow-der, maple syrup, vanilla, and salt. Whisk until the mixture is smooth. Serve immediately. Store in a sealed container in the refrigerator for up to 2 days. If the sauce hardens, place the sealed container in a bowl of warm water and let sit for 5 minutes, stirring often, until it's smooth and silky.

MAKES ¾ CUP

VARIATIONS:

‣ Add cinnamon, cardamom, or cayenne pepper for a spicy kick.

‣ In place of vanilla extract, substitute orange or almond extract.

‣ Use high-quality cocoa powder for a truly indulgent flavor.

gianduja classic
CHOCOLATE HAZELNUT SPREAD

This Italian-inspired hazelnut spread is the real deal. Say good-bye to your jar of processed Nutella and welcome this flavorful chocloate spread into your life. It's perfect to spread onto gluten-free whole-grain toast, Graceful Banana Almond Pancakes (page 132), dairy-free ice creams (pages 334–339), and my Morning Glory Carrot Muffins (page 127). You can also serve this as a topping on gluten-free cookies and biscuits in combination with the Blissful Dessert Cashew Cream (page 365).

1³⁄₄	cups raw hazelnuts
¹⁄₂	cup melted coconut oil
2¹⁄₂	tablespoons unsweetened cocoa powder
2¹⁄₂	tablespoons raw honey
¹⁄₄	teaspoon sea salt

Preheat the oven to 350°F.

Arrange the hazelnuts in a single layer on a rimmed baking sheet and toast in the oven for 10 minutes, or until fragrant. Let cool for 10 minutes. Rub the nuts between your hands to remove the skins.

Combine the hazelnuts with the oil, cocoa powder, honey, and salt in a food processor. Puree until very smooth, 3 to 4 minutes. Store in a sealed container in the refrigerator for up to 5 days.

MAKES 1³⁄₄ CUPS

APPENDICES

2-week detox
meal plan

This 2-week detox meal plan is to help you start your 21-Day Elimination Diet so you don't feel overwhelmed trying to figure out what to eat, how to eat it, and when! You'll be resetting your body by removing foods that may be causing inflammation and unwanted symptoms. This meal plan is filled with nutrient-dense foods to help you see results, remove toxic triggers, and reverse symptoms you may be experiencing such as bloating, gas, arthritis, acne, etc. There is no calorie counting; you'll eat one serving of the suggested meal plan recipes five times a day: breakfast, snack, lunch, snack, dinner, optional dessert, and soul-warming drinks. There's a lot of variation to keep you from getting bored or wanting to jump into a bag of potato chips! Feel free to add in more veggies, if desired. Snacks, optional desserts, and beverages are on page 374. Visit TheHealthyApple.com/EatingClean for a shopping list for week one; week two; and drinks, snacks, and desserts that you can print out and bring with you to the store.

time of day	day 1	day 2	day 3	day 4	day 5	day 6	day 7
Upon Rising	Warm Cleansing Tea (page 299) or warm water with fresh lemon	Dandelion Liver Detox Tea (page 299) or warm water with fresh lemon	Warm Cleansing Tea (page 299) or warm water with fresh lemon	Dandelion Liver Detox Tea (page 299) or warm water with fresh lemon	Warm Cleansing Tea (page 299) or warm water with fresh lemon	Dandelion Liver Detox Tea (page 299) or warm water with fresh lemon	Warm Cleansing Tea (page 299) or warm water with fresh lemon
Breakfast	Detoxing Greeny-licious Juice (page 289) with Overnight Black Rice and Berry Breakfast Bowl (page 138)	Splendid Macadamia Oatmeal Skillet (page 123)	Mango and Coconut Cream Parfait (page 135)	Creamy Breakfast Chia Pudding (page 112)	Millet 'n' Veggie Breakfast Tacos: Two Ways (page 130)	Detoxing Greeny-licious Juice (page 289) and Plentiful Coconut Granola with Peaches (page 115)	Beaming Raw Pecan Walnut Plum Crumble (page 136)
Lunch	Happy Swiss Chard–Wrapped Veggie Burgers (page 232)	"Creamy" Tarragon Cauliflower Soup with Chickpeas (page 185) (leftover from Day 1)	Coastal Carrot "Fettuccine" with Sun-Dried Tomatoes and Pumpkin Seeds (page 222)	Massaged Kale Salad with Spicy Hazelnuts (page 201)	East Coast Tarragon Grapefruit Salad with Macadamia Maple Dressing (page 216)	Purifying Raw Mint Zucchini "Noodles" (page 271)	Raw Jicama Romaine Wraps with Dilly Lime Drizzle (page 170)
Dinner	"Creamy" Tarragon Cauliflower Soup (page 185)	Spicy Chili Lime Chickpeas with Cauliflower "Rice" (page 255)	No-Eggplant Garden Herb Ratatouille (page 231)	Swiss Chard–Wrapped Portobello Burgers Stuffed with Dairy-Free Creamy Cashew Cheese (page 226)	Mini Black Rice and Almond Sliders in Radicchio Cups (page 225)	Moroccan Chickpea Skillet Pizza (page 239)	Warm-hearted Swiss Chard Lentil Bake (page 243)

Detox Week 2

time of day	*day 1*	*day 2*	*day 3*	*day 4*	*day 5*	*day 6*	*day 7*
Upon Rising	Warm Cleansing Tea (page 299) or warm water with fresh lemon	Dandelion Liver Detox Tea (page 299) or warm water with fresh lemon	Warm Cleansing Tea (page 299) or warm water with fresh lemon	Dandelion Liver Detox Tea (page 299) or warm water with fresh lemon	Warm Cleansing Tea (page 299) or warm water with fresh lemon	Dandelion Liver Detox Tea (page 299) or warm water with fresh lemon	Warm Cleansing Tea (page 299) or warm water with fresh lemon
Breakfast	Overnight Black Rice and Berry Breakfast Bowl (page 138)	Mushroom, Kale, and Caramel-ized Onion Savory Oats (page 117)	Energizing Maple Cranberry Amaranth "Granola" (page 122) with almond milk and fresh fruit	Creamy Breakfast Chia Pudding (page 112)	Graceful Banana Almond Pancakes (page 132)	Egg-Free Huevos Rancheros (page 133)	Grain-Free Golden Herbes de Provence Crackers (page 161) with creamy almond butter and a sliced banana
Lunch	Incredible Cranberry Curry Waldorf Salad (page 204)	Creamy Cashew Caesar Salad with Kale (page 209)	Plentiful Cherry Tomato and Portobello Dhal (page 258) (leftover from Day 1)	Roasted Onion and Sweet Pea Salad with Fresh Mint and Creamy Almond Dressing (page 207)	Coconut Curry Carrot Soup (page 197)	Humble Sriracha Roasted Wild Rice Buddha Bowl (page 253) (leftover from Day 5)	Raw and Grain-Free Zucchini Pad Thai (page 224)
Dinner	Plentiful Cherry Tomato and Portobello Dhal (page 258)	Carefree Carrot and Brussels Sprouts Medley with Maple Cashew Dressing (page 254)	Mucho Broccoli and Delicata Squash Bowl with Tahini Dressing (page 250)	Purifying Raw Mint Zucchini "Noodles" (page 271)	Humble Sriracha Roasted Wild Rice Buddha Bowl (page 253)	Open-Faced Pumpkin Enchiladas with Moo-Free Cashew Sour Cream (page 248)	Fabulous Lemon Basil Millet Burgers with Miraculous Mango Salsa (page 229)

Here are a few of my favorite snacks, treats, and drinks to help you through your detox plan. Note that desserts and drinks are optional (only a few options have been noted below). Desserts can be enjoyed on days when you're in the mood for something sweet without falling off the detox wagon—but not every night!

	day 1	*day 2*	*day 3*	*day 4*	*day 5*	*day 6*	*day 7*
Snacks	Inspiring Raw Layered Oat Squares (page 150)	Freckled Sesame Almond Clusters (page 140) with an apple	Grain-Free Perfect Parsley Sunflower Crackers (page 156) with Oil-Free White Bean and Basil Hummus (page 302)	Blanched Sea Salt Almonds (page 142) with a handful of fresh grapes	Creamy Tahini Tzatziki (page 303) and sliced raw veggies (zucchini, cucumbers, carrots)	Morning Glory Carrot Muffins (page 127)	Grain-Free Perfect Parsley Sunflower Crackers (page 156) with Oil-Free White Bean and Basil Hummus (page 302)
Desserts (Choose Your Own Dessert-Free Nights with these 5 options)		Totally Whipped Coconut Whippy Cream (page 364) with fresh berries	Everything-but-the-Gluten Cookies (page 348)	Playful Oaty Granola Clusters (page 343)	Coconut Milk Raspberry Basil Popsicles (page 342)	Lemon Cashew Dessert Cream (page 367) with fresh berries	
Soul-Warming Drinks (Choose Your Own Evening Drinks from these 3 options)			Cleansing Detox Veggie Broth (page 194)	Caffeine-Free Chai, (page 289), served chilled or gently warmed	Dairy-Free Nut (and Seed) Mylk (page 290) with ground cinnamon, served chilled or gently warmed		

anti-inflammatory pantry list

VEGGIES (ORGANIC)

Alfalfa sprouts

Artichokes

Arugula

Asparagus

Bamboo shoots

Beet greens

Beets

Bell peppers (red, green, orange, yellow)

Bok choy and other Asian greens

Broccoli

Broccoli rabe (rapini)

Brussels sprouts

Cabbage, green and red

Carrots

Cauliflower

Celery

Celery root

Chard, all colors

Chicory

Chinese cabbage

Chives

Collard greens

Cucumbers

Daikon radishes

Dandelion greens

Endive

Escarole

Fennel

Fiddleheads

Garlic

Jerusalem artichokes (sunchokes)

Jicama

Kale, all types (curly, lacina-to, dinosaur, red, etc.)

Kohlrabi

Leeks

Lettuce, all types of deep green, bright green, and red leaf (no iceberg)

Mizuna

Mushrooms

Mustard greens

Nettles

Okra

Olives (not canned)

Onions

Radicchio

Parsnips

Pumpkin

Radish leaves

Radishes

Ramps

Rhubarb

Romaine

Rutabagas

Scallions

Sea veggies (dulse, nori, kombu, kelp, wakame)

Shallots

Spinach

Sprouts

Squash, summer and winter varieties (acorn, butternut, etc.)

Sweet potatoes

Tomatoes (considered a fruit)

Tomatillos

Turnip greens

Turnips

Watercress

Yams

Zucchini

FRUITS (ORGANIC)

Acai

Apples

Apricots

Avocados

Bananas

Blackberries

Blood oranges

Blueberries

Cantaloupes

Cherries

Coconut

Cranberries

Currants

Dates

Dried fruit without sulfur/ added sugar/additives

Figs (fresh)

Goji berries

Grapefruit

Grapes

Guava

Honeydew melon

Kiwi

Lemons

Limes

Mangoes

Muskmelon

Nectarines

Oranges

Papayas

Peaches

Pears

Persimmons

Pineapples

Plums

Pomegranates

Prunes

Quinces

Raisins

Raspberries

Star fruits

Strawberries

Tangerines

Watermelon

UNSALTED RAW NUTS AND SEEDS (ORGANIC)

Almonds

Brazil nuts

Cashews

Chia seeds

Flaxseeds, ground

Hazelnuts

Hemp seeds

Macadamia nuts

Nut and seed butters
(almond, cashew, brazil,
pecan, walnut, pumpkin,
sesame, sunflower)

Pecans

Pine nuts

Pumpkin seeds

Sesame seeds

Sunflower seeds

Tahini (sesame paste)

Walnuts

BEANS AND LEGUMES (ORGANIC)

All beans and legumes,
except peanuts, including:

Chickpeas/garbanzo beans

Lentils

Peas (green, snow, and
sugar snap)

HERBS AND SPICES (ORGANIC)

Ancho pepper, ground

Basil

Bay leaves

Black pepper, freshly
ground

Cardamom

Cayenne pepper

Celery seeds

Chervil

Chili powder

Chilies, red and green

Chipotle powder

Cilantro

Cinnamon, sticks or ground

Cloves

Coriander, ground

Cumin

Curry powder

Dill

Fennel seeds

Five-spice powder

Garam masala

Garlic, fresh

Ginger, fresh and ground

Gomasio

Lemongrass

Marjoram

Mint

Mustard powder

Mustard seeds

Nutmeg

Oregano

Paprika

Parsley

Peppercorns, red and black

Red pepper flakes, crushed

Rosemary

Saffron

Sage

Sea salt

Star anise

Tarragon

Thyme

Turmeric

CONDIMENTS (ORGANIC)

Almond yogurt

Amie's mustard recipes
(Sweet Home Honey
Mustard, page 315, and
Surprisingly Easy
Make-Your-Own Mustard,
page 313)

Amie's Easy Home-Style
Sun-Dried Tomato
Ketchup (page 315)

Avocado oil

Balsamic vinegar

Cacao nibs

Cacao powder

Chickpea miso

Cocoa powder,
unsweetened

Coconut aminos

Coconut, unsweetened
flakes and shredded

Coconut meat (fresh)

Coconut oil

Coconut yogurt

Dulse flakes

Extra-virgin olive oil

Flaxseed oil

Hemp oil

Honey, raw

Horseradish

Kimchi

Low-sodium vegetable
broth

Medjool dates

Mustard, Dijon or whole-
grain

Pickles

Pure almond extract

Pure maple syrup

Pure vanilla extract

Raw unfiltered apple cider
vinegar

Red wine vinegar

Salsa

Sauerkraut

Seriously Sensational
Sriracha Sauce (page 318)
or hot sauce

Tomatoes, sun-dried or
in a glass jar

White wine vinegar

SUPERFOODS (ORGANIC)

Blue-green algae

Chlorella

Spirulina

GLUTEN-FREE GRAINS (ORGANIC)

Amaranth

Brown rice pasta

Buckwheat

Millet

Oats, gluten-free rolled
and steel-cut

Quinoa (white, red)

Rice (black, wild, brown)

Rice couscous

Sorghum

Teff

DAIRY-FREE MILKS— UNSWEETENED (ORGANIC)

Almond milk

Cashew milk

Coconut milk

Culinary coconut milk
(in BPA-free cans), in full
fat and light

Hemp milk

Oat milk (gluten-free)

Rice milk

BEVERAGES (ORGANIC)

Aloe vera juice

Filtered/purified water

Freshly squeezed and
pressed green juices

Green tea
(contains caffeine)

Herbal teas

Mineral water

Pure coconut water

Seltzer

FLOURS (ORGANIC)

Almond flour (page 39)

Almond meal

Chickpea (garbanzo bean)
flour

Coconut flour

Gluten-free oat flour
(page 39)

integrative and functional medicine testing

Western medical doctors typically perform only standard blood and urine tests. These don't detect toxins that accumulate over time and may be hurting you, nor do they take a deeper look into potential deficiencies in vitamins and minerals.

I recommend working with a Functional/Integrative medical doctor to get to your root cause of any symptoms you may be experiencing. My website, TheHealthyApple.com, has more information on Integrative and Functional medicine and how to find one of these doctors in your area. These tests do not take the place of a thorough medical evaluation. Other tests may need to be ordered that are not listed below. The language here may seem confusing, but don't let it discourage you. Bring this list to your Integrative MD and they will know what tests to run for you.

PREVENTATIVE LAB TESTS: These can detect CBC, CMP, nutritional deficiencies such as 25-OH vitamin D, vitamin B12, folic acid, ferritin, RBC-Mg (magnesium is usually depleted due to stress and poor diet), blood Hg (mercury) and Pb (lead), as well as homocysteine, lipoprotein, and hs-CRP (high-sensitivity C-reactive protein).

BLOOD TESTS FOR ALLERGIES: Serum IgE; ImmunoCAP for food, environmental, and mold allergies; Genova Diagnostics IgG4 food-allergy test; antigliadin antibody; antiendomysial antibody; antitransglutaminase antibody (gluten sensitivity); MELISA test (metal allergy). You can also do skin tests for allergies—provocation/neutralization testing for specific antigens or allergy triggers (food, mold, pollen, etc.).

FOOD SENSITIVITY TESTING: Cyrex Labs Array 10 tests for immune reactivity to 180 raw, cooked, and modified foods. This test will show you what foods are causing inflammation in your body. IgE and IgG antibody testing is also available through Genova Diagnostics. IgG tests for whole blood antibody levels and can be a sign of delayed type sensitivity (an allergy that may not create symptoms for one to three days after exposure). IgE allergy is an immediate allergy and can cause rashes and even anaphylaxis. This is a blood draw that assesses how your immune system responds to proteins in a variety of foods from grains, dairy, and vegetables to coffee, herbs, and spices. The current gold standard is an elimination diet (as I've outlined on page 22), but for a comprehensive analysis, ask your doctor about the Cyrex Array 10 test.

ADRENAL STRESS INDEX TEST: This measures cortisol (the stress hormone) at four different times throughout the day, with two measurements of DHEA. Adrenals are a huge part of the healing process; healing can only take place when your adrenals are healthy and your body is not in fight-or-flight mode. Available through Genova Diagnostics.

ORGANIC ACIDS TEST: This test helps you design a supplement regimen tailored for your needs, so you're not having to blindly take supplements that happen to be making the news. It will also help define pathophysiological areas of concern. It's designed to show the breakdown products of metabolism. High or low levels can give a wide variety of information, including whether there is an imbalance in producing mitochondrial ATP or an imbalance in intestinal bacteria or yeast. Once you have the results, you can use them to replenish any nutritional deficiencies that showed up. Review the results with your MD, who will be able to make recommendations based on your particular situation. Available through Genova Diagnostics.

INTESTINAL PERMEABILITY TEST FOR LEAKY GUT: This test is done through Genova Diagnostics. It will tell you if you have a leaky gut, which causes inflammation and food sensitivities.

THYROID TEST: This test looks at markers like TSH, free T3, free T4, and Reverse T3, as well as anti-TPO antibodies and antithyroglobulin antibodies. In essence, it shows you how well your thyroid is working, and whether or not it is overproducing or underproducing hormones.

GI FUNCTION TEST: This helps determine good bacteria and bad bacteria present in your digestive system. It also looks for things like yeast and parasites, as well as low levels of stomach acid and pancreatic enzymes. Testing is available by using the Genova Diagnostics GI Effects Profile.

HIGH-SENSITIVITY C-REACTIVE PROTEINS (CRP) TEST: This test measures the inflammation in your body. Find out why you have inflammation; is it coming from food sensitivities, nutritional deficiencies, or an infection such as a parasite? CRP test is run through a local lab such as Quest or Labcorp.

IODINE LEVEL TESTING: Iodine is needed for a healthy thyroid and almost every cell in the body, especially the salivary glands, breasts, ovaries, and uterus. Iodine testing is difficult and controversial. Spot urine or serum thyroglobulin tests can help. Twenty-four-hour urine iodine loading test is not yet a standard of care. The iodine absorption test is available at Doctor's Data laboratory.

LYME DISEASE TESTING: These are the tests that measure for exposure to *Borrelia burgdorferi* (Lyme disease) and the associated coinfections, through antibody production. They include IGenex or SUNY Stony Brook Lyme Western Blot IgG, IgM; Babesia antibody IgG, IgM; Bartonella antibody IgG, IgM; Babesia antibody IgG, IgM; Bartonella antibody IgG, IgM; Ehrlichia antibody IgG, IgM.

NEUROTRANSMITTER TESTING: This test measures epinephrine, norepinephrine, serotonin, and dopamine—chemical messengers in your body and brain. Testing from Neurorelie.com (Neuro Science) determines your balance of neurotransmitters. You can also evaluate the neurotransmitter balance with Organix organic acid testing through Genova Diagnostics. Note that not all doctors agree with Neuro Science urine neurotransmitter testing.

STOOL TESTS: These tests can assess your digestion

and how well food is absorbed. They can also detect parasites and bad bacteria that may exist. Genova comprehensive digestive stool analysis (CDSA 2.0) and parasitology test assesses digestion and absorption of food and parasite presence. Genova Diagnostics GI Effects stool analysis is for assessing digestion and absorption of food and parasite presence through a gene probe (which some believe is more sensitive). Hemoccult test assesses blood in stool.

MERCURY AND OTHER HEAVY METAL TESTING: Eating too much high-mercury fish, having mercury dental fillings, and other environmental sources can cause heavy-metal accumulation. The only reliable test is a twenty-four hour Urine Challenge Test with a chelating agent like DMSA. Genova Diagnostics and Doctors Data can both perform this test. See page 88 for a chart of heavy metals and possible sources of exposure.

OMEGA-3/OMEGA-6 RATIOS: A good indication of inflammation is the ratio between omega-3 and omega-6 fatty acids. Nutrasource Diagnostics Inc. and Genova perform RBC fatty acid analyses.

MINERAL ANALYSIS TESTS: Tests levels of magnesium, zinc, chromium, selenium, etc. Use Comprehensive Mineral Analysis available at Doctor's Data.

VITAMIN D TESTING: A lot of people are deficient in vitamin D and don't even know it. This test will let you know if you need to be getting more. The name of the test is the 25 OH Vitamin D test.

MTHFR-METHYLATION PATHWAYS TESTING: The official name is Methylenetetrahydrofolate Reductase, or MTHFR, for short. This is a DNA test that checks for genetic mutations C677T and A1298C. These variants in the MTHFR gene typically result in lower enzymatic activity, which in un-fancy talk simply means that people with these variants may potentially require higher doses of folate because their metabolic pathway inefficiently converts folic acid (synthetic) to folate (the biologically active form of the nutrient). Because folate is critical for disease prevention and has been implicated in recurrent pregnancy loss and other fertility issues, it is often recommended as an easy assessment to help the doctor gain further insight into his/her patient. Many Integrative doctors encourage women of childbearing age, who may or may not be trying to conceive, to take a prenatal with folate, not folic acid, since a high population has one or both of these mutations. The C677T apparently has higher risk than the A1298C variant and if you are homozygous (have two mutations for the C677T), your need for higher intake of folate (and other methylated B vitamins) is even that much more important. Elevated homocysteine levels and heart disease are possible side effects of having the MTHFR mutation; specifically the C677T mutation. MTHFR DNA single nucleotide mutations prevent optimization of your dose of folate, B12, and B6. This can be found through a blood test from your Integrative MD. A great deal has been discovered about the usefulness of the test, but the practical application of the information is very complicated due to genetic versus epigenetic expression. Ask your MD for the MTHFR test (provide both the full name and abbreviated) and if you have this mutation, ask your MD for multivitamins that have the methylated form of B vitamins, especially B9, or folate (not folic acid, which is synthetic).

HORMONE IMBALANCE TESTS: Men should check their testosterone, estradiol, DHEA-S, and IGF-1. Women should check their estradiol, total estrogen, progesterone, testosterone, and DHEA-S. Both genders should also assess SHBG to make sure this is not low, which is a sign of insulin resistance.

URINE OXIDATIVE STRESS TEST: This test from Genova Diagnostics tells you if you need more antioxidants in your diet.

Genova Diagnostics—gdx.net // 800-522-4762

Doctor's Data—doctorsdata.com // 800-323-2784

Cyrex Laboratories—joincyrex.com // 877-772-9739

Nutrasource Diagnostics Inc.—nutrasource.ca // 519-341-3367

amie-approved products and vendors

AIR PURIFIERS

Austin Air Purifiers—
austinairpurifiers.com

APPLIANCES/HOMEWARE

KitchenAid—kitchenaid.com

Omega—omegajuicers.com

Le Creuset—lecreuset.com

Sur La Table—surlatable.com

Oxo—oxo.com

Williams-Sonoma—williams-sonoma.com

Amazon—amazon.com

Onyx—onyxcontainers.com

Pyrex—pyrex.com

SUPPLEMENTS

Enzymedica—enzymedica.com

Flora—florahealth.com

NOW Foods—nowfoods.com

Natural Vitality—naturalvitality.com

Boiron—boironusa.com

Gaia—gaiaherbs.com

Vitahealth—vitahealthrx.com

Probiotics:

Enzymedica—enzymedica.com

Natren—natren.com

BEAUTY

CAP beauty—capbeauty.com

H. Gillerman Organics—
hgillermanorganics.com

Beautycounter—beautycounter.com

Badger Balm—badgerbalm.com

Crystal—thecrystal.com

CV Skinlabs—cvskinlabs.com

Rahua—rahua.com

Desert Essence—desertessence.com

EO Products—eoproducts.com

Erbaviva—erbaviva.com

RMS Beauty—rmsbeauty.com

Odacite—odacite.com

Tata Harper—tataharperskincare.com

Zoe Organics—zoeorganics.com

One Love Organics—
oneloveorganics.com

S.W. Basics—swbasicsofbk.com

Mini Organics—miniorganics.com

Raw Elements—rawelementsusa.com

Dr. Singha—drsingha.com

Lotus Wei—lotuswei.com

Lovely Lady Products—
lovelyladyproducts.com

BabyGanics—babyganics.com

Dr. Bronner's—drbronner.com

Aura Cacia—auracacia.com

Frontier Co-op—frontiercoop.com

NOW Solutions—nowfoods.com

California Baby—californiababy.com

BEDDING

Gaiam—gaiam.com

Green Sleep—greensleep.com

Natura—naturaworld.com

Organic Mattress Store—
organicmattressstore.com

Vivetique—vivetique.com

Hastens Beds—hastens.com

Naturepedic Mattress—naturepedic.com

Amenity Home—amenityhome.com

Lifekind—lifekind.com

Good Night Naturals—
goodnightnaturals.com

CAN-FREE/GLASS JAR PRODUCTS

Bionaturae—bionaturae.com

Jovial Foods—jovialfoods.com

Pacific Foods—pacificfoods.com

Farmers Market Foods—
farmersmarketfoods.com

CLEANING/LAUNDRY PRODUCTS

Branch Basics—branchbasics.com

Seventh Generation—
seventhgeneration.com

EO Products—eoproducts.com

Biokleen—biokleenhome.com

Ecover—us.ecover.com

Starfiber—starfibers.com

Norwex Cloths—norwex.com

People Towels—peopletowels.com

Molly's Suds—mollyssuds.com

Earth Friendly Products—ecos.com

Clean Well—cleanwelltoday.com

COCONUT PRODUCTS

NOW Foods—nowfoods.com

Barlean's—barleans.com

Bob's Red Mill—bobsredmill.com

Coconut Secret—coconutsecret.com

CONDIMENTS

Tessemae's—tessemaes.com

Green Garden by Litehouse—
greengardendressing.com

365 Whole Foods Market Organic
Mustard—wholefoodsmarket.com

Organicville Mustard—
organicvillefoods.com

Annie's Organic Dijon—annies.com

Amy's Organic Salsa—amys.com

CHOCOLATES (GLUTEN-FREE DAIRY-FREE)

Enjoy Life Foods—enjoylifefoods.com

Equal Exchange—equalexchange.coop

Alter Eco —alterecofoods.com

DETOX PRODUCTS

Frontier Co-op—frontier.com

Amazing Grass—amazinggrass.com

Sunlighten Infrared Saunas—
sunlighten.com

FLOURS (GLUTEN-FREE)

King Arthur Flour—
kingarthurflour.com

Bob's Red Mill—bobsredmill.com

Nutiva—nutiva.com

Coconut Secret—coconutsecret.com

Living NOW Foods—
livingnowfoods.com

FRUITS (DRIED)

Earthbound Farm—ebfarm.com

Navitas Naturals—navitasnaturals.com

Peeled Snacks—peeledsnacks.com

Made in Nature—madeinnature.com

GRAINS AND PASTAS (GLUTEN-FREE)

Arrowhead Mills—arrowheadmills.com

Bob's Red Mill—bobsredmill.com

Eden Organic—edenfoods.com

Lundberg—lundberg.com

Explore Asian—explore-asian.com

Emmy's Organics—
emmysorganics.com

Food for Life—foodforlife.com

Nature's Path—naturespath.com

Purely Elizabeth—purelyelizabeth.com

Shiloh Farms—shilohfarms.com

Tolerant Foods—tolerantfoods.com

TruRoots—truroots.com

Love Grown Foods—
lovegrownfoods.com

Stahlbush Island Farms—
stahlbush.com

Living NOW Foods—
livingnowfoods.com

HERBS, SPICES, AND SEASONINGS

Bragg—bragg.com

Eden Foods—edenfoods.com

Frontier Co-op—frontiercoop.com

iHerb—iherb.com

Miso Master Organic Chickpea Miso—
great-eastern-sun.com

Simply Organic—simplyorganic.com

LEGUMES

Bob's Red Mill—bobsredmill.com

Eden Organic BPA-free canned
beans—edenfoods.com

Shiloh Farms—shilohfarms.com

NON-DAIRY MILKS

Whole Foods Market 365—
wholefoodsmarket.com

Living Harvest—livingharvest.com

So Delicious—sodelicious.com

Natural Value (BPA-free canned
coconut milk)—naturalvalue.com

NUTS AND SEEDS

Barlean's—barleans.com

Bob's Red Mill—bobsredmill.com

Frontier Co-op—frontiercoop.com

Manna Organics—
mannaorganicbakery.com

Manitoba Harvest—
manitobaharvest.com

Maranatha—maranathafoods.com

Nuts—nuts.com

Raw Nuts and Seeds—
rawnutsandseeds.com

Sun Butter—sunbutter.com

NOW Foods—nowfoods.com

OILS

Nutiva—nutiva.com

Barlean's—barleans.com

Flora—florahealth.com

NOW Foods—nowfoods.com

PAINTS

Benjamin Moore—
benjaminmoore.com

The Silent Paint Remover—
silentpaintremover.com

PROBIOTIC-RICH FOODS

Real Pickles—realpickles.com

Farm House Culture—
farmhouseculture.com

Eden Organic Sauerkraut—
edenfoods.com

Zukay Live Foods—zukay.com

Woodstock Foods sauerkraut—
Woodstock-foods.com

Bubbies Sauerkraut—Bubbies.com

PRODUCE

Driscoll's Organic—Driscolls.com

Earthbound Farm—ebfarm.com

Whole Foods Market Organic 365
Everyday Value—
wholefoodsmarket.com

PROTEIN POWDERS

Nutiva—nutiva.com

Amazing Grass—amazinggrass.com

Manitoba Harvest—
manitobaharvest.com

Aloha—aloha.com

NOW Sports—nowfoods.com

SEA SALTS/HIMALAYAN PINK SALT

Frontier Co-op—frontiercoop.com

Simply Organic—simplyorganic.com

SEA VEGGIES

Eden Foods—edenfoods.com

Frontier Co-op—frontiercoop.com

Maine Coast—seaveg.com

SNACKS

Go Raw—Goraw.com

Vivapura Superfoods—vivapura.com

Essential Living Foods—
essentiallivingfoods.com

Foods Alive—foodsalive.com

Happy Family—
happyfamilybrands.com

SPROUTED FOODS

Wilderness Family Naturals—
wildernessfamilynaturals.com

Blue Mountain Organics—
bluemountainorganics.com

Living Intentions—
livingintentions.com

SUPERFOODS

Frontier Co-op—frontiercoop.com

Navitas Naturals—navitasnaturals.com

Organic India—organicindiausa.com

SWEETENERS

Coconut Secret Coconut Aminos—
coconutsecret.com

Frontier Co-op—frontiercoop.com

Medjool Dates—medjooldates.com

Navitas Naturals—navitasnaturals.com

NOW Foods—nowfoods.com

Wholesome Sweeteners—
wholesomesweeteners.com

Maple Valley Syrup—
maplevalleysyrup.com

Coombs Family Farms Maple Syrup—
coombsfamilyfarms.com

Y.S. Eco Bee Farms—ysorganic.com

TEAS

NOW Real Tea—nowfoods.com

Frontier Co-op—frontier.com

Organic India—organicindia.com

Traditional Medicinals—
traditionalmedicinals.com

Numi Organic Tea—numitea.com

Rishi—rishi-tea.com

Flora—Florahealth.com

VEGETABLE BROTHS

Pacific Foods Organic Simply Stock
Vegetables and Organic Vegetable
Broth—pacificfoods.com

VEGETABLES/FRUITS (FROZEN)

365 Whole Foods Market Organic
Frozen—wholefoodsmarkets.com

Earthbound Farm—ebfarm.com

WATER (SPRING)

Mountain Valley Spring Water—
mountainvalleyspring.com

ONLINE STORES

Abe's Market—abesmarket.com

Thrive Market—thrivemarket.com

Amazon—amazon.com

Vitacost—vitacost.com

Ecobags—ecobags.com

Eco Choices—ecochoices.com

Green Home—greenhome.com

Reuseit—reuseit.com

The Ultimate Green Store—
theultimategreenstore.com

Wild Mint Shop—wildmintshop.com

acknowledgments

This book has been a labor of love, but I definitely didn't do it alone. So many people were involved, and who worked with me to create a final product we all can be proud of.

First I want to thank my amazing agent, Joy Tutela, for helping this book find a home with Houghton Mifflin Harcourt. Giant hugs to my fabulous editor there, Justin Schwartz—I so appreciate your guidance and wisdom in taking this from final draft to published book and for believing in me; you are amazing. Thank you to the entire team at Houghton Mifflin Harcourt, including Cindy Brzostowski and Marina "Meatball" Padakis.

Colleen M. Story, thank you for your editing, advice, and everything! Additional thanks to Rachel Holtzman, Nora Isaacs, Daryn Eller, Terri Trespicio, and Hillari Dowdle for your great help with editing along the way. To Anthony Hawkins and Lindsay Dahl, thank you for your toxic-beauty-product expertise. Laura Enoch and Maria Whitas, thank you for being my right-hand recipe testers, amazing friends, and supporters. Many thanks to my other recipe testers, Claudia Bellini, Caitlin Tralka, Lisa Rector, and Tom Harnett. Thank you to my incredibly talented photo shoot team: Lauren Volo, Mariana Velasquez, April Valencia, and Austin Reavis.

For all the integrative doctors who have helped keep me alive: Dr. Sid Baker, Dr. Morton Teich, Dr. Jeffrey Morrison, John Fallon, Dr. Allan Warshowsky, Dr. Richard Horowitz, Dr. Susan Blum, Dr. Benjamin Ascher, Geri Brewster, Shane Hoffman, and Reid Winich. To the experts who so kindly reviewed the sections on medical testing, Dr. Jeffrey Morrison, Dr. Allan Warshowsky, and Lizzy Swick, MS, RDN, thank you for your expertise. Thank you Dr. Mark Hyman and Dhru Purohit for believing in me, and your beautiful foreword and ongoing support. I am forever grateful. And my heartfelt gratitude to my dear friend Kirstin Boncher, for your friendship, medical wisdom, and love that have helped me get well!

My deepest gratitude to my incredible mother—thank you for your unconditional love and tireless efforts running to the food store and buying all the food and supplies I needed when I was so sick, and for lending your shoulder to cry on when I was losing hope. I am so lucky to have your love and support. And to my father, for your support during my years of chronic pain, which finally brought us closer together, and for testing broccoli recipes for me at breakfast! Thank you to my sister, Aly, Aunt Val, Uncle Mike, Uncle Larry, and my buddies Alyssa MacKenzie, Jennifer Kass, and Meredith Campbell, for listening to me, understanding me, holding my hand, and helping me fight through countless years of chronic pain and tears—I love you.

A giant thank-you to all the readers of my blog, TheHealthyApple.com, and my followers of @TheHealthyApple on Facebook, Twitter, Instagram, Pinterest, Google+, and Tumblr! To all of you who believe in me, my detox knowledge, and my recipes—I wouldn't be here without you. Thank you for your support, comments, love, and trust through our challenging journeys to wellness.

Healing Hugs!

xox

INDEX